FTCE Prekindergarten /Primary PK-3

Teacher Certification Exam

By: Sharon Wynne, M.S.

XAMonline, INC.
Boston

To obtain permission(s) to use the material from this work for any purpose including workshops or seminars, please submit a written request to:

XAMonline, Inc.
21 Orient Ave.
Melrose, MA 02176
Toll Free 1-800-509-4128
Email: info@xamonline.com
Web: www.xamonline.com
Fax: 1-617-583-5552

Library of Congress Cataloging-in-Publication Data

Wynne, Sharon A.
    Prekindergarten/Primary PK-3: Teacher Certification / Sharon A. Wynne. -3rd
    ed. ISBN 978-1-60787-386-0
        1. Prekindergarten/Primary PK-3   2. Study Guides   3. FTCE
        4. Teachers' Certification & Licensure   5. Careers

Disclaimer:
The opinions expressed in this publication are the sole works of XAMonline and were created independently from the National Education Association, Educational Testing Service, or any State Department of Education, National Evaluation Systems or other testing affiliates.

Between the time of publication and printing, state specific standards as well as testing formats and website information may change and will not be included in part or in whole within this product. Sample test questions are developed by XAMonline and reflect similar content as on real tests; however, they are not former tests. XAMonline assembles content that aligns with state standards but makes no claims nor guarantees teacher candidates a passing score. Numerical scores are determined by testing companies such as NES or ETS and then are compared with individual state standards. A passing score varies from state to state.

Printed in the United States of America   œ-1

FTCE: Prekindergarten/Primary PK-3
ISBN: 978-1-60787-386-0

Project Manager: Sharon Wynne

Project Coordinator: Victoria Anderson

Content Coordinators/Authors: Fran Stanford
Victoria Anderson
Christina Godard
Kimberly Putney
Vickie Pittard
Deborah Suber
Kelley Eldredge
Bethany Chappel
Bonnie Lass
June Saunders
Kathy Morrison

Sample test: Shelley Wake
Deborah Harbin
Christina Godard
Kim Putney
Carol Moore
Vickie Pittard

Editors: Proof reader   Janis Mercer
Copy editor   Ann Weaver
Sample test   Shelley Wake
Production   David Aronson

Graphic Artist   Jenna Hamilton

Table of Contents

Great Study and Testing Tips!

What to study in order to prepare for the subject assessments is the focus of this study guide, but equally important is *how* you study.

You can increase your chances of truly mastering the information by taking some simple, but effective, steps.

Study Tips:

1.   <u>Some foods aid the learning process</u>. Foods such as milk, nuts, seeds, rice, and oats help your study efforts by releasing natural memory enhancers called CCKs (*cholecystokinin*) composed of *tryptophan*, *choline*, and *phenylalanine*. All of these chemicals enhance the neurotransmitters associated with memory. Before studying, try a light, protein-rich meal of eggs, turkey, and fish. All of these foods release the memory enhancing chemicals. The better the connections, the more you comprehend.

Likewise, before you take a test, stick to a light snack of energy boosting and relaxing foods. A glass of milk, a piece of fruit, or some peanuts will release various memory-boosting chemicals and help you relax and focus on the subject at hand.

2.   <u>Learn to take great notes</u>. A byproduct of our modern culture is that we have grown accustomed to getting our information in short doses (e.g., TV news sound bites or USA Today–style newspaper articles).

Consequently, we've subconsciously trained ourselves to assimilate information better in <u>neat little packages</u>. If your notes are scrawled all over the paper, the flow of the information is fragmented. Strive for clarity. Newspapers use a standard format to achieve clarity. Your notes can be much clearer through use of proper formatting. A very effective format is called the *Cornell Method.*

Take a sheet of loose-leaf, lined notebook paper and draw a line all the way down the paper about 1–2 inches from the left edge.

Draw another line across the width of the paper about 1–2 inches up from the bottom. Repeat this process on the reverse side of the page.

Look at the highly effective result. You have ample room for notes, a left-side margin for special emphasis items or inserting supplementary data from the textbook, a large area at the bottom for a brief summary, and a little rectangular space for just about anything you want.

3.   **Get the concept then the details.** Too often we focus on the details and don't gather an understanding of the concept. However, if you simply memorize only dates, places, or names, you may well miss the whole point of the subject.

A key way to understand information is to put it in your own words. If you are working from a textbook, automatically summarize each paragraph in your mind. If you are outlining text, don't simply copy the author's words.

Rephrase them in your own words. You remember your own thoughts and words much better than someone else's and subconsciously tend to associate the important details to the core concepts.

4.   **Ask Why?** Pull apart written material paragraph by paragraph and don't forget the captions under the illustrations.

Example: If the heading is "Stream Erosion," flip it around to read "Why do streams erode?" Then answer the questions.

If you train your mind to think in a series of questions and answers, you will not only learn more but also lessen test anxiety because you are used to answering questions.

5.   **Read for reinforcement and future needs.** Even if you only have 10 minutes, put your notes or a book in your hand. Your mind is similar to a computer; you have to input data in order to process it. *By reading, you are creating the neural connections for future retrieval.* The more times you read something, the more you reinforce the learning of ideas.

Even if you don't fully understand something on the first pass, *your mind stores much of the material for later recall.*

6.   **Relax to learn, so go into exile.** Our bodies respond to an inner clock called biorhythms. Burning the midnight oil works well for some people, but not everyone.

If possible, set aside a particular place to study that is free of distractions. Shut off the television, cell phone, and pager and exile your friends and family during your study period.

If you really are bothered by silence, try background music. Light classical music at a low volume has been shown to aid in concentration over other types. Music without lyrics that evokes pleasant emotions is highly suggested. Try just about anything by Mozart. It relaxes you.

7.   <u>**Use arrows, not highlighters**</u>. At best, it's difficult to read a page full of yellow, pink, blue, and green streaks. Try staring at a neon sign for a while and you'll soon see that the horde of colors obscures the message.

A quick note, a brief dash of color, an underline, and an arrow pointing to a particular passage is much clearer than a horde of highlighted words.

8.   <u>**Budget your study time**</u>. Although you shouldn't ignore any of the material, ***allocate your available study time in the same ratio that topics may appear on the test.***

Testing Tips:

1. Get smart; play dumb. Don't read anything into the question. Don't make an assumption that the test writer is looking for something else than what is asked. Stick to the question as written and don't read extra things into it.

2. Read the question and all the choices *twice* before answering the question. You may miss something by not reading carefully and then rereading both the question and the answers.

If you really don't have a clue as to the right answer, leave the question blank on the first time through. Go on to the other questions; they may provide a clue as to how to answer the skipped questions.

If later on, you still can't answer the skipped ones . . . *Guess.* The only penalty for guessing is that you *might* get it wrong. Only one thing is certain; if you don't put anything down, you will get it wrong!

3. Turn the question into a statement. Look at the way the questions are worded. The syntax of the question usually provides a clue. Does it seem more familiar as a statement rather than as a question? Does it sound strange? By turning a question into a statement, you may be able to spot if an answer sounds right, and it may also trigger memories of material you have read.

4. Look for hidden clues. It's actually very difficult to compose multiple-foil (choice) questions without giving away part of the answer in the options presented.
In most multiple-choice questions you can often readily eliminate one or two of the potential answers. Therefore, you have only two real possibilities and automatically your odds go to 50-50 with very little work.
5. Trust your instincts. For every fact that you have read, you subconsciously retain something of that knowledge. On questions that you aren't really certain about, go with your basic instincts. **Your first impression on how to answer a question is usually correct.**

6. Mark your answers directly on the test booklet. Don't bother trying to fill in the optical scan sheet on the first pass through the test.
Just be very careful not to missmark your answers when you eventually transcribe them to the scan sheet.
7. Watch the clock! You have a set amount of time to answer the questions. Don't get bogged down trying to answer a single question at the expense of 10 questions you can more readily answer.

SUBAREA 1   **DEVELOPMENTAL KNOWLEDGE**

COMPETENCY 1.0   KNOWLEDGE OF CHILD GROWTH, CHILD DEVELOPMENT, AND RELATIONSHIPS WITH

Skill 1.1   Identify the major effects of genetics, health, nutrition, public policy, environment, and economics on child development

In today's push toward academic achievement and standards, it is easy to forget the importance of a child's emotional and physical growth and health. New teachers may be tempted to just teach more or harder for fear that if they don't, their students will not learn. Yet, the new (and veteran) teacher must remember that child development plays a huge part in the academic development of individuals.

While all children develop at different rates, and every child will have unique attributes, we can generally say that teachers have some responsibility to note concerns regarding the emotional or physical states of their students. Indeed, this is a legal responsibility of teachers, particularly for cases in which abuse is noted. Other concerns may also be justifiable for discussion with counselors or administrators.

Genetics

Neurotic Disorders

Sometimes emotional disorders escalate so severely that the child's well-being is threatened. Teachers and parents must recognize the signs of severe emotional stress, which may become detrimental to the child. There are various forms of emotional disorders that can be potentially dangerous, including neurotic disorders. Neuroses are the second most common group of psychiatric disturbances of childhood, and symptoms include extreme anxiety related to overdependence, social isolation, sleep problems, unwarranted nausea, abdominal pain, diarrhea, or headaches.

Some children show characteristics of irrational fears of particular objects or situations, while others become consumed with particular thoughts, or ideas. One of the most serious neuroses is depression. A child suffering from depression may be sad, cry, show little or no interest in people or activities, have eating and sleeping problems, and may even sometimes talk about wanting to be dead. Teachers need to listen to what the child is saying and take these verbal expressions very seriously. Perhaps what happened at Columbine, CO, Jonesboro, AR, and Lake Worth, FL, could have been prevented if the signs had been recognized.

Psychotic Disorders

An even more serious emotional disorder is psychosis, which is characterized by a loss of contact with reality. Psychosis is rare in childhood, but when it does occur, it is often difficult to diagnose. One fairly constant sign is the child's failure to make normal emotional contact with other people. The most common psychosis of childhood is schizophrenia, in which the child loses touch with reality and withdraws from relationships with others. When this disorder occurs in childhood, the child will continue to have some contact with people; however, there is a curtain between him or her and the rest of the world. Schizophrenia is more common in boys than in girls. One of the major signs of this disorder is a habitually flat or habitually agitated facial expression. Children suffering from schizophrenia are occasionally mute, but at times they talk incessantly using bizarre words in ways that make no sense. Their incoherent speech often contributes to their frustration and compounds their fears and preoccupations; these speech patterns are the most significant sign of this very serious disturbance.

Early Infantile Autism

This disorder may occur as early as the fourth month of life. Suddenly the infant lies apathetic and oblivious in the crib. In other cases, the baby seems perfectly normal throughout infancy, and the symptoms appear without warning at about 18 months of age. Due to the nature of the symptoms, autistic children are often misdiagnosed as mentally retarded, deaf-mute, or organically brain-damaged. Autistic children are twice as likely to be boys as girls.

According to many psychologists who have been involved with treating autistic children, it seems that these children have built a wall between themselves and everyone else, including their families and even their parents. In some cases, they do not make eye contact with others and do not even appear to hear the voices of those who speak to them. They cannot empathize with others and have no ability to appreciate humor.

Autistic children usually have language disturbances. One third of them may never develop speech at all, but may grunt or whine. Others may repeat the same word or phrase over and over or parrot what someone else has said. They often lack even inner language as well and cannot play by themselves above a primitive, sensory-motor level.

Frequently, autistic children will appear to fill the void left by the absence of interpersonal relationships in their lives with a preoccupation with things. They may become compulsive about the arrangements of objects and often engage in simple, repetitive physical activities with objects for long periods of time. If these activities are interrupted, they may react with fear or rage. Others remain motionless for hours each day, sometimes moving only their eyes or hands.

On intelligence tests, autistic children score from severely subnormal to high average. Some exhibit astonishing ability in isolated skill areas while functioning poorly in general. They may be able to memorize volumes of material, sing beautifully, or perform complicated mathematical problems.

The cause of early infantile autism is unknown. Years ago some psychiatrists speculated that these children did not develop normally due to a lack of parental warmth. This has been found to be unlikely since the incidence of autism in families is usually limited to one child. Other theories once pointed to childhood vaccinations, but this also has been found to be untrue. Still other theories posit metabolic or chromosomal defects as causes; but again, there is no proof.

The prognosis for autistic children can be discouraging. Only about 5 percent of autistic children become socially well adjusted in adulthood. Another 20 percent make fair social adjustments. The remaining 75 percent are socially incapacitated and must be supervised for the duration of their lives. Treatment may include outpatient psychotherapy, drugs, or long-term treatment in a residential center, but neither the form of treatment nor even the lack of treatment seems to make a difference in the long run.

Environment

Let's start with the legal issues of abuse. While the symptoms of abuse are usually thought to be physical (and therefore visible), mental and emotional abuse is also possible. The best action is to immediately contact a superior at the school if abuse is suspected and follow your state and district's mandated reporting system. The impact of abuse of a child's development in other domains is often extensive. Abused children can be socially withdrawn, and typically, as one might suspect, their minds will not always be on their schoolwork. Significant emotional damage occurs as well, and teachers may notice very awkward social behavior around other children and around adults.

Health and Nutrition

Issues of physical health might include prenatal exposure to drugs, alcohol, or nicotine. In these cases, moderate to severe brain damage is possible; however, more subtle impairment can also occur (trouble with breathing, attention deficit disorder, and so on). Because drugs, alcohol, and nicotine can impair brain development, children exposed to these substances in the womb may need significant extra classroom support. Some of these children will also need to be referred to the Special Education teacher to be tested for learning disabilities.

Day-to-day issues, such as lack of sufficient sleep or nutrition, can harm children in a more temporal fashion. While a child who has had sleep disruptions or insufficient nutrition can bounce back easily when these things are attended to, it is often the case that children living in environments where sleep and proper nutrition are not available will continue through childhood to struggle for these things. Through federal and local funds, many schools are able to provide free or reduced-price breakfasts and lunches for children; however, consider that if this is a necessity, such children may not get a decent dinner, and during weekends and holidays they may struggle even more.

The most notable symptoms of a lack of nutrition and sleep include a lack of concentration, particularly in the classroom. Furthermore, children who lack sufficient sleep or nutrition may become agitated more easily than other children.

In summary, it is always a good idea for teachers to pay attention to the abnormalities in behavior of children—or even sudden drop-offs in achievement or attention—and to notify superiors at the school of their concerns.

Economics

The financial situation of a family has a tremendous effect on a child's development. Whether the family has enough money to provide for the child's needs in health and nutrition can impact the development in ensuring that there is enough food in the home and that the child can get needed medical attention. The family's economic situation also affects the child's experiences in having access to books or attending events that will help the child develop academically by providing prior experiences on which to draw in the school situation. For example, when the teacher talks about the circus or a fair, if the child does not have the background experience of attending these events, it will be hard to make any personal connections between the classroom and the world. Children who come from impoverished homes are often at a disadvantage in many regards when they enter school.

Skill 1.2	Identify development stages (e.g., social-emotional, cognitive, language, physical) and the milestones for the typically developing child

The teacher has a broad knowledge and thorough understanding of the development that typically occurs during the students' current period of life. More importantly, the teacher understands how children learn best during each period of development. The most important premise of child development is that all domains of development (physical, social, and academic) are integrated. Development in each dimension is influenced by the other dimensions. Moreover, today's educator must also have a knowledge of exceptionalities and how these exceptionalities effect all domains of a child's development.

Social-Emotional Development

Children progress through a variety of social stages, beginning with an awareness of peers but a lack of concern for their presence. Young children engage in "parallel" activities, playing alongside their peers without directly interacting with one another. During the primary years, children develop an intense interest in peers. They establish productive and positive social and working relationships with one another.

This stage of social growth continues to increase in importance throughout the child's school years including intermediate, middle school, and high school years. It is necessary for the teacher to recognize the importance of developing positive peer group relationships and to provide opportunities and support for cooperative small-group projects that not only develop cognitive ability but also promote peer interaction. The ability to work and relate effectively with peers is of major importance and contributes greatly to the child's sense of competence. To develop this sense of competence, children need to be successful in acquiring the knowledge and skills recognized by our culture as important, especially those skills that promote academic achievement.

Knowledge of age-appropriate expectations is fundamental to the teacher's positive relationship with students and to effective instructional strategies. Equally important is the knowledge of what is individually appropriate for the specific children in a classroom. Developmentally oriented teachers approach classroom groups and individual students with a respect for their emerging capabilities. Developmentalists recognize that kids grow in common patterns but at different rates, which usually cannot be accelerated by adult pressure or input. Developmentally oriented teachers know that variance in the school performance of different children often results from differences in their general growth. With the establishment of inclusionary classes throughout the schools, it is vital for all teachers to know the characteristics of students' exceptionalities and their implications for learning.

Cognitive (Academic) Development

Children go through patterns of learning, beginning with preoperational thought processes and moving to concrete operational thoughts. Eventually they begin to acquire the mental ability to think about and solve problems in their head because they can manipulate objects symbolically. Children of most ages can use symbols such as words and numbers to represent objects and relations, but they need concrete reference points. It is essential that children be encouraged to use and develop the thinking skills that they possess in solving problems that interest them. The content of the curriculum must be relevant, engaging, and meaningful to the students.

Physical Development

It is important for the teacher to be aware of each child's physical stage of development and how the child's physical growth and development affect the child's learning. Factors determined by the physical stage of development include the ability to sit and attend, the need for activity, the relationship between physical skills and self-esteem, and the degree to which physical involvement in an activity (as opposed to the ability to understand an abstract concept) affects learning.

Skill 1.3   **Identify atypical development (e.g., social-emotional, cognitive, language, physical)**

The effective teacher is cognizant of students' individual learning styles and human growth and development theory and applies these principles in the selection and implementation of appropriate instructional activities. In regards to the identification and implementation of appropriate learning activities, effective teachers select and implement instructional activities consistent with principles of human growth and development theory.

Learning activities selected for younger students (below age eight) should focus on short time frames in highly simplified form. The nature of the activity and the context in which the activity is presented affect the approach that the students will take in processing the information. Younger children tend to process information at a slower rate than older children (age eight and older).

On the other hand, when selecting and implementing learning activities for older children, teachers should focus on more complex ideas, because older students are capable of understanding more complex instructional activities. Moreover, effective teachers maintain a clear understanding of the developmental appropriateness of activities selected for providing educational instructions to students and select and present these activities in a manner consistent with the level of readiness of their students.

The early childhood educator takes care to select appropriate activities and classroom situations in which learning is optimized. The classroom teacher should manipulate instructional activities and classroom conditions in a manner that enhances group and individual learning opportunities. For example, the classroom teacher can organize group-learning activities in which students are placed in a situation in which cooperation, sharing ideas, and discussion occur. Cooperative learning activities can assist students in learning to collaborate and share personal and cultural ideas and values in a classroom learning environment.

The well-prepared teacher selects learning activities based on specific learning objectives. Ideally, teachers should not plan activities that fail to augment the specific objectives of the lesson. Learning activities should be planned with a learning objective in mind. Objective-driven learning activities tend to serve as a tool to reinforce the teacher's lesson presentation. Additionally, selected learning objectives should be consistent with state and district educational goals that focus on national educational goals (Goals 2000) and the specific strengths and weaknesses of individual students assigned to the teacher's class.

The effective teacher plans his or her learning activities to introduce them in a meaningful instructional sequence. Teachers should combine instructional activities to reinforce information by providing students with relevant learning experiences through instructional activities.

Skill 1.4　　　　**Identify and distinguish the influences of substance abuse, physical abuse, and emotional distress on child development**

Substance Abuse

Students are using drugs and alcohol at surprisingly young ages today. Cases exist of 10-year-old alcoholics. Young people start using drugs and alcohol for one of four reasons:

- Out of curiosity
- To party
- Due to peer pressure
- To avoid dealing with problems

In the school setting, hard signs of dependency are to be considered very serious. Any student who exhibits hard signs associated with substance ingestion must be treated by medical staff at a medical facility immediately. Seizures due to withdrawal are fatal 17 percent of the time, and overdoses due to mixed substances or overuse of a single substance are rapidly fatal, including overdoses with alcohol alone. Never, under any circumstances, should the teacher attempt to treat, protect, tolerate, or negotiate with a student who is showing signs of a physical crisis. Such students are to be removed from the school center by EMS or police as soon as possible and given constant one-on-one supervision away from the regular classroom before being taken to the hospital. Police must be called because such students are a danger to self or others in their condition. If it is questionable whether it is the teacher's responsibility to call the police, find out what the protocol is for each step.

Another hard sign is irresponsible, illogical, and dangerous use. The use of any substance by young people constitutes irresponsible, illogical, and dangerous use, if for no other reason than use of controlled substances, including alcohol, is illegal for minors. In the eyes of medical science, there exists a zero level of tolerance because of the inherent physical risk of ingesting street drugs, the possibility of brain damage, the loss of educational levels, and lost social development, diminishing a student's ability and chances in life. Psychologically, the use of drugs and alcohol prohibits the youth from learning non-chemical coping skills to solve problems. Typically, sophisticated anger modulation techniques usually learned in late adolescence are missed, leaving the young person limited in handling that most important of emotions. Substance abuse is also dangerous in light of the terrible number of automobile crash deaths, teen pregnancies that occur while intoxicated, overdose on contaminated substances, and the induction of mental disorders from exposure to harsh substances, such as activation of latent schizophrenia by use of hallucinogens.

There are three soft signs, less rapacious and life threatening, yet each a debilitating nightmare. They are the three psychosocial declines. The young substance abuser will exhibit losses in functional levels socially and academically previously attained. The adage, "Pot makes a smart kid average and an average kid dumb," is right on the mark. In some families, pot smoking is a known habit of the parents. The children may start their habit by stealing from the parents.

Typically, a student on drugs and/or alcohol will show:

- lack of muscle coordination
- wobbly, ataxic gait
- reddened, puffy eyes (reddened sclera)
- averted gaze
- dilated pupils
- dry eyes
- dry mouth (anticholinergia)
- excessive sneezing or sniffing
- gazing off into space
- nervousness
- fine trembling
- failure to respond to verbal prompts
- passive-aggressive behavior
- sudden sickness in class
- vomiting and chills
- slurred speech
- aggression
- sleep
- odd, sudden personality changes
- withdrawal
- an appearance of responding to internal stimuli
- the smell of alcohol or the smell of marijuana (pungent, sharp odor, similar to burning cane)

- the appearance of powder around the nasal opening, on the clothes, or on the hands

Students in early childhood classrooms would not have the same experience with drugs and alcohol as older students. They do, however, need to have instruction about the danger of taking prescription drugs. They see the medicine cabinet at home full of pills and medicine and need to know that these things, while legal, are very dangerous and that they should not take them. Teachers need to make this part of health class so that students know they only take medicine when needed.

Physical Abuse

Physical abuse is often not detected by teachers because the clothing covers the child's bruises. Also hidden is the traumatic effect that physical abuse has on the child's emotional state of mind. Fear affects how well the student learns and participates in class, and in young children, it is often hidden under a cloak of shyness.

Some of the signs that children who are abused may display include:

- a poor self-image
- difficulty trusting adults
- aggressive and disruptive behavior in the classroom
- displays of anger and rage over little things
- self-destructive behavior
- anxiety and fears
- fear of new situations
- failure in school

Early identification is essential for the child to continue to develop normally and without long-lasting effects.

Emotional Abuse

All students demonstrate some behaviors that may indicate emotional distress from time to time since all children experience stressful periods within their lives. However, emotionally healthy students can maintain control of their own behavior even during stressful times. Teachers need to be mindful that the difference between typical stressful behavior and severe emotional distress is determined by the frequency, duration, and intensity of stressful behavior.

Lying, stealing, and fighting are atypical behaviors that most children may exhibit occasionally, but if a child lies, steals, or fights regularly or blatantly, then these behaviors may be indicative of emotional distress. Lying is especially common among young children who feel the need to avoid punishment or as a means to make themselves feel more important. As children become older, lying is often a signal that the child is feeling insecure. These feelings of insecurity may escalate to the point of being habitual or obvious and then may indicate that the child is seeking attention because of emotional distress. Fighting, especially among siblings, is a common occurrence. However, if a child fights, is unduly aggressive, or is belligerent toward others on a long-term basis, teachers and parents need to consider the possibility of emotional problems.

How can a teacher know when a child needs help with his or her behavior? The child will indicate by what he or she does that he or she needs and wants help. Breaking rules established by parents, teachers, and other authorities and destroying property can signify that a student is losing control, especially when these behaviors occur frequently. Other signs that a child needs help may include frequent bouts of crying, a quarrelsome attitude, and constant complaints about school, friends, or life in general. Anytime a child's disposition, attitude, or habits change significantly, teachers and parents need to seriously consider the possibility of emotional difficulties.

Emotional disturbances in childhood are not uncommon and take a variety of forms. Usually these problems show up in the form of uncharacteristic behaviors. Most of the time, children respond favorably to brief treatment programs of psychotherapy. At other times, disturbances may need more intensive therapy and are harder to resolve. All stressful behaviors need to be addressed, and any type of chronic antisocial behavior needs to be examined as a possible symptom of deep-seated emotional upset.

Many safe and helpful interventions are available to the classroom teacher when dealing with a student who is suffering serious emotional disturbances. First and foremost, the teacher must maintain open communication with the parents and other professionals who are involved with the student whenever overt behavior characteristics are exhibited. Students with behavior disorders need constant behavior modification, which may involve communication between the home and school on a daily basis.

Other problems that cause students to have emotional pain include social awkwardness, depression, incipient major mental illnesses, personality disorders, learning disabilities, ADHD, conduct disorder, and substance abuse and dependency in family members. The most common emotional problems found in student populations are parent-child problems, that is, deficits in communication, authority, and respect between parent and child. A close second is conduct disorder, a behavior set characterized by aggression, exploitation, violence, disregard for the rights of others, animal cruelty, fire setting, bed wetting, defiance, running away, truancy, juvenile arrests, and associated ADHD, substance abuse, and parent-child problems.

The teacher must establish an environment that promotes appropriate behavior for all students as well as respect for one another. The students may need to be informed of any special needs that their classmates may have so they can give due consideration. The teacher should also initiate a behavior modification program for any student who might show emotional or behavioral disorders. Such behavior modification plans can be effective means of preventing deviant behavior. If deviant behavior does occur, the teacher should have arranged for a safe and secure time-out place where the student can go for a respite and an opportunity to regain self-control.

Often when a behavior disorder is more severe, the student must be involved in a more concentrated program aimed at alleviating deviant behavior, such as psychotherapy. In such instances, the school psychologist, guidance counselor, or behavior specialist is directly involved with the student and provides counseling and therapy on a regular basis. Frequently he or she is also involved with the student's family.

As a last resort, many families are turning to drug therapy. Once viewed as a radical step, administering drugs to children to balance their emotions or control their behavior has become a widely used form of therapy. Only a medical doctor can prescribe such drugs.

Skill 1.5	Identify diverse family systems and recognize their influences on children's early experiences which contribute to individual differences and development and learning

Our world is ever-changing, and the "typical" family dynamic that existed years ago is no longer quite as common. Households nowadays may contain larger families including grandparents, aunts, uncles, and cousins living under one roof. With divorce rates higher than they had been in the past, many students spend time with each of their parents separately, or they may be raised and cared for by a single parent.

Therefore, it is critical that the teacher identify with each child's situation. Being cautious when celebrating holidays in the classroom and making sure to include all parents/guardians in the child's education is critical. Students who are raised by their father rather than by their mother may feel uncomfortable when other learners are creating a craft to celebrate Mother's Day. As a way to help these children feel included, the teacher might suggest making a craft to give to another important figure in their lives.

The effective teacher will include both parents in parent-teacher conferences when applicable as well as in other school events. Understanding the situation and custody arrangements that are in place is important. The teacher will follow all court-ordered agreements for parental custody arrangements and will keep a close watch to make sure that each student within the classroom is dismissed to only the appropriate person who cares for him or her.

Keeping as many important parties as possible involved in a young learner's education is best for the student. It takes a team of family members, teachers, and administrators to ensure that each student is safe and well cared for and is therefore able to learn to the best of his or her ability each day.

Skill 1.6	Identify the influence of scientific research on theories of cognitive and social development, the principles of how children learn, and the development and implementation of instructional strategies

There are several learning theories that can be applied to classroom practices. One classic learning theory is Piaget's stages of development, which consist of four learning stages: sensorimotor (from birth to age 2); preoperation (ages 2 to 7 or early elementary); concrete operational (ages 7 to 11 or upper elementary); and formal operational (ages 7 to 15 or late elementary/high school). Piaget believed children passed through this series of stages to develop from the most basic forms of concrete thinking to sophisticated levels of abstract thinking.

Drawing on the studies of Piaget and other cognitive learning theorists, supporters of the cognitive approach maintained that children acquire knowledge of linguistic structures after they have acquired the cognitive structures necessary to process language. For example, joining words for specific meaning necessitates sensorimotor intelligence. The child must be able to coordinate movement and recognize objects before he or she can identify words to name the objects or word groups to describe the actions of these objects. Children must have developed the mental abilities for organizing concepts as well as performing concrete operations, predicting outcomes, and theorizing before they can assimilate and verbalize complex sentence structures, choose vocabulary for particular nuances of meaning, and examine semantic structures for tone and manipulative effect.

SEE Skill 2.1

Some of the most prominent learning theories in education today include brain-based learning and the multiple intelligences theory. Supported by recent brain research, brain-based learning suggests that knowledge about the way the brain retains information enables educators to design the most effective learning environments.

As a result, researchers have developed 12 principles that relate knowledge about the brain to teaching practices. These 12 principles are as follows:

- The brain is a complex adaptive system

- The brain is social
- The search for meaning is innate
- We use patterns to learn more effectively
- Emotions are crucial to developing patterns
- Each brain perceives and creates parts and whole simultaneously
- Learning involves focused and peripheral attention
- Learning involves conscious and unconscious processes
- We have at least two ways of organizing memory
- Learning is developmental
- Complex learning is enhanced by challenged (and inhibited by threat)
- Every brain is unique

(Caine & Caine, 1994, Mind/Brain Learning Principles)

Educators can use these principles to help design methods and environments in their classrooms to maximize student learning.

The multiple intelligences theory, developed by Howard Gardner, suggests that students learn in (at least) seven different ways. These include visually/spatially, musically, verbally, logically/mathematically, interpersonally, intrapersonally, and bodily/kinesthetically.

The most current learning theory, constructivist learning, allows students to construct learning opportunities. For constructivist teachers, the belief is that students create their own reality of knowledge and how to process and observe the world around them. Students are constantly constructing new ideas, which serve as frameworks for learning and teaching. Researchers have shown that the constructivist model is comprised of these four components:

1. Learner creates knowledge.
2. Learner constructs and makes meaningful new knowledge to existing knowledge.
3. Learner shapes and constructs knowledge by life experiences and social interactions.
4. In constructivist learning communities, the student, teacher, and classmates establish knowledge cooperatively on a daily basis.

Kelly (1969) states, "human beings construct knowledge systems based on their observations parallels Piaget's theory that individuals construct knowledge systems as they work with others who share a common background of thought and processes." Constructivist learning for students is dynamic and ongoing. For constructivist teachers, the classroom becomes a place where students are encouraged to interact with the instructional process by asking questions and posing new ideas to old theories. The use of cooperative learning that encourages students to work in supportive learning environments using their own ideas to stimulate questions and propose outcomes is a major aspect of a constructivist classroom.

The metacognition learning theory deals with "the study of how to help the learner gain understanding about how knowledge is constructed and about the conscious tools for constructing that knowledge" (Joyce and Weil 1996). The cognitive approach to learning involves the teacher's understanding that teaching the student to process his or her own learning and mastery of skill provides the greatest learning and retention opportunities in the classroom. Students are taught to develop concepts and teach themselves skills in problem solving and critical thinking. The student becomes an active participant in the learning process, and the teacher facilitates that conceptual and cognitive learning process.

Social and behavioral theories look at the social interactions of students in the classroom that instruct or impact learning opportunities in the classroom. The psychological approaches behind both theories are subject to individual variables that are learned and applied either proactively or negatively in the classroom. The stimulus of the classroom can be conducive to learning or can evoke behavior that is counterproductive for both students and teachers. Students are social beings that normally gravitate to action in the classroom, so teachers must be cognizant in planning classroom environments that provide both focus and engagement in maximizing learning opportunities.

Designing classrooms that provide optimal academic and behavioral support for diverse students in the classroom can be daunting for teachers. The ultimate goal for both students and teachers is creating a safe learning environment where students can construct knowledge in an engaging and positive classroom climate.

No single theory will work for every classroom, and a good approach is to incorporate a range of learning styles in a classroom. Still, under the guidance of any theory, good educators will differentiate their instructional practices to meet their students' abilities and interests using various instructional practices.

Skill 1.7   **Identify and apply strategies to involve families in their child's development and learning in all phases of school programs**

Parents and teachers should work together as a team to ensure a child is making sufficient progress developmentally and academically. Involving parents and guardians in a child's progress should be ongoing. Having a system in place for daily or weekly behavior and academic progress discussions is essential to a successful collaboration. Another way of interacting with families is the parent-teacher conference.

Parent-Teacher Conferences

The parent-teacher conference is generally for one of three purposes. First, the teacher may wish to share information with the parents concerning the performance and behavior of the child. Second, the teacher may be interested in obtaining information from the parents about the child. Such information may help answer questions or concerns that the teacher has. A third purpose may be to request parent support or involvement in specific activities or requirements. In many situations, more than one of the purposes may be involved.

Planning the Conference

When a conference is scheduled, whether at the request of the teacher or parent, the teacher should allow sufficient time to prepare thoroughly. Collect all relevant information, samples of student work, records of behavior, and other items needed to help the parent understand the circumstances. It is also a good idea to compile a list of questions or concerns you wish to address. Arrange the time and location of the conference to provide privacy and to avoid interruptions.

Conducting the Conference

Begin the conference by putting the parent as ease. Take the time to establish a comfortable mood, but do not waste time with unnecessary small talk. Begin your discussion with positive comments about the student. Identify strengths and desirable attributes, but do not exaggerate.

As you address issues or areas of concern, be sure to focus on observable behaviors and concrete results or information. Do not make judgmental statements about parent or child. Share specific work samples, anecdotal records of behavior, and so on, which demonstrate clearly the concerns you have. Be a good listener and hear the parent's comments and explanations. Such background information can be invaluable in understanding the needs and motivations of the child.

Finally, end the conference with an agreed plan of action between parents and teacher (and, when appropriate, the child). Bring the conference to a close politely but firmly and thank the parent for being involved.

After the Conference

A day or two after the conference, it is a good idea to send a follow-up note to the parent. In this note, briefly and concisely reiterate the plan or step agreed to in the conference. Be polite and professional; avoid the temptation to be too informal or chatty. If the issue is a long-term one, such as the behavior or ongoing work performance of the student, make periodic follow-up contacts to keep the parent informed of the student's progress.

The effective teacher will utilize applicable tools and reporting systems according to the school and district's expectations. These reports might occur each grading period, in the middle of a grading period, or once a month. As teachers report progress, it is crucial to be positive and share effective feedback about the child. Providing details about a child's weaknesses can help the guardian assist at home with extra reinforcement strategies.

Schools will plan social and learning events and invite parents and guardians to be a part of their parent-teacher organization. These are positive ways for parents to see the teachers in afterschool settings and also allow the children to see their parents and school personnel working together. Planning activity nights, family bingo, carnivals, plays, and other performances are all excellent ways to bring the school and community together.

Skill 1.8   **Identify and apply strategies to facilitate family and community partnerships**

Connecting School to the Outside World

According to Campbell, Campbell, and Dickinson (1992) "Teaching and Learning Through Multiple Intelligences," "The changing nature of demographics is one of the strongest rationales for multicultural education in the United States." The Census Bureau predicts a changing demographic for the American population and school communities, which includes the forecast that between 1990 and 2030, "while the white population will increase by 25%, the African American population will increase by 68%, the Asian-American, Pacific Island, and American Indian by 79%, and the Hispanic-American population by 187%." Reinforcing the learning beyond the classroom must include a diversity of instructional and learning strategies for any adult role models in a student's life.

Mentoring has become an instrumental tool in addressing student achievement and access to learning. Adult mentors work individually with identified students on specific subject areas to reinforce the learning through tutorial instruction and application of knowledge. Providing students with role models to reinforce the learning has become a crucial instructional strategy for teachers seeking to maximize student learning beyond the classroom. Students who work with adult mentors from culturally diverse backgrounds are given a multicultural aspect of learning that is cooperative and multimodal.

The interpersonal use of technology provides a mentoring tutorial support system and different conceptual learning modalities for students seeking to understand classroom material. Technology provides a networking opportunity for students to find study buddies and peer study groups, along with free academic support to problem-solve and develop critical thinking skills that are imperative in acquiring knowledge and conceptual learning. Distance learning is a technological strategy that keeps students and teachers interactively communicating about issues in the classroom and beyond. Students will communicate more freely using technology to ask teacher or adult mentors clarity questions than they will in a classroom of peers.

The Community as a Resource

The community is a vital link to increasing learning experiences for students. Community resources can supplement the minimized and marginal educational resources of school communities. With state and federal educational funding becoming increasingly subject to legislative budget cuts, school communities welcome the financial support that community resources can provide in terms of discounted prices on high-end supplies (such as computers, printers, and technology supplies), and often provide free notebooks, backpacks, and student supplies for low-income students who may have difficulty obtaining the basic supplies for school.

Community stores can provide cash rebates and teacher discounts for educators in struggling school districts and compromised school communities. Both professionally and personally, communities can enrich student learning experiences by including the following support strategies:

- Provide programs that support student learning outcomes and future educational goals
- Create mentoring opportunities that provide adult role models in various industries to students interested in studying in those industries
- Provide financial support for school communities to help low-income or homeless students begin the school year with the basic supplies
- Develop paid internships with local university students to provide tutorial services for identified students in school communities who are having academic and social difficulties processing various subject areas
- Provide parent-teen-community forums to create a public voice of change in communities
- Offer parents without computers or Internet connections stipends to purchase technology to create equitable opportunities for students to do research and complete word processing requirements
- Stop in classrooms and ask teachers and students what's needed to promote academic progress and growth

Community resources are vital in providing that additional support to students, school communities, and families struggling to remain engaged in declining educational institutions competing for federal funding and limited district funding. The commitment that a community shows to its educational communities is a valuable investment in the future. Community resources that are able to provide additional funding for tutors in marginalized classrooms or to help schools reduce classrooms of students needing additional remedial instruction, directly impact educational equity and facilitate teaching and learning for both teachers and students.

Promoting a Sense of Community

The bridge to effective learning for students begins with a collaborative approach by all stakeholders that support the educational needs of students. Underestimating the power and integral role of the community institutions in impacting the current and future goals of students can carry high stakes for students beyond the high school years who are competing for college access, student internships, and entry-level jobs in the community. Researchers have shown that school involvement and connections with community institutions have greater rates of students graduating and seeking higher education. The current disconnect and autonomy that has become commonplace in today's society must be reevaluated in terms of promoting tomorrow's citizens.

When community institutions provide students and teachers with meaningful connections and input, the commitment is apparent in terms of volunteering, loyalty, and professional promotion. Providing students with placements in leadership positions such as the ASB (Associated Student Body); the PTSA (Parent-Teacher-Student Association); school boards; neighborhood subcommittees addressing political or social issues; or government boards that impact and influence school communities creates an avenue for students to explore ethical, participatory, collaborative, transformational leadership that can be applied to all areas of a student's educational and personal life.

Community liaisons provide students with opportunities to experience accountability and responsibility so that students learn about life and how organizations use effective communication and teams working together to accomplish goals and objectives. These liaisons can teach students skills of inclusion and social and environmental responsibility, create public forums that represent student voices and foster student interest, and provide students an opportunity to develop and reflect on individual opinions and understand the dynamics of the world around them.

When a student sees that the various support systems are in place and consistently working to effectively provide resources and avenues of academic promotion and accountability, students have no fear of taking risks to grow by becoming a teen voice on a local committee about teen violence or volunteering in a local hospice for young children with terminal illnesses. The linkages of community institutions provide role models of a world in which the student will soon become an integral and vital member, so being a part of that world as a student makes the transition easier as a young adult.

COMPETENCY 2.0   KNOWLEDGE OF THE PROFESSION AND FOUNDATIONS OF EARLY CHILDHOOD (PREK–3) EDUCATION

Skill 2.1   Identify theorists, theories, and developmental domains in the fields of early childhood and elementary education and their implication for the classroom teacher of young children

Jean Piaget

Jean Piaget, a European scientist who died in the late twentieth century, developed many theories about the way humans learn. Most famously, he developed a theory about the stages of the development of human minds. It's very simple. The first stage is the sensorimotor stage, which lasts until a child is in the toddler years. In this stage, taking place from birth until about 18 or 24 months, children begin to understand their senses.

The next stage, from 18 to 24 months until age 7, called the preoperational stage, is when children begin to understand symbols. For example, as they learn language, they begin to realize that words are symbols of thoughts, actions, items, and other elements in the world. This stage lasts into early elementary school.

The third stage is referred to as the concrete operational stage, and takes place from ages 7 to 12. In this stage, children go one step beyond learning what a symbol is. They learn how to manipulate symbols, objects, and other elements. A common example of this stage is the displacement of water. In this stage, children can reason that a wide and short cup and a tall and thin cup can actually hold the same amount of water.

The next stage is called the formal operational stage. It usually starts in adolescence or early teen years and continues into adulthood. This stage is what allows critical thinking, hypotheses, systematic organization of knowledge, and so on.

Generally, when we say that children move from a stage of concrete thinking to logical and abstract thinking, we mean that they are moving from the preoperational and concrete operational stages to the formal operational stage. As anyone who spends time with children knows, there are many bumps in the road to a person's ability to be a strong critical thinker. Simply because a child has moved into a particular stage does not mean that the child will be able to complete functions at the specified level. For example, adolescents may be able to think critically, but they need plenty of instruction and assistance to do so at an adequate level. This does not necessarily mean that critical thinking skills should be taught out of context; rather, through all lessons, teachers should work to instill components that help develop children's thinking.

Benjamin Bloom

In 1956, Benjamin Bloom, an educational psychologist developed a detailed classification of critical thinking and learning skills/objectives into tiered levels. These hierarchal levels ordered thinking skills from the simplest (or lower-order) thinking skills to the highest (or higher-order) thinking skills. The goal of Bloom's taxonomy was to motivate teachers to teach at all levels of critical thinking, not just at the most common level—the lower-order thinking skills such as memorize, restate, and define. For details on the taxonomy, SEE Skill 6.14.

Lawrence Kohlberg

Lawrence Kohlberg outlined what is now known as Kohlberg's stages of moral development in 1958. Kohlberg's six stages are grouped into three levels: pre-conventional, conventional, and post-conventional. Each level consists of two stages according to Kohlberg.

- Pre-conventional (Egocentric: up to age 9)
  - Punishment/obedience: Morality is based on established rules. Children in this stage see that following the rules and/or avoiding negative consequences defines moral behavior.
  - Instrumental purpose: In this stage, whatever satisfies the child's needs is considered moral by that child.
- Conventional (Socio-centric: age 9 to adolescence)
  - Interpersonal: Children begin to understand that good behavior is expected, and achieving those expectations is moral.
  - Social system: Adolescents at this stage understand that there is a need for them to fulfill obligations and expectations, and that this fulfillment constitutes moral behavior.
- Post-conventional (adulthood)
  - Social contract: Individuals understand that various cultures, as well as individuals, have different definitions of morality, and good moral behavior is seen as living up to the moral standards of that person's social norm.
  - Universal ethical principles: At this stage, reasoning is based on ethical fairness, and individuals are able to judge themselves and others based on their own sense of morality.

Please refer to:

- http://allpsych.com/psychology101/moral_development.html
- http://www.utmem.edu/~vmurrell/dissertation/Kohlberg.htm

Skill 2.2   Identify curriculum models of early childhood (e.g., Montessori, Creative Curriculum)

Early curriculum models in elementary education programs have historical roots in Head Start programs in the early 1960s that were created to provide a comprehensive curriculum model for preparation of low-income students for success in school communities. During the 1970s and 1980s, curriculum models were replaced with a diversity of models that focused on academic achievement for all students in educational environments. The resurfacing of curriculum models in the early 1990s was rekindled by researchers who provided longitudinal research that the construction of curriculum models had an impact on early childhood development and academic success.

The emergence of Head Start programs and community-centered programs has provided conceptual and actual frameworks of well-defined curriculum models that are consistent in serving students at risk in academic acquisition.

There are many widely known curriculum models that continue to contribute to effective curriculum model development. The following models are used for early childhood curriculum:

- **Head Start**: This is a federally funded program designed to provide a comprehensive preschool program to children of underprivileged families. The focus is to ensure that children have the appropriate reading readiness skills by the time they enter kindergarten. It originated in 1965 and received a boost with the No Child Left Behind Act of 2001.

- **Montessori method**: In the Montessori curriculum model there are one or two uninterrupted three-hour work periods. During this time, the children are engaged in working at centers in mixed-age groups. The focus is on constant interaction, problem-solving, and socialization. The children are constantly challenged and are not bored.

- **Creative curriculum**: This type of curriculum focuses on thematic units as a way to teach young learners. Concepts are integrated across all subject areas. Students are engaged and are able to reflect on the information in various cross curricular ways.

- **High/scope curriculum**: This type of learning is based on the work of Jean Piaget and John Dewey. It also centers upon the ideas of Lev Vygotsky. The teacher is seen as a facilitator of learning, while children are actively engaged in their own problem-solving and discoveries.

Theoretical research has provided a definitive foundation in understanding how to develop curriculum models that frame how teachers instruct and how students learn in classrooms.

Curriculum models are conceptual frameworks that are structurally organized to impact and inform educational decision-making and policy direction. Acting as guides for program implementation and curriculum evaluation, curriculum models are foundation constructs for early elementary programs serving all students. Curriculum models vary in structure and school implementation. The goal of curriculum models is to provide consistency in instruction and create evaluation criteria for uniformity in programs designated for early childhood curriculum.

Researchers continue to show that childhood curriculum models produce effective academic outcomes. However, there are also limitations in curriculum reform that impact the implementation of specifically designed curriculum models that educate and accelerate the academic learning of students needing additional educational support in school communities. In designing early childhood curriculum models that raise academic standards and outcomes for students, the quality of instruction for students by experienced educators will ultimately improve elementary education programs.

Strategies used in the design and implementation of effective curriculum models should include the following instruction:

- Lesson concepts diversified for individual student learning goals
- Differentiated instruction for group/individual academic needs
- Best practices and instructional approaches
- Enhanced curriculum design that includes rigor and is relevant and relationship-oriented
- Portfolio of evaluation assessments for individual student performance
- Reading and writing level testing results for specified literacy skills and identified reading levels
- Worldwide application of curriculum design and reading resources

Curriculum models should contain predicative conceptual frameworks that outline specific academic expectations and evaluation components for those evaluating the effectiveness of implemented programs. Early childhood and elementary education programs must incorporate both the cognitive and social development of young learners in designing effective curriculum models. As educators increase their usage of curriculum models in elementary education, the ultimate educational goal and focus should be to improve curriculum programs for children.

Skill 2.3	Identify and analyze the impact of federal and state laws on education in the classroom (e.g., English for Speakers of Other Languages, Individuals with Disabilities Education Act)

ESOL

Teaching students who are learning English as a second language pose some unique challenges, particularly in a standards-based environment. The key is realizing that no matter how little English a student knows, the teacher should teach with the student's developmental level in mind. This means that instruction should not be "dumbed down" for ESOL (English to Speakers of Other Languages) students. Different approaches should be used, however, to ensure that these students get multiple opportunities to learn and practice English and still learn content.

Many ESOL approaches are based on social learning methods. By being placed in mixed-level groups or by being paired with a student of another ability level, students will get a chance to practice English in a natural, nonthreatening environment. Students should not be pushed in these groups to use complex language or to experiment with words that are too difficult. They should simply get a chance to practice with simple words and phrases.

In teacher-directed instructional situations, visual aids—such as pictures, objects, and video—are particularly effective at helping students make connections between words and items with which they are already familiar.

ESOL students may need additional accommodations with assessments, assignments, and projects. For example, teachers may find that written tests provide little or no information about a student's understanding of the content. Therefore, an oral test may be better suited for ESOL students. When students are somewhat comfortable and capable with written tests, a shortened test may actually be preferable; take note that they will need extra time to translate.

IDEA

IDEA (Individuals with Disabilities Act) passed in 1990, has a direct impact on classrooms. This law ensures that all children with disabilities and their families receive the help and support they need. It governs how states and public agencies can provide intervention services and how schools can provide special education services for these children. Part A of the law covers children from birth to age 2 and Part B covers children with disabilities from ages 3 to 21. The first step is to identify the specific learning disability and then to act upon getting the help the child needs. From the beginning and throughout the process, the family is involved along with a team at the school, which includes outside agencies that can provide support.

The referral of students for this process is usually relatively simple for the classroom teacher and requires little more than some initial paperwork and discussion. The services and resources the student receives as a result of the process typically prove to be invaluable to students with disabilities.

At times, the teacher must go beyond the school system to meet the needs of some students. An awareness of special services and resources and how to obtain them is essential for all teachers and their students. When the school system is unable to address the needs of a student, the teacher often must take the initiative and contact agencies within the community. Frequently there is no special policy for finding resources. It is up to the individual teacher to be creative and resourceful and to find whatever help the student needs. Meeting the needs of all students is certainly a team effort that is most often spearheaded by the classroom teacher.

Skill 2.4	Identify professional organizations, Websites, and scholarly journals in the field of early and elementary education

There are a variety of professional organizations, Websites, and scholarly journals/books that provide vital educational information on early and elementary education programs and models. The information will be categorized according to the defined criteria and presented as resources for educators seeking quality strategies to improve early childhood education for students.

Books

Epsteing, A.S., Schweinhart, L.J., & McAdoo, L. (1996). *Models of Early childhood education.* Ypsilanti, MI: High/Scope Press.

Essa, E.L. (2006). *Introduction to early childhood education.* (5th ed.). New York: Thomson Delmar Learning.

Harvey, S., & Goudvis, A. (2000). *Strategies that work: Teaching comprehension to enhance understanding.* York, Maine: Stenhouse Publishers.

Goffin, S.G., & Wilson, C. (2001). *Curriculum models and early childhood education: Appraising the relationship.* (2nd ed.). Upper Saddle River, NJ: Merrill/Prentice Hall.

Morrison, G.S. (2005). *Fundamentals of early childhood education.* (4th ed.). New York: Prentice Hall.

Morrison, G.S. (2001). *Early childhood education today.* (8th ed.). Columbus, OH: Merrill/Prentice Hall.

Powell, D.R. (1987). Comparing preschool curricula and practices: The state of research. In S. L. Kagan & E.F. Zigler (eds.), *Early schooling: The national debate* (190–211). New Haven, CT: Yale University Press.

Journals

Journal of Moral Education

Review of Educational Research

Teacher Magazine

Curriculum Design and Development

Educational Leadership

Marcon, R.A. (1999). "Differential impact of preschool models on development and early learning of inner-city children: A three-cohort study." *Developmental Psychology,* 35(2), 358–375.

Schweinhart, L.J., & Weikart, D.P. (1997). The High/Scope preschool curriculum comparison study through age 23. *Early Childhood Research Quarterly*, 12(2), 117–143.

Websites

Educational Archives

http://ceep.crc.uiuc,edu//eecearchive/digests/2000/goffin00.html. Goffin, S.G. (2000). The role of curriculum models in early childhood education. EDO-PS-00-8.

Education Week: News and Information about Education Reform and Concerns http://www/edweek.org/ew/index.html.

Professional Organizations

The Southern Early Childhood Association
P.O. Box 55930
Little Rock, AR 72215-5930
800-305-7322
E-mail: gbean@southernearlychildhood.org
Website: http://www.southernearlychildhood.org/postion_earlyliteracy.html

National Study of School Evaluation (NSSE)
1699 East Woodfield Road, Suite 406
Schaumburg, IL 60173
847-995-9080
Website: http://www.nsse.org

Center for the Improvement of Early Reading Achievement (CIERA)
University of Michigan School of Education
610 E. University, Room 1600 SEB
Ann Arbor, MI 48109-1259
734-647-6940
Website: http://www.ciera.org/

ERIC Clearinghouse on Reading, English, and Communication
Indiana University
Smith Research Center, Suite 150
Bloomington, IN 47408-2698
800-759-4723
Website: http://www.indiana.edu/~eric_rec/

National Institute for Literacy
1775 I St. N.W., Suite 730
Washington, DC 20006-2401
202-233-2025
Andrew Hartman, Director
Website: http://www.nifl.gov

Skill 2.5   **Interpret professional standards set by early childhood and elementary educational organizations (e.g., National Association for the Education of Young Children, Association for Childhood Educational International, National Council of Teachers of Mathematics, Southern Early Childhood Association)**

The following organizations have been instrumental in providing educational support for school communities; parents, legislators, and educators by promoting educational reform; designing innovative curriculum to address student academic needs; and providing a collaborative process for reform and instruction.

Professional Standards

International Reading Association (IRA)

The International Reading Association (IRA) is a comprehensive professional organization for effectively preparing teachers and educators for reading instruction. The guided mission and position for IRA is providing support in increasing literacy skills and reading instruction for students along with promoting effective instruction for parents, educators, and policymakers.

The governing board and mission of IRA are directed by Dr. Karen Douglas. Additional information can be obtained at the following e-mail address: kdouglas@reading.org. The IRA engages in studying the research and data from national organizations and school communities on effective reading instruction and strategies that promote reading acquisition.

Providing teachers with reading instruction in the newly created Status of Reading Instruction Institute has been beneficial in developing programs and initiatives promoting reading preparation programs for school communities. In preparing elementary teachers for reading instruction, the impact on school communities is in creating better readers and academic accessibility for students.

Association for Childhood Education International (ACEI)

The position statement for the Association for Childhood Education International (ACEI) is a collaborative one that extends its vision and mission of educational development for students into the global community. The position is progressive and demonstrates a strong commitment to students and staff in changing school communities and educational reform.

The mission of being influential in developing professional programs and training opportunities for educators and students benefiting from progressive and international educational programs remains an integral aspect of the position statement of ACEI. Providing consistent educational standards and equity are the cornerstones of the ACEI position statement in addressing the educational needs of elementary students.

National Association for the Education of Young Children (NAEYC)

The focus of the National Association for the Education of Young Children (NAEYC) is improving and developing programs and services for children from birth through age eight. The association was founded in 1926 and is considered the world's largest educational organization, with almost 100,000 members who work on behalf of the education of young children.

As a global organization, the NAEYC has a governing board that deals with educational issues relevant to childhood education policy and practices. With almost 300 affiliates working on behalf of educating young children, the NAEYC extends membership to anyone dedicated to promoting the educational needs of children.

The NAEYC provides position statements on a variety of educational issues related to childhood program development online at http://www.naeyc.org:

- Code of ethical conduct and statement of commitment with supplements for adult educators and program administrators
- Framework for conceptual professional development, early childhood curriculum, assessment, and program evaluation
- Early childhood mathematics and learning standards
- Learning to read and write

The influence of NAEYC on instructional practices for educators is extensive in providing a comprehensive educational approach in developing and promoting educational practices and policies that directly impact the learning acquisition of young children.

National Council of Teachers of Mathematics (NCTM)

The governing position for the National Council of Teachers of Mathematics (NCTM) directly impacts educational decision-making of administrators, teachers, and other professional staff in school communities. The principal positions for the NCTM are governed under the following six overarching themes impacting mathematics standards for Pre-Kindergarten through Grade 12:

- Equity—Curriculum design and implementation must have rigor and excellence, providing opportunity for all students.
- Curriculum—There must be a consistent and structured focus on mathematical conceptual design and instruction that is aligned from grade level to grade level.
- Teaching—Mathematical inclusion must provide a cultural and challenging instructional implementation effective for all students.
- Learning—Performance-based assessment opportunities for students must include assessments and evaluations that substantiate students' prior knowledge and skill base.
- Assessment—Congruent evaluations of mathematical conceptual learning must have real-life applications for students.
- Technology—Technology must be used to connect students with additional resources to study mathematical concepts and applications.

The comprehensive aspect of NCTM in providing an overview of standards for school mathematics directly influences how school communities construct curriculum design and direct teacher instruction for students in grades Pre-K through 12. With consistency in curriculum design and implementation, an alignment of evaluation tools can be constructed to assess student learning of mathematical concepts and applications.

Southern Early Childhood Association

The Southern Early Childhood Association provides a number of position statements on educational reform and curriculum models promoting student educational excellence. In its Early Literacy and Beginning to Read position statement, the Southern Early Childhood Association promotes early literacy for children learning to read and write. The association believes that literacy is collaborative and inclusive of all stakeholders in a young child's life: parents, teachers; invested adults, and neighborhood communities.

In promoting early literacy, the association understands that young children must be allowed opportunities to become active participants in activities that promote literacy skill development. Professional development opportunities for teachers must deal not only with literacy skill and curriculum model development but also with cultural influences of how students from different ethnic and cultural backgrounds acquire literacy skills. The framework for literacy development and reading proficiency must begin in the foundational years of childhood development, Pre-K through Grade 2, and formal educational training.

Other position statements promoted by the Southern Early Childhood Association include the following and all are available online at www.southernearlychildhood.org:

- Brain Research and Its Implications for Early Childhood Programs
- Assessing Development and Learning in Young Children
- Quality Child Care
- Supporting Learning with Technology in the Early Childhood Classroom
- Arts & Movement Education for Young Children
- Valuing Diversity for Young Children
- Invest in Children, Invest in Virginia: Universal Pre-Kindergarten, the Right Investment for the Right Reasons.

Skill 2.6 **Analyze the relationships among current educational issues, trends, and legislation and their impact on the field of early childhood education**

There are a variety of current issues, trends, educational innovations, and legislation that impact elementary school communities. National assessments and local evaluations of student academic performance in the areas of reading, writing, and math have shown that there are gaps in learning from one cultural group to another in classrooms. The issue of student learning and performance has become a national debate about whether providing additional educational funding will create academic access for students identified as at risk in schools.

Current Trends

Differentiating Instruction

The effective teacher will seek to connect all students to the subject matter through multiple techniques, with the goal that each student, through his or her own abilities, will relate to one or more techniques and excel in the learning process. Differentiated instruction encompasses several areas:

1. Content: What is the teacher going to teach? Or, perhaps better put, what does the teacher want the students to learn? Differentiating content means that students will have access to content that piques their interest about a topic, with a complexity that provides an appropriate challenge to their intellectual development.
2. Process: A classroom management technique in which instructional organization and delivery is maximized for the diverse student group. These techniques should include dynamic, flexible grouping activities, in which instruction and learning occurs as whole-class, teacher-led activities and as peer learning and teaching (while teacher observes and coaches) within small groups or pairs.
3. Product: The expectations and requirements placed on students to demonstrate their knowledge or understanding. The type of product expected from each student should reflect each student's own capabilities.

Creating programs for literacy development and mathematical acquisition have become both the issues and the trends in the construct of new educational innovations. Differentiating instruction for learners who come to school in the Pre-K grades has become a focus for educators seeking to increase the literacy and mathematical skills of their youngest learners. The development of effective programs and subsequent funding continue to be the goals of a legislative process dedicated to promoting educational equity for students.

Alternative Assessment

An alternative assessment is an assessment in which students create an answer or a response to a question or task, as opposed to traditional, inflexible assessments in which students choose a prepared response from among a selection of responses, such as matching, multiple-choice, or true/false.

When implemented effectively, an alternative assessment approach will exhibit these characteristics, among others:

- Requires higher-order thinking and problem-solving
- Provides opportunities for student self-reflection and self-assessment
- Uses real-world applications to connect students to the subject

- Provides opportunities for students to learn and examine subjects on their own as well as to collaborate with their peers.
- Encourages students to continuing learning beyond the requirements of the assignment
- Clearly defines objective and performance goals

Inquiry-based learning is performance-based learning in which students are actively involved in the learning process and in the construction of new knowledge. When students engage in inquiry-based learning to understand the world around them, the learning process involves the formulation of questions that convert new information into an active application of knowledge.

Figure 1 shows the contextual and interactive component of inquiry-based learning for students.

Figure 1 Inquiry-based learning model

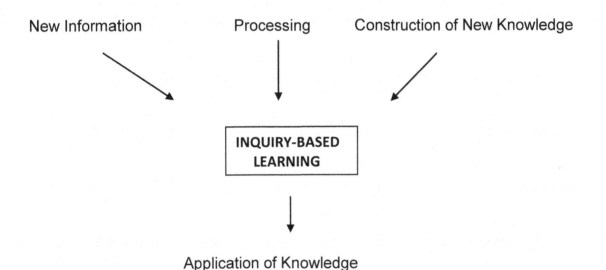

Application of Knowledge

When students are given new information to process, inquiry-based learning becomes a natural extension of knowledge acquisition and understanding. In traditional classrooms, the lecture becomes the mode of learning for students seeking to understand the context of mathematical application and real-life application of problem-solving skills learned in the traditional math class. In an inquiry-based learning format, students are shown how to apply mathematical learning and are actively involved in real-life application of newly constructed knowledge. Involving students in the active processing of mathematical learning increases their ability to construct frameworks of understanding into useful applications of new knowledge.

Legislation

Legislation issues of educational funding for teachers and program developments continue to impact existing educational implementations for students. With thousands of school communities failing to meet NCLB (No Child Left Behind) and AYP (Adequate Yearly Progress) standards, the cost of overhaul and providing additional financial support for effective school communities with over-capacity issues is a major reason for the decreased funding provided to current educational communities. Students who have been promoted from Pre-K to higher elementary grade levels but who have failed to attain the basic skills of reading, writing, and math are becoming increasingly frustrated by school systems designed to promote rather than hold accountability for student learning and evaluation.

Other Current Issues

The cost of teacher turnover in school communities has been estimated to be in the range of $5–7 billion, which further impacts the legislature's ability to provide enough funding for all educational communities. Professional development training and required certification classes for teachers in elementary education also contribute to the comprehensive cost of educating students.

Early violence in elementary school communities coupled with classroom management issues have contributed to a reduction in teaching and instructional time for young learners. Providing young learners with ethical and social strategies to improve cooperative learning and communication will go a long way toward reducing the time spent on conflict and increasing the time spent on learning acquisition.

Educational innovations in technology and educational reform must address the issues that are creating conflicting issues that impact educational development and implementation of effective curriculum for young learners. Current educational reform must continue to focus on addressing educational issues that promote learning opportunities and professional development for both students and educators.

Skill 2.7	**Analyze and apply ethical behavior and professional responsibilities as they relate to young children, families, colleagues, and the community (e.g., Florida Educator Accomplished Practices, Florida Department of Education Code of Ethics, National Association for the Education of Young Children Code of Ethics)**

Ethical behavior and professional responsibilities for early childhood educators are principles or codes of ethics that govern the practices of educators in school communities. The educators' role in guiding and building the learning capacity of young children is extremely important in developing a culture of learning and academic success that defines optimal student and teacher performance.

Character Education and the Early Childhood Program

Developing character and ethical responsibility in today's students has become the mainstay of teacher instruction, along with academic and social direction. Thinking about the issues of developing judgment and direction for young students with cognitive and physiological constructs that may prevent them from applying the learning is its own dilemma for educators.

Ethical instruction must come from a variety of alternative resources dedicated to the promotion of educational development of young learners. The inclusion of ethical dilemmas in curriculum design and instructional practice will allow educators the opportunity to address student ethical behavior within the guise of the curriculum expectations.

In elementary classrooms, teachers can use the following activities to develop character and ethical responsibility in early childhood programs:

- Artistic designs to help students think about everyday ethical dilemmas
- Ethical journals in which students keep a record of daily school experiences
- Cooperative team activities to build character education, such as role-playing school dilemmas and outcomes
- Assessments that provide students with scenarios to evaluate and apply solutions in ethical dilemmas and character education issues
- Classroom discussions on student-centered ethical issues

When students are able share their daily experiences and understanding of their world in a safe and nurturing learning environment, they are able to evaluate and redirect their own ethical issues that occur during the school day and build character in the process.

Working Well with Colleagues

Ethical expectations for students and staff should be included in handbooks with definitive outlines of behavioral and ethical operatives. Progressive school communities provide professional development on ethics training and strategies for constructing and implementing ethical discussion and activities in subject-area expectations.

By incorporating a core of ethical expectations for both students and staff, school communities can set the tone and school climate for accountability in action. To help students develop an ethical compass in behavior and performance in classrooms, educational staff must include ethical inclusion in classroom instruction and implementation. Professional modeling of expected student behavior and ethical standards by adults in the school community will provide an adult compass for students seeking to develop their inner source of ethical values and character development.

Professional development for staff on ethical inclusion in curriculum and instructional practices must provide a consistency of implementation throughout the school community. Practical strategies for dealing with the myriad of daily expectations and dilemmas in learning environments should be the cornerstone of staff development that improves staff collaboration and ethical character.

Connecting Ethics to the Community

School-wide community building activities that provide a connective bridge of ethical character building for students, parents, staff, and community members can present effective community outreach opportunities. Ethical development for students who take part in community programs after school can become aligned extensions of ethical expectations from the school community.

To connect the existing school code of ethical character building to the community, the following strategies can be employed to maintain effective networking between schools and communities:

- Create community links and technology Websites between schools and communities to develop a consistency of the school's ethical codes and expectations for students participating in community support programs.
- Share the schools' code of ethics by providing community members with a copy of the handbook or by directing members to the school's Website linkage on ethical expectations and character building.
- Develop a collaborative community/school ethics panel for consultation and a source for speakers on the subject of student and staff ethical character building.
- Engage in community-based professional development of ethics workshops and invite community members to school workshops on ethical implementation in classrooms.

COMPETENCY 3.0   KNOWLEDGE OF DEVELOPMENTALLY APPROPRIATE PRACTICES

Skill 3.1   Identify and apply developmentally appropriate practices that guide effective instruction

Knowledge of age-appropriate expectations is fundamental to the teacher's positive relationship with students and effective instructional strategies. Equally important is the knowledge of what is individually appropriate for the specific children in a classroom. Developmentally oriented teachers approach classroom groups and individual students with a respect for their emerging capabilities. Developmental professionals recognize that kids grow in common patterns but at different rates, which usually cannot be accelerated by adult pressure or input. Developmentally oriented teachers know that variance in the school performance of different children often results from differences in their general growth. With the establishment of inclusionary classes throughout the schools, it is vital for all teachers to know the characteristics of students' exceptionalities and their implications for learning.

If an educational program is child-centered, then it will surely address the abilities and needs of the students because it will take its cues from students' interests, concerns, and questions. Making an educational program child-centered involves building on the natural curiosity children bring to school and asking children what they want to learn.

Teachers help students identify their own questions, puzzles, and goals, and then structure for them widening circles of experience and investigation of those topics. Teachers manage to infuse all the skills, knowledge, and concepts that society mandates into a child-driven curriculum. This does not mean passive teachers who respond only to students' explicit cues. Teachers also draw on their understanding of children's developmentally characteristic needs and enthusiasms to design experiences that lead children into areas they might not choose but that they enjoy and find engaging. Teachers also bring their own interests and enthusiasms into the classroom to share and to act as a motivational means of guiding children.

Implementing such a child-centered curriculum is the result of very careful and deliberate planning. Planning serves as a means of organizing instruction and influences classroom teaching. Well-thought-out planning includes specifying behavioral objectives, specifying students' entry behavior (knowledge and skills), selecting and sequencing learning activities so as to move students from entry behavior to objective, and evaluating the outcomes of instruction to improve planning.

Planning for instructional activities entails identification or selection of the activities in which the teacher and students will engage during a period of instruction. Planning is a multifaceted activity that includes the following considerations: the determination of the order in which activities will be completed; the specification of the component parts of an activity, including their order; the materials to be used for each part; the particular roles of the teacher and students; decisions about the amount of time to be spent on a given activity and the number of activities to be completed during a period of instruction; judgment of the appropriateness of an activity for a particular situation; and specifications of the organization of the class for the activity.

Attention to learner needs during planning is foremost and includes the identification of what the students already know or need to know; the matching of learner needs with instructional elements such as content, materials, activities, and goals; and the determination of whether students have performed at an acceptable level following instruction.

SEE also Skill 1.3

Skill 3.2   **Identify the components of effective organization and management, such as classroom rituals, routines, and schedules**

Punctuality is defined as when a teacher begins class work promptly. If class is delayed for 10 minutes every day over the school year, almost two months of instruction is lost. Therefore, it is very important to begin class on time. Effective teachers are punctual. This is because punctuality leads to more on-task time, which results in greater subject matter retention among the students.

There are a number of things that hinder teachers from beginning instruction immediately. Some examples are attendance, discipline, or just getting students to settle down. Effective teachers have predetermined plans to deal with these distractions.

Dealing with the daily task of attendance can be done efficiently and quickly with the use of a seating chart. A teacher can spot absentees in seconds by noting the empty seats, rather than calling each student's name, which could take as long as five minutes. This laborious roll-calling time is also the ideal situation for deviant behaviors to occur, resulting in further off-task time. Therefore, the use of seating charts leads to more on-task time. Another timesaving technique is to laminate the seating chart. This allows the teacher to make daily notes right on the chart. The teacher may also efficiently keep track of who is volunteering and who is answering questions. The effective teacher uses this information to create an equitable classroom climate for all students.

Deviant behavior can lead to more off-task time than any other factor in today's classrooms. Effective teachers reduce the incidence of these behaviors through clear-cut rules and consistency. If the teacher is consistent, then the students know what to expect and learn very quickly that they, too, must be consistent.

Beginning-teacher programs teach that effective teachers state the rules, explain the rules, and then put the students through a guided practice of the rules. This will result in a clear understanding of what behaviors are expected in the classroom from each student. Moreover, it is more efficient to reduce the occurrence of deviant behaviors rather than dealing with them when they happen. Effective teachers achieve this through clear-cut rule explication and consistent monitoring.

Furthermore, effective teachers maintain a businesslike atmosphere in the classroom. This leads to the students getting on task quickly when instruction begins. There are many ways effective teachers begin instruction immediately. One method is through the use of on-screen projections.

The teacher turns on the projected lesson presentation the second class begins, and the students begin taking notes. The teacher is then free to circulate for the first few minutes of class and settle down individual students as necessary. Additionally, having a routine that is followed regularly at the beginning of class allows the students to begin without waiting for teacher instruction. By doing this, effective teachers maintain businesslike, consistent classrooms.

Effective teachers use class time efficiently. This results in higher student subject engagement and will likely result in more subject matter retention. One way teachers use class time efficiently is through a smooth transition from one activity to another; this is also known as management transition. Management transition is defined as shifts from one activity to another in a systemic, academically oriented way. One factor that contributes to efficient management transition is the teacher's management of instructional material. Management of instructional material is defined as teacher preparation of materials that are to be used for a particular segment of instruction. Effective teachers gather their materials during the planning stage of instruction. In other words, if a teacher is going to utilize a chart or a map in a lesson, the chart or map is already prepared and in place in the classroom before class begins. Furthermore, all materials are copied and in order ready to pass out as needed. This results in the efficient distribution of materials and leads to less off-task time. By doing this, a teacher avoids flipping through things looking for the items necessary for the current lesson. Momentum is lost and student concentration is broken when this occurs. This is also the ideal time for deviant behaviors to occur.

In conclusion, effective teachers utilize class time efficiently. The teacher understands it is important to begin class promptly because of the enormous amount of teaching time that can be lost. Therefore, effective teachers attend to attendance procedures and other nonacademic tasks routinely while maintaining on-task behavior among the students.

Additionally, teachers who keep students informed of the sequencing of instructional activities maintain systematic transitions because the students are prepared to move on to the next activity. Sequencing of instructional activity can be described as the teacher citing an order or pattern for a series of activities. For example, the teacher says, "When we finish with this guided practice together, we will turn to page 23, and each student will do the exercises. I will then circulate throughout the classroom helping on an individual basis. Okay, let's begin." Following an example such as this will lead to systematic, smooth transitions between activities because the students will be turning to page 23 when the class finishes the practice without a break in concentration.

Another method that leads to smooth transitions is to move students in groups and clusters rather than one by one. This is called group fragmentation. For example, if some students do seatwork while other students gather for a reading group, the teacher moves the students in predetermined groups. Instead of calling the individual names of the reading group members, which would be time consuming and laborious, the teacher simply says, "Will the blue reading group please assemble at the reading station. The red and yellow groups will quietly do the vocabulary assignment I am now passing out." As a result of this activity, the classroom is ready to move on in a matter of seconds rather than minutes.

Additionally, the teacher may employ academic transition signals, defined as teacher utterances that indicate movement of the lesson from one topic or activity to another by indicating where the lesson is and where it is going. For example, the teacher may say, "That completes our description of clouds, now we will examine weather fronts." Like the sequencing of instructional materials, this keeps the students informed about what is coming next so they will move to the next activity with little or no break in concentration.

In this way, effective teachers manage transitions from one activity to another in a systematically oriented way through efficient management of instructional matter, sequencing of instructional activities, moving students in groups, and employing academic transition signals. Through an efficient use of class time, achievement is increased because students spend more class time engaged in on-task behavior.

Effective teachers have rules that deal with controlled interruptions. Controlled interruptions happen when a teacher enforces rules and procedures to be followed by students who are tardy to class or who do not have their supplies and so on. The most efficient classrooms are run by teachers who give a high degree of direction. There is no better way to set the tone for this classroom atmosphere than by rule explication and monitoring. Rule explication and monitoring happen when a teacher specifies rules of conduct, explains them, provides practice in their use, and consistently checks student conduct by the rules.

For example, when a student returns to class after being absent, he or she places his or her parent note in the box on the teacher's desk designated for this. The student is aware that the teacher will deal with it after the class is engaged and when time allows. The student then proceeds to the side counter where extra copies of yesterday's work are located. The student takes the work and sits down to begin today's class work. The student is aware that the teacher will deal with individual instructions during seatwork time when it will not disrupt the class momentum. This is an example of rule explication because the teacher explained the procedures for this instance at the beginning of the year, and through constant monitoring the student is aware of what is expected of him or her in this situation. As a result of specifying classroom procedures for controlled interruptions, the classroom momentum is maintained, and thus on-task time is increased. This will result in increased achievement because on-task time directly correlates to student achievement.

Therefore, effective teachers have rules in place dealing with controlled interruptions. The teacher has ensured these rules will be followed through the use of rule explication and monitoring. For a rule to be effective, the teacher must state the rule, explain the rule, lead the students through a guided practice of the rule, and then consistently monitor the rule to insure compliance. The monitoring process is what teaches the students that they must also be consistent in these matters.

Effective teachers deal with daily classroom procedures efficiently and quickly because then students will spend the majority of class time engaged in academic tasks that will likely result in higher achievement. Various studies have shown that high-achieving classrooms spend less time on off-task behavior. For example, C.W. Fisher, et al., in a 1978 study, found that in the average classroom, students spent about eight minutes an hour engaged in off-task behavior. However, this was reduced to about four minutes in high-achieving classrooms. Therefore, effective teachers spend less time on daily housekeeping chores.

Housekeeping is when a teacher routinizes activities such as passing out papers, moving to get books, writing on the board, and so on, and has materials prepared, procedures worked out, and everything in order. It is recommended that teachers presort papers into rows and have the first person in the row distribute them. This achieves the laborious task of passing back papers in a few minutes. This same technique is useful for distributing books. The teacher may ask the students in the first seat to pick up enough books for their row and pass them out. Using this technique keeps the majority of the students in their seats and achieves the task quickly. Another possibility would be for the teacher to place the proper number of books on the front desks while finishing the last lesson. In this case, students have been pre-instructed not to pass back the books until instructed to do so. Regardless of the technique employed by the teacher, it is important that it is preplanned to utilize as little of class time as possible. Instructing the students of the daily routine activities early in the year leads to a more efficient use of class time on a daily basis.

To summarize, effective teachers make daily housekeeping activities a routine to minimize the amount of time spent on them. Additionally, they have all materials prepared and in order prior to class to facilitate speedy distribution.

Skill 3.3	**Identify ways to organize furniture, equipment, materials, and other resources in an indoor or outdoor environment in order to support early childhood development and curricula**

A well-organized classroom often begins with the room's physical arrangement—the arrangement of desks, the attractiveness of bulletin boards, and the storage of supplies and materials. By identifying various ways of organizing learning space, teachers can create a caring and child-centered environment.

The physical layout of a teacher's room should present the teacher as a warm and caring professional. Don't hesitate to give the classroom your personal touch with potted plants, colorful art, rugs, posters, and even some oversized cozy pillows for the reading corner.

Teachers can create different learning areas within the classroom; for example, a quiet reading corner with pillows to relax on, listening stations where students can listen to music through the use of headphones while completing work, a large table for group projects, multimedia centers, several learning stations, and individual work areas. If supplies and materials are easily accessible, delays and confusion can be eliminated as students prepare for activities.

In the majority of classrooms, the largest amount of floor space is devoted to the organization of student desks. Some teachers like to arrange desks in groups of four, while others utilize a U-shaped arrangement, allowing every student to have a front-row seat. Most importantly, arrange the desks so that eye contact can be made with every student. If the arrangement of the room doesn't work, don't be afraid to make changes.

Environmental preferences such as lighting, noise level, and room temperature are factors that can affect students in various ways and are often directly related to individual learning styles. A number of students learn best in bright light, but others learn considerably better in low-lighted areas. Bright light can actually cause some students to become restless and hyperactive. Teachers can provide listening stations with headsets for children who need sound and quiet, comfortable study areas for those who learn best in a silent environment. Teachers should encourage students to dress according to their body's temperature to assure that students are not uncomfortable and can concentrate fully on their schoolwork.

Skill 3.4   **Identify and analyze strategies for short- and long-term planning to set instructional goals in alignment with standards for developing teacher objectives**

Instructional goals are simply a clear statement of the planning that is needed to develop teacher objectives that are in accordance with required standards. By identifying strategies that specify the instructional goals that need to be aligned with the standards that need be achieved, teachers can plan effective objectives. The target objectives are clearer statements of the specific activities required to achieve the goals of the lessons.

After the goals have been developed, the objectives should be written for each goal. The objectives are the measurements that support the goals.

Objectives should be:

1. adaptable to timelines
2. concise and to the point
3. clear
4. observable

Teachers can plan short- and long-term goals that are achievable by designing realistic instructional objectives.

Skill 3.5   **Identify strategies for designing appropriate objectives and developing, implementing, and assessing lesson plans**

Successful lesson plans should have a logical sequence that enables learning to take place effectively. The material should be organized in a method that encourages student comprehension and learning. Effective lesson plans aid the teacher in preparing the lessons and provide the means for implementing the instructional material.

Objectives provide the basis for the entire lesson plan. Teachers should always give careful thought into the design and development of appropriate objectives. Teachers should consider addressing all levels of learning and critical thinking when developing their lesson objectives (see the section on Benjamin Bloom and Bloom's taxonomy in Skill 6.14). The objectives of a lesson plan must always be student centered. The phrase, "The student will . . ." should be used in writing the lesson objectives. By implementing this strategy, teachers can focus on what the student is expected to learn.

Implementing Lesson Plans

All lessons need an introduction, body, and conclusion. In many instances, it is desirable to develop the body of your lesson before writing the introduction and the conclusion. By constructing the body of the lesson first, you will be in a better position to decide how you want to introduce the lesson and then conclude the lesson by emphasizing the main ideas. The body of the lesson is where the teacher decides how to organize the main points and subpoints of the lesson.

Each lesson should include the definitions of new words or concepts. Teachers should include examples of these words and concepts and perhaps a personal experience to which the students can relate to help students connect with prior learning. If students are unfamiliar with the information, the teacher can do a compare-and-contrast concept.

Each lesson plan should include the 3 W's, WHAT? HOW? WHY? The introduction should outline the lesson and instruct the students of what they will be learning throughout the lesson. The introduction should spark the students' interest in the subject, thereby motivating them to eagerly learn the lesson. The introduction should flow smoothly and effortlessly into the body of the lesson.

The conclusion should emphasize the main points of the lesson. The final summary should also emphasize the objectives of the lesson plan. Teachers should also allow extra time at the end of the lesson for any and all questions that the students may have to clarify and explain the lesson.

Finally, teachers should reflect on a lesson when it has been completed to make notes of what to adapt and to evaluate for themselves if they feel the lesson achieved the objective(s).

Skill 3.6	Identify and select developmentally and/or age-appropriate instructional materials that enrich and extend active learning

In considering suitable learning materials for the classroom, the teacher must have a thorough understanding of the state-mandated competency-based curriculum. According to state requirements, certain objectives must be met in each subject taught at every designated level of instruction. It is necessary that the teacher become well acquainted with the curriculum for which he or she is assigned. The teacher must also be aware that it is unlawful to require students to study from textbooks or materials other than those approved by the state Department of Education.

In choosing materials, teachers should also keep in mind that students not only learn at different rates but also bring a variety of cognitive styles to the learning process. Prior experiences influence the individual's cognitive style, or method of accepting, processing, and retaining information. According to Marshall Rosenberg, students can be categorized as:

- rigid-inhibited
- undisciplined
- acceptance-anxious
- creative

Rosenberg states that, "The creative learner is an independent thinker, one who maximizes his/her abilities, can work by his/herself, enjoys learning, and is self-critical." This category constitutes the ideal, but teachers should make every effort to use materials that will stimulate and hold the attention of learners of all types.

Keeping in mind what is understood about the students' abilities and interests, the teacher should design a course of study that presents units of instruction in an orderly sequence. The instruction should be planned so as to advance all students toward the next level of instruction, although exit behaviors need not be identical due to the inevitability of individual differences.

Textbooks

Most teachers chose to use textbooks, which are suitable to the age and developmental level of specific student populations. Textbooks reflect the values and assumptions of the society that produces them, and they also represent the knowledge and skills considered to be essential in becoming an educated adult. Finally, textbooks are useful to the school bureaucracy and the community because they make public and accessible the private world of the classroom.

Though these factors may favor the adoption of textbooks, the individual teacher may have only limited choice about which textbooks to use, since such decisions are often made by the school administration or the local school district (in observance of the state guidelines). If teachers are consulted about textbook selection, it is likely that they have little training in evaluation techniques, and they are seldom granted leave time to encourage informed decisions. On those occasions when teachers are asked to assist in the selection process, they should ask, above all, whether the textbooks have real substance: Is World War II accurately chronicled? Does the science textbook correctly conceptualize electrical current? Do literary selections reflect a full range of genres?

From time to time, controversy has arisen about the possible weakness of textbooks—the preponderance of pictures and illustrations, the avoidance of controversy in social studies textbooks, the lack of emphasis on problem solving in science textbooks, and so on. In the 1980s, certain books were criticized for their attention to the "liberal" or "secular" values, and the creationism/evolution argument has resurfaced again and again. Finally, recent decades have witnessed a movement to grant more attention to women, African Americans, and other groups whose contributions to our developing culture may have been overlooked in earlier textbooks. Individual teachers would be well advised to keep themselves informed of current trends or developments so as to make more informed choices for their students and deal with the possibility of parental concern.

Focusing on the needs evident in almost any classroom population, the teacher will want to use textbooks that include some activities and selections to challenge the most advanced students as well as those who have difficulty in mastering the material at a moderate pace. Some of the exercises may be eliminated altogether for faster learners, while students who have difficulty may need to have material arranged into brief steps or sections. For almost any class, some experience in cooperative learning may be advisable. Thus, the faster learners will reinforce what they have already mastered, while those of lesser ability at the tasks in question can ask about their individual problems or areas of concern. Most textbook exercises intended for independent work can be used in cooperative learning, though in most cases, teachers will encourage better participation if the cooperating group is asked to hand in a single paper or project to represent their combined efforts rather than individual papers or projects.

Technological Materials

Aside from textbooks, there are a wide variety of materials available to today's teachers. Computers are now commonplace, and some schools can now afford laser discs to bring alive the content of a reference book in text, motion, and sound. Hand-held calculators eliminate the need for drill and practice in number facts, while they also support a problem solving and process to mathematics.

Textbook publishers often provide films, recordings, and software to accompany the text, as well as maps, graphics, and colorful posters to help students visualize what is being taught. Teachers can usually scan the educational publishers' brochures that arrive at their principal's or department head's office on a frequent basis. Another way to stay current in the field is by attending workshops or conferences. Teachers will be enthusiastically welcomed on those occasions when educational publishers are asked to display their latest productions and revised editions of materials.

In addition, yesterday's libraries are today's media centers. Teachers can usually have opaque projectors delivered to the classroom to project print or pictorial images (including student work) onto a screen for classroom viewing. Some teachers have chosen to replace chalkboards with projectors that reproduce the print or images present on the plastic sheets known as transparencies, which the teacher can write on during a presentation or have machine-printed in advance. In either case, the transparency can easily be stored for later use. In an art or photography class, or any class in which it is helpful to display visual materials, slides can easily be projected onto a wall or a screen.

Cameras are inexpensive enough to enable students to photograph and display their own work, as well as keep a record of their achievements in teacher files or student portfolios.

Studies have shown that students learn best when what is taught in lecture and textbook reading is presented more than once in various formats. In some instances, students themselves may be asked to reinforce what they have learned by completing some original production—for example, by drawing pictures to explain some scientific process, by writing a monologue or dialogue to express what some historical figure might have said on some occasion, by devising a board game to challenge the players' mathematical skills, or by acting out (and perhaps filming) episodes from a classroom reading selection. Students usually enjoy having their work displayed or presented to an audience of peers. Thus, their productions may supplement and personalize the learning experiences that the teacher has planned for them.

Factoring In Student Readiness

Keeping in mind the state requirements concerning the objectives and materials, the teacher must determine the abilities of the incoming students assigned to his or her class or supervision. It is essential to be aware of their entry behavior— that is, their current level of achievement in the relevant areas. The next step is to take a broad overview of students who are expected to learn before they are passed on to the next grade or level of instruction. Finally, the teacher must design a course of study that will enable students to reach the necessary level of achievement, as displayed in their final assessments or exit behaviors. Textbooks and learning materials must be chosen to fit into this context.

To determine the abilities of incoming students, it may be helpful to consult their prior academic records. Letter grades assigned at previous levels of instruction as well as scores on standardized tests may be taken into account. In addition, the teacher may choose to administer pretests at the beginning of the school year and perhaps also at the initial stage of each new unit of instruction. The textbooks available for classroom use may provide suitable pretests, tests of student progress, and posttests.

In selecting tests and other assessment tools, the teacher should keep in mind that different kinds of tests measure different aspects of student development. The tests included in most textbooks chosen for the classroom and in the teacher's edition that accompanies them are usually achievement tests. Few of these are the type of tests intended to measure the students' inherent ability or aptitude. Teachers will find it difficult to raise students' scores on ability tests, but students' scores on achievement tests may be expected to improve with proper instruction and application in the area being studied.

In addition to administering tests, the teacher may assess the readiness of students for a particular level of instruction by having them demonstrate their ability to perform some relevant task. In a class that emphasizes written composition, for example, students may be asked to submit writing samples. These may be used not only to assure the placement of the students into the proper level but also as a diagnostic tool to help students understand what aspects of their composition skills may need improvement. In the same way, students in a speech class may be asked to make an impromptu oral presentation before beginning a new or specific level of instruction. Others may be asked to demonstrate their psychomotor skills in a physical education class, display their computational skills in a mathematics class, and so on. Whatever the chosen task, the teacher will need to select or devise an appropriate assessment scale and interpret the results with care.

If students are informed of their entry behaviors on such a scale, they will be better motivated, especially if they are able to observe their progress by some objective means at suitable intervals during the course. For this reason, it may be advisable to record the results of such assessments in the students' portfolios as well as in the teacher's records.

Teachers may also gauge student readiness by simply asking them about their previous experience or knowledge of the subject or task at hand. While their comments may not be completely reliable indicators of what they know or understand, such discussions have the advantage of providing an idea of the students' interest in what is being taught. Teachers can have little impact unless they are able to demonstrate how the material being introduced is relevant to the students' lives.

Skill 3.7   **Apply a variety of methods of flexibly grouping children for the purposes of instruction**

Children learn at different paces due to reasons including prior experiences, personal situations, abilities, interests, and more. Today, teachers are using flexible grouping strategies to address the different learning needs of various students, and the ways they are organizing their classrooms are beginning to change.

Depending on the lesson objectives and classroom participants, teachers are starting to consider the dynamics of a group when planning instruction. Grouping flexibly also allows for various levels of differentiating learning when it is needed. Below are some of the most common organization methods for grouping students flexibly.

Teacher-led groups include the following:

- Whole-class instruction such as lectures or mini-lessons
- Small-group instruction such as guided reading
- Teacher-directed activities such as workshops

Student groups include the following:

- Collaborative groups such as circle sharing
- Performance-based groups such as group study or interviews
- Student dyads (pair work) such as "think, pair, share"

For more info:
http://www.eduplace.com/science/profdev/articles/valentino.html

The following is a small sampling of teacher-created team-building activities for elementary school children, available for sharing with colleagues via the Internet. There are thousands of similar lesson plans and activities available to address the development of social and academic skills through teamwork among young children in the classroom setting.

Arthur: Group Stories
This is an activity in which students can create stories as a group. There are several variations available.

Spider Web
In this team-building activity, students can get to know one another while creating a unique design.

Trading Cards
Children can share information about themselves by creating personalized trading cards. This could be used as an "ice-breaker" activity.

Can You Build It?
Students can work together toward a common goal in this team activity. It can also be used as an "ice-breaker."

Who Am I?
Children can use this activity to get to know one another by sharing about themselves and working together.

Ideas for Working with Kids
These are suggestions for games to help students get to know one another and build group cohesion.

Mad Minute Relay
Students can learn math in a team environment with this timed activity.

All of Me
This activity can help students get to know one another by drawing pictures that show some of the different aspects of their lives and sharing the pictures with classmates.

We're Different/We're Alike
Students can learn more about one another with this lesson by using Venn diagrams to describe the ways in which they are similar and different.

Make a Class Pictogram
Children can use this activity to help them understand the nature of social groups and their roles as members of various groups.

It's Too Loud in Here!
This lesson plan gives students the opportunity to work as a team and participate in decision-making processes in the classroom.

A–Z Teacher's Stuff: Teamwork
What does it mean to be a team? In this lesson plan, students can learn to define teamwork and work together in groups.

It is beneficial for the teacher to remain current with the studies and findings published in numerous journals related to child and educational psychology and physical and intellectual development in early childhood.

For example, several studies—past and present—have shown that girls tend to be more communicative with one another, while boys are more prone to be physically active together but less responsive to verbal interaction with one another. While this is a generalization, it still predicts that an effective grouping will include an approximately equal number of girls and boys, with the teacher monitoring and encouraging the participation of all in each aspect of the planned activity.

As in this example, awareness of research and findings in the study of childhood development will inform the teacher's application of appropriate groupings and goals for developing teamwork among younger students.

Skill 3.8   Identify characteristics of an integrated curriculum

An integrated curriculum is a program of study that describes a movement toward integrated lessons that enables students to make connections across curricula. This curriculum links lessons among the humanities, art, natural sciences, mathematics, music, and social studies.

Especially with young students, an integrated curriculum serves well to tie knowledge from various subjects together for students. Integrating subjects creates mental links across material, aiding in their retention of the material. The integrated curriculum is a method that teaches students to break down barriers between subjects. Lessons are planned around broad themes with which students can identify, such as "The Environment." Major concepts are pulled from this broad concept, and teachers then plan activities that teach these concepts.

Characteristics of an Integrated Curriculum

Characteristics of an integrated curriculum include the following:

- A combination of subjects
- An emphasis on projects
- Sources that go beyond textbooks
- Relationships among concepts
- Thematic units as organizing principles
- Flexible schedules
- Flexible student groupings

An integrated curriculum is an education that is organized in such a way that it cuts across subject-matter lines, bringing together various aspects of the curriculum into meaningful association to focus upon broad areas of study. It views learning and teaching in a holistic way and reflects the real world, which is interactive (Humphreys, Post, and Ellis).

Skill 3.9	Identify characteristics of play as related to the children's social, emotional, and cognitive development

Too often, recess and play are considered peripheral or unimportant to a child's development. They are sometimes seen as a way to allow kids to just get physical energy out or as a tradition of childhood. The truth is that play is very important to human development. First, an obvious point: In this country, even though we are very industrious, we believe strongly that all individuals deserve time to relax and enjoy the fruits of our labors.

But even more importantly, for the full development of children (who will soon be active citizens of our democracy, parents, spouses, friends, colleagues, and neighbors), play is an activity that helps teach basic values such as sharing and cooperation. It also teaches that taking care of oneself (as opposed to constantly working) is good for human beings and further creates a more enjoyable society.

The stages of play development move from solitary (particularly in infancy stages) to cooperative (in early childhood), but even in early childhood, children should be able to play on their own and entertain themselves from time to time. Children who do not know what to do with themselves when they are bored should be encouraged to think about particular activities that might be of interest.

But it is also extremely important that children play with peers. While the emerging stages of cooperative play may be awkward (as children will at first not want to share toys, for example), with some guidance and experience, children will learn how to be good peers and friends.

Play—both cooperative and solitary—helps develop very important attributes in children. For example, children learn and develop personal interests and practice particular skills. The play in which children engage may even develop future professional interests.

Finally, playing with objects helps develop motor skills. The objects that children play with should be varied and age appropriate. For example, playing with a doll can actually help develop hand-eye coordination. Sports, for both boys and girls, can be equally valuable. Parents and teachers, however, need to remember that sports at young ages should only be for the purpose of development of interests and motor skills—not competition. Many children will learn that they do not enjoy sports, and parents and teachers should be respectful of these decisions.

In general, play is an appropriate place for children to learn many things about themselves, their world, and their interests. Children should be encouraged to participate in different types of play, and they should be watched over as they encounter new types of play.

Skill 3.10   **Identify strategies for building and nurturing trusting relationships with students**

The effective teacher will establish routine within his or her classroom. As students become familiar with a teacher's expectations and understand the rules that have been established for safety and learning reasons, they will begin to feel welcome and comfortable in the classroom and school setting. As a teacher disciplines a student, he or she must be fair and consistent so each student can learn and understand the proper way to behave and be safe in the class.

At the beginning of the year, an effective way to build rapport with students is to share basic information (favorite hobbies, foods, books, family members, activities, and so on) and ask students to share similar things about themselves. Students understand that their teacher may share similar qualities.

Students also appreciate understanding that their teacher is involved in other activities outside the classroom. Attending soccer games, plays, musical performances, and parent meetings and events are all effective ways for a teacher to build a solid relationship with students.

Skill 3.11	Analyze and evaluate the use of evidence-based practices to improve student achievement

Student achievement should be evaluated and analyzed to effectively make decisions that meet the needs of learners in the classroom. Teachers and administrators should work to ensure that the best practices are being implemented. As trends change and more effective methodology is discovered, educators must implement these techniques, often replacing old and outdated ones.

Teaching strategies, testing methods, teaching methods, and overall data are looked at over a period of time, with adequate data collected before changes might take place. Only tried and true practices should be adjusted to continue to improve the education of young learners.

Educators and administrators should make it a practice to look over and analyze data at regular intervals (such as every month or every semester). The data will help show where adjustments need to be made.

COMPETENCY 4.0   KNOWLEDGE OF DEVELOPMENTALLY APPROPRIATE CURRICULA

Skill 4.1   Analyze and select developmentally appropriate curricula that provide for all areas of child development (i.e., physical, emotional, social, linguistic, aesthetic, cognitive)

Developmentally appropriate curricula are important in guiding instruction in the classroom. The curriculum should be age-appropriate, relevant to the students' real lives, and in their realm of anticipated interest. Should politically controversial issues be introduced or avoided? The teacher must make these decisions deliberatively on the basis of feedback from his or her students while keeping sight of her objectives.

The teacher must be very knowledgeable about the writing of behavioral objectives that fall within the guidelines of the state and local expectations, and the objectives must be measurable, so that when the unit or semester is complete, the teacher can know for sure whether they have been accomplished. The teacher should give careful consideration to how lessons will be implemented in the classroom. Some of the instructional techniques teachers can use are discussed below.

Whole language is an approach to instruction that is mainly used in language arts. It teaches the child to look for meaning instead of getting hung up on the individual components of language. In this approach, children learn about language by using it. They are encouraged to take risks, make mistakes, and learn from their mistakes, such as in spelling and writing. The teacher becomes a facilitator instead of spending large amounts of time instructing the whole class.

The classrooms of today are not the same as they were even 10 years ago. The students move from group to group and talk among themselves as they experience learning. It is important for the teacher to include physical and motor skills activities in the lessons so that students can see how the learning in the classroom helps them prepare for everyday life. Sitting at a desk working alone is not the way of the world any longer, and classrooms should reflect this change in society. Along with allowing students to move about, the physical aspect of the movement helps them develop physically. Lessons should have opportunities for students to get up and move about as well as demonstrate their learning in nontraditional ways, such as in dance. The teacher has to be cognizant of the needs of the child as well as the varied learning styles in the classroom so that the children develop to their potential.

In all areas of the curriculum, students learn important social skills from working in groups to solve problems. Through watching how the students interact with one another, the teacher can take advantage of opportunities to help students work better with others.

For young children, the language experience approach to teaching helps support their concept and vocabulary development through shared reading and writing experiences. In a classroom using the language experience approach, the students are involved in planning and experiencing learning as well as responding to and reflecting on the experience. They are immersed in books and writing, and through the reflections they can see where they did well and where they need to work harder. The teacher can work with the whole class or with a small group. As the group works through a concept or theme, the teacher or another person in the class records the students' ideas in the students' own language. This can then become a teaching focus as the teacher uses mini-lessons related to the experience.

Many classrooms have basal readers and textbooks for the students. The teacher can still use many different approaches with these resources and pick and choose which parts of the text to use. The main thing is that the lessons support the mandated curriculum outcomes. Even when using a basal reader, the teacher can use whole language or a balanced literacy approach to the instruction so that the children can succeed and advance to the next level of their development.

There are many opportunities in the curriculum for the teacher to bring in other domains of learning, such as music in social studies or math. When reading to children, the tone of voice and facial expressions are as important as the text itself. Through hearing different voices and sounds, for example, the child is better able to understand the story and will try to emulate this when reading the story alone.

Allowing children to demonstrate their learning through art is another way teachers can increase the aesthetic experiences in the classroom. It will also help students who may have difficulty with writing show that they have achieved the objectives of the lesson.

Skill 4.2   **Identify strategies that facilitate the development of literal, interpretive, and critical listening and thinking skills**

Some basic principles apply to the analysis of any text, whether magazine articles, newspaper articles, or even children's literature.

Understanding the literal meaning of written or spoken expression requires comprehending the vocabulary, the grammar, and the context. This may be difficult for young children, so teachers will need to check that students understand what they are reading and hearing. One way to do this is through discussion, in which children are asked to restate what they understand.

When literal interpretation is difficult, teachers will want to encourage children to use context clues, to guess at the meaning of words, and to use glossaries and dictionaries to check their knowledge and understanding. Comprehension may be checked verbally or through the administration of a formalized quiz or other written assessment.

Interpretive thinking skills require that children fit what they are hearing and reading into their own mental framework, perhaps relying upon already-acquired knowledge. It requires moving beyond a literal, objective understanding to a more subjective one. This is sometimes referred to as "meaning-making," in which the intended recipient of communication plays a role in assigning meaning to it.

Obviously, the younger a child is, the more the focus will be on merely understanding the literal meaning of something. Interpretive thinking skills develop partly through maturity and through having many other experiences and thoughts with which to compare new ones. Modeling is one way in which teachers can promote the development of interpretive thinking skills. According to Bloom's taxonomy, interpretive skills are higher-order thinking skills than understanding, so it would be unrealistic to expect small children to exhibit interpretive skills at a young age.

The six levels of Bloom's taxonomy and the skills each entails, from simplest to most complex, are as follows:

1. **Knowledge:** This is the most basic level of learning, in which students learn terminology and specific facts; tasks at this level ask students to define, label, recall, memorize, and list.
2. **Understanding/Comprehension:** This level of learning requires students to grasp the meaning of a concept; tasks at this level ask students to classify, explain, identify, locate, and review.
3. **Application:** This level of learning requires students to take previous learning and utilize it in a new way; tasks at this level ask students to demonstrate, illustrate, distinguish, solve, write, choose, and dramatize.
4. **Analysis:** This level of learning involves the breakdown of material to its component parts and requires students to utilize those parts; tasks at this level ask students to calculate, categorize, compare, contrast, criticize, distinguish, examine, and experiment.
5. **Synthesis:** This level of learning requires students to take the analyzed parts from the previous level and converge them into creative new wholes; tasks at this level ask students to collect, compose, design, manage, plan, organize, and formulate.
6. **Evaluation:** This is the highest level of learning on the taxonomy, and according to research, it is the level that is least often achieved. This level of learning requires students to judge the value of material based on experience, prior knowledge, opinions, and/or the resulting product; tasks

at this level ask students to assess, appraise, predict, rate, support, evaluate, judge, and argue.

Critical Listening Strategies

Oral speech can be very difficult to follow. First, we have no written record in which to reread things we didn't hear or understand. Second, oral speech can be much less structured and less even than written language. Yet, aside from rereading, many of the skills and strategies that help us in reading comprehension can help us in listening comprehension. For example, as soon as we start listening to something new, we should tap into our prior knowledge to attach new information to what we already know. This will not only help us understand the new information more quickly but also assist us in remembering the material.

We can also look for transitions between ideas. Sometimes, in oral speech, this is pretty simple when voice tone or body language changes. Of course, we don't have the luxury of looking at paragraphs in oral language, but we do have the animation that comes with live speech. Human beings have to try very hard to be completely nonexpressive in their speech. Listeners should take advantage of this and notice how the speaker changes character and voice to signal a transition between ideas.

In addition to animation of voice and body language, listeners can also better comprehend the underlying intents of speakers when they notice nonverbal cues. Simply looking to see expression on the face of a speaker can do more to signal irony, for example, than trying to extract irony from the spoken words. And often in oral speech, unlike written text, elements like irony are not indicated by the actual words, but rather by the tone and nonverbal cues.

One good way to follow oral speech is to take notes and outline major points. Because oral speech can be more circular (as opposed to linear) than written text, it can be of great assistance to keep track of a speaker's message. Students can learn this strategy in many ways in the classroom: for example, by taking notes of the teacher's oral messages and of other students' presentations and speeches.

Other classroom methods can help students learn good listening skills. For example, teachers can have students practice following complex directions. They can also have students orally retell stories or retell (in writing or in oral speech) oral presentations of stories or other materials. These activities give students direct practice in the very important skills of listening. They provide students with outlets in which they can slowly improve their abilities to comprehend oral language and take decisive action based on oral speech.

Effective Listening

Teachers should relate to students the specific purpose of their reading assignment. This will help them to

- ASSOCIATE: Relate ideas to one another.
- VISUALIZE: Try to see pictures in your mind as you read.
- CONCENTRATE: Have a specific purpose for reading.
- REPEAT: Keep telling yourself important points and associate details with these points.

Oral language (listening and speaking) involves receiving and understanding messages sent by other people and also expressing our own feelings and ideas. Students must learn that listening is a communication process, and to be successful, it must be an active process. In other words, they must be *active participant* in this communication process. In active listening, meaning and evaluation of a message must take place before a student can respond to the teacher.

Conversation requires more than just listening. It involves feedback and active involvement. This can be particularly challenging, because in our culture we are trained to move conversations along, to discourage silence in a conversation, and to always get the last word in. This poses significant problems for the art of listening. In a discussion, for example, when we are preparing our next response rather than listening to what others are saying we do a large disservice to the entire discussion. Children need to learn how listening carefully to others in discussions actually promotes better responses on the part of subsequent speakers. One way teachers can encourage this in both large- and small-group discussions is to expect students to respond directly to the previous student's comments before moving ahead with their new comments. This will encourage them to pose their new comments in light of the comments that came just before them.

Thinking Skills

Reasoning skills are higher-order skills, which involve recalling information, forming basic concepts and creative ideas, and critical thinking. These skills are essential across the curriculum, and they can be fostered through the language arts.

One way in which language arts teachers may encourage the development of these skills is through the use of age-appropriate detective novels. The following are a few good examples:

- *Private Eyes Club* mysteries by Crosby Bonsall
- *Nate the Great* by Marjorie Sharmat

- *Cam Jansen* by David Adler and Susanna Natti

These books require children to notice details, evaluate all aspects of a situation, guess at what is significant and what will happen next, relate clues to the environment, and solve problems. The mysteries require children to form associations, rely on past knowledge, and overlook irrelevant information. Their thinking may have to proceed through two or more steps to arrive at a conclusion. These are all factors in developing critical thinking skills. Of course, these critical thinking skills can also be applied to reading and interpreting any written work or to dissecting any conversation.

Skill 4.3   **Determine activities that support the development of both fine and gross motor skills**

Motor development is defined as how spontaneous actions within the structured central nervous system, environmental, and social fields assemble temporary linkings of muscle groups to do different and sequential kinds of work. Although the sequence of motor development is fairly uniform across children, differences still may exist individually. A baby may develop slowly in one stage but then catch up in the next. Concern arises if a child's motor development is delayed in many motor skill areas, not just one.

Listed below are the stages, sequences, and characteristics of motor development and motor learning and the general ages at which each stage occurs:

1. Newborn to 2 months: While lying on the stomach, pushes up on arms and lifts and holds head up
2. 2 to 6 months: Uses hands to support self in sitting; roles from back to tummy; while standing with support, accepts entire weight with legs
3. 7 to 8 months: Sits and reaches for toys without falling; moves from tummy or back into sitting position; creeps on hands and knees with alternate arm and leg movement (crawling)
4. 9 to 11 months: Pulls to stand and cruises along furniture; stands alone and takes several independent steps
5. 12 months on: Walks independently and seldom falls; squats to pick up toy(s)

Age-appropriate specific motor skills development:

- By age three, walking is automatic.
- By age four, the child has mostly achieved an adult style of walking.
- By age four to five, a child can run, stop, and turn.
- By age five to six, a child's running is in the style of an adult's running.
- Between ages three and six, a child should be able to climb using ladders.

- By age six, a child can hop and jump longer distances than before.

After age six, it becomes increasingly difficult to describe changes and differences in motor skills among children. Changes are usually to fine motor skills only and are more subtle. By age nine, eye-hand coordination normally has developed to a good point and growth continues, but slowly from this point. The motor skills that have been achieved are stabilized and perfected.

Motor-development learning theories that pertain to a general skill, activity, or age level are important and necessary for effective lesson planning. Motor-skill learning is unique to each individual, but does follow a general sequential skill pattern, starting with general gross-motor movements and progressing to specific or fine motor skills. Teachers must begin instruction at a level at which all students are successful and proceed through the activity to the point where frustration for the majority is hindering the activity. You need to learn the fundamentals or basics of a skill, or subsequent learning of more advanced skills becomes extremely difficult. Students must spend enough time learning beginning skills so they become second nature. Teaching in small groups with enough equipment for everyone is essential. Practice sessions that are too long or too demanding can cause physical and/or mental burnout. Teaching skills over a longer period of time, but with slightly different approaches, helps keep students attentive and involved as they internalize the skill. The instructor can then begin to teach more difficult skills while continuing to review the basics. If the skill is challenging for most students, allow plenty of practice time so that they retain it before having to use it in a game situation.

Visualizing and breaking down the skill mentally is another way to enhance the learning of motor movements. Instructors can teach students to picture the steps involved and see themselves executing the skill. Start by teaching the skill with a demonstration of the necessary steps. Beginning with the first skill taught, introduce key language terms and have students visualize performing the skill themselves. For example, when teaching dribbling in basketball, begin by demonstrating the skill followed by the component steps. Show students how to push the ball down toward the ground, let it bounce back up, and push it down again. Next, give students equipment to practice with while standing still. Then, add movement while dribbling. Finally, demonstrate how to control your dribbling while being guarded by another student.

The development of motor skills in children is a sequential process. We can classify motor skill competency into stages of development by observing children practicing physical skills. The sequence of development begins with simple reflexes and progresses to the learning of postural elements, locomotor skills, and, finally, fine motor skills. The stages of development consider both innate and learned behaviors.

Stages of Motor Learning

The stages of motor learning are as follows:

Stage 1—Children progress from simple reflexes to basic movements such as sitting, crawling, creeping, standing, and walking.

Stage 2—Children learn more complex motor patterns including running, climbing, jumping, balancing, catching, and throwing.

Stage 3—During late childhood, children learn more specific movement skills. In addition, the basic motor patterns learned in Stage 2 become more fluid and automatic.

Stage 4—During adolescence, children continue to develop general and specific motor skills and master specialized movements. At this point, factors including practice, motivation, and talent begin to affect the level of further development.

Locomotor Skills

Locomotor skills move an individual from one point to another.

1. **Walking**—With one foot contacting the surface at all times, walking shifts one's weight from one foot to the other while legs swing alternately in front of the body.
2. **Running**—An extension of walking that has a phase in which the body is propelled with no base of support (speed is faster, stride is longer, and arms add power).
3. **Jumping**—Projectile movements that momentarily suspend the body in midair.
4. **Vaulting**—Coordinated movements that allow one to spring over an obstacle.
5. **Leaping**—Similar to running, but leaping has greater height, flight, and distance.
6. **Hopping**—Using the same foot to take off from a surface and land.
7. **Galloping**—Forward or backward advanced elongation of walking combined and coordinated with a leap.
8. **Sliding**—Sideward stepping pattern that is uneven, long, or short.
9. **Body rolling**—Moving across a surface by rocking back and forth, by turning over and over, or by shaping the body into a revolving mass.
10. **Climbing**—Ascending or descending using the hands and feet with the upper body exerting the most control.

Nonlocomotor Skills

Nonlocomotor skills are stability skills in which the movement requires little or no movement of one's base of support and does not result in change of position.

1. **Bending**—Movement around a joint where two body parts meet
2. **Dodging**—Sharp change of direction from original line of movement, such as away from a person or object
3. **Stretching**—Extending/hyperextending joints to make body parts as straight or as long as possible
4. **Twisting**—Rotating body/body parts around an axis with a stationary base
5. **Turning**—Circular movements of the body through space releasing the base of support
6. **Swinging**—Circular/pendular movements of the body/body parts below an axis
7. **Swaying**—Same as swinging, but movement is above an axis
8. **Pushing**—Applying force against an object or person to move it away from one's body or to move one's body away from the object or person
9. **Pulling**—Executing force to cause objects/people to move toward one's body

Manipulative Skills

Manipulative skills use body parts to propel or receive an object, controlling objects primarily with the hands and feet. Two types of manipulative skills are receptive (catch + trap) and propulsive (throw, strike, kick).

1. **Bouncing/Dribbling**—Projecting a ball downward
2. **Catching**—Stopping momentum of an object (for control) using the hands
3. **Kicking**—Striking an object with the foot
4. **Rolling**—Initiating force to an object to instill contact with a surface
5. **Striking**—Giving impetus to an object with the use of the hands or an object
6. **Throwing**—Using one or both arms to project an object into midair away from the body
7. **Trapping**—Without the use of the hands, receiving and controlling a ball

Knowledge of Activities for Body Management Skill Development

Sequential Development and Activities for Locomotor Skills Acquisition

Sequential Development = crawl, creep, walk, run, jump, hop, gallop, slide, leap, skip, step-hop

- **Activities to develop walking skills** include walking slower and faster in place; walking forward, backward, and sideways with slower and faster paces in straight, curving, and zigzag pathways with various lengths of steps; pausing between steps; and changing the height of the body.

- **Activities to develop running skills** include having students pretend they are playing basketball, trying to score a touchdown, trying to catch a bus, finishing a lengthy race, or running on a hot surface.
- **Activities to develop jumping skills** include alternating jumping with feet together and feet apart, taking off and landing on the balls of the feet, clicking the heels together while airborne, and landing with a foot forward and a foot backward.
- **Activities to develop galloping skills** include having students play a game of Fox and Hound, with the lead foot representing the fox and the back foot the hound trying to catch the fox (alternate the lead foot).
- **Activities to develop sliding skills** include having students hold hands in a circle and sliding in one direction, then sliding in the other direction.
- **Activities to develop hopping skills** include having students hop all the way around a hoop and hopping in and out of a hoop, reversing direction. Students can also place ropes in straight lines and hop side-to-side over the rope from one end to the other and change (reverse) the direction.
- **Activities to develop skipping skills** include having students combine walking and hopping activities leading up to skipping.
- **Activities to develop step-hopping skills** include having students practice stepping and hopping activities while clapping hands to an uneven beat.

Sequential Development and Activities for Nonlocomotor Skill Acquisition

Sequential Development = stretch, bend, sit, shake, turn, rock and sway, swing, twist, dodge, and fall

- **Activities to develop stretching** include lying on the back and stomach and stretching as far as possible; stretching as though one is reaching for a star, picking fruit off a tree, climbing a ladder, shooting a basketball, or placing an item on a high shelf; waking and yawning.
- **Activities to develop bending** include touching knees and toes, then straightening the entire body and straightening the body halfway; bending as though picking up a coin, tying shoes, picking flowers/vegetables, and petting animals of different sizes.
- **Activities to develop sitting** include practicing sitting from standing, kneeling, and lying positions without the use of hands.
- **Activities to develop falling** include first collapsing in one's own space and then pretending to fall like bowling pins, raindrops, snowflakes, a rag doll, or Humpty Dumpty.

Sequential Development and Activities for Manipulative Skill Development

Sequential Development = striking, throwing, kicking, ball rolling, volleying, bouncing, catching, and trapping

- **Activities to develop striking** begin with the striking of stationary objects by a participant in a stationary position. Next, the person remains still while trying to strike a moving object. Then, both the object and the participant are in motion as the participant attempts to strike the moving object.
- **Activities to develop throwing** include throwing yarn/foam balls against a wall, then at a big target, and finally at targets decreasing in size.
- **Activities to develop kicking** include alternating feet to kick balloons/beach balls, then kicking them under and over ropes. Change the type of ball as proficiency develops.
- **Activities to develop ball rolling** include rolling different size balls to a wall, then to targets decreasing in size.
- **Activities to develop volleying** include using a large balloon, first hitting it with both hands, then with one hand (alternating hands), and then using different parts of the body. Change the object as students progress (from balloon to beach ball, to foam ball, and so on).
- **Activities to develop bouncing** include starting with large balls, first using both hands to bounce and then using one hand (alternate hands).

- **Activities to develop catching** include using various objects (such as balloons, beanbags, and balls) to catch, first catching the object the participant has thrown himself or herself, then catching objects someone else threw, and finally increasing the distance between the catcher and the thrower.

- **Activities to develop trapping** include trapping slow and fast rolling balls; trapping balls (or other objects such as beanbags) that are lightly thrown at waist, chest, and stomach levels; and trapping different size balls.

Skill 4.4	Select and apply strategies, including the use of technology, for presenting instruction and concepts related to health, safety, and nutrition

Teaching Styles

Common teaching styles that teachers can use to facilitate learning include command style, practice style, reciprocal style, and inclusion style.

In the **command style**, the teacher makes all decisions and controls all activities. The command style is particularly useful in teaching students a skill in a short period of time. Because command style allows very little student-teacher and student-student interaction, instructors should limit its use to initial demonstrations and explanations.

Practice style allows students to make decisions and move according to their own skill level during the implementation phase of skill development. Practice style is particularly useful when students have achieved basic skill competency because it allows self-paced practice and individualized feedback.

Reciprocal style involves the interaction of pairs of students. Reciprocal style provides needed social interaction and allows students to learn from each other through observation. The instructor is also free to interact with the students.

Inclusion style gives all students the chance to participate in the same task regardless of skill level. Students make decisions on how best to go about practicing and developing their skills. They learn their strengths and weaknesses through trial and error. For example, when learning to throw objects at a target, students can choose the size and type of target and the distance between themselves and the target that best suits their ability level.

Communication Delivery Systems

Three basic types of communication delivery systems relevant to physical education are written, verbal, and visual.

Written communication is particularly effective in communicating large amounts of information. In addition, instructors may choose to provide students with written instructions for classroom activities to eliminate the need for extended and repeated explanation.

Verbal communication is traditionally the foundation of teacher-student interaction. Verbal communication is an effective method of explaining skills and concepts. Physical education instructors should, however, attempt to limit verbal instructions and explanations to allow for maximum physical activity during class time.

Visual communication is an important and often underutilized method of communication in physical education. Visual demonstrations are often the most effective way to introduce athletic skills and activities.

Motivation is essential to student learning in education. Instructors should recognize and understand the important elements of student motivation. Important theories and concepts in student motivation include attribution theory, social learning theory, learned helplessness, and self-efficacy.

Attribution theory describes how people make causal explanations and how they answer questions beginning with "Why?" The theory deals with the information people use in making causal inferences and with how they utilize this information to answer causal questions. For instance, a student's aggressively competitive behavior may reflect his or her personality, or it may be a response to situational pressures. Attribution theory describes the processes of explaining events and the behavioral and emotional consequences of those explanations. Attribution theory also claims that students' perceptions of their educational experience affect their motivation more than the experience itself.

Social learning theory focuses on the learning that occurs within a social context. It emphasizes that people learn from one another and includes such concepts as observational learning, imitation, and modeling. Social learning theory asserts that people can learn by observing the behaviors of others and the outcomes of those behaviors. It further states that learning can occur without a permanent change in behavior. Instructors should also note that cognition plays an important role in learning. Awareness and expectations of future rewards or punishments can have a major effect on the behaviors that people exhibit. Thus, socialization and reward/punishment can motivate students to learn.

Learned helplessness occurs in situations in which continued failure may inhibit somebody from trying again and can also lead to many forms of depression. Thus, it is very important how physical education instructors respond to children's failures and successes. If a student feels as though he or she cannot control his or her environment, this lack of control will impair learning in certain situations. That is, learned helplessness often occurs in environments in which people experience events in which they have, or feel as though they have, no control over what happens to them.

Self-efficacy describes a person's belief about his or her capability to produce designated levels of performance that exercise influence over events that affect his or her life. Self-efficacy beliefs determine how people feel, think, motivate themselves, and behave. Such beliefs produce these diverse effects through cognitive, motivational, affective, and selection processes. A strong sense of efficacy enhances human accomplishment and personal well-being in many ways. People with high assurance in their capabilities view difficult tasks as challenges rather than threats. A student with high self-efficacy will be highly motivated to participate in sports and game-related activities. To build efficacy, the instructor must not only raise the student's belief in his or her capabilities but also structure situations that breed success and limit repeated failure. Students with high self-efficacy measure success in terms of self-improvement rather than by triumphs over others.

Technology is the application of science to commercial, educational, health-related, military, or industrial objectives. Technology includes the use of computers and communication devices (telephones and videoconference devices), or other entities and methodologies to achieve those objectives.

Technology has become vital to the instructional process because all grades, lesson plans, semester grades, descriptions of tests, test grades, absences, tardiness, and behavior issues are recorded and exchanged with the appropriate parties via computers.

Successful teachers integrate technology into the instructional process. Technology is not simply a practice tool or device without purpose. The use of a particular technological device or product of technology should be appropriate to the lesson content.

Instructors can use technology in a variety of ways to help students and athletes improve or learn. Some ways in which instructors can use technology include the following:

1. Actual use of technology: The teacher and the students use the technology in a hands-on setting. For example, students use a digital recording device in physical education to analyze their skills.

2. Use of products of technology: The use of products of technology in instruction and learning may include gathering information or resources from the Internet, imaging results for analyzing a motor skill, and so on. In such a situation, the teacher can use the technology or the products of technology to present information, to provide examples and illustrations, and as the medium or object of instruction.

Some of the offered examples currently available in technology-mediated instruction include audio technologies such as radio, telephone, voice mail, and audiocassettes; video technologies such as television, teleconferencing, compressed video, and prerecorded videocassettes; and information technologies such as standalone workstations, CD ROM prepackaged multimedia, e-mail, chat rooms, bulletin boards, and the Internet.

Technology Resources

The best sources for identifying current technological resources for accessing information on physical activity and health are the Internet and local district technology workshops. District workshops are an extremely valuable resource in obtaining additional knowledge of how to use technology to obtain more information on each teacher's specific subject matter, including physical education.

Internet resources form an important part of current technology. Internet resources enable educators, students, performers, parents, and athletes to keep up to date on information and programs about physical activity and health.

Numerous Websites also exist that allow educators as well as performers to know about the developments in the activity and health training systems. Technological resources also give students more knowledge about physical activity and health-related issues.

Some organizations such as the NASPE also provide information on physical fitness and health. For example, NASPE invites school districts nationwide to post their school wellness policy on the NASPE Forum.

Research also shows there are different types of devices that athletes can use to monitor physical activity and health. Such devices include health pyramids and diagrams, virtual bicycles, rowing machines, and treadmills. Such technology helps plan and implement workouts and view workout results.

Skill 4.5   **Select and apply strategies, including the use of technology, for presenting instruction and concepts related to visual arts, music, drama, and dance**

Visual Arts

The components and strands of visual art encompass many areas. Students are expected to fine-tune observation skills and be able to identify and recreate the experiences that teachers provide for them as learning tools. For example, students may walk as a group on a nature hike taking in the surrounding elements and then begin to discuss the repetition found in the leaves of trees, or the bricks of the sidewalk, or the size and shapes of the buildings and how they may relate. They may also use such an experience to describe lines, colors, shapes, forms, and textures. Basic elements of perspective are noticed at an early age. The questions of why buildings look smaller when they are far away and bigger when they are closer are sure to spark the imagination of early childhood students. Students can then take their inquiry to a higher level of learning with some hands-on activities such as building three-dimensional buildings and constructions using paper and geometric shapes. Eventually students should acquire higher-level thinking skills such as analysis, in which they will begin to question artists and artwork and analyze many different aspects of visual art.

An excellent opportunity is to have students create an art sample book. Such books could include a variety of materials that would serve as examples, such as sandpaper and cotton balls to represent texture elements. Samples of square pieces of construction paper folded or cut into various shapes could represent shape. String samples could represent the element of lines.

The sampling of art should also focus clearly on colors necessary for the early childhood student. Color can be introduced in more depth when discussing **intensity**, the strength of the colors, and **value**, the lightness or darkness of the colors. Another valuable tool for teaching about color is the color wheel, and it's helpful to allow students to experiment with the mixing of colors to create their own art experience.

Works of art should most often be interpreted through a wide variety of rich art and literature experiences. Students will be able to react to art experiences by understanding the definitions of the basic principles such as line, color, value, space, texture, shape, and form in art. Early childhood students are most greatly affected by these experiences. A resource is the author Eric Carle. His books are age appropriate for young children and include a wide variety of shape, color, line, and media for young students to explore. Once students have been introduced to a wide range of materials, they are able to better relate and explain the elements they have observed through artwork and illustrated literature. Literature is the most common form of exposure for young students, but video and other types of media also provide rich art experiences.

Music

Students can explore creating moods with music, analyzing stories and creating musical compositions that reflect or enhance them. Their daily routines can include exploration, interpretation, and understanding of musical sound. Immersing them in musical conversations as they sing, speak rhythmically, and walk in step stimulates their awareness of the beauty and structure of musical sound.

In some schools, computer-assisted programs provide students with opportunities to evaluate music. Programs are designed to present two performances of one or more musical pieces so students can work with the teacher to compare and contrast the pieces. The Internet allows students to collect musical information for evaluation and provide information about studied or performed compositions. These resources and tools enable teachers to provide the richest possible education in music.

Drama

In theater, students should learn to use all of their five senses to observe their environment and recreate experiences through drama and other theater skills. Using role-play and prior knowledge and experiences, students should develop the ability to react to a feeling or a situation to expand their ability to develop character. Using sight, smell, taste, touch, hearing, and memory recall, students should be able to retell stories, myths, and fables. Experience using costumes and props for performances should be provided. Students can relate to familiar jobs that are relevant to their everyday experiences and should be provided experiences to "act out" some of the following professions: firefighters, police officers, teachers, doctors, nurses, postal employees, clerks, and other service-related professions that students may have witnessed.

Dance

Begin with primitive patterns of **rhythm**. Rhythm is the basis of dance. Children can sit in chairs and clap or tap their hands on their legs to express thoughts of rhythm. With older children, imagery enables them to visualize and internalize the particular qualities of a specific movement.

Because younger children are usually unsteady, the initial emphasis is not on gracefulness but rather on developing **body awareness**. The uniqueness of dance is that it is self-expression that can be guided through instruction. The student is taught the elements that are available, such as **time and space.** The student incorporates **listening skills** to develop a sense of tempo.

Creative dance is the type of dance that is most natural for a young child. Creative dance depicts feelings through movement. It is the initial reaction to sound and movement. The older elementary student will incorporate mood and expressiveness. Stories can be told to release the dancer into imagination.

Isadora Duncan is credited with being the mother of modern dance. **Modern dance** today refers to a concept of dance in which the expressions of opposites are developed, such as fast-slow and contract-release, varying height and level to fall and recover. Modern dance is based on four principles: substance, dynamism, metakinesis, and form.

Students should be able to judge the effectiveness of a dance composition based on the intent, structure, meaning, and purpose. Dance is a way of expressing everything from feelings of mood to appreciation of cultures and historical time periods. Students express empathy for others as they take on various roles within the dance. Participation in dances helps students develop self-confidence, body awareness, and communication skills and provides experiences in areas otherwise left undiscovered. School settings for dance have a feel of community. Therefore, a good way to evaluate dance in a school setting is as a group experience rather than as the technical skill level of individuals, which is best left to dance schools. Dance is a way of expressing the connections and relationships among the dancers and an appreciation of dance as creative expression.

Skill 4.6   Select and apply strategies, including the use of technology, in developmentally appropriate ways to teach reading, mathematics, science, and social studies

Reading

SEE Skill 4.1

Mathematics

For young children, mathematics concepts are very hard to understand through pencil and paper activities. By using manipulatives that they can handle themselves, they can visualize the concept and therefore internalize it more easily. When teaching addition and subtraction, for example, using blocks so that the children can count out the amounts and then add or take away blocks will help them understand the concepts better. However, some children do catch on right away and do not need to use manipulatives. They are hindered if they are forced to use them, and this takes away from their learning. The teacher has to watch the children carefully to determine which ones would benefit from this approach.

Science

Children are naturally curious, and what better way to satisfy that curiosity and help them learn about the world than through an inquiry-based science program? The lessons in science should include opportunities for the students to experiment and find answers for themselves. Of course, it is easier for the teacher to do the experiments for the children, but they internalize the concepts much better when they do the experiments and find the answers for themselves. The students can be grouped for the activities and then work together to formulate hypotheses and reach conclusions about what they are doing.

When teachers allow students to engage in activities and search for answers to problems, they not only help them achieve the outcomes in science but also teach them problem-solving techniques to use in the real world. The skills of inquiry include asking questions, proposing ideas, observing, experimenting, and interpreting the results. The inquiry could be based on a single question from the teacher or posed by a student, or it could arise out of the results of another classroom activity.

Social Studies

It is the goal of an effective teacher to teach young learners that as a citizen of the world, one is expected to respect the rights of other nations and the people of those nations. Social studies provides an opportunity for students to broaden their general academic skills in many areas. By encouraging students to ask and investigate questions, they gain skill in making meaningful inquiries into social issues. Providing them with a range of sources requires students to make judgments about the best sources for investigating a line of inquiry and develops the ability to determine authenticity among those sources. Collaboration develops the ability to work as part of a team and to respect the viewpoints of others.

Historic events and social issues cannot be considered in isolation. People and their actions are connected in many ways, and events are linked through cause and effect over time. Identifying and analyzing these social and historic links is a primary goal of social studies. The methods used to analyze social phenomena borrow from several of the social sciences. Interviews, statistical evaluation, observation, and experimentation are just some of the ways that people's opinions and motivations can be measured. From these opinions, larger social beliefs and movements can be interpreted, and events, issues, and social problems can be placed in context to provide a fuller view of their importance.

Technology

SEE Skill 1.8

Skill 4.7   **Select and apply strategies, including the use of technology, in developmentally appropriate ways to increase receptive and expressive vocabulary**

SEE Skill 4.6

COMPETENCY 5.0	KNOWLEDGE OF DEVELOPMENTALLY APPROPRIATE INTERVENTION STRATEGIES AND RESOURCES AVAILABLE TO MEET THE NEEDS OF ALL STUDENTS
Skill 5.1	Select and analyze evidence-based instructional strategies to adapt curriculum for children with diverse needs

No two students are alike. It follows, then, that no students *learn* alike. To apply a one-dimensional instructional approach and a strict tunnel-vision perspective of testing is to impose learning limits on students. All students have the right to an education, but there cannot be a single path to that education. A teacher must acknowledge the variety of learning styles and abilities among students within a class (and, indeed, from class to class) and apply multiple instructional and assessment processes to ensure that every child has appropriate opportunities to master the subject matter, demonstrate such mastery, and improve and enhance learning skills with each lesson.

Students' attitudes and perceptions about learning are the most powerful factors influencing academic focus and success. When instructional objectives center on students' interests and are relevant to their lives, effective learning occurs. Learners must believe that the tasks that they are asked to perform have some value and that they have the ability and resources to perform them. If a student thinks a task is unimportant, he or she will not put much effort into it.

If a student thinks he or she lacks the ability or resources to successfully complete a task, even attempting the task becomes too great a risk. Not only must the teacher understand the students' abilities and interests, he or she must also help students develop positive attitudes and perceptions about tasks and learning.

Differentiated Instruction

SEE Skill 2.6

Alternative Assessment

SEE Skill 2.6

Testing Modifications

The intent of testing modifications is to minimize the effect of a student's disability or learning challenge and to provide an equal opportunity to participate in assessments to demonstrate and express knowledge and ability.

Testing modifications should be identified in the student's IEP, be consistently implemented, and be used to the least extent possible. Types of testing modifications include the following:

- Flexible scheduling: Providing time extensions or altering testing duration (for example, by inserting appropriate breaks)
- Flexible setting: Using special lighting or acoustics, minimizing distractions (for example, testing the student in a separate location), or using adaptive equipment
- Alternate test format: Using large print or Braille, increasing the space allocated for student response, or realigning the format of question and answer selections (for example, vertically rather than horizontally)
- Use of mechanical aids: Digital recording devices, word processors, visual and auditory magnification devices, calculators, or spell check and grammar check software (where spelling and grammar are not the focus of assessment)

Most classrooms contain a mixture of the following:

- Differences among learners, classroom settings, and academic outcomes
- Biological, sociological, ethnic, socioeconomic, psychological, and learning modality and style differences among learners
- Differences in classroom settings that promote learning opportunities such as collaborative, participatory, and individualized learning groupings
- Expected learning outcomes that are theoretical, affective, and cognitive for students

Students generally do not realize their own abilities and frequently lack self-confidence. Teachers can instill positive self-concepts in children and thereby enhance their innate abilities by providing certain types of feedback. Such feedback includes attributing students' successes to their effort and specifying what the student did that produced the success. Qualitative comments influence attitudes more than quantitative feedback such as grades.

Teachers must avoid teaching tasks that fit their own interests and goals and design activities that address the students' concerns. To do this, it is necessary to learn about students and to have a sense of their interests and goals. Teachers can do this by conducting student surveys and simply by questioning and listening to students. Once this information is obtained, the teacher can link students' interests with classroom tasks.

Teachers are learning the value of giving assignments that meet the individual abilities and needs of students. After instruction, discussion, questioning, and practice have been provided, rather than assigning one task to all students teachers are asking students to generate tasks that will show their knowledge of the information presented. Students are given choices and thereby have the opportunity to demonstrate more effectively the skills, concepts, or topics that they as individuals have learned.

It has been established that student choice increases student originality, intrinsic motivation, and higher mental processes.

A diverse classroom should also address children who are learning English and those with disabilities and exceptionalities. The types of disabilities in children are very numerous. Some disabilities are entirely physical, while others are entirely related to learning and the mind or background. Some involve a combination of both. While it would be a disservice to say that all kids should display the same types of characteristics to be considered "normal," when abnormalities are noticed, such as a student's incredible ability to solve a math problem without working it out (a potential attribute of giftedness) or another student's extreme trouble with spelling (a potential attribute of dyslexia), a teacher may assume that a disability or exceptional ability is present.

Common learning disabilities include attention deficit hyperactivity disorder or ADHD (in which concentration can be very tough), auditory processing disorders (in which listening comprehension is very difficult), visual processing disorders (in which reading can be tough and visual memory may be impaired), dyslexia (in which reading can be confusing), and many others. Physical disabilities include Down's Syndrome, in which mental retardation may be a factor; cerebral palsy, in which physical movement is impaired; and many others. Developmental disabilities might include the lack of ability to use fine motor skills.

When giftedness is observed, teachers should concern themselves with ensuring that such children get the attention they need and deserve so that they can continue to learn and grow.

Below are some of the more common approaches used in today's K–12 classrooms for children still acquiring English. Cognitive approaches to language learning focus on concepts. While words and grammar are important, when teachers use the cognitive approach, they focus on using language for conceptual purposes rather than on learning words and grammar for the sake of simply learning new words and grammatical structures. This approach focuses heavily on students' learning styles, and it cannot necessarily be pinned down as having specific techniques. Rather, it is a philosophy of instruction.

Another very common motivational approach is total physical response (TPR). This is a kinesthetic approach that combines language learning and physical movement. In essence, students learn new vocabulary and grammar by responding with physical motion to verbal commands. Some people say it is particularly effective because the physical actions create good brain connections with the words.

In general, the best methods do not treat students as if they have a language deficit. Rather, they build upon what students already know, and they help instill the target language as a communicative process rather than a list of vocabulary words that have to be memorized.

To ensure the maximum education for all learners, teachers must plan to meet the needs of all their students. The target of diversity allows teachers a variety of opportunities to expand their experiences with students, staff, community members, and parents from culturally diverse backgrounds so that their experiences can be proactively applied in promoting cultural diversity inclusion in the classroom. Teachers are able to engage and challenge students to develop and incorporate their own diversity skills in building character and relationships with cultures beyond their own. By changing the thinking patterns of students to become more culturally inclusive in the twenty-first century, teachers are addressing the globalization of our world.

Skill 5.2   **Identify the characteristics of children with diverse needs in order to support their learning**

The most successful teacher is one who regards parents as partners and friends. Although all parents are different, they are alike in their desire to secure the best education for their child. Parents want to provide a chance for their own children to have a richer, more rewarding life than they themselves enjoyed.

Teachers today will deal with an increasingly diverse group of cultures in their classrooms. And while this is an exciting prospect for most teachers, it creates new challenges in dealing with a variety of family expectations for school and teachers. Diversity in classroom makeup may not be as distinctive as race, ethnicity, gender, and so forth. Students who are physically or intellectually challenged may also add diversity to a general student population. A student population including members from varying socioeconomic situations also provides diversity. All students must be included in the learning process. Students' acceptance of this diversity and any specific requirements necessary to help individual students accomplish on par with classmates must be incorporated in lesson planning, teacher presentation, and classroom activities.

First, teachers must show respect to all parents and families. They need to set the tone that suggests that their mission is to develop students into the best people they can be. Then they need to realize that various cultures have different views of how children should be educated.

Second, teachers will have better success when they talk personally about their children. Even though teachers may have many students, when they share personal things about each child, parents will feel more confident that their child is in the right hands.

Third, it is very important that teachers act like they are partners in the children's education and development. Parents know their children best, and it is important to get feedback, information, and advice from them.

Finally, teachers will need to be patient with difficult families, realizing that certain methods of criticism (including verbal attacks) are unacceptable. Such circumstances would require the teacher to get assistance from an administrator. This situation, however, is very unusual, and most teachers will find that when they really attempt to be friendly and personable with parents, the parents will reciprocate and assist in the educational program.

For example, access to technology and media, generally, may vary greatly within the student population. In planning classroom work, homework assignments, and other projects, the teacher must take this into account. First, be knowledgeable about the resources available to the students within the school, the library system, and the community. Be sure that any issues that might restrict a student's access (such as physical impediments, language difficulties, or expenses) are addressed. Second, never plan for work or assignments in which every student would not have equal access to information and technology. As in all aspects of education, each student must have an equal opportunity to succeed.

A positive self-concept for a child or adolescent is a very important element in terms of the student's ability to learn and to be an integral member of society. If students think poorly of themselves or have sustained feelings of inferiority, they probably will not be able to optimize their potential for learning. It is therefore part of the teacher's task to ensure that each student develops a positive self-concept.

A positive self-concept does not imply feelings of superiority, perfection, or competence/efficacy. Instead, a positive self-concept involves self-acceptance as a person, liking oneself, and having a proper respect for oneself. The teacher who encourages these factors has contributed to the development of a positive self-concept in students.

Teachers may take a number of approaches to enhancement of self-concept among students. One such scheme is the process approach, which proposes a three-phase model for teaching. This model includes a sensing function, a transforming function, and an acting function. These three factors can be simplified into the words by which the model is usually given: reach, touch, and teach. The sensing, or perceptual, function incorporates information or stimuli in an intuitive manner. The transforming function conceptualizes, abstracts, evaluates, and provides meaning and value to perceived information. The acting function chooses actions from several different alternatives to be set forth overtly. The process model may be applied to almost any curricular field.

An approach that aims directly at the enhancement of self-concept is called invitational education. According to this approach, teachers and their behaviors may be inviting or they may be disinviting. Inviting behaviors enhance self-concept among students, while disinviting behaviors diminish self-concept. Students are "invited" or "disinvited" depending on teacher behaviors.

Disinviting behaviors include those that demean students and those that may be chauvinistic, sexist, condescending, thoughtless, or insensitive to student feelings. Inviting behaviors are the opposite of these, and they characterize teachers who act with consistency and sensitivity. Inviting teacher behaviors reflect an attitude of "doing with" rather than "doing to."

Invitational teachers exhibit the following skills *(Biehler and Snowman, 394)*:

- Reaching each student (for example, learning names, having one-to-one contact)
- Listening with care (for example, picking up subtle cues)
- Being real with students (for example, providing only realistic praise)
- Being real with oneself (for example, honestly appraising your own feelings and disappointments)
- Inviting good discipline (for example, showing students you have respect in personal ways)
- Handling rejection (for example, not taking lack of student response in personal ways)
- Inviting oneself (for example, thinking positively about oneself)

When diversity is promoted in learning environments and curriculum, both students and teachers are the beneficiaries of increased academic success.

Using classrooms as vital resources for cultural and ethnic inclusion can assist students in contributing cultural norms and artifacts to the acquisition of learning. Teachers are able to create global thinkers by helping students identify cultural assumptions and biases that may direct the type of social and academic groupings that occur in the classroom and influence the type of thinking and construction of learning that happens within a classroom. For example, if a student is struggling in math, a teacher can examine the cultural aspect of learning math. For some students, math is insignificant because socioeconomic issues of poverty and survival are the daily reality of existence. When students see parents juggling finances, the only math that becomes important for them is that less is never enough to keep the lights on and the mortgage paid.

When there is equity pedagogy, teachers can use a variety of instructional styles to facilitate diversity in cooperative learning and individualized instruction that will provide more opportunities for positive student experiences and academic success. Empowering the school culture and climate by establishing an anti-bias learning environment and promoting multicultural learning inclusion will discourage disproportionality and unfair labeling of certain students.

Teachers can use various toolkits to assess integration and incorporation of ethnic and cultural inclusion in classroom. Effective promotion should translate into increased academic success and opportunities for all students. Looking at diverse or homogenous groupings in the classroom can provide teachers with opportunities to restructure cooperative learning groupings and increase diverse student interactions, which can provide increased improvements for school communities.

Using CultureGrams to help students understand different cultures and research cultural diversity helps teachers profile students' learning styles and engagement in the classroom. Students can use technology to discover how students in other cultures and in other states learn. The ability to communicate with other learners provides another way of compiling and categorizing cultural profiles that may assist teachers in identifying learning styles and how students acquire learning. An interesting aspect of using CultureGrams is how they help students connect to other cultures and their perceptions of students who identify with different cultures.

| Skill 5.3 | Identify and select resources and procedures that support children with diverse needs and their families |

SEE Skill 5.2

| Skill 5.4 | Identify characteristics of children at risk for school failure and select appropriate intervention strategies for these children |

SEE Skills 5.1 and 7.1

| Skill 5.5 | Identify major trends in educating children with exceptionalities and incorporate such trends in early childhood settings as appropriate |

An exceptional child is one who is different in some way from the "normal" or "average" child. The term "exceptional child" includes those with special problems related to physical disabilities, sensory impairments, emotional disturbances, learning disabilities, and mental retardation. With developmental disabilities on the rise, there is much that remains poorly understood, from cause to cure. However, there is one widely accepted fact: Early and intensive intervention can have a profound impact on the quality of life for both children at risk and their families. The key is early detection. But recognizing the first signs of a developmental delay or disorder, such as autism, can be a challenge for parents and health care professionals alike.

After nearly 50 years of research, there is evidence—both quantitative (data-based) and qualitative (reports of parents and teachers)—that early intervention increases the developmental and educational gains for the child, improves the functioning of the family, and reaps long-term benefits for society.

Early intervention has been shown to result in the child

- needing fewer special education and other rehabilitative services later in life
- being retained in grade less often
- in some cases, being indistinguishable from non-handicapped classmates years after intervention

Most exceptional children require a lot of understanding and patience, but profit from being included in "regular" classes with varied teaching procedures and modified materials selected based on the needs of each child. It has become less customary to isolate children with special needs or areas of delay.

It is never too early for the exceptional child to have opportunities to become friends and play with other children. All children learn from one another how to give and to take, the rules to follow, and to share and to have things shared with them. The exceptional child should be treated as other children and be allowed to share in appropriate tasks with his or her peers. He or she will also need special opportunities to practice and develop skills and to have experiences adapted to his or her special needs and abilities.

Interventions should be understood as part of *caring* for a child rather than *curing* a child. Children have complex and variable developmental pathways; accordingly, any interventions should be based on the unique needs of an individual child. The following are some considerations:

- Physical space and materials are adapted to promote active engagement with responsive toys and structured and clearly defined spaces.
- The social environment is structured to promote interaction and communication with peer models and responsive and imitative adults who expand the child's play and behavior.
- Routines and transitions should be structured, and a visual cue system should be used.
- As much as possible, the environment should encourage the child's independence rather than dependence on the adult's presence.
- The child's current skills and behaviors should be used to establish reasonable targets for growth and achievement, and these goals should be tracked using data.
- Teachers should strive to accelerate learning by communicating goals, instructional activities, and progress across environments with all caregivers.

Skill 5.6   **Select and apply strategies for working with children who are in foster care and children who are migrant, transient, orphaned, or homeless**

Migrant, homeless, and abandoned children endure many educational challenges resulting from mobility and poverty. Particular challenges include moving from one school to another several times during the year, facing difficulties in enrollment, or being placed in inappropriate classes due to missing school records. Poor attendance or nonattendance, language barriers, and social isolation are all conditions that can lead to poor school performance.

The unfortunate circumstances that can cause students' high mobility include abandonment, poverty, job relocation of caregivers, changes in family arrangements, lack of affordable accommodations, and other determining factors. Children who had been neglected or abandoned or were in failed placements often have more medical problems and experience nutrition deficiencies. Teachers and school personnel should work to provide healthy school lunches and offer medical attention to students of high mobility while they are within their school jurisdiction.

The following organizations provide legal representation and strive to enforce the rights of foster, migrant, abandoned, and homeless children:

- The National Association for the Education of Homeless Children and Youth (NAEHCY) http://www.naehcy.org/
- Migrant Legal Action Program (MLAP) http://www.mlap.org/
- National Alliance to END HOMELESSNESS http://www.endhomelessness.org/

Skill 5.7   **Identify ways for accessing and appropriately using health information to monitor children's medical needs (e.g., medications for allergies) and/or other health impairments**

Students may experience a wide range of diverse medical needs. Some may require little or no treatment, but for others, treatment may be essential to their lives.

Excellent communication is required to successfully integrate a child with special health care needs safely into the school day. Teachers, school professionals, and especially the school nurse should regularly communicate via a logbook, e-mail, phone calls, or another method with the student's caregivers. Any new treatments, procedures, or medications need to be carefully and fully documented. Medical equipment, supplies, and/or medications should be provided to the school by the caregivers and stored in a secured place.

The original container should be labeled with the student's name, name of medication, directions for dosage, frequency of administration, and the licensed prescriber's name.

In school districts in which nurses are available on a daily basis, it is recommended that the school nurses assume responsibility for the administration of medication to students. In schools in which school nurses are not available on a daily basis, it is recommended that the principal assume responsibility for the administration of the medication.

In cases of life-saving medication where time is of the essence, particularly asthma inhalers, students may be allowed to carry and self-administer such medication on school grounds. However, a release form signed by the health care provider, the parent/guardian, and the student is required to be documented and on file at the school.

If a student with a medical or health impairment or disability is entering school for the first time, a specially designed instruction IEP (Individualized Educational Program) is required.

Skill 5.8	Identify needs for, and methods of, collaboration with other professionals in order to positively impact student learning

In school settings, teachers and administrators work together in various situations including during meetings, planning times, team teaching, and parent conferences, and they collaborate to plan curriculum and school-wide needs. Teachers and educational leaders need to work alongside one another to ensure that all aspects of the school year run smoothly.

Early childhood educators might work with paraeducators who assist with learning needs in the classroom. By working as a team, this allows activities like learning centers to run smoothly. The school may also utilize other professional personnel including guidance counselors, a school nurse, physical therapists, occupational therapists, related arts teachers, ELL teachers, and speech and language teachers, among others. By collaborating to meet student needs, these professionals can help ensure that each child is getting the best education possible.

Skill 5.9	Identify programs, curricula, and activities that address the language needs of children and their families who have limited English proficiency

SEE Skill 2.3

COMPETENCY 6.0   KNOWLEDGE OF DIAGNOSIS, ASSESSMENT, AND EVALUATION

Skill 6.1   Select and apply developmentally appropriate, reliable, and valid formal and informal screening, progress monitoring, and diagnostic instruments and procedures that measure specific characteristics

The process of collecting, quantifying, and qualifying student performance data using multiple sources of information on student learning is called assessment. A comprehensive assessment system must include a variety of assessment tools such as norm-referenced tools, criterion-referenced tools, performance-based tools, or any student-generated alternative assessments that can measure learning outcomes and goals for student achievement and success in school communities. There are four main kinds of assessment:

1. Observation: Noticing someone and judging his or her action.
2. Informal continuous assessment: This type of assessment is less structured and not formal like a test or exam. It is continuous because it occurs periodically (usually on a daily or weekly basis).
3. Formal continuous assessment: This type of assessment is more structured and includes setting up assessment situations periodically. An assessment situation is an activity you organize to assess learners. It could be a quiz, or it could be a group activity in which the participants will be assessed.
4. Formal assessment: This type of assessment is a structured, infrequent measure of learner achievement. Tests and exams are formal assessments. Exams are used to measure the learner's progress.

The purpose of informal assessment is to help learners learn better. This form of assessment helps the teacher determine how well the learners are learning and progressing. Informal assessment can be applied to homework assignments, field journals, and daily classwork, which are good indicators of student progress and comprehension.

Formal assessment, in contrast, is highly structured. It must be done at regular intervals, and if the progress is not satisfactory, parent involvement is absolutely essential. A test or exam is a good example of formal assessment. A science project is also a formal assessment.

Informal Assessments

There are many ways to evaluate a child's knowledge and assess his or her learning needs. In recent years, the emphasis has shifted from mastery testing of isolated skills to authentic assessments of what children know. Authentic assessments allow the teacher to know more precisely what each individual student knows, can do, and needs to do. Authentic assessments can help both the student and the teacher become more responsible for learning.

One of the simplest and most efficient ways for the teacher to get to know his or her students is to conduct an entry survey. This is a record that provides useful background information about the students as they enter a class or school. Collecting information through an entry survey will give valuable insights into a student's background knowledge and experience. Teachers can customize entry surveys according to the type of information considered valuable. Some of the information that may be incorporated includes the student's name and age, family members, health factors, special interests, strengths, needs, fears, parent expectations, languages spoken in the home, what the child likes about school, and so on.

At the beginning of each school term, the teacher will likely feel compelled to conduct some informal evaluations to obtain a general awareness of his or her students. These informal evaluations should be the result of a learning activity rather than a test and may include classroom observations, collections of reading and writing samples, and notations about the students' cognitive abilities as demonstrated by classroom discussions and participation, including the students' command of language. The value of these informal evaluations cannot be overstated. These evaluations, if utilized effectively, will drive instruction and facilitate learning.

Structured Assessments

After initial informal evaluations have been conducted and appropriate instruction follows, teachers need to fine-tune individual evaluations to provide optimum learning experiences. Some of the same types of evaluations that were used to determine initial general learning needs can be used on an ongoing basis to determine individual learning needs. It is somewhat more difficult to choose an appropriate evaluation instrument for elementary-aged students than for older students. Therefore, teachers must be mindful of developmentally appropriate instruments. At the same time, teachers must be cognizant of the information that they wish to attain from a specific evaluation instrument. Ultimately, these two factors—students' developmental stage and the information to be derived—will determine which type of evaluation will be most appropriate and valuable. There are few commercially designed assessment tools that may prove to be as effective as the tool that is constructed by the teacher.

A simple-to-administer, information-rich evaluation of a child's reading strengths and weaknesses is the running reading record. According to Traill (1993), "This technique for recording reading behavior is the most insightful, informative, and instructionally useful assessment procedure you can use for monitoring a child's progress in learning to read." The teacher uses a simple coding system to record what a child does while reading text out loud. At a later time the teacher can go back to the record and assess what the child knows about reading and what the teacher needs to address in an effort to help the student become a better reader.

If the teacher is evaluating a child's writing, it is a good idea to discourage the child from erasing his or her errors and to train the child to cross out errors with a single line so that the teacher can actually see the process that the student went through to complete a writing assignment. This writing becomes an important means of getting to know about students' writing and is an effective, valuable writing evaluation.

Mathematics skills can be evaluated informally by observing students as they work at their seats or perform at the board. Teachers can see if the students know basic computation skills, if they understand place value, or if they transpose numbers simply by watching them as they solve computation problems. Some teachers may prefer to administer some basic computation tests to determine a student's mathematics strengths and weaknesses. Although these tests are not as effective or thorough as observation in assessing students, they are quick and easy to administer.

Classroom observations can provide teachers with one of the most comprehensive means of knowing their students. Teachers can observe students to see how they interact with their peers, which activities they choose, what they like to read, and how frequently they choose to work alone. "Everything you hear a child say and see a child do is a glimpse into a mind and a source of information to 'know' from" (Traill, 1993).

Formal Assessments

Norm-Referenced Assessments

Norm-referenced tests (NRT) are used to classify student learners for homogenous groupings based on ability levels or basic skills into a ranking category. In many school communities, NRTs are used to classify students into AP (Advanced Placement), honors, regular, or remedial classes that can significantly impact students' future educational opportunities or success. NRTs are also used by national testing companies such as Iowa Test of Basic Skills (Riverside), Florida Achievement Test (McGraw-Hill), and other major test publishers to test a national sample of students to norm against standard test-takers. Stiggins (1994) states, "Norm-referenced tests (NRT) are designed to highlight achievement differences between and among students to produce a dependable rank order of students across a continuum of achievement from high achievers to low achievers."

Educators may select NRTs to focus on student learners with lower basic skills that could limit the development of curriculum content that needs to provide students with academic learning that accelerates student skills from basic to higher skill application to address the state assessments and core subject expectations. NRT ranking ranges from 1 to 99, with 25 percent of students scoring in the lower ranking of 1 to 25 and 25 percent of students scoring in the higher ranking of 76 to 99. Florida uses a variety of NRTs for student assessments that range from Iowa Test of Basic Skills to California Battery Achievement testing to measure student learning in reading and math.

Criterion-Referenced Assessments

Criterion-referenced assessments look at specific student learning goals and performance compared to a norm group of student learners. According to Bond (1996), "Educators or policymakers may choose to use a criterion-referenced test (CRT) when they wish to see how well students have learned the knowledge and skills which they are expected to have mastered." Many school districts and state legislation use CRTs to ascertain whether schools are meeting national and state learning standards. The latest national educational mandate of No Child Left Behind (NCLB) and Adequate Yearly Progress (AYP) use CRTs to measure student learning, school performance, and school improvement goals as structured accountability expectations in school communities. CRTs are generally used in learning environments to reflect the effectiveness of curriculum implementation and learning outcomes.

Performance-Based Assessments

Performance-based assessments are currently being used in a number of state testing programs to measure the learning outcomes of individual students in subject content areas. Washington State uses performance-based assessments for the WASL (Washington Assessment of Student Learning) in Reading, Writing, Math and Science to measure student-learning performance. Attaching a graduation requirement to passing the required state assessment for the class of 2008 has created a high-stakes testing and educational accountability for both students and teachers in meeting the expected skill based requirements for Grade 10 students taking the test.

In today's classrooms, performance-based assessments in core subject areas must have established and specific performance criteria that start with pretesting in a subject area and maintain daily or weekly testing to gauge student learning goals and objectives. To understand a student's learning is to understand how a student processes information. Effective performance assessments will show the gaps or holes in student learning, which allows for an intense concentration on providing fillers to bridge non-sequential learning gaps. Typical performance assessments include oral and written student work in the form of research papers, oral presentations, class projects, journals, student portfolio collections of work, and community service projects.

Tests

Tests and similar direct assessment methods represent the most easily identified types of assessment. Thorndike (1997, 199) identifies three types of assessment instruments:

1. Standardized achievement tests
2. Assessment material packaged with curricular materials
3. Teacher-made assessment instruments
   Pencil-and-paper tests
   Oral tests
   Product evaluations
   Performance tests
   Effective measures

Kellough and Roberts (1991, 343) take a slightly different perspective. They describe "three avenues for assessing student achievement:

a) what the learner says
b) what the learner does, and
c) what the learner writes."

See also Skill 6.2

Skill 6.2	Identify procedures for accurately establishing, maintaining, and using formal and informal student records

Student Records

The information contained within student records, teacher observations, and diagnostic tests is only as valuable as the teacher's ability to understand it. Although the student's cumulative record will contain this information, it is the responsibility of each teacher to read and interpret the information. Diagnostic test results are somewhat uniform and easy to interpret. They usually include a scoring guide that tells the teacher what the numbers actually mean. Teachers also need to realize that these number scores leave room for uncontrollable factors and are not the ultimate indicator of a child's ability or learning needs. Many factors influence these scores, including the rapport the child had with the tester, how the child was feeling when the test was administered, and how the child regarded the value or importance of the test. Therefore, the teacher should regard these scores as a "ballpark" figure.

When a teacher reads another teacher's observations, it is important to keep in mind that each person brings to an observation certain biases. The reader may also influence the information contained within an observation with his or her own interpretation. When using teacher observations as a basis for designing learning programs, it is necessary to be aware of these shortcomings.

Student records may provide the most assistance in guiding instruction. These records contain information that was gathered over a period of time and may show student growth and progress. They also contain information provided by several people including teachers, parents, and other educational professionals. By reading this compilation of information, the teacher may get a more accurate picture of a student's needs. All of this information is only a stepping stone in determining how a child learns, what a child knows, and what a child needs to know to further his or her education.

Other Assessments

It is useful to consider the types of assessment procedures that are available to the classroom teacher. The types of assessment discussed below represent many of the more common types, but the list is not comprehensive.

Anecdotal Records

These are notes recorded by the teacher concerning an area of interest or concern with a particular student. These records should focus on observable behaviors and should be descriptive in nature. They should not include assumptions or speculations regarding effective areas such as motivation or interest. These records are usually compiled over a period of several days to several weeks.

Rating Scales and Checklists

These assessments are generally self-appraisal instruments completed by the students or observation-based instruments completed by the teacher. The focus of these is frequently on behavior or effective areas such as interest and motivation.

Portfolio Assessment

The use of student portfolios for some aspect of assessment has become quite common. The purpose, nature, and policies of portfolio assessment vary greatly from one setting to another. In general, though, a student's portfolio contains samples of work collected over an extended period of time. The nature of the subject, age of the student, and scope of the portfolio all contribute to the specific mechanics of analyzing, synthesizing, and otherwise evaluating the portfolio contents.

In most cases, the student and teacher make joint decisions as to which work samples go into the student's portfolio. A collection of work compiled over an extended time period allows teacher, student, and parents to view the student's progress from a unique perspective. Qualitative changes over time can be readily apparent from work samples. Such changes are difficult to establish with strictly quantitative records like the scores recorded in the teacher's grade book.

Questioning

One of the most frequently occurring forms of assessment in the classroom is oral questioning by the teacher. As the teacher questions the students, he or she collects a great deal of information about the degree of student learning and potential sources of confusion for the students. While questioning is often viewed as a component of instructional methodology, it is also a powerful assessment tool.

See also Skill 6.1

Skill 6.3	**Interpret formal and informal assessment data to make instructional decisions about the educational needs of children**

See Skill 6.2

Skill 6.4	**Identify procedures for appropriately using authentic assessments (e.g., portfolios, observations, journals) to plan instruction that better extends the child's level of learning and interest**

Portfolios are a focused collection of student work that exhibits the student's efforts, progress, and achievements in one or more areas of the curriculum, representing a variety of work assignments. The portfolio should represent a collection of the student's best work or best efforts and include student-selected samples of work experiences related to outcomes being assessed. A portfolio charts growth and developmental patterns toward achieving expected outcomes. The portfolio may also contain one or more works in progress that demonstrate the formation of a project, such as a story that is developing through the stages of origin, drafting, and revision.

Procedures for Planning Instruction

Keep the following in mind when planning portfolio creation and assessment:

- Portfolio assessment is a continuous and ongoing, providing both formative (ongoing) and summative (culminating) opportunities for monitoring students' progress toward achieving essential outcomes.

- Portfolio assessment is multidimensional, that is, it reflects a varied collection of student work and work in progress that demonstrates various aspects of students' learning processes.
- Portfolio assessment provides for collaborative reflection, including ways for students to reflect on their own thinking processes as they monitor their own comprehension and reflect on their approaches to problem solving and decision making.

In today's classrooms, portfolios are appreciated by teachers as an assessment tool because they are representations of classroom-based performance. Students are also greatly benefited by portfolio instruction, which encourages self-directed learning.

See also Skill 6.1

| Skill 6.5 | Identify procedures and legal requirements that provide for productive family conferences and/or home visits, regarding the assessment, education, and development of children, in accordance with due process (e.g., IEP, RtI) and confidentiality |

See Skill 1.7

| Skill 6.6 | Identify methods of observing, facilitating, and extending children's play to practice newly acquired abilities (e.g., through problem solving, imitation, persistence, and creativity) |

Today's hurried lifestyles, changes in family structure, and increased attention to academics have reduced play time. It is important to remove barriers to children's opportunities to play. When children's lives are overscheduled with activities, sports, and classes, they do not have time to themselves and time for unstructured play. When children watch too much TV, their play often mimics what they see on TV (or the computer screen), and it robs them of valuable time when imagination and creativity take hold. When a child says, "I'm bored," this may be a signal to add more unstructured time for play, not less.

Play allows children to create and explore a world they can master, conquering their fears while practicing their adult roles, sometimes with other children and sometimes with adult caregivers. This is turn leads to increased confidence and the resiliency they will need to face challenges in the future. While adults are often involved in playing with young children, adults should be careful not to control the play. Undirected play teaches children decision-making skills, creativity, leadership, and group skills.

Adults should join in on what the child is doing and talk with the child. Children are endlessly curious and often ask "Why?" Instead of being exasperated by the continuous questioning, adults should encourage questions and answer them to the best of their ability. Be sure to respect the unusual ideas of children and show them that their ideas have value. As you interact with a child at play, offer help when needed, raise questions to stimulate thought, and give wholehearted approval of the child's honest attempts.

Passive toys like computers require limited imagination. Imaginative play allows children to create situations for themselves and work out solutions and reactions. Providing toys likes blocks, dolls, and dress-up clothes encourages this kind of play. Creative play is supported by providing raw materials of all kinds such as sand, paint, and scraps of paper. Adventure play involves overcoming obstacles, gaining new skills, exercising, and using coordination.

Repetition is an important aspect of children's play. Doing the same thing over and over may be boring to the adult caregiver, but the repetition allows the child to master the new skill and then move on to experimentation and creativity.

Children at play reveal many things about themselves. Adults should observe and listen for the hopes, fears, and joys of the child to be revealed. With this knowledge, the adult can provide materials and opportunities for continued learning in the areas of interest.

Most importantly, adults should provide opportunities for learning and discovery without the threat of immediate evaluation. Teachers and parents should help each child experience some success every day, develop a healthy attitude toward mistakes, and gradually assume responsibilities in the care of materials. This feeling of security will leave the child free to think, imagine, select, and make decisions.

Skill 6.7   **Identify different types of assessments (e.g., norm-referenced, criterion-referenced, diagnostic, curriculum-based) and the purposes of each**

There are several types of assessments that will be utilized in the early childhood classroom.

Norm-Referenced Assessments

Norm-referenced tests are assessments that look at one student's score compared to the scores of students of the same age or grade level. This type of test allows a teacher to understand where his or her students may be in comparison to other learners across the nation or state, but does not necessarily give specific information about how much material a student might know in comparison to what he or she needs to know and understand at that point in time.

See also Skill 6.1

Criterion-Referenced Assessments

Most assessments written by teachers fall into the category of criterion-referenced tests. This type of assessment allows a teacher to obtain a grade, or score, and shows what a student understood or needs to relearn. Rubrics and checklists are two ways that this type of assessment can be scored. Many school districts and states use criterion-referenced tests (CRTs) to ascertain whether schools are meeting national and state learning standards. CRTs are generally used in learning environments to reflect the effectiveness of curriculum implementation and learning outcomes.

See also Skill 6.1

Diagnostic Assessments

Diagnostic assessments allow a teacher to see what a student already knows and understands. Diagnostic assessments might be used before beginning a chapter or even a section of a lesson. This is a way to ensure that learning will not be limited because the student is ready for the new material that will be taught.

Curriculum-Based Assessments

This type of assessment shows the teacher what a student understands that has been taught in class. By collecting this data via assessment, a teacher has concrete information about which objectives have been mastered from the classroom and which others might need to be reviewed to make sure a student is successful.

| Skill 6.8 | Identify and apply appropriate processes for monitoring struggling students (e.g., RtI, tiered interventions) and planning and implementing intervention strategies |

There may be various times when a student is demonstrating difficulty with certain abilities (social, emotional, academic, or developmental). Observation and data collection are crucial in allowing the teacher to analyze what a student's strengths and weaknesses are. If a student is demonstrating serious weakness in an area, a teacher should communicate this with the child's guardian. A teacher may then begin to look at ways to differentiate instruction for the student to see if adjustments can be made to allow the student to become more successful in the classroom.

Sometimes more serious needs will require further means of intervention. The teacher, after collecting data, will meet with a team of professional within the school setting to discuss the student's needs and will come up with possible solutions and interventions. This process, known as RTI, or Response to Intervention, is a way to strategize how to get a student back on track.

Minor adjustments like visual cues, moving a student's seat, working with the student in a small-group setting, and allowing the student extra time to complete an assessment are all strategies that might help a student become more productive within the classroom. Engaging the student in social groups or utilizing individual behavior charts are other possible ways to assist a student within the school setting.

After meeting and deciding upon some strategies to implement, the team meets again and can recommend any other changes or even formal evaluation for special education services.

COMPETENCY 7.0   KNOWLEDGE OF CHILD GUIDANCE AND CLASSROOM
BEHAVIORAL MANAGEMENT

Skill 7.1   Identify and analyze developmentally appropriate components of a positive and effective classroom behavioral management system

Behavior management techniques should focus on positive procedures that can be used at home and at school. When an intervention is needed, the least restrictive method should be used first, except in severe situations (such as fighting or dangerous behaviors). For example, a child who begins talking instead of working in class would not be immediately placed into time-out, because the teacher can use less intrusive techniques to prompt the child to return to task. The teacher could use a signal or verbal prompt to gain the child's attention, then praise the child when he or she is back on task.

Classroom management plans should be in place when the school year begins. Developing a management plan takes a proactive approach—that is, decide what behaviors will be expected of the class as a whole, anticipate possible problems, and teach the behaviors early in the school year. Involving the students in the development of the classroom rules lets the students know the rationale for the rules and allows them to assume responsibility in the rules because they had a part in developing them.

Procedures that use social humiliation, withholding of basic needs, pain, or extreme discomfort should never be used in a behavior management plan.

Emergency intervention procedures used when the student is a danger to himself or herself or others are not considered behavior management procedures. Throughout the year, the teacher should periodically review the types of interventions being used, assess the effectiveness of the interventions used in the management plan, and make revisions as needed for the best interests of the child.

Behavior Management Plan Strategies

Prompts

A prompt is a visual or verbal cue that assists the child through the behavior-shaping process. In some cases, the teacher may use a physical prompt such as guiding a child's hand. Visual cues include signs or other visual aids. Verbal cues include talking a child through the steps of a task. The gradual removal of the prompt as the child masters the target behavior is called *fading*.

Modeling

For modeling to be effective, the child must first be at a cognitive and developmental level to imitate the model. Teachers are behavior models in the classroom, but peers are powerful models as well, especially in adolescence. A child who does not perceive a model as acceptable will not likely copy the model's behavior. This is why teachers should be careful to reinforce appropriate behavior and not fall into the trap of attending to inappropriate behaviors. Children who see that the students who misbehave get the teacher's constant attention will most likely begin to model those students' behaviors.

Token Economy

A token economy mirrors our money system in that the students earn tokens ("money"), which are of little value in themselves but can be traded for tangible or activity rewards, just as currency can be spent for merchandise. Using stamps, stickers, stars, or point cards instead of items like poker chips decreases the likelihood of theft, loss, and noise in the classroom.

The following are tips for a token economy:

- Keep the system simple to understand and administer.
- Develop a reward "menu" that is deliverable and varied.
- Decide on the target behaviors.
- Explain the system completely and in positive terms before beginning the economy.
- Periodically review the rules.
- Price the rewards and costs fairly, and post the menu where it will be easily read.
- Gradually fade to a variable schedule of reinforcement.

Skill 7.2	Apply developmentally appropriate positive strategies for guiding children's behavior and responding to challenging behaviors

Teaching social skills can be rather difficult because social competence requires a repertoire of skills in a number of areas. The socially competent person must be able to get along with family and friends, function in a work environment, take care of personal needs, solve problems in daily living, and identify sources of help. A class of emotionally handicapped students may present several deficits in a few areas or a few deficits in many areas. Therefore, the teacher must begin with an assessment of the skill deficits and prioritize the ones to teach first.

Type of Assessment	Description
Direct Observation	Teacher observes student in various settings with a checklist.
Role-Play	Teacher observes students in structured scenarios.
Teacher Ratings	Teacher rates student with a checklist or formal assessment instrument
Sociometric Measures: Peer Nomination	Student names specific classmates who meet a stated criterion (such as playmate). Score is the number of times a child is nominated.
Peer Rating Paired-Comparison	Students rank all their classmates on a Likert-type scale (such as a 1–3 or 1–5 scale) on stated criterion. Individual score is the average of the total ratings of their classmates. Student is presented with paired classmate combinations and asked to choose who is most or least liked in the pair.
Context Observation	Student is observed to determine if the skill deficit is present in one setting but not in others.
Comparison with Other Student	Student's social skill behavior is compared to two other students in the same situation to determine if there is a deficit or if the behavior is not really a problem.

Social skills instruction can include teaching conversation skills, assertiveness, play and peer interaction, problem solving and coping skills, self-help, task-related behaviors, self-concept related skills (such as expressing feelings and accepting consequences), and job-related skills.

Methods for Guiding Behavior

Punishment should not be the first strategy in behavior management plans because it tends to suppress behavior, not eliminate it. Punishment focuses on negative rather than positive behaviors. There is also the chance that the child will comply out of fear, stress, or tension rather than a genuine behavior change. Furthermore, there is the chance that punishment may be misused to the point where it is no longer effective. Forms of punishment include the following:

1. Subtracting something that the child likes (such as recess)

2. Response Cost
In token economies, response cost results in loss of points or tokens. Response cost or loss of privileges is preferred to adding aversives, but for long-term changes in behavior, punishment is less effective than other forms of decreasing misbehavior, such as extinction and ignoring.

3. Time-Out
Time-out means removing a child from the reinforcing situation to a setting that is not reinforcing. Time out may be **observational** (for example, sitting at the end of the basketball court for five minutes or putting one's head down at the desk). The point is to have the child observe the others engaging in the appropriate behavior. **Exclusion time-out** involves placing a visual barrier between the student and the rest of the class. This could mean placing a divider between the desks and the time-out area or removing the child to another room.

4. Seclusion time-out
This type of time-out necessitates a special time-out room that adheres to mandated standards as well as a log of the children who are taken to time out, the reasons, and the time spent there.

To be effective, time-out must be consistently applied, and the child must know why he or she is being sent to the time-out area and for how long. The teacher briefly explains the reason for time-out, directs the child to the area, and refrains from long explanations, arguments, or debates. The time-out area should be as neutral as possible, away from busy areas, and easily observed by the monitor but not by the rest of the class. The duration of time-out should vary according to the age of the child and should be timed so the child knows when the end of time-out has arrived.

Time-out as part of a behavior management plan needs to be periodically evaluated for its effectiveness. By analyzing records of time-out (as required and directed by the school district), the teacher can see if the technique is working. If a student regularly goes to time-out at a certain time, the student may be avoiding a frustrating situation or a difficult academic subject. Seclusion time-out may be effective for children who tend to be group-oriented, acting out, or aggressive. Isolation from the group is not rewarding for them. Shy, solitary, or withdrawn children may actually prefer to be in time-out and increase the target behavior to go to time-out.

5. Overcorrection
Overcorrection is most effective with severe and profoundly handicapped students. The student is required to repeat an appropriate behavior a specified number of times when the inappropriate behavior is exhibited.

6. Suspension

Suspension is the punishment of last resort. In addition to restrictions on suspension for students with disabilities, suspension translates into a "vacation" from school for many students with behavioral problems. Furthermore, suspension does not relieve the teacher of the responsibility of exploring alternatives that may be effective with the child. An alternative to out-of-school suspension is in-school suspension, in which the student is placed in a special area to do his or her class work for a specified time and with minimal privileges.

Other Strategies for Behavior Management

Other strategies for behavior management include the following:

1. Counseling Techniques
   These techniques include life-space interview, reality therapy, and active listening.

2. Consequences
   Consequences should be as close as possible to the outside world, especially for adolescents.

3. Student Participation
   Students, especially older students, should participate as much as possible in the planning, goal setting, and evaluation of their behavior management plans.

4. Contingency Plans
   Because adolescents frequently have a number of reinforcers outside school, the teacher should try to incorporate contingencies for school behavior at home, since parents can control important reinforcers such as movies, going out with friends, and car privileges.

5. Consistency
   Consistency, especially with adolescents, reduces the occurrence of power struggles and teaches them that predictable consequences follow for their choice of actions.

Initially, the target behavior may increase or worsen when the student realizes that the behavior is no longer reinforced. However, if the behavior management plan is properly administered, the teacher should begin to see results. Behavior management plan evaluation is a continuous process, since changes in behavior require changes in the target behavior, looking for outside variables that may account for behavior change, or changes in reinforcement schedules and menus.

It has already been established that appropriate verbal techniques include a soft nonthreatening voice, void of undue roughness, anger, or impatience, regardless of whether the teacher is instructing, providing student alert, or giving a behavior reprimand.

Verbal techniques, which may be effective in modifying student behavior, include simply stating the student's name and then explaining briefly and succinctly what the student is doing that is inappropriate and what the student should be doing. Verbal techniques for reinforcing behavior include both encouragement and praise delivered by the teacher.

In addition, for verbal techniques to positively affect student behavior and learning, the teacher must give clear, concise directives while implying his or her warmth toward the students.

Other factors that contribute to enhanced student learning have to do with body language. The teacher needs to make eye contact with individual students; smile and nod approvingly; move closer to the students; give gentle pats on the shoulder, arm, or head; and bend over so that he or she is face to face with the students. Some of these techniques can be applied as a means of desisting student misbehaviors. Rather than smiling, the teacher may need to make eye contact first and then nod disapprovingly. Again, a gentle tap on the shoulder or arm can be used to get a student's attention in an attempt to stop deviancy.

It is also helpful for the teacher to prominently display the classroom rules. This will serve as a visual reminder of the students' expected behaviors. In a study of classroom management procedures, it was established that the combination of conspicuously displayed rules, frequent verbal references to the rules, and appropriate consequences for appropriate behaviors led to increased levels of on-task behavior.

Skill 7.3   **Identify opportunities for promoting positive self-concept, self-esteem, prosocial skills, and social-emotional development through interaction with peers and familiar adults**

See Skill 7.2

Skill 7.4   **Select developmentally appropriate problem-solving strategies for conflict resolution, self-regulatory behavior, and social interaction**

Instructors can foster critical thinking and evaluative skills by making children active partners in the entire learning and training process. Instructors should encourage students to employ self-assessment and self-monitoring techniques and skills.

Problem Solving

Problem solving is a higher-order cognitive process that requires the modulation and control of more routine or fundamental skills. It is the ability to solve a problem. A teacher might have the students call upon their problem-solving skills during a game of chess. Alternatively, they could strategize during a time-out in the last few seconds of a basketball game in which their team is down by two points. Development of adequate problem-solving skills also provides the student with self-confidence and a sense of accomplishment.

Goal Setting, Problem Solving, and Decision Making

There are three key elements necessary for promoting students' goal-setting, problem-solving, and decision-making skills. First, instructors must give students a clear understanding of the goals they need to attain, problems they need to solve, and decisions they need to make. Second, instructors must give students the requisite information needed to attain the goals, solve the problems, and make the decisions. Third, instructors need to give students the opportunity to assume active responsibility for these matters and create opportunities for them to act on those responsibilities.

Finally, instructors should emphasize to students that taking action is their responsibility. The more they get accustomed to making decisions and following through, the better equipped they will be to act similarly in future situations.

Conflict Management

Interpersonal conflict is a major source of stress and worry. Common sources of interpersonal conflict include problems with family relationships, competition, and disagreement over values or decisions. Teaching students to successfully manage conflict will help them reduce stress levels throughout their lives, thereby limiting the adverse health effects of stress. The following is a list of conflict resolution principles and techniques.

1. Think before reacting. In a conflict situation, it is important to resist the temptation to react immediately. You should step back, consider the situation, and plan an appropriate response. In addition, do not react to petty situations with anger.
2. Listen. Be sure to listen carefully to the opposing party. Try to understand the other person's point of view.
3. Find common ground. Try to find some common ground as soon as possible. Early compromise can help ease the tension.
4. Accept responsibility. In every conflict there is plenty of blame to go around. Admitting when you are wrong shows you are committed to resolving the conflict.

5. Attack the problem, not the person. Personal attacks are never beneficial and usually lead to greater conflict and hard feelings.
6. Focus on the future. Instead of trying to assign blame for past events, focus on what needs to be done differently to avoid future conflict.

Skill 7.5   **Identify and analyze appropriate strategies for teaching character development to young children**

Many individual schools, school districts, and even states are now requiring that character education be taught in the classroom. Teachers can build a caring atmosphere within their classroom that supports character building by implementing character development examples. The most identifiable and common character development traits are:

Responsibility, Caring, Self-discipline, Citizenship, Honesty, Respect, and Patriotism.

Strategies for Teaching Character Development

The following are some strategies for teaching character development:

- Hold class meetings in which students can establish group goals.
- Allow students to decide on rules of conduct.
- Teach conflict resolution so that students can become skilled at settling conflicts peacefully.
- Concentrate on problem solving rather than rewards and punishments.

Teachers can incorporate daily lessons, current events, movies, television programs, and so on to engage students in thinking about characters and their value systems. For example, when reading a book, have the students analyze the characters of the story. What were their strengths and weaknesses?

Teachers can also ask classic hypothetical questions such as: What would you do if you found a wallet with money in it? What would you do if your best friend begged you to help him or her cheat on a test?

The best strategies of a character development education always involve students in honest, thoughtful discussions concerning the moral implications of everyday life around them.

Skill 7.6   Identify the roles of early childhood professionals in collaboration with other professionals (e.g., social workers, school counselors, community liaisons) in helping children and their families cope with stressors

Although what's considered normal or acceptable behavior can vary a great deal depending upon a student's age and level of maturity, here are a few signs that a student may be experiencing stress:

- Behavioral problems (such as excessive anger, bullying, or eating disorders)
- A significant drop in grades
- Episodes of sadness
- Nightmares
- Decreased interest in previously enjoyed activities
- Overly aggressive behavior (such as biting, kicking, or hitting)
- An increase in physical complaints (such as headache or stomachache)

Parents need to spend time with their children; sometimes just listening to them talk about their day gives children peace of mind that everything is all right. Often children do not have time to play creatively or relax after school. Time should be allotted for children to be children with no responsibilities. Parents can ensure that children get plenty of sleep at night. Children also need to eat a healthy diet including each of the food groups. Adequate preventive health care is also crucial to the mental and physical well-being of a child.

Teachers and other professionals can also identify when a student is displaying symptoms of stress and then take steps to alleviate the stress. Many times just asking students what problem is bothering them will alleviate the stress. Children need to feel that their teachers care about them and their daily lives. Let students know that it's okay to feel angry, scared, lonely, or anxious.

Teachers can also read books to young students. Books can allow children to identify with characters in stressful situations. Some examples of helpful books are *Alexander and the Terrible, Horrible, No Good, Very Bad Day* by Judith Viorst; *Tear Soup* by Pat Schweibert, Chuck DeKlyen, and Taylor Bills; and *Dinosaurs Divorce* by Marc Brown and Laurene Krasny Brown.

SUBAREA 2   **LANGUAGE ARTS AND READING**

COMPETENCY 1.0   KNOWLEDGE OF LITERACY AND LITERACY INSTRUCTION

Skill 1.1   Identify the content of emergent literacy (e.g., oral language development, phonological awareness, alphabet knowledge, concepts of print, motivation, written language development)

Research supports that oral language development lays the foundation for phonological awareness, which leads to reading ability. As young children begin to learn to read, connections are made between the printed letters on the page and the sounds they have heard in language.

Phonemic awareness is a specific type of phonological awareness that focuses on the ability to distinguish, manipulate, and blend specific sounds or phonemes within an individual word.

Since the ability to distinguish among individual sounds, or phonemes, within words is a prerequisite to associating sounds with letters and manipulating sounds to blend words—a fancy way of saying "reading"—the teaching of phonemic awareness is crucial to emergent literacy (early childhood K–2 reading instruction).

The alphabetic principle is sometimes called *graphophonemic awareness*. This technical reading foundation term represents the understanding that written words are composed of patterns of letters that represent the sounds of spoken words. The correspondence between sounds and letters leads to phonological reading—reading regular and irregular words and performing advanced word analysis.

Since the English language is dependent on the alphabet, the ability to recognize and sound out letters is the first step for beginning readers. Relying simply on memorization for recognition of words is not feasible as a way for children to learn to read. Therefore, decoding is essential. Teaching students to decode text is the beginning reading teacher's most important goal.

Concepts of print include the understanding that print carries a message; that books are organized by title, cover, and author; and the directionality of print—left-to-right progression, top-to-bottom order, and one-to-one correspondence. Children also recognize print consistencies, which is the understanding that text is made up of letters that form words, which are then combined to form sentences. As the beginning reader makes these connections, he or she will next develop the concept of capital letters at the beginning of sentences and basic punctuation marks. The final stage of the concepts of print involves the identification of both upper- and lower-case letters. More advanced students may begin to recognize some of the most common spelling patterns in beginning texts.

The creation of a meeting area and a reading chair (sometimes a rocking chair) with throw pillows around it promotes a love of reading. Many classrooms also have children's storyboards, artwork, story maps, pop-up books, and "in the style of" writing inspired by specific authors. Some teachers buy calendars for the daily schedule that celebrate children's authors or types of literature. Children are also encouraged to bring in public library books and special books from their home libraries. The teacher can model this habit by sharing beautiful books and stories from his or her home library.

In addition, news stories about children's authors, series books, television versions of books, film versions of books, stuffed toy book character decorations, and other memorabilia related to books can be used to decorate the room.

One of the centerpieces of the K–2 classroom is the high-frequency word chart. This is a growing list of commonly used words that the teacher tapes under the appropriate beginning letter according to the children's directions. At the end of each month, the newest high-frequency words go into the children's folders and become part of their spelling words. In this way, reading, writing, and spelling are all intricately connected and reinforced as desirable achievements.

Successful reading and writing go hand in hand. Children develop writing skills through a series of steps. The first step is Role-Play Writing, in which children write in scribbles and assign a message to the symbols. The next step is Experimental Writing, in which children write in simple forms of language, often writing letters according to the way they sound (such as the word *are* written as *r*). At this step, they are aware of a correspondence between written words and oral language. The following step is Early Writing, in which children start to use a small range of familiar text forms and sight words in their writing. They learn that they have to correct their writing so that others can easily read it. The last step is Conventional Writing. By the time students reach this stage of writing, they can proofread their writing and edit it for mistakes. They can transfer between reading and writing and get ideas for writing from what they read. By this time, students also have a sense of what correct spelling and grammar look like.

Skill 1.2   **Identify common emergent literacy difficulties and apply strategies for prevention and intervention**

Common difficulties in emergent literacy begin early in childhood development and provide the foundation for how children acquire literacy skills and apply them in reading and writing development. Providing children with the tools for successful literacy acquisition enhances the reading and writing experience and provides ongoing successful development in literacy application and comprehension.

Some of the factors that cause difficulties for children in emergent literacy include the following:

- They do not have the requisite phonemic awareness skills to begin reading.
- They have difficulty with phonological memory.
- They experience problems with lexical access and lack the ability to rapidly name colors, pictures, and objects.

In today's educational communities, emergent literacy development poses critical issues and difficulties. Early childhood literacy development begins with exposing children to literacy-enriched environments, which include pictorial and written activities that provide examples of reading acquisition and cognitive development. Phonics application, whole language understanding, alphabetical construction in word development, and literacy skills provide strong bases for reading development. Students without these skills exhibit risk factors in literacy development.

Given that literacy development begins early in a child's cognitive development and provides the foundation for emergent literacy construction, educational researchers continue to promote the importance of parents and preschool educators.

Any child who is not in a home, daycare or preschool environment in which English phonology operates may have difficulty perceiving and demonstrating the differences between English language phonemes. If children cannot hear the difference between words that sound the same, like "grow" and "glow," they will be confused when these words appear in a print context. Sadly, this confusion will impact their comprehension.

Highly proficient readers can be paired as buddy tutors for ELL or special needs classroom members or to assist the resource room teacher during their reading time. They can use the CVC game developed by Jacki Montrieth to support their peers and can even modify the game to meet the needs of classroom peers. Of course, this also offers the highly proficient reader the opportunity to do a service learning project while still in elementary school.

Early Warning Signs

Parents and teachers should be aware of early warning signs of emergent literacy difficulties. These include the following:

- Failure in identifying or recognizing letters in the child's own name

- Lack of interest in singsong rhymes
- Difficulty learning and remembering names and shapes of letters
- Trouble comprehending simple instructions

Intervention and prevention of emergent literacy difficulties is most advantageous when these difficulties are diagnosed early in the preschool period. If not caught early, they are often persistent and influence the children's language and literacy learning throughout the following school years.

Methods for Intervention

Methods for intervention include the following:

- Encourage the child to name or describe objects, people, and events in his or her everyday life.
- Read picture and story books that focus on sounds and rhymes.
- Introduce new vocabulary words during holidays and special activities.
- Encourage the child to describe a story about his or her drawing and write down the words.

Parents and teachers must understand the difference between developmental speech, word development, and language delays/differences that may prevent oral language acquisition. The ability to differentiate between the natural development of children's language patterns and the delayed development of those patterns should be the focus of the adult caregivers who provide the environmental stimuli and language experience for children.

Skill 1.3	**Apply various approaches for developing emergent and early literacy skills (e.g., oral language and listening, phonological awareness, alphabet knowledge, background knowledge, concepts of print)**

In 2000, the National Reading Panel released its now well-known report on teaching children to read. In a way, this report put to rest the debate between phonics and whole language. It argued, essentially, that both word-letter recognition and reading comprehension were important. The report's *Big 5* critical areas of reading instruction are phonemic awareness, phonics, fluency, comprehension, and vocabulary.

Methods used to teach these skills are often featured in a *balanced literacy* curriculum that focuses on the use of skills in various instructional contexts. For example, with independent reading, students choose and read books that are at their reading levels; with guided reading, teachers work with small groups of students to help them with their particular reading problems; with whole-group reading, the entire class reads the same text, and the teacher incorporates activities to help students learn phonics, comprehension, fluency, and vocabulary. In addition to these components of balanced literacy, teachers incorporate writing so that students can learn to communicate through text. Emergent literacy research examines early literacy knowledge and the contexts and conditions that foster that knowledge. Despite differing viewpoints on the relation between emerging literacy skills and reading acquisition, the literature strongly supports the important contribution that early childhood exposure to oral and written language makes to the facility with which children learn to read.

Learn more about the National Reading Panel:

http://www.nationalreadingpanel.org/

Early theories of language development were formulated from learning theory research. The assumption was that language development evolved from learning the rules of language structures and applying them through imitation and reinforcement. This approach also assumed that language, cognitive, and social development were independent of one another and that children would learn language from patterning after adults who spoke and wrote standard English.

Linguistic Approach

In the linguistic approach, studies spearheaded by Noam Chomsky in the 1950s formulated the theory that language ability is innate and develops through natural human maturation as environmental stimuli trigger acquisition of syntactical structures appropriate to each exposure level. Linguists attributed language development to biological rather than cognitive or social influences.

Cognitive Approach

Researchers in the 1970s proposed that language knowledge derives from both syntactic and semantic structures. Drawing on the studies of Piaget and other cognitive learning theorists, supporters of the cognitive approach maintained that children acquire knowledge of linguistic structures after they have acquired the cognitive structures necessary to process language. For example, joining words for specific meaning necessitates sensorimotor intelligence. Children must be able to coordinate movement and recognize objects before they can identify words to name the objects or word groups to describe the actions performed with those objects. Children must have the mental abilities for organizing concepts and concrete operations, predicting outcomes, and theorizing before they can assimilate and verbalize complex sentence structures, choose vocabulary for particular nuances of meaning, and examine semantic structures for tone and manipulative effect.

Socio-Cognitive Approach

During the preschool years, children acquire cognitive skills in oral language that they later apply to reading comprehension. Reading aloud to young children is one of the most important things that an adult can do because adults are teaching them how to monitor, question, predict, and confirm what they hear in the stories. Reid (1988, 165) described four metalinguistic abilities that young children acquire through early involvement in reading activities:

1. Word consciousness. Children who have access to books can tell the story through the pictures before they can read. Gradually they begin to realize the connection between the spoken words and the printed words.
2. Language and conventions of print. During this stage, children learn how to hold a book, where to begin to read, the left-to-right motion, and how to continue from one line to another.
3. Functions of print. Children discover that print can be used for a variety of purposes and functions, including entertainment and information.
4. Fluency. Through listening to adult models, children learn to read in phrases and use intonation.

Importance of Background Knowledge

All children bring some level of background knowledge to beginning reading. Teachers can use this background knowledge to help children link their personal literacy experiences to beginning reading instruction and also close the gap between students with rich experiences and those with impoverished literacy experiences. Activities that draw upon background knowledge include incorporating oral language activities that discriminate between printed letters and words into daily read-alouds and frequent opportunities to retell stories, look at books with predictable patterns, write messages with invented spellings, and respond to literature through drawing.

Phonemic Awareness

Phonemic awareness is the ability to hear, identify, and manipulate the individual sounds or phonemes in spoken words. Language games, such as listening games, counting syllables games, rhyming games, and word and sentence building games encourage phonological and phonemic awareness and help students understand that language is a series of sounds that form words, which ultimately form sentences. Structured computer programs can also help teach or reinforce these skills. Daily reading sessions with the students (one on one or group) help develop their understanding of print concepts.

Alphabet Knowledge

For those children with previous knowledge of the alphabetic principle, instruction extends their knowledge as they learn more about the formal features of letters and their sound correspondences. Other students with fewer prior experiences must be taught the beginning alphabetic principle—that the alphabet comprises a limited set of letters and that these letters stand for the sounds of spoken words. These students will require more focused and direct instruction. In all cases, however, children need to interact with a rich variety of print materials.

| Skill 1.4 | Identify appropriate emergent and early literacy activities |

Teaching phonemic awareness is crucial to emergent literacy or early childhood K–2 reading instruction. Children need a strong background in phonemic awareness for effective phonics instruction—sound and spelling relationships in printed materials.

The following Instructional methods may be effective for teaching phonemic awareness:

- Clapping syllables in words
- Distinguishing between a word and a sound
- Using visual cues and movements to help children understand when the speaker goes from one sound to another
- Oral segmentation activities that focus on easily distinguished syllables rather than sounds
- Singing such familiar songs as *Happy Birthday* and *Knick Knack Paddy Whack* and replacing key words in the song with words having a different ending or middle sound (oral segmentation)
- Dealing children a deck of picture cards and having them sound out the words for the pictures on their cards or calling for a picture by asking for its first and second sound

Storybook reading affects children's knowledge about, strategies for, and attitudes toward reading. Of all the strategies intended to promote growth in literacy acquisition, none is as commonly practiced or as strongly supported across the emergent literacy literature as storybook reading. During storybook reading teachers can show students how to recognize the fronts and backs of books, locate titles, or look at pictures and predict the story, rather than assume children will learn this through incidental exposure. Teachers can also use repeated readings to give students multiple exposures to unfamiliar words or extended opportunities to look at books with predictable patterns, as well as provide support by modeling the behaviors associated with reading.

Activities to teach phonological awareness may also include any or all of the following:

1. Auditory games during which children recognize and manipulate the sounds of words, separate or segment the sounds of words, take out sounds, blend sounds, add in new sounds, or take apart sounds to recombine them in new formations.

2. Snap game in which the teacher says two words. The children snap their fingers if the two words share a sound, which might be at the beginning or end of the words. Children hear initial phonemes most easily, followed by final ones. Medial or middle sounds are most difficult for young children to discriminate. One sees this in their oral responses as well as in their invented spelling. Silence occurs if the words share no sounds. Children love this simple game, and it also helps with classroom management.

3. Language games model for children identification of rhyming words. These games help inspire children to create their own rhymes.

4. Read books that rhyme, such as *Sheep in a Jeep* by Nancy Shaw or *The Fox on a Box* by Barbara Gregorich.

5. Share books with children that use alliteration (words that begin with the same sound) such as *Avalanche, A to Z*.

The use of big books, poems, and charts are strategies teachers can use in both large- and small-group instruction. Simple questions can engage the students to pay closer attention to these skills (for example, "We are going to read this passage; where should I put my pointer to start reading?").

Provide children with a sample of a single-letter book (or create one from environmental sources, newspapers, coupons, circulars, magazines, or your own text ideas). Make sure that your already published or created sample includes a printed version of the letter in both uppercase and lowercase forms. Make certain that each page contains a picture of something that starts with that specific letter and also has the word for the picture. The book you select or create should be a predictable one in that when the picture is identified, the word can be read.

Once the children have been provided with your sample and have listened to it being read, challenge them to each make a one-letter book. Often it is best to focus on familiar consonants for the single-letter book or the first letter of the child's first name. By using the first letter of the child's first name, he or she is invited to develop a book that tells about him or her and the words that he or she finds.

While young children in Grades K–1 will do better with the one-letter-book authoring activity, children in Grade 2 and beyond can truly be inspired and motivated by alphabet books to enhance their own reading, writing, and alphabetic skills. Furthermore, use of these books—which have been and are being produced in a variety of formats to enhance social studies, science, and mathematical themes—provides an opportunity for even young children to create a meaningful product that authenticates their content study as it enhances alphabetic skills and, of course, print awareness

Skill 1.5	Select specific instructional methods (e.g., whole group, small group, explicit, systematic) for developing emergent literacy

Teachers should look at flexible grouping within the classroom setting. Although students may be grouped for ability at different times, this should not be the standard. The following are some of the instructional grouping strategies that teachers can use in the classroom:

- Whole-class instruction—Used to introduce new materials and strategies to the whole class.
- Small-group instruction—Used for small groups of students who need more instruction on an objective.
- Students working alone in teacher-directed activities—This enables the teacher to give one-on-one instruction or to assess how students are progressing.
- Collaborative groups—Students working together on a project.
- Circle sharing—Student discussion, such as author's chair.
- Partner groups—Paired reading, think pare share, and so on.

A variety of texts are available from a number of publishers for use within the classroom. If students struggle, it may be necessary to utilize a more specific systematic and explicit phonics program.

Examples of such programs include Wilson Reading, Early Intervention Reading, and Open Court. Children develop the ability to decode and recognize words automatically. They can then extend their ability to decode to multisyllabic words.

Explicitly teaching vocabulary works best when teachers connect new words to words, ideas, and experiences with which students are already familiar. This helps reduce the strangeness of the new words. Furthermore, the more concrete the examples are, the more likely students will know how to use the word in context.

The explicit teaching of word analysis requires that the teacher preselect words from a given text for vocabulary learning. These words should be chosen based on the storyline and main ideas of the text. The educator may even want to create a story map for a narrative text or develop a graphic organizer for an expository text. Once the story mapping and/or graphic organizing have been done, the educator can compile a list of words that relate to the storyline and/or main ideas.

The number of words that require explicit teaching should only be two or three. If the number is higher than that, the children need guided reading, and the text needs to be broken down into smaller sections for teaching. Some researchers, including Tierney and Cunningham, believe that a few words should be taught as a means of improving comprehension. It is up to the educator whether the vocabulary selected for teaching needs review before reading, during reading, or after reading.

See also Skill 1.3

Skill 1.6	Identify the components of and techniques for creating a print-rich environment reflecting diverse cultures and the impact of such an environment on classroom instruction

Components of a Print-Rich Environment

Classroom Libraries

Students need many opportunities to read and comprehend a wide assortment of print material, and the teacher should offer students a variety of reading materials, books, and other texts. Classroom libraries should attempt to build a collection with various genres of children's literature. The reading difficulty should vary to include multiple levels of reading. Libraries should include a variety of topics to interest all students, and diversity of books and their themes should also be considered.

Labeling

Labeling items in the classroom takes word walls to another level. Labels provide another everyday visual of words that are commonly encountered in a classroom. Labeling can also be done in multiple languages to promote diversity.

Displays

Teachers should display the students' work throughout the room. Children can be encouraged to dictate titles for their own artwork and stories. The students' work should be placed at the children's eye level for the other students to read, recognize, and enjoy.

Experiences with print (through writing and reading) help young children develop a better appreciation and understanding of the purposes and functions of print. A print-rich environment contributes to the students' phonological awareness and letter recognition. Children can then begin to acquire early reading proficiency by developing word-recognition skills.

The concept that print carries meaning is demonstrated every day in the elementary classroom as the teacher holds up a selected book to read it aloud to the class. The teacher explicitly and deliberately thinks out loud about how to hold the book, how to focus the class on looking at its cover, where to start reading, and in what direction to begin. Even in writing the morning message on the board, the teacher provides a lesson on print concepts.

When the teacher challenges children to take a single letter and name the items in the classroom, their home, or their knowledge base that start with that letter, the children are making the abstraction that print carries meaning concrete.

When reading to children, teachers point to words as they read them. Illustrations and pictures also contribute to understanding the text. Therefore, teachers should discuss illustrations related to the text. When reading to students, teachers should also discuss the common characteristics of books such as author, title page, and table of contents. Asking students to predict the story based on the cover teaches students about the importance of the book cover to the story. Pocket charts, big books, and song charts provide ample opportunity for teachers to point to words as they read, demonstrating that print has meaning.

1. Using big books in the classroom
    The teacher gathers the children in a group with the big book placed on a stand so that all children can see the words and pictures. The teacher reads and points to each word. By using a pointer, the teacher does not cover any other words or parts of the page. When students read from the big book on their own, they can also use the pointer for each word.
    When students begin reading from smaller books, they can transfer what they have learned about pointing to the words; they can use their fingers to track the reading. Observation is a key point in assessing a student's ability to track words and speech.

2. A classroom rich in print
    Having words from a familiar rhyme or poem in a pocket chart lends itself to the following activity: The students arrange the words in the correct order and then read the rhyme. This instructional strategy reinforces concepts of print. It also reinforces punctuation and capitalization and matching print to speech. Using highlighters or sticky tabs to locate uppercase and lowercase letters or specific words can help students isolate words and develop concepts about the structure of language that they need for reading.

The classroom should have plenty of books for children to read on their own or in small groups. While students read on their own, the teacher should note how the child holds the book and tracks and reads the words.

3. Word wall
   A word wall is a great teaching tool for words in isolation and with writing. Each of the letters of the alphabet is displayed with words under each one that begin with that letter. Students are able to find the letter on the wall and read the words under it.

   The words should include the words students encounter in their daily reading and writing and words they frequently misspell. Word-wall words can be arranged alphabetically, or they can be arranged by spelling patterns or by themes. Activities with a word wall include clapping out the letters in a word, solving mystery words, making word cards, and organizing words by parts of speech, by letters, or by subjects and themes.

4. Sounds of the letters
   In addition to letter names, students should learn the corresponding sound of each letter. This skill is a key feature of decoding when a student is beginning to read. The use of rhyming words is an effective way to teach letter sounds.

Classrooms that value people of all cultures integrate multicultural materials into many different areas of the classroom, and the print-rich environment should include printed materials from other languages and cultures.

Skill 1.7   **Analyze the structure (e.g., small group, whole group) and components (e.g., vocabulary, phonics) of a balanced literacy program**

J. David Cooper (2004) and other advocates of the balanced literacy approach feel that children become literate, effective communicators and able to comprehend by learning phonics and other aspects of word identification through the use of engaging reading texts. Engaging text, as defined by the balanced literacy group, are those texts that contain highly predictable elements of rhyme, sound patterns, and plot. What is more, advocates of balanced literacy believe in the use of "real literature"—recognized works of the best of children's fiction and nonfiction trade books and winners of such awards as the Newberry and Caldecott medals—for helping children develop literacy. They say:

- real literature engages young readers and assures that they will become lifelong readers
- real literature also offers readers a language base that can help them expand their expressiveness as readers and as writers
- real literature is easier to read and understand than grade-level texts

Other researchers, such as Jeanne Chall (1983) and Rudolf Flesch (1981), support a phonics-centered foundation before the use of engaging reading texts. This is the crux of the phonics versus whole language/balanced literacy/integrated language arts teaching of reading controversy.

It is important for the new teacher to be informed about both sides of this controversy as well as the work of theorists who attempt to reconcile these two perspectives, such as Kenneth Goodman (1994). There are powerful arguments on both sides of this controversy, and each approach works wonderfully with some students and does not succeed with others.

As far as the examinations go, all that is asked of you is the ability to demonstrate that you are familiar with these varied perspectives. If asked on a constructed response question, you need to be able to show that you can talk about teaching some aspect of reading using strategies from one or the other or a combination of both approaches.

The framework for organizing the balanced literacy classroom is referred to as the one book–whole class mode. What this means is that everyone in the class has experiences with the same book. Everyone in the class discusses the literature. The teacher starts by activating prior knowledge and developing the context or background for the piece of literature. Some of the children within the class may have less prior knowledge or context with which to frame the book. The teacher will need to provide a preview of the book or develop key concepts to provide a stronger base for what the class will read together.

Some children will have to work with a paraprofessional or with a reading tutor before the class studies the book. Different modes of reading are accommodated within the class; for example, by the books being read as a read-aloud, as part of shared reading, or as guided reading. Student reader choices can also include cooperative reading, reading with a partner, or independent reading.

Following the reading, the children respond to it, which can be done through a literature circle, with the whole class, or in writing. Based on assessments, the teacher will often form small ability groups for guided reading and mini-lessons. In this situation, the small group of children will all be working on the same skill(s). These ability groups are not permanent; they will change as the children's needs change. Guided reading with groups of six children is a major part of the balanced literacy approach.

In some U.S. districts a phonics-only approach is heavily embedded. However, the majority of school districts would describe their approach to reading as the balanced literacy approach, which includes phonics work as well as the use of real literature texts. To contrast the phonics and balanced literacy approaches as opposite is inaccurate, since a balanced approach includes both.

It is important to go online and to visit the key resources of the National Council of Teachers of English (NCTE) and the International Reading Association (IRA) to keep abreast of the latest research in the field.

Reading aloud to students is a main part of balanced literacy. However, the focus is on modeling the skills and strategies and then allowing students time to practice on their own. The components of a balanced literacy curriculum are the following:

- Shared reading
- Guided reading
- Independent reading
- Shared writing
- Guided writing
- Independent writing

J. David Cooper believes that children should not be "taught" vocabulary and structural analysis skills. Flesch and E.D. Hirsch, who are key theorists of the phonics approach and advocates of cultural literacy (a term coined by and associated with E.D. Hirsch), believe that specific vocabulary words at various grade and age levels need to be mastered and *must* be explicitly taught in schools. For Cooper, it is far more important that children be made aware of and become interested in learning words by themselves. Cooper feels that by reading and writing, children develop a love for and a sense of ownership of words.

Read-alouds are the corner piece of the balanced literacy approach for teaching reading. The book selected should be one taken from the classroom library that is appropriate for a read-aloud. Before reading the book to the class, the teacher needs to be familiar with it. The teachers should also plan or at least know what nuances of content, style, rhythm, and vocabulary will be emphasized in the reading. In addition, specifically for the younger grades, the teacher should select a text that also enhances the development of phonemic awareness. This might include a text that can be used to teach rhyming, alliteration, or poetry.

Generally teachers aim to teach one strategy during the read-aloud, which the children will practice in small groups or independently. Among these strategies for the first-grader could be print strategies and talking about books.

As the teacher reads aloud, the teacher's voice quality should highlight his or her enjoyment of the read-aloud and involvement with the text. Often in a balanced literacy classroom, the teacher reads from a specially decorated Reader's Chair, as do the guest readers. This chair's decorativeness, complete with comfortable throwback pillows or rocking chair–style frame, is meant to set an atmosphere that will promote the children's engagement in and love for lifelong reading.

The balanced literacy approach also advocates that teachers select books that children will enjoy hearing read aloud. Particularly accessible texts for the elementary school classroom read-alouds are collections of poetry.

Skill 1.8   **Apply instructional approaches and strategies for teaching informational literacy skills (e.g., reading labels, signs, newspapers)**

Uta Frith has identified three phases that describe the progression of children's phonic learning from ages four through eight. The first of these three phases, which relates to informational literacy skills, is the logographic phase. In this phase, children recognize whole words that have significance for them, such as their own names or the names of stores they frequent or products that their parents buy. Examples are McDonald's, SuperValu, and the like. Strategies that nurture development in this phase include explicit labeling of classroom objects, components, furniture, and materials and showing the children's names in print as often as possible. Toward the end of this phase, children start to notice initial letters in words and the sounds that they represent.

Use of Environmental Print

Sometimes children have not yet experienced an awareness of the conventions of print and labeling in their own home environments. The teacher or an aide may have to go on a label adventure and support children in recognizing or affixing labels to parts of the classroom, halls, and school building. A neighborhood walk with a digital camera may be required to help children identify uses and functions of print in society. A classroom photo essay or bulletin board could be the outgrowth of such an activity.

The teacher can also use the strategy of highlighting the uses of print products found in the classroom such as labels, yellow sticky pad notes, labels on shelves and lockers, calendars, signs, and directions.

Children can create an environmental print book, which contains collaged symbols of their favorite lunch or breakfast foods. The children cut and clip symbols from food packages and then place them in alphabetical order in their class-made book. Magazines and catalogues with ads for child-centered products are another accessible source of environmental print. Supermarket circulars and coupons from the newspaper are also excellent for engaging children in using environmental print as reading, especially when combined with dramatic play centers or prop boxes.

What is particularly effective in using environmental print is that it immediately invites the child from an ELL background into print awareness through the familiarity of commercial logos and packaging symbols used.

Play "letter leap" with the children and have them look carefully at the room to identify labeled items that begin with a specific letter by "leaping" over to them and placing a large lettered placard next to them. Children who are advanced in letter formation can then be challenged to "leap" through the classroom when called upon to literally "letter" unlabeled objects.

Children can literally realize the goal of making words their own and exploring word structures through creating concrete objects or displays that demonstrate the words they own. Children can create and maintain their own files of words they have learned or are interested in learning.

The files can be categorized by the children according to their own interests. They should be encouraged to develop files using science, history, physical education, fine arts, dance, and technology content. Newspapers and web resources, which the teacher has approved, are excellent sources of such words. In addition, this provides the teacher with the opportunity to instruct the children in appropriate age- and grade-level research skills. Even children in Grades 2 and 3 can begin simplified bibliographies and webliographies for their found words. Children can learn how to annotate and note the page of a newspaper, book, or URL for a particular word.

Students can also copy down the word as it appears in the text (print or electronic). If appropriate, the child can place the particular words found for a given topic or content in an actual bank of the child's own making. The words can be printed on cards. This allows for differentiated word study and appeals to those children who are kinesthetic and spatial learners. Of course, children can also choose to create their own word books that include their specialized vocabulary and descriptions of how they identified or hunted down their words.

The expository text structure of a *collection text* may be helpful. This text presents ideas in a group. The writer presents a set of related points or ideas. This text structure is also called a listing or a sequence. The author frequently uses clue words such as first, second, third, finally, and next to alert the reader to the sequence. Based on how well the writer structures the sequence of points or ideas, the reader should be able to make connections. It is important the writer make clear in the expository text how the items are related and why they follow in that given sequence. Simple collection texts that can be modeled for young children include recipe making. A class of first-graders, beginning readers and writers, was spellbound by a teacher's presentation of a widely known copyrighted collection text. The children were thrilled as the author followed the sequences of the recipe, and the children finally took turns stirring the food until it was creamy and smooth. The children enjoyed eating their Cream of Farina from a commercial cereal box, which had cooking directions on it.

The children had constructed meaning from this five-minute class demonstration and would now pay close attention to collection texts on other food and product instruction boxes because this text had become an authentic part of their lives.

Skill 1.9   **Identify effective methods and strategies to integrate reading, writing, speaking, listening, viewing, and presenting across the curriculum**

Some of the activities that teachers can use to integrate language arts into the content areas of the curriculum include the following:

- Use thematic units that incorporate reading, writing, math, social studies, and science with activities that are interrelated.
- Have a quick-write at the end of content-area instruction in which students record what they learned in this class. This is often referred to as using a Learning Log.
- Use shared reading with students paired for reading the text.
- Introduce content-area topics by reading from a picture book about the topic.
- Use process writing for all writing activities across the curriculum.
- Use interactive writing.
- Use oral reports.
- Use cartoons in writing assignments.
- Use written retellings of the text material.
- Create math journals (science journals, social studies journals).
- Write informational texts.
- Jot notes for research.

Research presentations are structured like essays. They often present a thesis or overarching claim or argument. Then they explicate, or explain, the thesis or argument with examples and details. The point of a research presentation is to provide an audience with enough details that they will: (a) remember the presentation, and (b) believe the argument—but not so many details that they will become bored with the presentation.

Responding to literature, particularly in discussions, involves making claims about the literature and then defending those claims with specific details from the text or personal experience. Good responses to literature make claims about a character's intent, for example, or the importance of the setting in a story. It is important to provide details to support one's claim. Often, though, a good piece of literature will elicit many different viewpoints, so while not everyone must agree on a claim, everyone involved in a conversation about the literature should at least be able to see how responder arrived at the claim.

Although speaking in class may seem natural for some students, listening is something that has to be nurtured and taught. Good listeners will respond emotionally, imaginatively, and intellectually to what they hear. Students need to be taught how to respond to presentations by their classmates in ways that are not harmful or derogatory in any way. There are different types of listening that the teacher can develop in the students:

- Appreciative listening to enjoy an experience
- Attentive listening to gain knowledge
- Critical listening to evaluate arguments and ideas

Listening is not a skill that is talked about much, except when someone clearly does not listen. The truth is, though, that listening is a very specific skill for very specific circumstances.

For young children, listening discrimination aids children's learning and further oral development. Games that encourage students to distinguish among animal sounds or that ask students to match a sound with the picture that makes the sound are two excellent activities teachers can use with students to practice listening discrimination. Phoneme games that, for example, ask students to circle the letter that is the beginning sound or a rhyming sound also aid listening skills. In addition, music games that encourage children to pat a beat, hear a rhyme, or follow an instruction (such as Simon Says) all allow children to practice listening in a fun environment.

For older students, there are two aspects to listening that warrant attention. The first is comprehension. Comprehension is understanding what someone says, the purposes behind the message, and the contexts in which it is said. The second is purpose. While a listener may understand a message, what is he or she supposed to do with it? Just nod and smile? Go out and take action? While listening comprehension is indeed a significant skill in itself that deserves focus in the classroom (much as reading comprehension does), we will focus on purpose here. Often, when we understand the purpose of listening in various contexts, comprehension becomes much easier. Furthermore, when we know the purpose of listening, we can better adjust our comprehension strategies.

See also Skill 4.2

Skill 1.10	Determine effective techniques for motivating students to engage in academic and personal reading (e.g., student interest in texts, student reading goals, student self-selection of texts)

There are many ways teachers can encourage reading for pleasure in their classrooms. One of the best ways is to read aloud from a novel each day, even with grades as young as Grade 2. For Kindergarten and Grade 1, choosing picture books by one author at a time will help students realize that different authors write on different topics and in different ways. Author studies in all grades will encourage students to seek out books by that author and read them on their own.

Monthly book clubs are also an excellent way of getting age-appropriate reading material into students' hands. Since these book clubs offer books at fairly inexpensive prices, parents realize that they can get more value for their money when they order each month. Book fairs at school provide students with the chance to win books for themselves and their classrooms.

Read-a-thons encourage reading because students realize that by reading they are helping a cause. Some of these offers, which include prizes for the students or for the teacher or school, could initiate this kind of motivation.

Some of the strategies that teachers can use to provide opportunities for students to give creative and personal responses to their reading include the following:

- Reading conferences—Ask a student to read a section of the text and then tell why he or she chose that section. Teachers can also ask students why they are reading a certain book or ask about their favorite author.
- Reading surveys—Teachers can devise a list of questions to find out what students are reading, how they decide what books to read, and how students feel about the topics or language used in the book.
- Daily reading time—This could be a set time when everyone in the class is reading, including the teacher, or it could be a center activity for a small group of children.
- Literature circles—Using the role sheets developed by Harvey Daniels in *Voice and Choice in a Student-Centered Classroom*, students take on different roles each day. They discuss the chapter or book, find new vocabulary words, illustrate a scene, or pose questions for the group.
- Reader's theater—Students adapt part of the book or story and make it into a choral reading with expression that shows how they felt about what they have read.

Deliberately assign a child or a pair of children to read big books. These are a guaranteed success for the children because they have already been shared in class. Some children enjoy reading these independently using big rulers to point at words. This provides them with a sense of mastery over the words and ownership of their independent reading.

Some children enjoy working on their own strategy sheet, such as a story map, character map, or storyboard panel, to demonstrate how they can apply a strategy to their own independent learning.

Another thing teachers can do to inspire students to become readers is to assign a book that you have never read before and read along with them, chapter by chapter. Run a contest in which the winner gets to pick a book that you and they will read chapter by chapter. If you are excited about it and are experiencing satisfaction from the reading, that excitement will be contagious. Be sure that the discussion sessions allow for students to relate what they are thinking and feeling about what they are reading. Lively discussions and the opportunity to express feelings will lead to more spontaneous reading.

You can also hand out a reading list of your favorite books and spend some time telling the students what you liked about each. Make sure the list is diverse. It's good to include nonfiction along with fiction. Don't forget that a good biography or autobiography may encourage students to read beyond thrillers and detective stories.

When the class is discussing the latest movie, whether formally as a part of the curriculum or informally and incidentally, if the movie is based on a book, this is a good opportunity to demonstrate how much more can be derived from the reading than from the watching or how the two combined make the experience more satisfying and worthwhile.

Matching young children with "just right" books fosters their reading independently no matter how young they are. The teacher needs to have an extensive classroom library of books. Books that emergent readers and early readers can be matched with should have fairly large print, appropriate spacing so that the reader can easily see where word begins and ends, and few words on each page so that the young reader can focus on the important concerns of top-to-bottom and left-to-right directionality and the one-to-one match of word to print.

Illustrations for young children should support the meaning of the text and language patterns, and predictable text structures should make these texts appealing to young readers. Most important, the content of the story should relate to the children's interests and experiences as the teacher knows them.

One of the most interesting ways in which the web complements the Reading and Writing Workshop involves the proliferation of author-specific Websites. If used judiciously, these web resources allow authors to be "present" in the classroom and allow children to write, question, discuss, and share their literacy experiences with the authors themselves. Children can also readily become part of a distance community of peers who are also reading works by a given author.

For instance, children who have been introduced to the work of Faith Ringgold, the author of *Tar Beach*, can easily visit her Website, www.faithringgold.com. Here they will not only find extensive biographic data on Ringgold but also be able to learn a song inspired by her main character, Cassie. They will be able to help illustrate a new story Ringgold has put up on the Website and also see if any of the questions they may have generated in their shared or independent reading of her books has already been answered in the "frequently asked questions" section of her web resource. A few of the author Websites respond online to individual children's questions.

There are even some reader response web resources such as the Spaghetti Review Website where young readers can post their response to different books they are reading. See http://www.book-club-review.com/view.php?cid=1.

COMPETENCY 2.0   KNOWLEDGE OF FICTION AND NONFICTION GENRES INCLUDING READING INFORMATIONAL TEXTS (E.G., LITERARY NONFICTION, HISTORICAL, SCIENTIFIC, AND TECHNICAL TEXTS)

Skill 2.1   Select literature (e.g., pattern books, concept books) from a variety of narrative texts that build language skills and concept development

Note: Books marked with an asterisk (*) have won the Caldecott Medal.

Fine children's literature opens children up to vicarious experiences that enrich their worlds. From being read to by parents and caregivers from the earliest ages, toddlers can handle **board books** with sturdy pages such as Kit Allen's *Sweater,* Donald Crews's **Freight Train,* and Margaret Wise Brown's *Goodnight, Moon.* Children ages two and three enjoy what are called **toy books**, that is, those that have flaps to lift up, textures to touch, or holes to peek through. Examples include Dorothy Kunhardt's *Pat the Bunny* and Eric Hill's *Where's Spot?*

From ages three to seven, children enjoy a variety of nonfiction **concept books**. These books combine language and pictures to show concrete examples of abstract concepts. Hundreds of beautiful books make up this genre, such as Lois Ehlert's **Color Zoo* (animals, shapes, and colors), counting books such as Eric Carle's **Ten Little Rubber Ducks* (directions, numbers, and up and down) Tana Hoban's *Count and See* (numbers and sets of 10 up to 100), and Molly Bang's **Ten, Nine, Eight* (a gentle lullaby as an African American father readies his daughter for bed).

Another category of concept books is **alphabet books**, popular with children from preschool through Grade 2. Outstanding examples include Arnold Lobel's **On Market Street* (every item purchased from the market is in alphabetical order); Lois Ehlert's *Eating the Alphabet: Fruits and Vegetables from A to Z;* Betsy Bowen's *Antler, Bear, Canoe: A Northwoods Alphabet Year;* Margaret Musgrove's *Ashanti to Zulu: African Traditions;* and Lara Rankin's *The Handmade Alphabet* (gives the American Sign Language signal for each alphabet letter in sequence).

In Grades K–2, when children are becoming early readers, two other genres of literature become salient: **wordless picture books** and **easy-to-read books**. The first of these, the wordless picture book, is excellent for children just breaking into reading. The books accommodate readers and nonreaders alike, because there is no text. Children must be capable of "reading" the pictures and be creative enough to supply the dialogue and descriptive language to accompany them. Many children have enjoyed Mercer Mayer's *Frog Goes to Dinner,* Emily Arnold McCully's *Picnic,* Peter Sis's *Dinosaur!,* and Mitsumasa Anno's *Anno's Journey.* Teachers should be discriminating about easy-to-read books because some are of questionable literary quality. Among the best are such familiars as Arnold Lobel's *Frog and Toad Are Friends*, Cynthia Rylant's *Henry and Mudge* books, and Else Minarik's *Little Bear* books, illustrated by Maurice Sendak.

From the preschool years onward, the **picture book**, characterized by illustrations and a plot that are closely related (one usually cannot exist independently of the other) are suitable for children. With the explosion of picture books in the last 15 years, there are some that can even be used with children in Grade 6 and above. Each year the Caldecott committee awards a medal to the best illustrated picture book in the United States. The committee also chooses one or two honor books. Teachers of children ages four to eight should be intimately familiar with the Caldecott list, which can be found in any children's library or on the Internet, as these books are exemplary reading choices. Well-illustrated children's books show sensitivity to line, color, shape, texture, and overall composition.

Illustrators use various media, from watercolor (David Wiesner's *Tuesday*) to oil painting (Paul Zelinsky's *Rapunzel* and Lane Smith's illustrations of Jon Scieszka's *The True Story of the Three Little Pigs!*), collage, used extensively by Eric Carle (*The Very Hungry Caterpillar*) and Ezra Jack Keats (*The Snowy Day* and *Goggles!*), to pastels (Ed Young's *Lon Po Po: A Red Riding Hood Story from China*). Other outstanding picture books include Maurice Sendak's *Where the Wild Things Are*, Vera B. Williams's *More More More, Said the Baby*, Barbara Joosse's *Mama, Do You Love Me?*, Jane Yolen's *Owl Moon,* and Leo Lionni's *Swimmy*.

Predictable texts or pattern books allow the beginning reader to feel successful with the process of reading in a rapid manner. Words or phrases are repeated over and over so that students can participate in the act of reading. They are also generally much enjoyed by students due to the natural rhythm that develops via the repetitions. However, teachers should quickly move on from this type of text so that children can begin to attend to the words and not rely on their auditory memory alone.

Chapter books are appropriate for readers in Grades 2, 3, and 4 and beyond. They are characterized by occasional illustrations, relatively short chapters to begin with, and interesting plots that appeal to children ages eight and up. High-quality chapter books for children ages 8–10 include: Patricia McKissack's, *Porch Lies: Tales of Slicksters, Tricksters, and Other Wily Characters*; Kate DiCamillo's *Because of Winn-Dixie*, and E. B. White's *Charlotte's Web*.

The following is a list of sample authors to choose for books in the classroom:

- Eric Carle
- Mem Fox
- Betsy Byars

- Tomie de Paola
- Leo Lionni
- Kristine O'Connell George
- Joan Holub
- Kevin Henkes

Skill 2.2　　　　　　Identify and distinguish the elements of various literary genres and formats of prose and poetry (e.g., multicultural literature, fables, legends, biographies, realistic fiction, fantasy)

Authors use various ways to tell a story while employing various literary techniques. If teachers want students to understand the technique, they need to teach them the characteristics of each narrative genre. It may be necessary to draw the students' attention to the elements and structure of narratives as well as the strategies they can use for reading each of the genres. Before students actually read a selection, the teacher can address the literary techniques, forms, and vocabulary in mini-lessons to provide them with knowledge about what they will be reading. This helps students become more engaged with the text and have an idea of what they should think about as they are reading.

Prose fiction is literature about imaginary people, places, and events. This narrative genre can be used to stimulate students' imaginations while considering the author's view of the world. This genre includes novels, short stories, and plays, each of which has its own distinctive characteristics. To varying degrees, they all have a setting, conflict, plot, climax, and resolution.

For younger elementary children, the following types of stories in big book format are ideal for providing predictable and repetitive elements that can be grasped by these children.

Folktales/Fairy Tales: Some examples are The Three Bears, Little Red Riding Hood, Snow White, Sleeping Beauty, Puss-in-Boots, Rapunzel, and Rumpelstiltskin. Adventures of animals or humans and the supernatural characterize these stories. The hero is usually on a quest and is aided by otherworldly helpers. More often than not, the story focuses on good and evil and reward and punishment.

Fables: Terse tales offering a moral or exemplum, in which animals often speak and act in characteristically human ways, illustrating human foibles. Aesop's fables have been adapted and repeated for centuries.

Legends: Traditional narratives or collections of related narratives, popularly regarded as historically factual but usually a mixture of fact and fiction.

Myths: Stories that are more or less universally shared within a culture to explain its history and traditions.

Tall Tales: Examples include Paul Bunyan, John Henry, and Pecos Bill. These are purposely exaggerated accounts of individuals with superhuman strength.

Modern Fantasy: Many of the themes found in these stories are similar to those in traditional literature. The stories start out based in reality, which makes it easier for the reader to suspend disbelief and enter worlds of unreality. Little people live in the walls in *The Borrowers*, and time travel is possible in *The Trolley to Yesterday*. Including some fantasy tales in the curriculum helps elementary-grade children develop their senses of imagination. These often appeal to ideals of justice and issues having to do with good and evil; because children tend to identify with the characters, the message is more likely to be retained.

Science Fiction: Robots, spacecraft, mystery, and civilizations from other ages often appear in these stories. Most presume advances in science on other planets or in a future time. Most children like these stories because of their interest in space and the "what if" aspect of the stories. Examples are *Outer Space and All That Junk* and *A Wrinkle in Time*.

Modern Realistic Fiction: These stories are about real problems that real children face. By finding that their hopes and fears are shared by others, young children can find insight into their own problems. Young readers also tend to experience a broadening of interests as a result of this kind of reading. It's good for them to know that a child can be brave and intelligent and can solve difficult problems.

Historical Fiction: *Rifles for Watie* is an example of this kind of story. Presented in a historically accurate setting, it's about a 16-year-old boy who serves in the Union army. He experiences great hardship but discovers that his enemy is an admirable human being. It provides a good opportunity to introduce younger children to history in a beneficial way.

Poetry: Poetry communicates ideas and feelings through an arrangement of words and sounds. Poetry can be used to capture a mood, tell a story, or explore different ideas. There are various literary techniques authors use in writing poetry, which the teacher can discuss with the class through mini-lessons.

Prose Nonfiction: Prose nonfiction is literature that is about real events, times, and places. It includes essays, journals, articles, letters, biographies, and autobiographies.

Essays: Essays are short works of nonfiction that give the author's opinion on a specific topic.

Biographies: Biographies are written accounts of a person's life. They usually highlight specific aspects of personality, give insight into events in someone's life, and often include intimate details that are not widely known. A biography is written about a subject and so is in third-person point of view.

Autobiographies: Autobiographies are accounts of a person's life written by that person. When one is telling about one's life, the opinions expressed may be exaggerated, or events may be omitted. They are written in the first-person point of view.

Memoirs: Memoirs are a type of autobiography, but usually deal with only one or two aspects of the author's life. They are not as structured as autobiographies because they are usually only about one section of the author's life rather than the entire life. Like autobiographies, memoirs are usually written in the first-person point of view.

Editorials: Editorials are statements or news articles written by a news organization. They express the opinion of the editor or writer on topics that may be of interest to the readers. Such writing is usually short and always labeled as being an editorial or opinion piece.

Textbooks: Textbooks present information on a subject area and include many different topics. They are divided into chapters, each one focusing on a topic. There are many features in a textbook, such as a table of contents, index, and glossary, along with photos, charts, maps, and diagrams.

News Articles: News articles present information on recent events of interest. These writings answer the 5W's and How and may be accompanied by photos or illustrations.

Skill 2.3 **Analyze and compare literature with common themes written from different viewpoints and cultural perspectives.**

There are many fine children's books that show children how people are alike. Differences then become interesting and tantalizing. Allowing children to see their own culture reflected in the books and activities in the classroom is deeply affirming. The following books give all children a glimpse of the delights and challenges we all face at times:

- Linda Jacobs Altman, *Amelia's Road* (migrant farm workers)
- Paul Goble, *The Girl Who Loved Wild Horses* (Native American)
- Bill Martin, *Knots on a Counting Rope* (Native American)
- Eve Bunting, *Going Home* (from California to Mexico)
- Pat Mora, *Uno, Dos, Tres: One, Two, Three* (shopping in a Mexican market)
- Gary Soto, *Too Many Tamales* (did a wedding ring get lost in the tamales?)
- Joseph Bruchac, *Crazy Horse's Vision* (Native American)

- Carole Boston Weatherford, *Freedom on the Menu* (sit-in movement at lunch counters)

Classroom Activities

The following are classroom activities to use with literature that shows different viewpoints and cultural perspectives:

1. Make a graph showing the sizes of families represented in the classroom.
2. Take snapshots of the children in your classroom, laminate them, and create a concentration game.
3. Enlarge the children's pictures and make face puzzles of them.
4. Make classroom books about My Family after reading a book such as Rebecca Doltich's *A Family Like Yours*.
5. Provide children with playdough and a variety of powdered colors, along with a mirror. Allow them to match their skin colors. This is an opportunity to learn new descriptive words. It demystifies skin color.
6. After reading *Hairs/Pelitos* by Sandra Cisneros (different kinds of hairs within Latino cultures) and Camille Yarborough's *Cornrows* (an African American hairstyle), provide a microscope for children to look at their hair, comparing and contrasting it.
7. Have older children make a family tree after interviewing their relatives.
8. Do creative dramatics, acting out powerful stories such as Eloise Greenfield's *Rosa Parks*.
9. Use persona dolls to tell stories of difficulties such as teasing or name-calling. Use class discussion to help children recognize the unfairness of this and brainstorm ways one could stand up for himself or herself.
10. Use oral stories along with pictures to tell the story of local, regional, and national heroes like Barack Obama.
11. Bake different kinds of breads in the classroom after reading Ann Morris's *Bread, Bread, Bread* (from all around the world).
12. Use Mitsumasa Anno's *All in a Day* (showing eight children from eight different countries at the same time each day for two days) as inspiration for essays the children write about a typical day in their lives.
13. Create a shoe store in the dramatic play area after reading Ann Morris's *Shoes, Shoes, Shoes* (from all over the world) or assemble an interesting collection of different kinds of shoes and allow children to make shoeprints in art.
14. Use Karin Luisa Badt's *Good Morning, Let's Eat!* (breakfast in different cultures) as inspiration for a math graphing activity of different foods children eat for breakfast.
15. After reading Laura Ingalls Wilder's *Little House on the Prairie* and Louise Erdrich's *The Birchbark House* (about an Ojibway girl who lives on Madelaine Island on Lake Superior in approximately the same time period as Laura), have children use a Venn diagram to show similarities and differences between the two characters and stories.

Classrooms that value people of all cultures reflect this by integrating multicultural materials into many different areas of the classroom. Teachers post art prints on the walls showing scenes and people from many different racial and ethnic backgrounds as well as people with disabilities. In the block area, teachers may post pictures showing different kinds of houses from different cultures. Miniature play people of different ethnicities (available from Lakeshore Company) are props sometimes provided in this area. In the music area, there can be rhythm instruments from a variety of cultures. In the dramatic play area, teachers may provide items and clothing from different cultures. For example, a sombrero might be available as well as a construction hardhat and a tortilla press as well as a play mixer in the kitchen area. Dolls of various ethnicities should be available for dramatic play. Many teachers also use persona dolls to educate children about ethnicities not represented in the classroom. The book area should have a wide variety of materials so children can see themselves in the stories as well as learn about others and their cultures. Providing a rich multicultural classroom environment for children is extremely important.

Skill 2.4   **Identify instructional approaches and apply strategies for developing literary analysis (e.g., story-mapping, plot structure, elements of literary devices)**

There are many exciting ways to sensitize and teach children about the features and formats of different literary genres. First and foremost, the teacher should choose fine children's literature as the basis for teaching literary analysis skills. Typically for younger children, teachers turn to picture books. The best-illustrated picture book published in the United States each year wins the Caldecott Medal, named for Randolph Caldecott, who was a nineteenth-century English illustrator. There is one winning book selected yearly as well as one, two, or three honor books. Teachers cannot go wrong in selecting Caldecott books to share with children. In recent years, more and more picture books are being written for older children as well.

Another award in children's literature that is critically important is the Newbery Medal, presented for the most distinguished children's book written by a U.S. author in any given year. The Newbery award–winning books tend to be suitable for intermediate and middle-level children. The award is named for John Newbery, an eighteenth-century English bookseller. Like the Caldecott awards, there is one winner as well as several honor books selected each year.

Strategy One: Genre Switch–Reader and Writer Transformation

This strategy should be introduced as a read-aloud with young children or with children who are struggling readers. In a similar fashion, it would be introduced as a read-aloud for ELL learners. Older children in Grades 3–6 might just be started by a teacher prompt and do the required reading on their own.

To begin, the teacher selects a particular genre book. If it is close to Halloween, a goblin or suspense story will do well. The teacher begins to read the story with the open invitation to the students to determine, as the story is being read, what type of story it is and what makes it that type of story.

Older children take notes in their reading journals, while younger children and those more in need of explicit teacher support contribute their ideas and responses as part of the discussion in class. Their responses are recorded on a chart.

As the reading continues, the story type components are listed on the chart (most of the responses are those that have been elicited from the children).

At some point in what is either an oral read-aloud, guided reading, or independent reading, the teacher directs the children's attention to the components that have emerged on the chart. They then use these components that are generally components of character—setting, plot, style, conflict, language—to identify the story genre.

The teacher provides the children with an opportunity to expound at length on why this story is an example of the genre that they have identified. Once they have done so, the teacher challenges them to consider how this story, with its set of given characters, plot, and setting, would be changed if the genre were different. The teacher can challenge the class as a whole with the idea of changing the story to a radically different genre—for example, from suspense to a fairy tale or a comedy—or allow the children to come up with another genre.

Then, depending on the children's developed writing abilities, they might be given time to rewrite the story on their own or retell it in class prior to writing and illustrating it.

In the balanced literacy approach, this transformation of the story into another genre is done as part of the Writing Workshop component that uses the reading material as the source for writing. The strategy will result in the children having had the experience of an in-depth analysis of a particular genre as well as hands-on writing (or telling, if they cannot yet write or cannot yet write in English) experience of restyling that basic plot and characters into another genre. This authenticates the children's participation as readers and writers.

Strategy Two: Analyzing Story Elements

Story elements include plot (including conflict and resolution), setting (including time and place), characters (flat and round; static and dynamic), and theme (the main idea of the story). Students can use graphic organizers such as story maps, compare/contrast displays, and sequence boxes to display their understanding of these critical features of stories.

Strategy Three: Analyzing Character Development

Characters in children's literature may be flat or round. A flat character is one-dimensional and is often defined by one characteristic. Rosie in *Rosie's Walk* is an example. A round character seems like someone you know, such as Jess in *Bridge to Terabithia*. Static characters do not change from the beginning to the end of the story, while dynamic ones do. Characters reveal themselves through their actions, their interactions, and through what they say.

Strategy Four: Interpreting Figurative Language

Similes are direct comparisons between two things using "like" or "as." "Her eyes were like stars" is a simile. Metaphors are indirect comparisons, such as "The earth is a big blue marble." Personification is giving human characteristics to nonhumans. Frances, Shrek, and the animals in *Mr. Gumpy's Outing* are all examples of personification.

Strategy Five: Identifying Literary Allusions

Children can understand allusions best when they read a lot. A literary allusion when it appears in a story is also called *intertextuality*. That is when a reference, character, or symbol from one story appears or is alluded to in another. Recently, many popular children's books use literary allusions, from the Ahlbergs' *Each Peach Pear Plum* to Jon Scieszka's *The True Story of the Three Little Pigs*. Note that any character or plot element can become an allusion, not just references from fairy tales.

Strategy Six: Analyzing the Author's Point of View

In fiction, point of view is the vantage point from which the narrator tells the story. We determine point of view by asking, Where is the narrator standing in relation to the characters? Is the narrator inside or outside of the story? If inside, is the narrator one of the characters? This is *first-person point of view*. If outside, can the narrator "see" into anyone else's mind besides his or her own? If the narrator cannot see into the mind and heart of other characters, then the point of view is *third-person limited*. Narrators who can see what other characters are thinking and feeling are using the *third-person omniscient* point of view.

Skill 2.5	Select appropriate techniques for encouraging students to respond to literature and informational texts in a variety of ways (e.g., retelling, dramatizing, writing)

Responding to literature through art, writing, and drama helps children reflect on the books they have read and make them a part of their lives. The following list suggests a few activities teachers can facilitate using children's books to make them come alive:

- Have younger children make puppets to retell the story.
- Allow children to act out the story with the teacher as the first narrator. Books like John Burningham's *Mr. Gumpy's Outing* work well for this.
- Do an art project using the same artistic medium used in the book, such as collage after reading Ezra Jack Keats or Eric Carle.
- Have children create a tableau (a montage of still figures) that captures a critical scene from a book.
- Use the interlocking structure of Bill Martin's *Brown Bear, Brown Bear* as the template for a new story in which the children draw new characters. This can be made into a classroom big book.
- After reading a book like *The Village of Round and Square Houses*, have the children create a village of box sculptures.
- Have children create a story map to show critical places in the setting.
- Ask students to write telegraphs or e-mails to characters explaining how to handle a problem.
- Encourage older children to retell a story from another character's point of view, as in Jon Scieszka's *The True Story of the Three Little Pigs*, which is told from the point of view of the wolf.
- Children can create a newspaper based on a book, such as the multiple perspectives in Anthony Browne's *Voices in the Park*.
- In writing, have children connect a book to their own lives. For example, after reading *Jamaica's Friend*, ask them to write about something they do together with their best friend.

Retelling needs to be very clearly defined so that the child reader does not think that the teacher wants him or her to spill the *whole* story back in the retelling. A child should be able to talk comfortably and fluently about the story he or she has just read. He or she should be able to tell the main things that happened in the story.

When a child retells a story to a teacher, the teacher needs ways to help him or her assess the child's understanding. The teacher can use some of the same strategies he or she suggests to the child to assess the child's understanding of a book that is not familiar to the teacher. These strategies include back cover reading, scanning the table of contents, looking at the pictures, and reading the book jacket.

If the child can explain how the story turned out and provide examples to support these explanations, try not to interrupt him or her with too many questions. Children can use the text of the book to reinforce what they are saying, and they can even read from it if they wish. It is also important to note that some children need to reread the text twice, and that their rereading of it is out of enjoyment.

Even young children will enjoy and gain tremendous additional expository comprehension facility when they are asked to dramatize a well-known historical document or song. They may act out the preamble to the Constitution, read aloud as a chorus the Declaration of Independence, or dramatize the "Battle Hymn of the Republic." This gives children an opportunity to examine in deep form the vocabulary, syntactic, and semantic clues of these texts. They then have to use their oral instruments (voices) to appropriately express the texts.

In addition to the activities already mentioned, the activities below will promote literary response and analysis:

- Have children take a particular passage from a story and retell it from another character's perspective.
- Challenge children to suggest a sequel or a prequel to any given story they have read.
- Ask the children to recast a story in which the key characters are male into one in which the key characters are female (or vice versa). Have them explain how these changes alter the narrative, plot, or outcome.
- Encourage the children to transform a story or book into a Reader's Theater format and record it, complete with sound effects for the multimedia center of the classroom.
- Have the children produce a newspaper as the characters of a given story would have reported the news in their community.
- Transform the story into a ballad poem or a picture book version for younger peers.
- Give ELL children an opportunity to translate stories into their native language or to author in English with a buddy a favorite story that was originally published in their native language.

Skill 2.6   **Identify a variety of uses and purposes for multiple representations of information (e.g., maps, timelines, charts, tables, graphs, pictures, print and nonprint media)**

Traditionally, the aspects of expository text reading comprehension have been taught in a dry format using reference books from the school or public library, particularly the atlas, almanac, and large geography books. Although these worthy library and perhaps classroom library books can still be used, it is much easier to take a simple newspaper to introduce and provide children with daily, ongoing, authentic experiences in learning these necessary skills as they also keep up with real-world events that affect their daily lives.

Students can go on a chronological hunt through the daily newspaper and discover the many formats of schedules contained therein. For instance, some newspapers include a calendar of the week with literary, sports, social, movie, and other public events. Children can also go on scavenger hunts through various sections of the newspaper and on certain days find timelines detailing famous individual's careers, business histories, and milestones in the political history of a nation or even key movies made by a famous movie director up for an Oscar.

The nature of the newspaper reportage and the public's need to know the why and wherefore behind the story of natural disasters, company takeovers, political downfalls, and uprisings leads newspapers to represent events graphically and to use cause/effect diagramming and comparison/contrast wording. If the teacher specifically wants to make certain that the students come away with this material, he or she can pre-clip "teaching" stories from the news for the children and introduce them in a special News Center.

After children have been walked through these comparison/contrast news writings and cause/effect diagramming as it appears in the newspaper, they can be challenged to find additional examples of these text structures in the news or challenged to reframe or rewrite familiar stories using these text structures. They can even use word processing to re-author the stories using the same text structures.

If a class participates in a local Newspapers in Education program, in which the children receive a free newspaper two to three times a week in the classroom, the teacher can teach index skills using the index of the newspaper by having children compete or cooperate in small groups to find various features.

Map and chart skills take on much more relevance and excitement when the children work on these skills using sport charts detailing the batting averages and pass completions of their favorite players or perhaps the box scores of their older siblings' football and baseball games. Maps dealing with holiday weather become meaningful to children as they anticipate a vacation.

What is really intriguing about the use of newspapers as a model and an authentic platform for introducing children to recognizing and using expository text structures, features, and references is that the children can demonstrate their mastery of these structures by putting out their own newspapers detailing their school universe. They can also create their own timelines for projects or research papers using newspaper models.

If the class gets newspapers in the classroom as part of an ongoing Newspapers in Education program, it is natural and easy for the teacher to take the time to show children how the same news is covered online. All newspapers have e-news. Children can first do a K-W-L on what they know or think they know about e-news and then review their specific daily newspaper's site. With the support of the teacher or an older peer, they can examine the resource and perhaps note the following differences in electronic text:

- use of moving pictures and video to document events
- use of sound clips in addition to written text
- use of music/sound effects not in printed text
- links to other web resources and to other archived articles

Naturally, this can lead to much rich discussion and to further detailed web versus print news resource analysis.

Quantitative data are often easily presented in graphs and charts in many content areas. However, if students are unable to decipher a graph, it is of limited use to them. Since information can clearly be displayed in a graph or chart form, accurate interpretation of the information is an important skill for students.

Students should be taught to evaluate all of the features of the graph, including the main title, what the horizontal axis represents, and what the vertical axis represents. Also, students should locate and evaluate the graph's key (if there is one) if there is more than one variable represented on the graph. For example, line graphs are often used to plot data from a scientific experiment. If more than one variable was used, a key or legend would indicate what each line on the graph represented. Then, once students have evaluated the axes and titles, they can begin to assess the results of the experiment.

Students need to be taught how to read and interpret graphs, charts, and maps that are found within reference materials and content-specific materials. Being able to correctly interpret these types of information will better allow the students to draw the appropriate conclusions. It will enhance the knowledge the students gain from reading and provide further clarification.

Once children understand how to access and interpret the information contained in content-specific materials or reference materials, they can then begin to analyze it to clarify their thinking process and make the connections to their own life or information from other texts. Sometimes, the students will find conflicting pieces of information that they will be able to examine more deeply.

Processing information in this way takes reading to an even higher, more involved level. It also requires students to find their own method for integrating it into their personal schema for later recall.

Skill 2.7   **Identify instructional methods and strategies (e.g., using graphic organizers, summarizing, oral questioning, inferring) for facilitating students' reading comprehension across the curriculum**

Reading is an inherent component of every subject area taught in schools today. Content-area reading (such as in science and social studies) can sometimes be much more difficult for students. Typically, the information is nonfiction and contained in smaller amounts of text. Deciphering content-area reading requires a unique set of strategies to best acquire the necessary information.

There are five key strategies for children reading informational/expository texts.

Inferencing is a process that involves the reader making a reasonable judgment based on the information given and engages children to construct meaning. To develop and enhance this key skill in children, they might have a mini-lesson in which the teacher demonstrates this by reading an expository book aloud (such as one on skyscrapers for young children) and then demonstrating for them the following reading habits: looking for clues, reflecting on what the reader already knows about the topic, and using the clues to figure out what the author means/intends.

Identifying main ideas in an expository text can be improved when the children have an explicit strategy for identifying important information. They can make this strategy part of their everyday reading style, "walking" through the following exercises during guided reading sessions. The child should read the passage so that the topic is readily identifiable to him or her. It will be what most of the text is about.

Next, the child should be asked to be on the lookout for a sentence within the expository passage that summarizes the key information in the paragraph. Then the child should read the rest of the passage or excerpt in light of this information and also note which information in the paragraph is less important. The important information the child has identified in the paragraph can be used to formulate the author's main idea. The child reader may even want to use some of the author's own language in stating that idea.

Summarizing engages the reader in pulling together into a cohesive whole the essential bits of information within a longer passage or excerpt of text. Children can be taught to summarize informational or expository text by following these guidelines. First, they should look at the topic sentence of the paragraph or the text and ignore the trivia. Then they should search for information that has been mentioned more than once and make sure it is included only once in their summary. They should then find related ideas or items and group them under a unifying heading. Next, they should search for and identify a main idea sentence. Finally, they should put together the summary using all these guidelines.

Generating questions can motivate and enhance children's comprehension of reading because they are actively involved. The following guidelines will help children generate meaningful questions that will trigger constructive reading of expository texts. First, children should preview the text by reading the titles and subheadings. Then they should look at the illustrations and the pictures. Finally, they should read the first paragraph. These previews should yield an impressive batch of specific questions.

Next, children should get into a Dr. Seuss mode and ask themselves a "think" question. Make certain that the children write down the question. Then have them read to find important information to answer their "think" question. Ask that they write down the answer they found and copy the sentence or sentences where they found the answer. Also have them consider whether, in light of their further reading through the text, their original question was a good one.

Ask them to be prepared to explain why their original question was a good one or not. Once the children have answered their original "think" question, have them generate additional "think" questions, find their answers, and judge whether these questions were good ones in light of the text.

Graphic organizers are pictorial methods of organizing information to help the student remember it more efficiently. Graphic organizers can be complex or simple, provided to the student or drawn from memory. The key is that the method or organizing tool used will help the students classify the information to be learned into smaller pieces with common characteristics. They also help the students begin to see relationships among the concepts. Graphic organizers work well as study aids to help students acquire more information. Some graphic organizers can use pictures or other visual cues to help the students remember the items to be learned.

Semantic mapping is a strategy of organizing information in which the students use a visual representation to show how words or concepts are related. This is a form of graphic organizer. In semantic mapping, the new knowledge is directly linked to the prior information. Sometimes called concept mapping, semantic maps allow the learner to see relationships among words or concepts and tie them to their own background knowledge in a meaningful manner.

| Skill 2.8 | Identify and appropriately use text structures (e.g., cause and effect, chronological order, compare and contrast) to develop student comprehension |

The five types of expository texts (also called text structures) to which the children should be introduced through modeled reading and a teacher facilitated walk through are as follows:

Description text: This usually gives the characteristics or qualities of a particular topic. It can be depended upon to be factual. Within this type of text, the child reader has to use all of his or her basic reading strategies, because these types of expository texts do not have explicit clue words.

Causation or cause-effect text: This text is one in which faulty reasoning may come into play, and the child reader has to use inferential and self-questioning skills to assess whether the stated cause-effect relationship is a valid one. Clue words to look for are: *therefore, the reasons for, as a result of, because, as a consequence of,* and *since.* The reader must then decide whether the relationship is valid. For example, does the ventricle pump blood into the heart?

Comparison text: This is an expository text that gives contrasts and similarities between two or more objects and ideas. Many social studies, art, and science textbooks and nonfiction books include this contrast. Key words to look for are: *like, unlike, resemble, different, different from, similar to, in contrast with, in comparison to,* and *in a different vein.* It is important that as children examine texts that are talking about illustrated or photographed entities, they review the graphic representations for clues to support or contradict the text.

Collection text: This text presents ideas in a group. The writer presents a set of related points or ideas. This text structure is also called a listing or a sequence. The author frequently uses clue words such as *first, second, third, finally,* and *next* to alert the reader to the sequence.

Based on how well the writer structures the sequence of points or ideas, the reader should be able to make connections. It is important the writer make clear in the expository text how the items are related and why they follow in that given sequence.

SEE also Skill 2.6

Response structure expository texts: These texts present a question or response followed by an answer or solution. Of course, entire mathematics textbooks and some science and social studies textbooks are filled with these types of structures. Again, it is important to walk the child reader through the excerpt and to sensitize the child to the clue words that signal this type of structure. These words include, but are not limited to: *the problem is, the question is, you need to solve for, one probable solution would be, an intervention could be, the concern is,* and *another way to solve this would be.*

Skill 2.9	Identify informational text features and their purposes (e.g., index, glossary, heading/subheading, table of contents, bibliography, references)

Children need to understand and be comfortable with the fact that not every expository text is meant to be read thoroughly and completely. It is important for the teacher to model for them that in research on a social studies or science exploration, it may not be necessary to read every single word of a given expository information text. For instance, if the child is trying to find out about hieroglyphics, he or she might only read through those sections of a book on Egyptian or Sumerian civilization that deal with picture writing. The teacher,

assisted by a child, should model how to go through the table of contents and the index of the book to identify those pages that deal with picture writing.
With the advent of the Internet, the art of research and study skills in texts is being lost. It is, however, a skill that needs to be emphasized and explained to students. Understanding reference materials will provide the students with the necessary foundational skills to prepare them for future learning.

Students should be able to locate the information they need for projects or to further their learning. To be able to find the information they need, students will need knowledge of using indexes, tables of contents, and other time-saving helpers.

In writing or reading a report or preparing any written information to address specific topics, the use of reference resources to locate information is crucial for supplying data. Information can be obtained from a variety of locations within the media, reference, and technological resources that serve as databases of organized facts and files.

In reference books, the table of contents and the glossary contain content chapters that are organized according to specific topic areas. Readers are able to locate specific information with page numbers to guide them quickly to the content areas that will provide data. Indexes contain more specific, detailed information that helps the researcher locate content to support his or her research.

A glossary, for example, provides definitions for words in the text. Throughout the text, words that are included in the glossary are written in bold so that they are easily identifiable. A glossary is similar to a dictionary in that it provides definitions of words; however, a glossary is typically a collection of difficult, unfamiliar, or new words located in one section of a reading. Most textbooks have a glossary at the end that includes all of the bolded terms in the book. Often, magazine articles for students have a glossary box of unfamiliar terms somewhere within the reading. Glossaries can be used as a study review or a springboard for flashcards for the challenged reader.

When searching for information, students can become much more efficient if they learn to use an index, which is an alphabetical listing of important topics covered in the book. The bibliography, a list of book titles that were used as references for the material in the book, refers the student to further explorations or a search for the origins of the information presented.

All these text features help students cope with the fact that in content-area subjects there are often texts with a great deal of information—typically, more information than students need at one time. In cases like this, students need to develop specific study skills to help them distinguish the more important information from the less important information and attain specific information without having to read every word of a book.

As they are becoming familiar with books, children need to be shown the following book features: front and back cover, title and half-title page, dedication page, table of contents, prologue and epilogue, and foreword and after notes. For factual books, children need to be familiar with terms such as labels, captions, glossary, index, headings and subheadings of chapters, charts and diagrams, and sidebars.

Knowing these text features can save children a lot of time and frustration as they understand how to hone in on needed information without having to plow through it all in an unorganized way.

SEE also Skill 2.6

COMPETENCY 3.0   KNOWLEDGE OF READING FOUNDATIONAL SKILLS

Skill 3.1   Identify appropriate stages of word recognition (e.g., pre-alphabetic, partial-alphabetic, full-alphabetic) and cueing strategies (e.g., graphophonic, syntactic, semantic) that effective readers use in the decoding process

Alphabetic Principle

The following are the four basic features of the alphabetic principle:

1. Students must be able to hear the separate sounds in spoken words.
2. Students must be able to blend separate sounds together to make words.
3. Teachers must use a systematic, effective program to teach children to decode.
4. The teaching of the alphabetic principle usually begins in kindergarten.

Teachers must remember that some children already know the letters and sounds before they come to school. Others may catch on to this quite quickly, and still others need one-on-one instruction to learn decoding.

See also Skill 1.1

Morphology, Syntax, and Semantics

Morphology is the study of word structure. When readers develop morphemic skills, they begin to understand the meaningful parts in words (phonemes have no meaning by themselves, morphemes do). For example, they realize that *cat, cats*, and *catfish* are related words. Using this skill, readers can identify and understand words faster and more easily.

Syntax refers to the rules or patterned relationships that create phrases and sentences from words. When readers develop an understanding of syntax, they begin to understand sentence structure and, eventually, grammar.

Example: "I am going to the movies." This statement is syntactically and grammatically correct.

Example: "They am going to the movies." This statement is syntactically correct since all the words are in their correct place, but it is grammatically incorrect with the use of the word *they* instead of *I*.

The meaning expressed when words are arranged in a specific way is called *semantics*. Knowledge of word meanings—their connotation and denotation— has an essential role with speakers and readers of any language.

The alphabetic principle, morphology, syntax, and semantics are all-important for building the effective word identification skills that help emerging readers develop fluency.

Decoding

Decoding refers to the students' abilities to sound out a word by translating different letters or groups of letters into the sounds they represent. If students do not understand that spoken words are made of sequences of speech sounds, and they do not have the ability to hear, identify, and then blend individual sounds in spoken words, they will have difficulty with decoding.

Tasks for assessing word-analysis and decoding skills can be grouped into three categories:

- comparing sounds
- blending phonemes into words
- segmenting words into phonemes

Teachers need to assess the students' general level of phonemic awareness to adjust the instructional time and effort in accordance with students' prior knowledge and needs. The following are some strategies for doing this:

- Procedures for assessing how students compare sounds are the easiest to use. Teachers can ask students to find which words begin with the same sound or words that rhyme.
- Teachers can present a list of words and ask students to read them. When students have difficulty, the teacher asks them to sound out the word and makes note of the strategies used.
- Another informal assessment is to use cards with letters on them. Ask the students to make the sound of the letter.

A checklist is helpful in recording what students can and cannot yet do. The checklist includes such subskills as the following:

- identify individual phonemes
- identify patterns of phonemes
- categorize phonemes
- identify blends
- segment words into phonemes
- add phonemes to words
- substitute phonemes in words

Using decodable texts is another way to assess students' continuing needs in phonics. Beginning readers are presented with words they should be able to decode if they use the phonics skills they have been taught.

Skill 3.2	Identify the components of reading fluency (i.e., accuracy, automaticity, rate, prosody)

Accuracy

Assessing student accuracy is one way to evaluate reading, and teachers can assess it by keeping running records of students as they read orally. Calculating the reading level lets teachers know what level a book is at—one at which the child can comfortably read independently, one at which the child can read with guidance, or one that frustrates the child.

As part of the informal assessment of primary-grade reading, the teacher should record the child's word insertions, omissions, requests for help, and other attempts to read the word. In informal assessment, the teacher can estimate the rate of accuracy from the ratio of errors to total words read.

Results of running record informal assessment can be used for teaching based on text accuracy. If students read from 95 to 100 percent correctly, they are ready to read that level of text independently. If they read from 92 to 97 percent of that level correctly, they are ready for guided or instructional reading at that level. Students who read words correctly less than 92 percent of the time need an easier level to avoid frustration and failure.

Automaticity

Fluency in reading is dependent on automatic word identification. Even slight difficulties in word identification can significantly increase the time it takes a student to read material, may require rereading parts or passages of the material, and can reduce the level of comprehension. If students experience reading as a constant struggle or an arduous chore, they will avoid reading whenever possible and consider it a negative experience. Obviously, the ability to read for comprehension and learning in general will suffer if all aspects of reading fluency are not presented to students as acquirable skills that they can readily develop with the appropriate effort.

Automatic reading involves developing strong orthographic representations, which allow fast and accurate identification of whole words made of specific letter patterns (such as ate, late, plate). Most young students move easily from the use of alphabetic strategies to the use of orthographic representations that can be accessed automatically. But for others, repeated practice in pattern recognition is often necessary. Practice techniques may include speed drills, which may consist of the same word lists repeated in sessions until students achieve the goal for several succeeding sessions.

Rate

A student with a slow, halting, or inconsistent reading rate has not developed reading fluency. According to an article by Mastropieri, Leinart, and Scruggs (1999), some students develop accurate word pronunciation skills but read at a slow rate. They have not moved to the phase where decoding is automatic, and their limited fluency may affect performance in the following ways:

1. They read less text than peers and have less time to remember, review, or comprehend the text.
2. In trying to identify individual words, they expend more cognitive energy than their peers.
3. They may be less able to retain text in their memories and be less likely to integrate those segments with other parts of the text.

Teachers can apply the following general guidelines for reading lists of words in a one-minute speed drill: 30 correct words per minute for first- and second-grade children; 40 for third-grade children; 60 for mid-third-grade children; and 80 for students in fourth grade and higher.

Various techniques are useful with students who need to increase their reading rate. Students can listen to the well-paced reading of material at their instructional level as they follow along with the print by using their fingers as guides. They can also practice repeated readings of independent-level material, timing the readings to chart progress.

Prosody

Prosody is the study of poetic meters and versification. Prosody, because it includes such matters as which syllable of a word is accented, translates reading into the same experience as listening. It involves intonation and rhythm through such devices as syllable accent and punctuation.

In their article for *Perspectives* (Winter 2002), Pamela Hook and Sandra Jones proposed that teachers begin to develop awareness of the prosodic features of language by introducing a short three-word sentence with each of the three words underlined for stress; for example, *He is sick. He is sick. He is sick*. The teacher models the three sentences and discusses the possible meaning for each variation. The students practice reading them with different stress until they are fluent. Teachers can modify and expand these simple three-word sentences to include various verbs, pronouns, and tenses; for example, *You are sick. I am sick. They are sick.* Teachers can increase the length of phrases and emphasize different meanings; for example, *Get out of bed. Get out of bed. Get out of bed now*.

Teachers also need to alert students to the prosodic features present in punctuation marks. In the early learning stages, using the alphabet helps students focus on the punctuation marks without dealing with meaning. The teacher models for the students and then has them use the intonation patterns that correctly fit the punctuation marks: ABC. DE? FGH! IJKL? ABCD! EFGHI? KL. Teachers can then move to simple two-word or three-word sentences. The sentences are punctuated with periods, question marks, and exclamation points, and the class discusses the differences in meaning that occur with each different punctuation mark; for example, *Chris hops. Chris hops? Chris hops!*

For older, more able readers dealing with longer sentences, teachers can mark the phrase boundaries with slashes for short, easy-to-read passages. Eventually, students can mark passages into phrases by themselves and then read the passages aloud, pausing as the divisions dictate.

Skill 3.3	Select instructional methods and strategies for increasing vocabulary acquisition and development (e.g., concept maps, morphemic and contextual analysis) across the curriculum

Vocabulary from Texts

The explicit teaching of vocabulary requires that teachers preselect words from a given text for vocabulary learning. They should choose words appropriate to the storyline and main ideas of the text and may even want to create a word-meaning map to prepare for the reading of a text. Teachers can differentiate among these key words; for example, some will already be well defined in the text and will therefore need less instructional time. (See also the section below on Context Clues.)

The teacher then decides whether the vocabulary selected needs review before reading, during reading, and/or after reading.

The teacher may want to introduce vocabulary before reading if:

- children are having difficulty constructing meaning on their own.
- children themselves have previewed the text and indicated words they want to know.
- the teacher has seen that some words within the text are definitely keys necessary for reading comprehension
- the text itself, in the judgment of the teacher, contains difficult concepts for the children to grasp

Introduce vocabulary during reading if:

- children are already doing guided reading
- the text has words that are crucial for comprehension, and the children will have trouble comprehending the text if they are not helped with it

Introduce vocabulary after reading if:

- the children themselves have shared words that they found difficult or interesting
- the text itself is one that is particularly suited for vocabulary building

Use the following strategies to support word analysis and as vehicles for enhancing and enriching reading comprehension:

- a graphic organizer such as a word map
- semantic mapping
- semantic feature analysis
- hierarchical and linear arrays
- previews in context
- contextual redefinition
- vocabulary self-collection

Context Clues

Authors often define words explicitly (for example, *Autumn is the season between summer and winter that includes the months September, October, and November.*) Sometimes, however, the definition is implicit (for example, *Denise was in a foul mood. Her head, eyes, and mouth were all pointed downward, and she talked to no one.*)

Helping students use these kinds of author devices constitutes the context clue strategy, which allows them to make informed guesses, or hypotheses, about word meanings.

To help students use this strategy, first select two or three unfamiliar words for teaching. Write them on the board or on cards to show to students. Then write one or more sentences with the unknown words that supply sufficient clues to help the students figure out their meaning. You will later read these sentence(s) with students.

Next, challenge students to read and define each word on display. When students offer more than one definition, encourage them to decide as a group what the definition is and write down their agreed-upon definition with no comment about its true meaning.

Now read aloud the sentences with the context clues that you wrote and continue the discussion of the words with students, directing their attention to their previously agreed-upon definitions of the words and the contrasts between these definitions and their ideas about meanings when they heard the words in context. Finally, have the children use a dictionary to check their use of context skills to correctly define the words.

Extending Vocabulary Knowledge

Pre-K through Grade 3 teachers will want to extend vocabulary study beyond stories and articles students read, although such study may be prompted by these texts. For example, after reading a story about bears, students may explore a concept/vocabulary study of other forest animals—their names, habits, ranges, and the like—both deepening their background knowledge and encouraging new vocabulary acquisition for all the language arts.

Another way to extend vocabulary is through the study of morphemes, or prefixes, roots, and suffixes. Let's say that one pre-taught word in a text is *transport*. Related words such as *transportation, translate, transfer, transnational,* and *transmigration* can be studied so that students can define the prefix *trans-* (across) and later have an advantage defining other words that begin with it.

Skill 3.4	Select effective instructional methods for teaching essential comprehension skills (e.g., main idea, supporting details, author's purpose, inference)

Topic, Main Idea, and Supporting Details

The topic of a paragraph or story is what the paragraph or story is about. The main idea of a paragraph or story is the important idea(s) that the author wants the reader to know about a topic. The supporting details are sentences that provide more information about the topic and the main idea.

The topic and main idea of a paragraph or story are sometimes directly stated. There are times, however, when the topic and main idea are not directly stated, but simply implied.

Read this paragraph:

Henry Ford was an inventor who developed the first affordable automobile. The cars that were being built before Mr. Ford created his Model T were very expensive. Only rich people could afford to have cars.

The topic of this paragraph is Henry Ford. The main idea is that Henry Ford built the first affordable automobile.

The supporting details are that Ford was an inventor and that before he created his Model T only rich people could afford cars because they were too expensive.

Teachers can help students find main ideas by examining how paragraphs are written. A paragraph is a group of sentences about one main idea. Paragraphs often have a topic sentence, which contains the main idea, and two or more detail sentences that support, prove, provide more information, explain, or give examples. You can only tell if you have a detail or topic sentence by comparing the sentences within a paragraph with one another.

Read this paragraph:

Fall is the best of the four seasons. The leaves change colors to create a beautiful display of golds, reds, and oranges. The air turns crisp and windy. The scent of pumpkin muffins and apple pies fills the air. Finally, Halloween marks the start of the holiday season. Fall is my favorite time of year!

Breakdown of sentences:

Fall is the best of the four seasons. (topic sentence)

The leaves change colors to create a beautiful display of golds, reds, and oranges. (detail)

The air turns crisp and windy. (detail)

The scent of pumpkin muffins and apple pies fill the air. (detail)

Finally, Halloween marks the start of the holiday season. (detail)

Fall is my favorite time of year! (restatement of topic sentence)

Tips for Finding the Topic Sentence

The following are tips for finding the topic sentence of a paragraph:

- The topic sentence is usually first, but could be in any position in the paragraph.
- A topic sentence is usually more general than the other sentences; that is, it talks about many things and looks at the big picture. Sometimes it refers to more than one thing. Plurals and the words *many, numerous,* or *several* often signal a topic sentence.
- Detail sentences are usually more specific than the topic sentence, that is, they usually talk about one single or small part of an idea. The words *for example, i.e., that is, first, second, third, etc.,* and *finally* often signal a

detail sentence. Detail sentences support, give examples, prove, talk about, or point toward the topic sentence in some way.

- How can you be sure that you have a topic sentence? Try this trick: Switch the sentence you think is the topic sentence into a question. If the other sentences seem to answer the question, then you've got it.

For example, reword the topic sentence "Fall is the best of the four seasons" in one of the following ways:

- "Why is fall the best of the four seasons?"
- "Which season is the best season?"
- "Is fall the best season of the year?"

Then, as you read the remaining sentences (the ones you didn't pick), you will find that they answer (support) your question. If you attempt this with a sentence other than the topic sentence, it won't work.

Author's Purpose

An author's purpose may be to entertain, to persuade, to inform, to describe, or to narrate. There are no tricks or rules to follow in attempting to determine an author's purpose. It is up to the reader to use his or her judgment. With Pre-K through Grade 3 students, teachers usually model, via think-alouds (teacher monologues about how they think through a problem to find its answer), how they themselves have come to understand the author's purpose. A couple of examples of how to do a think-aloud follow.

Read the following paragraph to students:

Charles Lindbergh had no intention of becoming a pilot. He was enrolled in the University of Wisconsin until a flying lesson changed the entire course of his life. He began his career as a pilot by performing daredevil stunts at fairs.

Then, think aloud:

I think the author wrote this to tell us about Charles Lindbergh. He thinks Lindbergh is important and wants to inform us about why he thinks this is so. It doesn't seem as though he's trying to persuade us to do something. And what he's written isn't particularly entertaining. So I think informing readers is the author's purpose.

Author's Tone

Read the following letter to students:

Dear Teri,

I was shocked when you said that having breakfast at home is a thing of the past. Many families consider breakfast time to be family time. A healthy breakfast provides the energy needed for an active morning. Are you joking? I cannot believe that you are serious.

Sincerely,
Jean

Then, think aloud:

I think that Jean's purpose in this letter is to express her disbelief and disagreement with what Teri said. Jean argues that breakfast is important and directly states that she "cannot believe" that Teri is really telling the truth about the importance of breakfast and may actually be joking.

Inferences and Conclusions

Early instruction in making inferences usually involves having students look at pictures and listen to stories about characters (usually children their own age) whose feelings are evident but not stated. Children can bring their own experiences with feeling glad, sad, and mad to a literacy event and identify with story characters, inferring feelings from the events, dialogue, and illustrations. When *Corduroy* the toy teddy bear is lost in a department store, his expressions and plight gain sympathy from children. Children know Corduroy is sad, even though the author doesn't directly say so.

To make inferences and draw conclusions, readers must use prior knowledge and common sense about how their world works and apply it to what they read. If students haven't had the experience of waiting for luggage after an airplane flight, they might not be able to draw a conclusion about what has actually happened to the Smith family's bags in the following story:

The Smith family waited patiently around carousel number 7 for their luggage to arrive. They were exhausted after their five-hour trip and eager to get to their hotel. After about a half-hour, they realized that they no longer recognized any of the other passengers' faces. Mrs. Smith asked the person in charge if they were waiting at the right place. The man replied, "Yes, this is it, but we finished unloading that baggage 15 minutes ago."

When students are required to read content for which they have little or no prior knowledge, it is essential for teachers to prepare them by explaining and discussing the concepts necessary for making inferences and drawing conclusions.

Skill 3.5   **Apply instructional strategies (e.g., utilizing graphic organizers, activating background knowledge) for helping students comprehend content area texts**

Most early readers are attracted to illustrations, and as beginning readers they should be encouraged to use them as they try to make sense of print. Children can use pictures and prior knowledge to construct a story, often with little attention to the print.

Teachers can demonstrate the value of visual clues in reading comprehension by reading a storybook that, in part, depends on pictorial representations for meaning. Teachers can also show students how to use the pictures in nonfiction books—photos, drawings, maps, graphs, charts, posters, and diagrams—to bring meaning to text.

Graphic Organizers

Graphic organizers are pictorial representations of content within a text. For example, use of Venn diagrams can highlight the differences and similarities between two characters in a story, two branches of Congress, and two kinds of plants. Teachers can use flowcharts with students to talk about the order of events in a story, the stages of life, or the steps for a science experiment.

Semantic organizers also graphically display information. They focus on words or concepts. For example, a word web can help students extend word meaning by mapping from a central word all the similar and related concepts of that word.

Text Structure

Nonfiction texts are often structured differently from fiction, which is the more familiar genre for beginning readers. It is important to point out to students what will give them important clues about key information. Often, students do not know how to make sense of the headings in a nonfiction text and do not realize that, for example, the sidebar story about a character in history is not the main text on a particular page. Teaching students how to interpret nonfiction text structures gives them important tools for understanding content-area reading.

Skill 3.6   Identify instructional strategies (e.g., making connections, questioning, summarizing) for developing critical thinking skills (e.g., critiquing, analyzing, problem-solving)

The point of instruction in strategies is not necessarily to focus just on the texts students are reading at the moment, but to help them learn the strategies that they can use independently with any text. The following are the most useful comprehension strategies for beginning readers.

Students need to be aware of their comprehension, or lack of it, in particular texts. So teaching students what to do when the text suddenly stops making sense is important. For example, students can go back and reread the description of a character, or go back to the first paragraph of a chapter to refresh their memory about where they are headed. This is often called monitoring comprehension.

Students should also know that, when they are responding to a text—analyzing and critiquing it—there are additional strategies that can help them. These include questioning, summarizing, and making connections.

Questioning

Students are often asked questions about what they have read. To facilitate success with answering questions and to help them become critical thinkers, students should be encouraged to generate questions as they read. (For example, Why did this author or character make a difficult and puzzling choice?) The best questions for critical thinking are those that cause students to have to think about the text rather than just finding an answer within the text.

But students should raise all kinds of questions—critical, inferential, and literal—especially for peer-group discussions. Encouraging them to create their own questions will help them understand the nature of the questions asked of them and facilitate answering.

Summarizing

For beginning readers especially, identifying the most important or main ideas in a text and distinguishing them from details is often difficult. Therefore, summarizing or gathering together the most important ideas and using them to create an oral or written summary is difficult for Pre-K–Grade 3 students. Teachers should guide the creation of summaries at first, making sure to teach the difference between main ideas and details. You may wish to have students mark copies of texts, using one color for highlighting main ideas and another for details. Then have them copy the main ideas to create a written summary.

SEE also Skill 3.4

Making Connections

Making connections involves three areas: text-to-self, text-to-text, and text-to-world. In text-to-self, the students connect what they are reading to their personal prior knowledge, something they have experienced or are knowledgeable about. In text-to-text, the students connect what they are reading to a previous reading passage. In text-to-world, the students connect something they are reading to prior knowledge that involves the world around them.

Prompts that help a student make connections in reading include the following:

- Text-to-self: That reminds me of . . . That made me think of the time . . . I can relate . . .
- Text-to-text: This part is just like . . . That reminds me of . . . I read another book where . . . This is similar to . . .
- Text-to-world: That reminds me of . . . This is like . . . I know about this . . . but I didn't know that

Teachers should help their beginning readers make connections between what they already know (their background knowledge and experience) and what they are reading or about to read. In fact, it isn't possible for students to understand what they read without thinking about what they already know.

When students have had an experience similar to a character in a story, they are more likely to understand and appreciate what that character is going through and feeling. Similarly, when students already have some knowledge about content they are about to read, they are more likely to understand the new knowledge more completely.

It is important for Pre-K–Grade 3 teachers to capitalize on students' prior knowledge and interests when selecting texts for them to read and be sure to activate that prior knowledge when introducing texts. To help students use this strategy themselves, the K-W-L activity is a good one to teach them. On a sheet of paper horizontally folded into thirds, students write in the first column what they already Know about a topic or a character, for example. In the second column they write what they Want to know about the character or topic, and in the third column they write what they Learn about it.

Skill 3.7	Select and apply instructional methods for developing reading fluency (e.g., practice with high-frequency words, timed readings, repeated readings)

Instructional methods that help students develop fluency in reading include the following:

- modeling fluent reading
- using shared and choral reading
- using repeated readings
- providing appropriate level materials
- providing practice with high-frequency words and phrases

Some of the first experiences in school involve being read to. When teachers and other adults read aloud to students, they are modeling fluent reading. Listening to fluent reading on headphones, sometimes following along with the printed story provides another source of fluent reading. Oral reading by classmates is often the opposite experience, and when beginning readers take turns reading aloud, they often provide models of halting, inarticulate reading, which should be avoided.

Shared, or choral, reading of stories, particularly those with repeated language patterns, can also promote fluency. Better readers provide models and pull the group along with them. When students are sufficiently familiar with the texts they may want to use them independently for repeated readings.

Repeated readings of the same text ensure that students recognize the words readily and can read at a normal pace. You may wish to time and chart results of repeated readings if students enjoy a challenge. Some students may memorize texts, but teachers can easily check this by choosing pages or individual words at random for the students to read aloud.

Choose texts for students at both their independent and instructional levels, avoiding frustration-level material. (You may wish to use the Fountas and Pinnell formulas for finding text levels.) After teacher guidance for instructional-level material is complete, students can practice rereading all or part of that text for fluency. Independent-level texts can be reread without teacher support.

Some students benefit from practice (timed or not) with individual high-frequency words (want, went, saw, they, when) and phrases (in the house, on top of, with my friends), via games, word drills, and word finds. Improved automaticity with word identification helps improve fluency.

Skill 3.8   **Apply effective reading strategies to comprehend complex literature and informational texts (e.g., stories, drama, poetry, biographies, technical texts)**

Teachers should have a toolkit of instructional strategies, materials, and technologies to encourage and teach students how to problem solve and think critically about subject content.

Higher-Order Thinking Skills

Critical thinking skills can be taught within the context of specific subject matter. For example, when instructing in the language arts, teachers can teach critical thinking skills through stories; when instructing in social studies, teachers can teach critical thinking skills through primary source documents or current events; and when instructing in science, teachers can teach critical thinking skills by having students develop hypotheses prior to conducting experiments.

Encouraging Independent Critical Thinking

Questioning is an effective tool in building higher-order thinking skills. But lower-order questions are useful to begin the process. If the objective is for students to be able to read and understand the story "Goldilocks and the Three Bears," the teacher may wish to start with lower-order questions; for example, "What are some things Goldilocks did while in the bears' home?" or "Why didn't Goldilocks like the Papa Bear's chair?" Then the teacher can move students up the taxonomy; for example, "If Goldilocks had come to your house, what are some things she might have used?", "How might the story been different if Goldilocks had visited the seven dwarfs?", or "Do you think Goldilocks was good or bad? Why?"

Understanding Nonfiction

Text Structure

Teach children how nonfiction texts look different from fictional texts. The format of the nonfiction text provides an organizational tool to help chunk information. Key word boxes help by providing students with word phrases to remember. Tables of contents, headings, and indexes help students scan a large amount of information to find what they need when answering a particular comprehension question. Most nonfiction text has boldfaced headings and subheadings. Students can use these as the main points or ideas and can then read the information below the headings for supporting details.

Graphic Aids

It is important to teach students how to interpret the graphic aids often featured in content area texts. Graphic aids help to clarify the text and provide another format to help with accurate interpretation. Being able to read graphs, maps, and charts, for examples, is necessary for students to understand these additions to content area texts.

Summarizing

Content-area subjects often attempt to convey a great deal of information. Generally, there is so much known information about topics that authors try to share all of that information with the reader. This is where summarizing can be so valuable and productive. Teach students how to take large amounts of information and consolidate it into four or five sentences so they can manage, record, and remember content area text.

Note Taking

Learning how to take notes when reading is a tough skill to master and teach. It requires readers to find the main ideas in a text and summarize those ideas into something meaningful. This process requires a great deal of support for younger students. A method of providing support is to provide main ideas listed in story or chapter order with a few missing so that the students can find the missing ideas while they are reading.

SEE also Skill 2.7

Prior Knowledge

Prior knowledge influences and, in some cases, determines comprehension. The more closely the reader's experiences and knowledge approximate those of the text, the more likely the reader is to comprehend the text. It is obvious that many Pre-K–Grade 3 children will not have the prior knowledge and experiences necessary to comprehend content-area texts.

Teachers at this level are required to provide before-reading experiences with aspects of the content to provide prior knowledge. Providing real, concrete, hands-on, motivating experiences will ensure the most meaningful acquisition of the background knowledge needed to comprehend content-area texts.

COMPETENCY 4.0   KNOWLEDGE OF LANGUAGE ELEMENTS USED FOR ORAL AND WRITTEN COMMUNICATION

Skill 4.1   Distinguish among the developmental stages of writing (e.g., drawing, scribbling, letter-like formations, strings of letters)

For children to write, they must first begin to develop certain fine motor skills. Before being required to manipulate a pencil, children should have dexterity and strength in their fingers, which helps them to gain more control of small muscles.

Children develop writing skills through a series of steps. The steps and their characteristics are discussed in the following sections.

Role-Play Writing

At this stage, children write in scribbles and assign a message to the symbols. Even though adults are not able to read the writing, children can read what is written although it may not be the same each time they read it. Children at this stage will also dictate to adults who can write down their message or story.

Experimental Writing

At this stage, children write in simple forms of language. The words usually contain letters according to the way they sound; for example, the word *are* may be written with the letter *r*. Children at this stage often display a sense of sentence formation and write in groups of words with a period at the end. In short, there is evidence of an awareness of the correspondence between written words and oral language.

Early Writing

Children start to use a small range of familiar text forms and sight words in their writing. The topics they choose for writing are ones that have some importance for them, such as their family, friends, or pets. Because they are used to hearing stories, they have a sense of how a story sounds and begin to write simple narratives. They learn that they do have to correct their writing so that others can easily read it.

Conventional Writing

By the time children reach this stage of writing, they have a sense of audience and purpose for writing. They are able to proofread their writing and edit it for mistakes. They have gained the ability to connect their writing to their reading, getting ideas for writing from what they read. By this time, children also have a sense of what correct spelling and grammar look like, and they can change the order of events in the writing so that it makes sense for the reader.

Skill 4.2 Identify developmentally appropriate writing strategies for developing concepts of print and conventions, including spelling and punctuation

Concepts of Print

At the early stages of print awareness, children who have access to books can tell the story through the pictures. Gradually they begin to realize the connection between the spoken words and the printed words and they become word conscious. Often they will ask an adult who is reading aloud to point to the word the adult just said. Adults then will point to each word as they say it, and soon children will imitate them, gradually acquiring a sense of where a word begins and ends. Also during this stage, many children learn the correct way to hold a book, where to begin reading, the left-to-right motion, and how to continue from one line to another. When children have not had access to books and reading aloud at home, teachers need to provide that experience in a school setting so students can informally acquire concept of print and book orientation.

Spelling

The acquisition of word spellings follows a developmental sequence. The following are developmental stages of spelling:

1. **Pre-phonemic spelling**—Children know that letters stand for a message, but they do not know the relationship between spelling and pronunciation.
2. **Early phonemic spelling**—Children are beginning to understand spelling. They usually write the beginning letter correctly and finish with consonants or long vowels.
3. **Letter-name spelling**—Some words are consistently spelled correctly. The student is developing a sight vocabulary and a stable understanding of letters as representing sounds. Long vowels are usually used accurately, but silent vowels are omitted. The child spells unknown words by attempting to match the name of the letter to the sound.

In the early grades, spelling strategies should include:

- spelling words that children ask for in their personal writing and words misspelled in writing that is corrected
- spelling words that students know from their phonics instruction, words they can sound out
- high-frequency words (Dolch list) that need to be repeated often for memorization

Punctuation

Through exposure and direct instruction, children in the preprimary and primary grades come to understand that there are functional marks in text that are not letters. These are punctuation marks that end sentences (such as periods, commas, and question marks) and punctuation marks that divide parts of sentences for easier reading and understanding (such as commas and dashes). There are also marks that show when someone is talking or has talked (open quotation mark) and when they stop (closed quotation mark). There is also a punctuation mark that tells you that you have read an abbreviation (period).

There are also spaces that "mark" text. An indent to the left of a line of text shows that a new paragraph has begun, as does an extra space between chunks of text.

Capitalization

The use of capital letters is an important convention of print for Pre-K–Grade 3 students. Capital letters begin names and show when new sentences begin. At first children tend to write with all capital letters, or use both capital and lowercase letters unconventionally, at the beginning, middle and/or end of words. Here are some of the most useful capitalization rules for this age group. Use a capital letter for the first letter of:

- all names of persons and places
- a word that follows an open quotation mark
- a title such as President, Senator, Mr., or Mrs.
- the first word in a tile and each main word that follows (*The Cat in the Hat*)

Skill 4.3   **Determine the stages of the writing process (e.g., prewriting, editing, publishing)**

As students engage in the various stages of writing process, they develop and improve not only their writing skills but also their thinking skills. Guide students to understand that writing is a process and typically involves these steps: prewriting, drafting, revising and editing, proofreading, and publishing.

Prewriting

Students gather their ideas before writing. Prewriting may include brainstorming with the teacher and/or other students or free thinking or writing by the individual student to see what surfaces. Remind students that, as they prewrite, they need to think about who their audience will be. Here are some ideas about: encouraging prewriting. Have students:

- keep an idea book for jotting down ideas that come to mind.
- write in a daily journal.
- write down whatever comes to mind; this is called free writing. Students do not stop to make corrections or interrupt the flow of ideas.

Drafting

After students have chosen a topic to write about, they write a first draft, using their notes or writing plan from the prewriting stage. Encourage students to write as freely as possible, since there will be time later to make changes and correct spelling and grammar.

Revising and Editing

The word revise comes from *revidere,* a Latin word meaning "to see again." Revising is probably the most important step in the writing process, because it is here that students examine their work critically and attempt to make it better. Often, students write a draft and feel that they're done. On the contrary, they must be encouraged to develop, change, and enhance their writing, analyzing it carefully as they complete a second draft. Probably the most effective way students can analyze their draft is to read it aloud to themselves or others. In fact, it's a good idea for revising to be practiced in small groups or pairs, so students can help each other. "Group think" is especially helpful for:

- analyzing sentences for variety and completeness
- asking questions about unclear areas in the writing
- prompting peers to add details or more information

Proofreading

Once students have a second draft of their writing, they need to proofread it to be sure it is correct. Working on their own or with a partner, they should:

- make sure all sentences are complete
- correct misspellings
- check for the correct use of capital letters, punctuation, verb tense, and word usage

Finally, students should recopy their corrected work neatly for publication.

Publishing

Students may illustrate their work and have it displayed on a bulletin board, read aloud in class, and/or printed in a class magazine or newspaper. They may send it (via snail mail or e-mail) to a friend or relative. The most important thing is to share a job well done.

Skill 4.4   **Identify and distinguish characteristics of various modes of writing (e.g., narrative, expository, persuasive, descriptive)**

Modes of Writing

Discourse, whether spoken or written, falls naturally into four different forms: narrative, descriptive, expository, and persuasive.

Narrative writing is discourse that is arranged chronologically: Something happened, and then something else happened, and then something else happened. News reports are often narrative in nature, as are records of trips, many stories, and nonfiction, especially history.

Descriptive writing is discourse that makes an experience available through one or more of the five senses: seeing, smelling, hearing, feeling, or tasting. Descriptive words make it possible for the reader to see with the mind's eye, hear through the mind's ear, smell through the mind's nose, taste with the mind's tongue, and feel with the mind's fingers. Language helps readers experience an event by involving the senses and thereby engaging the emotions. Poets are often experts in descriptive language.

Expository writing is discourse that is informative in nature. Examples of expository writing include driving directions, instructions for putting together an unassembled toy, unbiased news stories, and most content-area reading.

Persuasive writing is a piece of writing—a poem, a play, or an essay—whose purpose is to change the minds of readers or audience members or to get them to do something. This can be achieved in several ways:

- The language the writer uses may lead readers to a change of mind or a recommended action.
- A well-thought-out, reasonable, logical argument is important in persuasive writing. No one wants to accept a new viewpoint or go out and take action just because he or she likes the person who recommends it.
- Perhaps the most powerful force that leads to acceptance of a request or action suggested in persuasive writing is emotional appeal. Even if people have been persuaded logically and reasonably that they should believe something, they are unlikely to act on it unless they are moved emotionally. Descriptions that contain adjectives that evoke feelings (sad, hilarious, scary, exciting) help persuade readers, as do appealing illustrations.

Skill 4.5   Select and analyze the appropriate mode of writing for a variety of occasions, purposes and audiences, and use textual support, reader response, and research as needed

Audiences for Writing

Writing is communication, either with the self or others. For students to be meaningfully engaged in their writing and able to function in contemporary society, they need to write for a variety of purposes and often for different audiences. Writing for the self includes journaling and note taking. It's important to emphasize to students that certain writing is for their eyes only, that free writing is personal and its content and purpose need not be shared. Writing for an audience is an entirely different matter. Use these questions to help students figure out how to take their audience into account when planning a writing project:

- What does my audience already know about my topic?
- What does the audience want or need to know? What will interest them? Amuse them? Entertain them?
- What type of language and tone, formal or informal, suits my audience?
- What does my audience need to understand about my purpose or what my words mean? Should I include an introduction or a glossary?
- What was the audience response to what I wrote? How can I find out more about what they thought and felt about it?

Writing Projects in Varied Modes

Narrative Writing

Invite students to write a personal narrative about a trip they've taken with their family, a visit to a friend's house, or a typical fall Saturday afternoon at home. You might want to encourage them to write a fictional narrative in any genre, for example, realism, animal fantasy, or science fiction. They may enjoy narrating an important event, something they've read in a social studies text, or something they know about from an interest in sports history.

Descriptive Writing

Ask students to write a description of their favorite food, toy, book, or TV program. Remind them that they need to engage the senses in their description by using adjectives that will help their audience imagine (see, hear, feel, smell, and/or taste) what they are describing. You may want to prepare them for this activity by hiding an object and using only adjectives to have them guess what is hidden. (Yellow, fruity, curved, ready to peel . . . a banana, of course!)

Expository Writing

Research reports are a special kind of expository writing. A topic is researched—explored by searching literature, interviewing experts, or conducting experiments—and the findings are written up in such a way that a particular audience can know what was discovered. One way beginning researchers can start research reporting is by reading two books on the same topic and reporting on the same and different ways the topic is explored in each source. Book reports that require reading at least two books by a favorite author and doing an online search to find information about the author via her Website and biography are another way.

Persuasive Writing

Have students write persuasive letters to friends and family members or create posters for the school community, inviting them to a class art show, play, or festival. Remind student that their writing should contain adjectives that will help persuade visitors (funny, fancy, yummy) and bright, inviting illustrations, which will add to the appeal.

Skill 4.6	Identify developmentally appropriate strategies for enhancing writer's craft (e.g., supporting details, dialogue, transition words)

The difference between adequate writing and good writing is often in the use of details, dialogue, and transitions. Help your beginning writers become better by using several of the following techniques when they are revising their writing.

Transitions

Transitional words help writing to flow smoothly and enhance comprehension. Teach students the following ways to use transitions:

- Introduce another detail to their writing by adding one of these words: *and then, also, too, next,* or *another.*
- Compare two similar things in their writing by using the phrases *just like, similar to,* or *in the same way.*
- Contrast dissimilar things they are writing about by using *but, or, instead, yet,* or *otherwise.*
- Indicate the sequence of time in what they are writing by using these words: *today, tomorrow, now, soon, after, later, earlier, first, second, third, next,* or *before.*
- Show what causes something to happen by using these words: *because, so, then,* or *as a result.*

- • Summarize, emphasize, and highlight important ideas by adding these words to their writing: *as I said before, clearly, of course, I think, certainly,* or *definitely.*

Details

To help children add detail to their narratives, first ask them to answer the questions below that make sense for their story:

- • Who or what is the writing about?
- • When does it take place?
- • Where does it take place?
- • What happened?
- • How did it happen?
- • Why did it happen?

Next, ask them to tell three details about each answer. Have them make sure that all three things get written into the revision of their story.

With expository writing, have students make sure they have written at least three supporting details for every main idea in their essay.

Dialogue

Tell students that dialogue is an author's attempt to write down what people might say to one another. Help students recognize dialogue in their reading of realistic fiction, noting the quotation marks and other punctuation. Read together the dialogue only from several stories. Ask students to identify the ways the dialogue sounds like real people talking and the ways it does not. Then ask them to listen to some conversations in the classroom, the playground, and at home and imagine putting some of those conversations into a story. Suggest that students think about similarities and differences among their characters. If their characters are too alike and always agree with one another, the dialogue won't be as interesting as when there is something to argue about or debate.

You might also have students play What Will They Say Next? Prepare some two-person dialogues, supply only what one character says, and let students supply the retort. Later, supply both parts of the beginning of the dialogue and let students supply the next bit.

Character 1: How fast can you run? I'm pretty sure I'm faster than you are.
Character 2: (to be supplied by students)
Character 3: "Excuse me, I think I stepped on your toe!"
Character 4: "That was a Lego sticking out from under the table, not my toe!"
Character 3: (to be supplied by students)
Character 4: (to be supplied by students)

Skill 4.7   **Determine effective strategies for comprehension and collaboration (e.g., following multiple-step directions, following group rules, participating in group discussions)**

Discussion

Small-group or whole-class discussion stimulates ideas about texts and gives students a larger picture of the impact of those texts. Students learn to consider texts within larger social concepts. By listening to their peers, students see the wide range of possible interpretations and thoughts regarding one text.

Discussion groups in which individuals have a particular job encourages multitasking. Students are part of the discussion but may also lead it, do visual representations for it (designated Group Artist), or look up definitions and inform the group about specific vocabulary words (designated Word Master). Along with group discussion rules, these jobs assist the group in maintaining a conversation without teacher assistance.

SEE also Skill 4.2

Following Complex Directions

To encourage independent work and not have to constantly remind students what step comes next in their instructional routines, teachers need to help students practice following complex directions. Written directions given to students need to be read aloud first and then posted and/or distributed. It's best to number each direction and have students check it off when it is accomplished. Whenever possible, the text in the directions should be decodable by the group; for example, the directions could include small icons that represent each step. An example would be a chart of the steps in the writing process:

- Prewriting (art: a small group of kids—stick figures are okay—discussing ideas)
- Drafting (art: a blank paper and pencil)
- Revising and editing (art: a paper with text, one word circled with arrow showing where the word should be moved)
- Proofreading (art: paper with a misspelling—for example, *ran* for *rain*—marked for correction)
- Publishing (art: show several final drafts on a bulletin board labeled Our Best Work)

Multistep oral directions are often harder to follow because they involve memory. Making oral directions simple, logical, and habitual will help students remember them. In addition, processes that enhance students' ability to remember should be discussed and practiced with them:

- Association: Find a way to remember things by relating them to one another in some way.
- Visualization: Create a strong, vivid memory. Try to picture in your mind what you wish to remember.
- Concentration: Focus your attention on one thing only (the directions) and get rid of distractions.
- Repetition: Say the directions several times aloud.
- Paired learning: Two heads are better than one! Ask a study buddy to remember oral directions with you.

Collaborative Learning

Collaborative, or cooperative, learning situations as practiced in today's classrooms grew out of research conducted by several groups in the early 1970s. Collaborative learning is now firmly recognized and established as a teaching and learning technique in U.S. schools.

Collaborative learning groups can operate smoothly and enhance learning when students interact constructively with one another. Learning to work together takes time and effort on the part of students and their teacher. (It also takes maturity, so some students in the Pre-K–Grade 3 spectrum may have difficulty with cooperative learning and may need to be exempted from it.) Rules that are group determined are more readily followed. Teachers may want to role-play conflict situations in which different points of view are constructively entertained and resolved.

Skill 4.8	Identify key elements in students' presentations of ideas (e.g., visual and digital components, organization of ideas, clarity of thought)

Technology in the classroom is multifaceted. One teacher might allow students to surf the Internet to do research while she guards against misuse and inappropriate access; another may allow students access to only preapproved, preselected audio and visual sources to use in their presentations.

What is most important is that students learn to use some elements in their presentations that go beyond the words they speak or read. Not only is that what's required of them in the twenty-first century but a multimedia presentation of content also helps learners better understand and process the material. In some instances, they are able to read the written words, see an image, and hear the sounds—all at the same time. Combining these sensory modalities helps a child more efficiently internalize information about a topic.

Other kinds of reports can also make use of classroom media. Pre-K–Grade 3 students enjoy hearing their voices, so they may want to read their reports into a recording device, making them smooth by multiple attempts, and play the recording for the group.

When child has some sort of fine motor or large motor problem so that his or her handwriting is slow and sloppy, preparing the child's research reports and other presentations on a word processor allows him or her to hand in or read from papers that are clean and neat.

A number of computer programs allow children with information-processing difficulties to get a multimedia presentation of content so that they can better understand and process the material. These programs also supply models for all students to follow when they are creating their own multimedia presentations.

Skill 4.9   **Analyze the increasing complexity of conventions of English (e.g., common prepositions, personal and possessive pronouns, compound and complex sentences)**

Pre-K through Grade 3 teachers should be cognizant of proper rules and conventions of punctuation, capitalization, and spelling, even though their students aren't ready to learn the full scope of those rules. Competency exams generally test the ability to apply the more advanced grammar and usage skills; thus, a limited number of more frustrating rules are presented here. Rules should be applied according to the American style of English, for example, spelling *theater* instead of *theatre* and placing terminal marks of punctuation almost exclusively within other marks of punctuation.

Subject-Verb Agreement

A verb should always agree in number with its subject. Making them agree relies on the ability to properly identify the subject.

Examples:
One of the boys was playing too rough.
No one in the class, neither the teacher nor any student, was listening to the message from the intercom.
The candidates, including a grandmother and a teenager, are debating some controversial issues.

If two singular subjects are connected by *and*, the verb must be plural.

Example:
A man and his dog were jogging on the beach.

If two singular subjects are connected by *or* or *nor*, a singular verb is required.

Example:
Neither Dot nor Joyce has missed a day of school this year. Either Fran or Paul is missing.

If one singular subject and one plural subject are connected by *or* or *nor*, the verb agrees with the subject nearest to the verb.

Example:
Neither the coach nor the players were able to sleep on the bus.

If the subject is a collective noun, its sense of number in the sentence determines the verb: It is singular if the noun represents a group or unit and plural if the noun represents individuals.

Example:
The House of Representatives has adjourned for the holidays.

Pronoun-Antecedent Agreement

A noun is any word that names a person, place, thing, idea, quality, or activity. A pronoun is a word that is used in place of a noun or other pronoun. The word or word group that a pronoun stands for (or refers to) is called its antecedent.

We use pronouns in many of the sentences that we write. Pronouns enable us to avoid monotonous repetition of nouns. They also help us maintain coherence within and among sentences. Pronouns must agree with their antecedents in number and person. Therefore, if the antecedent is plural, use a plural pronoun; if the antecedent is feminine, use a feminine pronoun.

Specific types of pronouns include: personal, possessive, indefinite, reflexive, reciprocal, intensive, interrogative, relative, and demonstrative.

Verbs (Tense)

Present tense is used to express that which is currently happening or is always true.

Example:
Randy is playing the piano. Randy plays the piano like a pro.

Past tense is used to express an action that happened in the past.

Example:
Randy learned to play the piano when he was six years old.

Future tense is used to express an action that will or may happen in the future.

Example:
Randy will probably earn a music scholarship.

Present perfect tense is used to express action or a condition that started in in the past and continues.

Example:
Randy has practiced the piano every day for the last 10 years. Randy has never been bored with practice.

Past perfect tense expresses action or a condition that occurred as a precedent.

Example:
Randy had considered playing clarinet before he discovered the piano.

Future perfect tense expresses action that started in the past or the present and will conclude at some time in the future.

Example:
By the time he goes to college, Randy will have been an accomplished pianist for more than half of his life.

Verbs (Mood)

Indicative mood is used to make unconditional statements; subjunctive mood is used for conditional clauses or wish statements that pose conditions that are untrue. Verbs in subjunctive mood are plural with both singular and plural nouns and pronouns.

Examples:
If I were a bird, I would fly.
I wish I were as rich as Donald Trump.

Conjugation of Verbs

The conjugation of verbs follows the patterns used in the discussion of tense above. However, the most common errors in verb use stem from the improper formation of the past and past participial forms.

Examples:
Regular verb: believe, believed, (have) believed
Irregular verbs: run, ran, run; sit, sat, sat; teach, taught, taught

Other errors stem from the use of verbs that are the same in some tenses but have different forms and different meanings in other tenses.

Examples:
I lie on the ground.
I lay on the ground yesterday.
I have lain down.
I lay the blanket on the bed.
I laid the blanket there yesterday.
I have laid the blanket down every night.

The sun rises.
The sun rose.
The sun has risen.

He raises the flag.
He raised the flag.
He had raised the flag.

I sit on the porch.
I sat on the porch.
I have sat in the porch swing.

I set the plate on the table.
I set the plate there yesterday.
I had set the table before dinner.

Two other common verb problems stem from misuse of the preposition *of* for the verb auxiliary *have* and misuse of the verb *ought* (now rare).

Examples:
Incorrect: *I should of gone to bed.* **Correct:** *I should have gone to bed.*

Incorrect: *He hadn't ought to get so angry.* **Correct:** *He ought not to get so angry.*

Adjectives

An adjective should agree in number with the word it modifies.

Examples:
Those apples are rotten.
This one is ripe.
These peaches are hard.

With some exceptions *(worse, worst),* comparative adjectives end in *-er* and superlatives end in *-est.* Some adjectives that cannot easily make comparative and superlative inflections should be preceded by *more* and *most,* respectively.

Avoid double comparatives and superlatives.

Examples:
Incorrect: *This is the worstest headache I ever had.*
Correct: *This is the worst headache I ever had.*

When comparing one thing to others in a group, exclude the thing under comparison from the rest of the group.

Examples:
Incorrect: *Joey is larger than any baby I have ever seen. (Since you have seen him, he cannot be larger than himself.)*
Correct: *Joey is larger than any other baby I have ever seen.*

Include all necessary words to make a comparison clear in meaning.

Examples:
I am as tall as my mother. I am as tall as she (is).
My cats are better behaved than those of my neighbor.

Plurals

Most plurals that end in hard consonant sounds followed by a silent *e* are made by adding *-s*. (*fingers, numerals, banks, bugs, riots, homes, gates*)

Plurals of some words ending in vowels are formed by adding only *-s*. (*radios, bananas*)

For nouns that end in soft consonant sounds—*s, j, x, z, ch,* and *sh*—the plurals are formed by adding *-es*. (*dresses, waxes, churches, brushes*)

Plurals of some nouns ending in *o* are formed by adding *–es*. (*tomatoes, potatoes*)

Plural of words ending in a *y* not preceded by a vowel are formed by changing *y* to *i* and adding *-es*. (*dry, dries, baby, babies*) When *y* is preceded by a vowel, add only *–s*. (*boys, alleys, buoys*)

Make the plurals of open or hyphenated compounds by adding the change in inflection to the word that changes in number. (*fathers-in-law, courts-martial, masters of art, doctors of medicine*)

Some irregularly formed plurals are: *sheep, deer, children, leaves, hooves, oxen, indices,* and *crises.*

Possessives

Make the possessives of singular nouns by adding an apostrophe followed by the letter *s* (*'s*). (*baby's bottle, mother's job, elephant's eye, teacher's desk*)

Make the possessives of singular nouns ending in *s* by adding either an apostrophe or an apostrophe followed by the letter *s*, depending upon common usage or sound. When the possessive sounds awkward, use a prepositional phrase instead. (*the dress's color* or *the color of the dress, the species' characteristics, James' hat* or *James's hat, Dolores's shirt*)

Make the possessives of plural nouns ending in *s* by adding an apostrophe after the *s*. (*horses' coats, jockeys' times, four days' time*)

Make the possessives of plural nouns that do not end in *s* by adding *'s*. However, if the word following the noun is a gerund, no inflection is added. (*children's shoes, deer's antlers, cattle's horns*, but *The general was perturbed to see the private sleeping on duty.*)

Make the possessives of compound nouns by adding the inflection at the end of the last noun. (*the mayor of Los Angeles' campaign, the mailman's new truck, the mailmen's new trucks, my father-in-law's first wife*)

Pronouns

A pronoun used as a direct object, indirect object, or object of a preposition requires the objective case form.

Examples:
The teacher praised him. She gave him an A on the test. Her praise of him was appreciated. The students whom she did not praise will work harder next time.

Common pronoun errors occur from misuse of reflexive pronouns (*myself, yourself, herself, himself, itself, ourselves, yourselves, themselves*).

Examples:
Incorrect: *Jack cut hisself shaving.* **Correct:** *Jack cut himself shaving.*
Incorrect: *They backed theirselves into a corner.* **Correct:** *They backed themselves into a corner.*

Commas

Separate two or more coordinate adjectives that modify the same word and three or more nouns, phrases, or clauses in a list.

Examples:
It was a dank, dark day. Maggie's hair was dull, dirty, and lice-ridden.
Dickens portrayed the Artful Dodger as a skillful pickpocket, loyal follower of Fagin, and defender of Oliver Twist.

Use commas to separate antithetical or complementary expressions from the rest of the sentence.

Examples:
The veterinarian, not his assistant, would perform the delicate surgery.
The more he knew about her, the less he wished he had known.
Randy hopes to, and probably will, get an appointment to the Naval Academy.

Semicolons

Use semicolons to separate independent clauses when the second clause is introduced by a transitional adverb. (These clauses may also be written as separate sentences, preferably by placing the adverb within the second sentence.)

Example:
The Elizabethans modified the rhyme scheme of the sonnet; thus, it was called the English sonnet.
or
The Elizabethans modified the rhyme scheme of the sonnet. Thus, it was called the English sonnet.

Use semicolons to separate items in a series that are long and complex or have internal punctuation.

The leading scorers in the WNBA were Zheng Haixia, averaging 23.9 points per game; Lisa Leslie, 22; and Cynthia Cooper, 19.5.

Colons

Place a colon at the beginning of a list of items.

Example:
Three of Faulkner's symbolic novels are: *Absalom, Absalom, As I Lay Dying,* and *Light in August.*

Dashes and Italics

Place em dashes to denote sudden breaks in thought.

Examples:
Some periods in literature—the Romantic Age, for example—spanned different periods in different countries.

Use em dashes instead of commas if commas are already used elsewhere in the sentence for amplification or explanation.

Example:
The Fireside Poets included three Brahmans—James Russell Lowell, Henry David Wadsworth, and Oliver Wendell Holmes.

Use italics to punctuate the titles of works of literature, names of periodical publications, musical scores, works of art, and motion picture, television, and radio programs. If italic type is unavailable, students should be instructed to use underlining instead. *(Mary Poppins, Hiawatha, Newsweek, The Sound and the Fury, The Nutcracker Suite)*

Skill 4.10   **Compare characteristics and uses of formal and informal language (e.g., oral, written)**

The appropriateness of language in a given situation, often known as its social construct, is as important as understanding its semantic and syntactic structures. Sociolinguistics is something students usually learn implicitly. Conversation, or **informal oral language,** is only one mode of communication, although usually the first to be acquired. Conversation satisfies the learner's need to listen, copy, innovate, be heard and understood, and influence others. It often lacks full sentences and is bound by the situation in which one is communicating to supply the context for telegraphic snatches of language.

Similarly, **informal written language**—such as shopping lists, homemade cards, or the caption for a child's drawing—tends to be telegraphic and context-bound.

Writing sentences that link together in meaning tends not to occur until children enter school, although when children are read aloud to, they hear **formal written language**, which they quickly learn to comprehend.

The beginnings of producing **formal written language,** with its demands for complete sentences, supporting details, restatements of topic, and the like, usually occur exclusively in school settings.

The Pre-K–Grade 3 teacher, along with the parent, needs to make clear to students which modes belong in school and where in school they belong. Just as early educators talk about inside and outside voices, we need to make students aware of and encourage them to use appropriate inside and outside language modes.

COMPETENCY 5.0   KNOWLEDGE OF ASSESSMENTS TO INFORM LITERACY
                   INSTRUCTION

Skill 5.1   Identify appropriate oral and written methods for assessing
                   individual student progress in reading and writing (e.g., fluency
                   probes, conferencing, rubrics, running records, portfolios)

Oral retellings can be used to test children's comprehension. Children who are
retelling a story to be tested for comprehension should be told that that is the
purpose when they sit down with the teacher. It is a good idea to let the child
start the retelling on his or her own because then the teacher can see whether he
or she needs prompts to retell the story. Often more experienced readers
summarize what they have read. This summary usually flows out along with the
characters, the problem of the story, and other details.

Other signs that children understand what they are reading when they give an
oral retelling include their use of illustrations to support the retelling, references to
the exact text in the retelling, emotional reaction to the text, making connections
between the text and other stories or experiences they have had, and giving
information about the text without the teacher asking for it.

Teachers can maintain ongoing logs and rubrics for assessment throughout the
year of phonemic awareness for individual children. Such assessments would
identify particular stated reading behaviors or performance standards, the date of
observation of the child's behavior (in this context, phonemic activity or exercise),
and comments.

The rubric or legend for assessing these behaviors might include the following
descriptors:

- Demonstrates or exhibits reading behavior consistently
- Makes progress/strides toward this reading behavior
- Has not yet demonstrated or exhibited this behavior

Depending on the particular phonemic task the teacher models, the performance
task might include the following:

- Saying rhyming words in response to an oral prompt
- Segmenting a word spoken by the teacher into its beginning, middle, and
  ending sounds
- Counting correctly the number of syllables in a spoken word

Informal Reading Inventories (IRI) is a series of samples of texts prearranged in
stages of increasing difficulty. Listening to children read through these
inventories, the teacher can pinpoint their skill level and the additional concepts
they need to work on.

Running Records

A running record of children's oral reading progress in Grades K–3 is a pivotal informal assessment. It supports the teacher in deciding whether a book a child is reading is matched to his or her stage of reading development. In addition, this assessment allows the teacher to analyze a child's miscues to see which cueing systems and strategies the child uses and to determine which other systems the child might use more effectively. Finally, the running record offers a graphic account of a child's oral reading.

Generally, a teacher should maintain an annotated class notebook with pages set aside for all the children or maintain an individual notebook for each child. One of the benefits of using running records as an informal assessment is that they can be used with any text and can serve as a tool for teaching rather than an instrument to report on children's status in class.

Another advantage of using running records is that they can be taken repeatedly and frequently by the teacher, so he or she can truly observe a pattern of errors. This in turn provides the educator with sufficient information to analyze the child's reading over time. As any mathematician or scientist knows, the more samples of a process you gather over time, the more likely you are to get an accurate picture—in this case, a picture of the child's reading needs.

As part of the informal assessment of primary-grade reading, it is important to record the child's word insertions, omissions, requests for help, and attempts to get the word. In informal assessment, the rate of accuracy can be estimated by dividing the child's errors by the total words read.

Results of a running record assessment can be used to select the best setting for the child's reading. If a child reads from 95 percent to 100 percent correct, the child is ready for independent reading. If the child reads from 92 percent to 97 percent right, the child is ready for guided reading. Below 92 percent, the child needs a read-aloud or shared reading activity. Note that these percentages are slightly different from those one would use to match books to readers.

Portfolios

One of the increasingly popular and meaningful forms of informal assessment is the compilation of the literacy portfolio. What is particularly compelling about this type of informal portfolio is that artists, television directors, authors, architects, and photographers use portfolios in their careers. This is an authentic format for documenting children's literacy growth over time. The portfolio is not only a significant professional informal assessment tool for the teacher but also a vehicle and format for the child reader to take ownership of his or her progress over time. It models a way of compiling one's reading and writing products as a lifelong learner, which is the ultimate goal of reading instruction.

Portfolios can include the following six categories of materials:

- *Work samples:* These can include children's story maps, webs, K-W-L charts, pictures, illustrations, storyboards, and writings about the stories they have read.

- *Records of independent reading and writing:* These can include the children's journals, notebooks, or logs of books read with the names of the authors, titles of the books, date completed, and pieces related to books completed or in progress.

- *Checklists and surveys:* These include checklists designed by the teacher for reading development, writing development, ownership checklists, and general interest surveys.

- *Self-evaluation forms:* These are the children's own evaluations of their reading and writing process framed in their own words. They can be simple templates with starting sentences such as the following:

  I am really proud of the way I _____

  I feel one of my strengths as a reader is _____

  To improve the way I read aloud I need to _____

  To improve my reading I should _____

When teachers are maintaining the portfolios for mandated school administrative review, district review, or even for their own research, they often prepare portfolio summary sheets. These provide identifying data on the children and then a timeline of their review of the portfolio contents plus professional comments on the extent to which the portfolio documents satisfactory and ongoing growth in reading.

Portfolios can be used beneficially for child-teacher, and of course parent-teacher, conversations to review the child's progress, discuss areas of strength, set future goals, make plans for future learning activities, and evaluate what should remain in the portfolio and what needs to be cleared out for new materials.

Skill 5.2   Interpret and analyze data from informal and formal reading assessments using qualitative and quantitative measures (e.g., screening, progress monitoring, diagnostic) to guide differentiated instruction

Assessment and evaluation are intricately connected in the literacy classroom. Assessment is necessary because teachers need ways to determine what students are learning and how they are progressing. In addition, assessment can be a tool that can also help students take ownership of their own learning and become partners in their ongoing development as readers and writers. In this time of public accountability, clear, definite, and reliable assessment creates confidence in public education.

There are two broad categories of assessment: informal assessment and formal assessment.

Informal Assessment

Informal assessment utilizes observations and other nonstandardized procedures to compile anecdotal and observation data/evidence of children's progress. It includes but is not limited to checklists, observations, and performance tasks. Formal assessment is composed of standardized tests and procedures carried out under circumscribed conditions. Formal assessments include state tests, standardized achievement tests, NAEP tests, and the like.

Assessment needs to be a collaborative and reflective process. Teachers can learn from what the children reveal about their own individual assessments. Children, even as early as Grade 2, should be supported by their teacher to continually and routinely ask themselves questions assessing their reading. They might ask: "Am I understanding what the author wanted to say?" "What can I do to improve my reading?" and "How can I use what I have read to learn more about this topic?" Teachers need to be informed by their own professional observation *and* by children's comments as they assess and customize instruction.

Quality assessment is multidimensional and may include, but not be limited to, samples of writings, student retellings, running records, anecdotal teacher observations, self-evaluations, and records of independent reading. From this multidimensional data, the teacher can derive a consistent level of performance and design additional instruction that will enhance the child's reading performance.

Assessment must take into account children's ages and their ethnic/cultural patterns of learning. Assess to teach children from their strengths, not their weaknesses. Find out what reading behaviors children demonstrate well and then design instruction to support those behaviors. Assessment should be part of children's learning process; they should not be done *to* children, but rather done *with* them.

Formal Assessment

Formal assessment includes criterion-referenced tests and norm-referenced tests, among others.

Criterion-Referenced Tests

Criterion-referenced tests are tests in which the children are measured against criteria or guidelines that are uniform for all test-takers. Therefore, by definition, no special questions, formats, or considerations are made for the test-taker who is either from a different linguistic/cultural background or is already identified as a struggling reader/writer. On a criterion-referenced test, it is possible that a child test-taker can score 100 percent because the child may have actually been exposed to all of the concepts taught and mastered them. A child's score on such a test would indicate which of the concepts have already been taught and what he or she needs additional review or support to master.

Two criterion-referenced tests that are commonly used to assess children's reading achievement are the Diagnostic Indicators of Basic Early Literacy Skills (DIBELS) and the Stanford Achievement Test. DIBELS measures progress in literacy from kindergarten to Grade 3. It can be downloaded from the Internet free at dibels.uoregon.edu. The Stanford test is designed to measure individual children's achievement in key school subjects. Subtests covering various reading skills are part of this test. Both DIBELS and the Stanford Achievement Test are group-administered.

The Degrees of Reading Power (DRP) test is targeted to assess how well children understand the meaning of written text in real-life situations. This test is supposed to measure the process of children's reading, not the products of reading such as identifying the main idea and author's purpose.

The CTPIII is a criterion-referenced test that measures verbal and quantitative ability in Grades 3–12. It is targeted to help differentiate among the most capable students, that is, those who rank above the 80th percentile on other standardized tests. This is a test that emphasizes higher-order thinking skills and process-related reading comprehension questions.

Norm-Referenced Tests

There are many more standardized norm-referenced tests to assess children's reading than there are criterion-referenced tests. In these tests, scores are based on how well a child does compared to others, usually on the local, state and national level. Scores on these tests are reported in percentiles. Each percentile indicates the percent of the testing population whose scores were lower than or the same as a particular child's score. Percentile is defined as a score on a scale of 100 showing the percentage of a distribution that is equal to it or below it. This type of state-standardized norm-referenced test is being used in most districts today in response to the No Child Left Behind Act. While this type of test does not help track the individual reader's progress in his or her ongoing reading development, it does permit comparisons across groups. If the norming groups on the tests are reflective of the children being tested (that is, they have the same spread of minority, low-income, and gifted students), the results are more trustworthy.

One of the best-known norm-referenced tests is the Iowa Test of Basic Skills. It assesses student achievement in various school subjects and has several subtests in reading. Other examples of norm-referenced tests used around the country are the Metropolitan Achievement Tests, the Terra Nova-2, and the Stanford Diagnostic Reading Test-4. These are all group tests. An individual test that reading specialists use with students is the Woodcock Reading Mastery Test.

Assessment skills should be an integral part of teacher training so teachers are able to monitor student learning using pre- and post-assessments of content areas; analyze assessment data in terms of individualized support for students and instructional practice for teachers; and design lesson plans that have measurable outcomes and definitive learning standards. Assessment information should be used to provide performance-based criteria and academic expectations for all students in evaluating whether students have learned the expected skills and content of the subject area.

Teachers can use assessment data to inform instructional practices by making inferences regarding teaching methods and gathering clues about student performance. By analyzing the various types of assessments, teachers can gather more definitive information on projected student academic performance. Instructional strategies for teachers would provide learning targets for student behavior, cognitive thinking skills, and processing skills that can be employed to diversify student learning opportunities.

Assessment for learning should be the main focus for teachers. Instead of testing just to determine what students have learned, teachers need to assess to determine what students need to learn. In this way, assessment drives the instruction. By assessing students' prior knowledge and keeping notes on what they can and cannot do, teachers are better able to help students who need extra instruction and allow those who are succeeding to move on to higher-order skills and challenges.

SUBAREA 3   **MATHEMATICS**

COMPETENCY 1.0   **KNOWLEDGE OF EFFECTIVE MATHEMATICS INSTRUCTION**

Skill 1.1   Identify and analyze developmentally appropriate strategies for presenting mathematical concepts progressing from concrete to semi-concrete to abstract

Teaching young children mathematics requires a progression from the tangible to the abstract. As new concepts are introduced, the teacher should use concrete objects so that the students can manipulate, touch, and explore and be actively engaged in the learning. In this way, students can construct their own foundations, questions, and concepts related to numbers.

Providing the students with concrete and meaningful learning experiences is more involved than simply passing out blocks or beans to help introduce a concept. It involves using and developing the language of math. Through inquiry-based learning, the students can not only explore the materials and concepts but also begin to organize the information so that they can communicate their ideas of mathematics.

Without this concrete level of exploration, students may be able to memorize rote processes for solving problems (algorithms), but they may lack the foundational understanding necessary to make mathematical connections to everyday situations and experiences. Some students will be unable to see the broader generalizations found throughout math unless they are exposed to the concepts through concrete learning experiences.

When introducing a new mathematical concept to students, teachers should utilize the concrete-to-representational-to-abstract sequence of instruction. The first step of the instructional progression is the introduction of a concept modeled with concrete materials. The second step is the translation of concrete models into representational diagrams or pictures. The third and final step is the translation of representational models into abstract models using only numbers and symbols.

One way to provide children with valuable, concrete learning experiences is through centers or exploration activities. These types of centers/opportunities might include weighing themselves or other items on scales, covering the area of a shape with tiles, filling a shape with solids or liquids, comparing the size of objects, putting objects in order by size, sorting shapes, duplicating simple patterns with colored beads, and looking at books about numbers. Stations could be set up around the room at which two or three children can work together to answer specific questions using physical objects. The teacher could circulate around to each station checking on the work and perhaps making suggestions, while still letting the children work things out for themselves as much as possible.

Once the students are successful at completing learning activities at the concrete level, they should be exposed to the semi-concrete level (use of pictures and symbols) and, finally, to the abstract level (use of symbols or letters to represent numbers or concepts).

Skill 1.2   **Identify and apply related mathematical concepts, computation, problem solving, and reasoning**

Problem solving requires belief in the notion that there can be more than one way to reach a conclusion. This lets students of varying mathematical skills and abilities look at the same situation and find their best way to solve it. Providing students with the means to investigate a problem, rather than restricting them to one mode of solution, lets them be flexible in their approach. For example, a kindergartener has the following problem: If you have 3 pies and 12 people to feed, how can you easily divide the pies? This student can easily use pieces of real pie to work out an appropriate solution, which is one way to find the answer. However, the parent or teacher who insists that the student use the division algorithm to solve the problem may automatically set up this same student for failure.

We should incorporate real-world mathematics use into daily classroom activities so that students will understand, appreciate, and value the subject. Having the students help with lunch count and attendance, count the number of days left in the school year, or calculate the time left until recess are examples of including realistic math problem solving in the classroom.

Teachers are important role models. Thinking aloud as you come across a problem in the course of the day will help the students realize the necessity and real-world implications of reasoning and solving problems. Encouraging students to be reflective will also help build the necessary mathematical language. Also, students can share their ideas and methods with one another, which is an excellent strategy for learning about problem solving.

Typically, problem solving has five steps. Teachers should teach each of the following steps explicitly and model them regularly:

1. Identify the problem.
2. Determine the question.
3. Find a strategy to solve the problem.
4. Gather the materials and method to record your work.
5. Solve the problem.
6. Explain the method used to solve the problem.

While solving problems together in the classroom, the teacher can promote numerous useful strategies. The **guess-and-check** strategy, for instance, calls for students to make an initial guess at the solution, check the answer, and use the outcome to guide the next guess. With each successive guess, the student should get closer to the correct answer. Constructing a table from the guesses can help organize the data.

Example:
There are 100 coins in a jar, and 10 are dimes. The rest are pennies and nickels. There are twice as many pennies as nickels. How many pennies and nickels are in the jar?

There are 90 total nickels and pennies in the jar (100 coins – 10 dimes).

There are twice as many pennies as nickels. Make guesses that fulfill the criteria and adjust based on the answer found. Continue until you find the correct answer: 60 pennies and 30 nickels.

Number of Pennies	Number of Nickels	Total Number of Pennies and Nickels
40	20	60
80	40	120
70	35	105
60	30	90

When solving a problem in which the final result and the steps to reach the result are given, students must **work backward** to determine what the starting point must have been.

Example:
John subtracted 7 from his age and divided the result by 3. The final result was 4. What is John's age?

Work backward by reversing the operations:
$4 \times 3 = 12$
$12 + 7 = 19$
John is 19 years old.

Estimation and testing for **reasonableness** are related skills students should employ prior to and after solving a problem. These skills are particularly important when students use calculators to find answers.

Example:
Find the sum of 4387 + 7226 + 5893.

$4300 + 7200 + 5800 = 17300$ Estimation
$4387 + 7226 + 5893 = 17506$ Actual sum

By comparing the estimate to the actual sum, students can determine that their answer is reasonable.

Skill 1.3 **Identify and analyze opportunities and strategies to integrate mathematics with other subject areas**

Teachers should incorporate math-related activities into all subject areas. In science, children can graph the daily temperatures and make predictions for future temperatures. In social studies, they can gather, tabulate, and calculate the data related to the topic presented (for example, how many classmates agree that drugs are bad for your body). In language arts, children can solve problems found in children's literature. Charting favorite books, calculating ages of characters in stories, and drawing maps of the setting(s) of books are examples of connecting language arts and math. Numerous exciting books have a mathematical basis and can be used to cover both subjects in a fun manner.

Too often, mathematics problem solving is misinterpreted as mathematical word problems. In fact, if a child is unaware of the answer, any problem presented is a problem to be solved, and numbers and math can be a valuable tool. From the very beginning, children need to experience a variety of mathematical situations across all subject areas. Exposing children to a variety of contexts in which to use math allows children to develop their own constructs upon which they can build new learning.

Skill 1.4 **Identify mathematical concepts appropriate for the Pre-K–Grade 3 curriculum**

Children are born with an innate curiosity about the world around them. Toddlers group their toys and explore early mathematical concepts through their play as they complete their shape sorters or manipulate their building blocks into piles or towers. Some of the most up-to-date research in the area of mathematics indicates children may have an inborn sense that helps them solve some complex problems before they understand the number and symbol system used in later mathematics. This intuitive ability to understand numbers and problems is typically referred to as a child's *number sense*.

Number sense is the foundation upon which all future math topics are built, and providing young children with the opportunity to interact with objects across multiple contexts helps them develop number sense. During the beginning levels of mathematics, students progress at different levels at different times. For example, one student may be able to count and identify a group of five but not recognize the pattern of five on a die. Another student may count the group, recognize the pattern, and understand the concept of grouping things into piles of five and counting by the groups.

Number sense develops into the understanding of place value and number relationships. The students identify and explain how they can group numbers into *tens*, *ones*, and eventually *hundreds* or more. Using trading games, place value mats, and base ten blocks, students can develop these skills. These activities will progress until the student understands that the *one* in *sixteen* represents *ten*, not simply *one*.

In kindergarten, children learn to read the numbers 0 through 10, and in Grade 1, they should be able to read through the number 20. At first, this activity could involve connecting a pictorial representation of the number with a corresponding number of items. This exercise may or may not involve assistive technology. Assistive technology is defined as devices that help students, such as calculators, an abacus, or manipulatives such as blocks.

As students advance, they should be able to read the numbers as sight words. Students should be taught that we have a naming procedure for our number system. The numbers *0* through *12* have unique names. The numbers *13* through *19* are the *teens*. These names are a combination of earlier names, and the *ones* place is named first. For example, fourteen is short for *four ten*, which means *ten plus four*. The numbers *20* through *99* are also combinations of earlier names, but the *tens* place is named first. For example, forty-eight means *four tens plus eight*. The numbers *100* through *999* are combinations of hundreds and previous names. Once a number has more than three digits, groups of three digits are set off by commas.

Eventually, children develop the necessary skills to extrapolate these beginning concepts to more difficult situations and problems. They will make generalizations about number situations, even when they cannot use traditional computational methods to solve problems. For example, young children may be able to solve a multiplication problem, such *as four rows of three chairs, how many chairs*, using manipulatives and their number sense; however, they would not be able to solve the more traditional problem of *4 × 3*.

Using a variety of materials, teachers should present concepts of numeracy and other math concepts to children across situations until they reach levels of proficiency. As concepts of math build upon one another, the appropriate foundation must be in place for future learning to progress. By presenting concepts and ideas early, teachers give students the opportunity to experience and construct their own competencies.

Skill 1.5   Select and apply the appropriate use of available tools, including technology (e.g., interactive white boards, computers) and manipulatives in teaching mathematics

Teachers must understand that mathematics is not just about learning abstract concepts that involve numbers. Students' understanding of mathematical concepts is strengthened when they use tools to help make the abstract concepts concrete realities. Teachers have a wide variety of tools available to help students learn mathematics.

Manipulatives: Various assortments of cubes, counters, and tiles give students the opportunity to physically interact with the concepts being developed.

Rulers: Rulers are used to help students learn about measurement—the length of an object or distance. Rulers teach students about fractions and teach the relationship between standard units (inch, foot, yard, and mile) and metric units (millimeters, centimeters, meters, and kilometers). Understanding measurement will lead student to understand perimeter, circumference, and area in geometry.

Measuring containers: Measuring containers teach students about fractions and the relationship between the standard units (pint, quart, and gallon) and metric units (milliliter, liter). Students also learn about the volume of available space in different sized containers.

Scales: Scales are a good tool to use to teach the concept of equality in equations. In an equation, both sides must have the same value. This only happens when the scales balance.

Money: Students are exposed to money at a very early age. Money helps students understand the value associated with each denomination. Students learn the basic concepts of money management and personal finances using their addition and subtraction skills. In understanding the use and value of money in their lives, students are better prepared.

Computers: Technology becomes part of students' lives at a very young age. Math programs can enhance the teaching and learning of mathematical concepts. Programs, such as tutorials, can be individualized so each student has a course tailored to his or her specific needs. Students can strengthen mathematical understanding by playing games in which they need to use their math skills to advance.

Interactive white boards: Individual presentations of mathematical processes can be easily shared with the whole class when work is displayed at the front of the room. The unique tactile properties of the board let students be directly involved with the onscreen process in a large-group setting.

Skill 1.6   **Identify the use of mathematical practices to promote critical thinking (e.g., construct viable arguments, make use of structure, express regularity in repeated reasoning)**

Reasoning is the crux of all mathematics. Without the ability to reason, students cannot make adequate progress through future mathematical processes. Young children have already developed reasoning skills before they come to school, but they may be unable to identify or classify those skills.

Children use reasoning skills to explore, justify, and use mathematical knowledge. The underlying premise for mathematical reasoning is that students make conjectures, use models to investigate their conjectures, and draw logical conclusions from the entire process.

- **Making conjectures**—Conjectures are assumptions, hypotheses, predictions, or estimates about the problem presented. When making conjectures, students should be able to justify their thinking. At the very young level, they may use objects, pictures, and words. As students become more confident, they incorporate numbers or algorithms into their justification. As part of the process of making a conjecture, the children should be able to describe a plan for validating their suppositions.
- **Using models**—At this stage, the students use objects or models to investigate their conjectures, and children aged 4 through 10 must have access to pictures, objects, or other tangibles. This part of the process directly involves working through the plan developed to prove or disprove the conjecture. The process may be simplistic at this level but should not be skipped; working through the entire process is important for building later reasoning skills.
- **Drawing logical conclusions**—Students have completed the plan and have a solution. By working through the entire process, the children determine whether the conjecture made at the beginning is an accurate hypothesis. Children should be able to explain how they arrived at the conclusion and make appropriate connections to all of the previous steps.

The more exposure students have to meaningful mathematical processes and strategies, the better they will be able to think critically in their approach to future problems.

Skill 1.7   **Select and analyze uses of a variety of assessments to plan instruction**

Student assessment is an important part of the educational process. High-quality assessment methods are necessary for the development and maintenance of a successful learning environment. Teachers must develop and implement assessment procedures that accurately evaluate student progress, test content areas of greatest importance, and enhance and improve learning. To enhance learning and accurately evaluate student progress, teachers should use a variety of assessment tasks to gain a better understanding of a student's strengths and weaknesses. Finally, teachers should implement scoring patterns that fairly and accurately evaluate student performance.

A variety of assessment procedures help to better evaluate student knowledge and understanding. In addition to the traditional methods of performance assessment like multiple choice, true/false, and matching tests, there are many other methods of student assessment available to teachers. Partner quizzes are a good way to introduce testing in a nonthreatening manner. In this testing method, students work in pairs and turn in a single paper as their joint quiz work, in which they have agreed, after discussion, on the correct answers.

Alternative assessment is any type of assessment in which students express their understanding in a way other than just providing a question's answer. Student portfolios are one method of alternative assessment. In creating a portfolio, students collect samples of their work, self-assessments, and teacher evaluations over a period of time. Such a collection allows students, parents, and teachers to evaluate student progress and achievements. In addition, portfolios provide insight into a student's thought process and learning style.

Projects, demonstrations, and oral presentations are means of alternative assessment that require students to use different skills than those used on traditional tests. Such assessments require higher-order thinking, creativity, and the integration of reasoning and communication skills. The use of predetermined rubrics, with specific criteria for performance assessment, is the accepted method of evaluation for projects, demonstrations, and presentations.

Skill 1.8	Select and analyze structured experiences for small and large groups of students according to mathematical concepts

Successful teachers select and implement instructional delivery methods that best fit the needs of a particular classroom and the characteristics of the concepts to be taught. Individual, small-group, and large-group classroom formats require different techniques and methods of instruction, and they address multiple learning styles and varied content.

Individual instruction allows the teacher to interact closely with the student. Teachers may use a variety of methods in an individual setting that are not practical when working with a large number of students. For example, teachers can use manipulatives to illustrate a mathematical concept. In addition, teachers can observe and evaluate the student's reasoning and problem-solving skills through verbal questioning and by checking the student's written work. Finally, individual instruction allows the teacher to work problems directly with the student, thus familiarizing the student with the problem-solving process.

Small-group formats require the teacher to provide instruction to multiple students at the same time. Because the group is small, instructional methods that encourage student interaction and cooperative learning are particularly effective. This instructional method often works well when introducing a new concept to students. It gives them an opportunity to experiment and discover new ideas as they work with their small group. Group projects, inquiries, discussions, and question-and-answer sessions promote cooperative learning and maintain student interest. In addition, working problems as a group or in pairs can help students learn problem-solving strategies from one another.

Large-group formats require instructional methods that can effectively deliver information to a large number of students. Lecture is a common instructional method for large groups. In addition, demonstrating methods of problem solving and allowing students to ask questions about homework and test problems is an effective strategy for teaching large groups.

| Skill 1.9 | Identify and analyze attitudes and dispositions underlying mathematical thinking |

When teaching mathematics to young students, delivery of instruction and exposure to new concepts should be promoted with a positive approach of inquiry and discovery whenever possible. In this way, children will develop a sense of ownership of the study of math. If students first see math as pleasing, logical structure that exists in the world around them, they will continue to see it as a valuable and necessary subject of intrigue and study.

Furthermore, successful math teachers introduce their students to multiple problem-solving strategies and create a classroom environment where free thought, curiosity, and experimentation are encouraged. Teachers can nurture successful problem solving by allowing multiple attempts at problems, arranging for students to support one another and work together to solve problems, and encouraging the sharing of ideas through class discussion. As the students achieve success with their math and problem-solving activities, they will continue to have a favorable approach to the subject.

COMPETENCY 2.0   KNOWLEDGE OF ALGEBRAIC THINKING

Skill 2.1   Identify and extend simple number and nonnumeric repeating and
                                growing patterns using words, variables, tables, and graphs

In the primary grades, the concept of algebra is significantly different from what
an adult remembers as algebra class. Adults will typically recall letters being
used to hold the place of numbers and solving various equations to find the
answer for a variable. However, for young children the basis for this concept
develops through learning about patterns, the attributes of objects, and how to
describe objects in detail. These ideas help students develop the fundamental
thinking and concepts behind algebraic reasoning. These patterns may begin
through concrete objects, but they will be further developed into counting
patterns and other recognition of the patterns of numbers as well as variable
representation.

Beginning with the basic understanding of the symbols used throughout math
(numerical representations), students can investigate things around them. They
can gather this information and begin to report it in a way that means something
to others who look at it. These facts related to their own thinking can be
expanded. As students look at a variety of situations and manipulate the objects
to draw new conclusions, their problem-solving skills are advanced. These skills
will allow students to begin to solve missing number problems or solve for
unknown pieces to a situation. This can be done with the youngest students as
well. An example of a preschool missing object problem might be:

Red   yellow   red   _____   red   yellow   red   yellow   red

In this case, the students would be shown real objects of two colors set in a
pattern and need to determine which one is missing from the center of the
pattern. This type of thinking is more complex than "what comes next" types of
questions.

As children begin to compare, sort, order, and demonstrate seriating of objects
using various characteristics, their thinking changes. These changes are the
beginning of algebraic thought. As they add on to patterns, make changes to
patterns, build their own patterns, or convert patterns into new formats, they are
thinking in more complex ways. Connecting this new thinking with the
understanding of the number system is the beginning of using variables to define
the relationships among mathematical concepts. This method of problem solving
is then defined further into the expression of these relationships in a more
traditional mathematical manner.

Pre-K children should be able to recognize and extend simple repeating patterns
using objects and pictures. By patterns, we mean a sequence of symbols,
sounds, movements, or objects that follow a simple rule, such as ABBABBABB.

Students should be presented with a simple pattern that they try to understand. Once they have an understanding of the pattern, they should copy it and extend it. Students at this age are capable of assigning letters to their patterns to verbalize how the pattern repeats. This is the very early fundamental stage of algebra.

Algebraic concepts and reasoning can be used to investigate patterns, make generalizations, formulate models, make predictions, and validate results by providing an organized system to display the data. To help young children begin to see these relationships, the teacher must share data with students and explore possibilities. The data can be displayed in various formats, such as tables, graphs, and equations, to help define the pattern. Once the student has determined a model for the data, the model can be used to make predictions using larger input values or to follow the development of the pattern over time. All data and results need to be validated. Without validation, there could be a flaw in the pattern or the mathematical model that could skew results without the student knowing.

Example 1: Find the next term in the pattern:

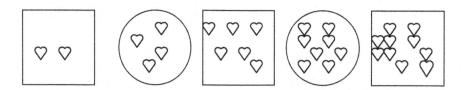

Examining the pattern, one observes that it has alternating squares and circles that include a number of hearts that increases by two for each subsequent term. Hence, the next term in the pattern will be as follows:

Example 2: 1, 4, 9, 16... is a sequence that consists of the squares of the natural numbers. Using this rule, the next term in the series, 25, can be found by squaring the next natural number, 5.

Example 3: Find the next term in the series 1, 1, 2, 3, 5, 8...

Inspecting the terms in the series, one finds that every term in the series is a sum of the previous two terms.
Thus, the next term is 5 + 8 = 13.
This particular sequence is a well-known series named the Fibonacci sequence.

Example 4: Consider the function $y = 2x + 1$.

The relationship could be written in words by saying "The value of y is equal to two times the value of x, plus one." This function can also be represented as a table of values or as a graph, as shown below.

x	y
-2	-3
-1	-1
0	1
1	3
2	5

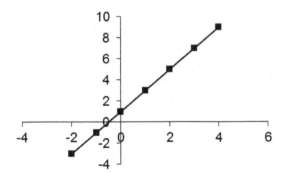

It is clear that all the points lie on a straight line, and the difference between successive y's is constant. We therefore can determine any value of y by picking an x-coordinate and finding the corresponding point on the line. For example, if we want to know the value of y when x is equal to 4, we find the corresponding point and see that y is equal to 9.

Example 5: Sometimes a diagram makes it easier to see the next number in a series. Take the following:

$$1, 3, 6, 10, 15$$

Organizing the diagram gives:

				*	*		
			*	**	**		
		*	**	***	***		
	*	**	***	****	****		
	*	**	***	****	*****		
Total	1	3	6	10	15		
# Added:	1	2	3	4	5		
	1st term	2nd term	3rd term	4th term	5th term	6th term	nth term

The 6th term will be $1 + 2 + 3 + 4 + 5 + 6 = 21$
The 10th term will be $1 + 2 + 3 + 4 + 5 + 6 + 7 + 8 + 9 + 10 = 55$
The nth terms will be $1 + 2 + 3 + 4 + \ldots + n$

Skill 2.2   Determine and apply the concepts of equality and inequality in real-world situations (e.g., balancing and comparing quantities)

In the early childhood classroom, comparing quantities may start with the beginning vocabulary of position words (such as first, next, last, third, above, and below). These are terms students will need to understand to complete math tasks, but they also will come across these terms in reading, will use them in writing, and will be expected to follow correctly in listening situations.

The following are examples of how these terms will be utilized in each area:

- **Mathematics**—patterns (The Green block is first. The purple block is third in line. The red block is between the green and purple. The blue block is last.)
- **Reading**—simple text references (The cat is on the mat. The cat is under the mat.)
- **Writing**—paragraph and transitioning (First, the cat walked inside. Next, the cat went to eat.)
- **Listening**—teacher directions (I would like you to all line up. I want Susie to be first, and John to be fifth.)

Specifically drawing comparisons and showing the students the connection is important. Using phrases similar to "remember when we learned about 'next to' in math? Now the author is saying the cat is *next to* the window. What does that mean?" can help the students draw these comparisons in a clear, concise manner. The opposite can be done when introducing a new concept in math class.

Children at this age should be able to begin to use simple quantity words such as *more, fewer, same, enough, some, many,* and *lots of* and apply these words to daily situations: "May I have one more cookie?" "She has fewer blocks than I do." "I have some toys."

Further concrete experiences with quantity comparison can be done with volume and mass. Pour water from one container to another to assess which one holds *more*. Set objects on a balance scale to determine which side has *less* mass and what could be done to equalize the sides. Actual volume and mass measurements can then be used to show numerical quantitative comparison. Additionally, students can read product labels to see this concept applied to product comparison. Symbolically, students should eventually be able to express their comparisons with (in) equality notation: = *equals*, > *greater than*, and < *less than*. Working with formalized comparison statements builds a foundation for the algebraic concept of balanced sides of equations.

Linear Programming

Linear programming is the optimization of a linear quantity that is subject to constraints expressed as linear equations or inequalities. It is often used in various industries, ecological sciences, and governmental organizations to determine or project production costs, the amount of pollutants dispersed into the air, and so on. The key to most linear programming problems is to organize the information in the word problem into a chart or graph of some type.

Example: A printer manufacturer makes two types of printers: a Printmaster and a Speedmaster. The Printmaster requires 10 cubic feet of space and weighs 5,000 pounds, and the Speedmaster takes up 5 cubic feet of space and weighs 600 pounds. The total available space for storage before shipping is 2,000 cubic feet, and the weight limit for the space is 300,000 pounds. The profit on the Printmaster is $125,000, and the profit on the Speedmaster is $30,000. How many of each machine should be stored to maximize profitability, and what is the maximum possible profit?

First, let x represent the number of Printmaster units sold, and let y represent the number of Speedmaster units sold. Then, the equation for the space required to store the units is the following.

$$10x + 5y \leq 2000$$
$$2x + y \leq 400$$

Since the number of units for both models must be no less than zero, also impose the restrictions that $x \geq 0$ and $y \geq 0$. The restriction on the total weight can be expressed as follows.

$$5000x + 600y \leq 300000$$
$$25x + 3y \leq 1500$$

The expression for the profit P from sales of the printer units is the following.

$$P = \$125,000x + \$30,000y$$

The solution to this problem, then, is found by maximizing P subject to the constraints given in the preceding inequalities, along with the constraints that $x \geq 0$ and $y \geq 0$. The equations are grouped below for clarity.

$$x \geq 0$$
$$y \geq 0$$
$$2x + y \leq 400$$
$$25x + 3y \leq 1500$$
$$P = \$125,000x + \$30,000y$$

The two inequalities in two variables are plotted in the graph below. The shaded region represents the set of solutions that obey both inequalities. (Note that the shaded region only includes points where both x and y are whole numbers.)

Note that the border of the shaded region that is formed by the two inequalities includes the solutions that constitute the maximum value of y for a given value of x. Note also that x cannot exceed 60 (since it would violate the second inequality). The solution to the problem, then, must lie on the border of the shaded region, since the border spans all the possible solutions that maximize the use of space and weight for a given number x.

To visualize the solution, plot the profit as a function of the solutions to the inequalities that lie along the border of the shaded area. Then students can identify specific solutions by choosing points from the shaded region.

Skill 2.3   **Identify and apply function rules using addition and subtraction (e.g., input-output machines, tables)**

Students can experiment with functions using basic addition and subtraction. The notion of a function machine helps children see the numerical changes in data as a process, as does giving them the opportunity to make lists or charts as they work the function and record their answers.

For instance, give children the following list of numbers: 10, 6, 7, 15, 2. Tell them to subtract 2 from each value and record their answers in a table.

10	6	7	15	2		
8	4	5	13	0		

They may want to extend the table with new inputs of their own.

This exercise can be worked in reverse: The teacher can show the students a function machine at work by putting numbers in a box and then pulling out the results, or outputs. Once students have observed the pattern, they can make predictions using other inputs and eventually express the rule, or function, that the machine is using.

Showing the students a function's pattern in terms of a situation that they can visualize will also help explain the process of the function. Consider the following example.

Suppose a daycare center gives children a snack amount depending on how old they are. The number of crackers given to each child is 3 more than the child's age.

The data can be discussed, demonstrated, and presented in multiple formats.

$$y = x + 3$$

x	1	2	3
y	4	5	6

Skill 2.4	Identify and analyze appropriate instructional strategies (e.g., draw a picture, make a table, act it out) to facilitate student understanding of problem solving

Problem solving is not about one strategy or right way; rather, it is about allowing students of varying mathematical skills and abilities to look at the same problem situation and find a way to solve it. Providing students with the means to investigate a problem allows them to be flexible in their approach. (SEE Skill 1.2) How perfect, then, that the patterns of mathematics can be expressed in multiple ways. Individual students can adjust their problem-solving strategies as their skills and insights allow. Once students discern the pattern, whether in a table, graph, or demonstration, they can extend the format to make predictions and solve the problem.

Example: The following table represents the number of children in a reading group each day, starting with the first day of the group.

Day	1	2	3	4	5	6	7	8	9	10	11
Number of Children	1	1	2	3	5	8	13				

If this pattern is continued, how many children will be in the reading group on the eleventh day?

The table can first be experienced in its most concrete form by acting out the grouping of children with actual classroom members. Then, if we look for a pattern, it appears that the number of children in the group each day is equal to the sum of the participating children for the previous two days. We test this as follows:

Day 2 = 1 + 0 = 1
Day 3 = 1 + 1 = 2
Day 4 = 2 + 1 = 3
Day 5 = 3 + 2 = 5
Day 6 = 5 + 3 = 8
Day 7 = 8 + 5 = 13

Therefore, Day 8 would have 21 children; Day 9, 34 children; and Day 10, 55 children.

In another example, suppose a rancher needs to purchase horseshoes for his horses. We show the students a table representing horses and the number of hooves. We construct a table of values and graph the equation to see if we can find a pattern.

Horses	Hooves
1	4
2	8
3	12
4	16
5	

The pattern formed by the points is that they all lie in a line. We therefore can determine any solution of y by picking an x-coordinate and finding the corresponding point on the line. For example, if we want to know how many shoes to buy for 6 horses, we find the corresponding point and see that y is equal to 24.

A solution to this problem can also be expressed in variable format. To start, the discussion can lead the students to recognize that there will always be 4 hooves, and therefore 4 shoes, for each horse. Next, shorten the word use to "(horse) shoes = 4 for each horse" and then finish with the equation S = 4H. The equation can then be used to yield further values. In this way, students are able to interpret the problem on multiple levels, which strengthens their problem-solving skills.

COMPETENCY 3.0   KNOWLEDGE OF NUMBER CONCEPTS AND OPERATIONS IN BASE TEN

Skill 3.1   Identify the cardinal number for a set, various ways to count efficiently (e.g., counting by ones, skip counting, counting on, counting backwards, counting collections), and ordinal numbers

When experiencing math at an early age, students should learn not only how numbers represent actual quantity (see one-to-one correspondence, Skill 3.2) but also that they form a counting pattern. A good way to show this is with a number line. The number line can also give students a tactile opportunity to practice the skill of counting on, which mimics addition.

Suppose we want to count from 3 to 6 or show *6 + 3* on a number line.

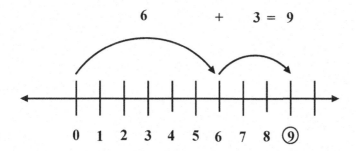

We can think of addition as starting from 0 and counting 6 units to the right on the line in the positive direction and then counting 3 more units to the right. The number line shows that this activity is the same as counting 9 units to the right. The number line can also help students master the patterns of counting backwards and skip counting (counting by 2s, by 5s, and so on) which are important foundations for efficiency of counting and for grouping sets of numbers.

As with other subjects, it is important to provide explicit instruction for students as to the relationship between the oral numbers and their written form. Typically, this begins by showing students examples of numbers in their written form. Then, provide students with direct instruction in the mechanical formation of the numbers.

There are many different instructional procedures for both numerical identification and the formation of the numbers. Children may look at number books or work with puzzles that connect numerals with sets of objects. There are also math mats with print numbers and the same number of dots on which students must match manipulatives to each dot. No matter the procedure used, students need specific, explicit instruction in this area. One example of a format for teaching students to identify numbers is based on a direct instructional model. In this format, students are shown the number to be taught more times than other numbers. As skills build, the newly introduced numbers are shown more times than those previously learned (some recommend at least seven representations of the new information). Consistent review and direct instruction with specific correction procedures are hallmarks of the direct instruction model.

Similarly, students need to be able to make the connection between a numerically named quantity and a numerical descriptor such as relative sizes (greater or smaller, SEE Skill 2.2) and the ordinal numbers (first, second, third, and so on). Exposure to this can be done by sharing with the class specifically chosen stories containing such math vocabulary or by demonstrating relationships with manipulatives or actual class members. For instance, the teacher can ask students to line up by height, and then identify who is tallest, or first, who is second, and so forth.

Regardless of the instructional method used, it is important to expose children to various ways numbers can be represented. As students gain a broader understanding of numbers and can read them, we should teach them to apply these concepts to everyday life.

Skill 3.2   Identify pre-number concepts, one-to-one correspondence, conservation of numbers, constructing sets to match given criteria, and rote counting

All future math topics are built on early foundations of number sense, and providing young children with the opportunity to interact with objects across multiple contexts helps ensure the strength of this foundation. During these early years of mathematics, students progress at different levels at different times. Typically, students will have some beginning oral counting system (1-10 or 1-20) but may only begin with identifying the relationships between groups of objects such as size, quantity, more, less, bigger, and smaller.

In order to ensure children's strong math foundations, they must develop an understanding of one-to-one correspondence and be able to link a single number name with one object at a time. For example, a child counts four blocks in a row and says the number as each block is touched. Getting a carton of milk for each of the other children at a table is another example of practicing this concept. Preschool children should also be able to use one-to-one correspondence to compare the size of a group of objects. For example, a child should be able to compare the actual number of cars with the number another child has and say, "I have more…or less."

Children first learn to count using the counting numbers (1, 2, 3). Preschool children should be able to recite the names of the numerals in order or sequence (rote counting). Activities that practice this skill include singing counting songs. Eventually, students should be able to attach a number name to a series of objects. A preschool child should understand that the last number spoken when counting a group of objects represents the total number of objects.

Additionally, classroom activities should ensure that students have opportunities to construct a set, either with manipulatives or by making a diagram that represents a specific numeric quantity. With continued attention to these number concepts, the early childhood educator will ensure each child starts his or her study of mathematics with a solid foundation.

Skill 3.3	Use knowledge of place value to name, compare, and flexibly represent numbers in base ten (e.g., 22 = 2 tens and 2 ones, 1 ten and 12 ones, or 22 ones)

Place value is the basis of our entire number system. A place value system is one in which the position of a digit in a number determines its value. In the standard system, called base ten, each place represents ten times the value of the place to its right. This can also be thought of as making groups of ten of the smaller unit and combining them to make a new unit.

Ten ones make up one of the next larger unit, tens. Ten of those units make up one of the next larger unit, hundreds. This pattern continues for greater values (ten hundreds = one thousand, ten thousands = one ten thousand, etc.), and lesser, decimal values (ten tenths = one one, ten hundredths = one tenth, etc.). In standard form, the number modeled above is 233.

A place-value chart is a way to make sure digits are in the correct places. The value of each digit depends on its position or "place". A great way to see the place-value relationships in a number is to model the number with actual objects (place-value blocks, bundles of craft sticks, etc.), write the digits in the chart, and then write the number in the usual, or standard form.

Place value is vitally important to all later mathematics. Without it, keeping track of greater numbers rapidly becomes impossible. (Think of how hard it would be to write 999 with only ones?) A thorough mastery of place value is essential to learning the operations with greater numbers. Using trading games, place value mats, and base ten blocks, students can develop these place value skills. These activities will progress until the student understands that the *one* in *sixteen* represents *ten*, not simply *one*. With this foundational understanding, students will be prepared for base 10 regrouping ("borrowing" and "carrying") in addition, subtraction, multiplication, and division.

It should be shown to students that the naming procedure for our number system demonstrates place value. The numbers *0* through *12* have unique names. The numbers *13* through *19* are the *teens*. These names are a combination of earlier names, and the *ones* place is named first. For example, fourteen is short for *four ten*, which means *ten plus four*. The numbers *20* through *99* are also combinations of earlier names, but the *tens* place is named first. For example, forty-eight means *four tens plus eight*. The numbers *100* through *999* are combinations of hundreds and previous names.

It is also important to expose children to various ways numbers can be represented. For example, the number ten can be represented in the following ways (and more):

10	ten	12-2	6+4	X

Teaching students from the beginning that there are different ways to represent a number helps to build their number sense and helps them begin to see the relationships and patterns of numbers.

Skill 3.4	Use place value (e.g., flexibility of numbers) and properties of numbers (i.e., commutative, associative, distributive, identity) to solve problems involving addition and subtraction of multi-digit numbers and multiplication facts through 100

Once students begin to see numbers flexibly, they can reorganize quantities and apply mathematical number properties to master numerical problem solving. Properties are rules that apply for addition, subtraction, multiplication, or division of real numbers.

Commutative Property: You can change the order of the terms or factors as follows.

For addition: $a + b = b + a$
For multiplication: $ab = ba$

Since addition is the inverse operation of subtraction and multiplication is the inverse operation of division, no separate laws are needed for subtraction and division.

Example: $5 + 8 = 8 + 5 = 13$
Example: $2 \times 6 = 6 \times 2 = 12$

Associative Property: You can regroup the terms as you like.

For addition: $a + (b + c) = (a + b) + c$
For multiplication: $a(bc) = (ab)c$

This rule does not apply to division and subtraction.

Example: (2 + 7) + 5 = 2 + (7 + 5)
9 + 5 = 2 + 12 = 14

Example: (3 × 7) × 5 = 3 × (7 × 5)
21 × 5 = 3 × 35 = 105

Identity: Finding a number such that when added to a term results in that number (additive identity); finding a number such that when multiplied by a term results in that number (multiplicative identity).

For addition: $a + 0 = a$ (zero is additive identity)
For multiplication: $a \times 1 = a$ (one is multiplicative identity)

Example: 17 + 0 = 17

The sum of any number and zero is that number.

Example: 34 × 1 = 34

The product of any number and one is that number.

Distributive Property: Using this technique, we can operate on terms inside the parentheses without first performing the operations inside the parentheses. This technique is especially helpful when you cannot combine the terms inside the parentheses.

$a (b + c) = ab + ac$
Example: 6 × (4 + 9) = (6 × 4) + (6 × 9)
6 × 13 = 24 + 54 = 78

To multiply a sum by a number, multiply each addend by the number, then add the products.

Addition of Whole Numbers

The above properties along with number flexibility lay the groundwork for a child's understanding of addition. Once children know these properties, they can use them as thinking strategies and remember addition facts for *0* through *9*. If we think of these facts in terms of a table, a child must learn 100 addition facts.

+	0	1	2	3	4	5	6	7	8	9
0	0	1	2	3	4	5	6	7	8	9
1	1	2	3	4	5	6	7	8	9	10
2	2	3	4	5	6	7	8	9	10	11
3	3	4	5	6	7	8	9	10	11	12
4	4	5	6	7	8	9	10	11	12	13
5	5	6	7	8	9	10	11	12	13	14
6	6	7	8	9	10	11	12	13	14	15
7	7	8	9	10	11	12	13	14	15	16
8	8	9	10	11	12	13	14	15	16	17
9	9	10	11	12	13	14	15	16	17	18

Now we start to highlight patterns in the table.

1. **Commutativity:** If children understand commutativity, when they learn the first 55 addition facts, they will automatically know the remaining 45 facts; that is, *4 + 1 = 5* just as *1 + 4 = 5*, as highlighted in the table.

+	0	1	2	3	4	5	6	7	8	9
0		1	2	3	4	5	6	7	8	9
1			3	4	5	6	7	8	9	10
2				5	6	7	8	9	10	11
3					7	8	9	10	11	12
4						9	10	11	12	13
5							11	12	13	14
6								13	14	15
7									15	16
8										17
9										

2. **Adding zero:** Teaching children that $a + 0 = a$ adds another 10 addition facts; that is, $0 + 0 = 0, 1 + 0 = 1 \ldots 9 + 0 = 9$.

+	0	1	2	3	4	5	6	7	8	9
0	0	1	2	3	4	5	6	7	8	9
1	1		3	4	5	6	7	8	9	10
2	2			5	6	7	8	9	10	11
3	3				7	8	9	10	11	12
4	4					9	10	11	12	13
5	5						11	12	13	14
6	6							13	14	15
7	7								15	16
8	8									17
9	9									

3. **Counting on by 1 and 2:** Children find close sums, or sums obtained by adding 1 or 2, by counting on; for example, to find 8 + 2, think 8, then 9, 10.

+	0	1	2	3	4	5	6	7	8	9
0	0	1	2	3	4	5	6	7	8	9
1	1	2	3	4	5	6	7	8	9	10
2	2	3	4	5	6	7	8	9	10	11
3	3	4	5		7	8	9	10	11	12
4	4	5	6			9	10	11	12	13
5	5	6	7				11	12	13	14
6	6	7	8					13	14	15
7	7	8	9						15	16
8	8	9	10							17
9	9	10	11							

4. **Combinations to 10**: Children use combinations of their 10 fingers to find such sums as 7 + 3, 6 + 4, and 5 + 5. There is now overlap in the table.

+	0	1	2	3	4	5	6	7	8	9
0	0	1	2	3	4	5	6	7	8	9
1	1	2	3	4	5	6	7	8	9	10
2	2	3	4	5	6	7	8	9	10	11
3	3	4	5		7	8	9	10	11	12
4	4	5	6			9	10	11	12	13
5	5	6	7			10	11	12	13	14
6	6	7	8		10			13	14	15
7	7	8	9	10					15	16
8	8	9	10							17
9	9	10	11							

5. **Doubles:** Children easily learn such addition facts as *1 + 1 = 2, 2 + 2 = 4,* and *3 + 3 = 6* because they are also the results of counting by twos.

+	0	1	2	3	4	5	6	7	8	9
0	0	1	2	3	4	5	6	7	8	9
1	1	2	3	4	5	6	7	8	9	10
2	2	3	4	5	6	7	8	9	10	11
3	3	4	5	6	7	8	9	10	11	12
4	4	5	6		8	9	10	11	12	13
5	5	6	7			10	11	12	13	14
6	6	7	8		10		12	13	14	15
7	7	8	9	10				14	15	16
8	8	9	10						16	17
9	9	10	11							18

6. **Associativity:** When children understand associativity as regrouping, they can understand that *8 + 7 = 15* is the same as *8 + (2 + 5) = 15* is the same as *(8 + 2) + 5 = 15* is the same as *10 + 5 = 15*. This completes the table.

+	0	1	2	3	4	5	6	7	8	9
0	0	1	2	3	4	5	6	7	8	9
1	1	2	3	4	5	6	7	8	9	10
2	2	3	4	5	6	7	8	9	10	11
3	3	4	5	6	7	8	9	10	11	12
4	4	5	6	7	8	9	10	11	12	13
5	5	6	7	8	9	10	11	12	13	14
6	6	7	8	9	10	11	12	13	14	15
7	7	8	9	10	11	12	13	14	15	16
8	8	9	10	11	12	13	14	15	16	17
9	9	10	11	12	13	14	15	16	17	18

7. **Doubles + 1 and + 2:** As an example, *7 + 8 = 7 + 7 + 1 = 14 + 1 = 15*. This procedure overlaps the other procedures.

Subtraction of Whole Numbers

Subtraction is expressed as *a – b,* read "*a* minus *b,*" where *a* is the minuend and *b* is the subtrahend. Just as properties and methods aid students in understanding addition, conceptual models can help students with subtraction.

1. Take-away:
   Start with 10 objects.
   Take away 4 objects.
   How many objects are left?

2. Missing addend:
   Start with 4 objects.
   How many more objects are needed to give a total of 10 objects?
3. Comparison:
   Start with two sets of objects with 10 objects in one set and 4 in the other set.
   How many more objects are in the larger set?
4. Number line:
   Move forward (to the right) 10 units.
   Move backward (to the left) 4 units.
   What is the distance from 0?

Multiplication of Whole Numbers

Multiplication is another of the four basic number operations. In simple terms, multiplication is the addition of a number to itself a specified number of times.

Multiplication is simply repeated addition. This relationship explains the concept of variable addition. We can show that the expression *4x + 3x = 7x* is true by rewriting 4 times *x* and 3 times *x* as repeated addition, yielding the expression *(x + x + x + x) + (x + x + x)*. Thus, because of the relationship between multiplication and addition, variable addition is accomplished by coefficient addition.

For example, 4 multiplied by 3 is equal to *4 + 4 + 4* or *3 + 3 + 3 +3*. Thinking in terms of groups is another way of conceptualizing multiplication. For example, if we have 4 groups of 3 students, the total number of students is 4 multiplied by 3. We call the solution to a multiplication problem the *product*.

The same number properties that make the problem set of addition facts easy to learn can apply to multiplication patterns. If students learn multiplication tables in a logical order, the process is less daunting, more streamlined, and foundationally sound. Students should recognize the following patterns:

- The commutative property of multiplication cuts the product possibilities in half (that is, $8 \times 4 = 4 \times 8$).
- The identity property of multiplication ($5 \times 1 = 5$) should be quickly applied.
- Multiplication by zero always results in zero.
- Multiplying by 10 increases place value ($8 \times 10 = 80, 75 \times 10 = 750$).
- Multiplying by 2 is equivalent to doubles addition ($6 \times 2 = 6 + 6$).

Multi-digit Addition

Typically used algorithms provide students with a structured way to perform multi-digit operations. All of these algorithms rely on the commutative and associative properties, allowing regrouping and reordering of numbers.

Three common algorithms for addition of integers are the partial sums method, column addition method, and fast method. The partial sums method is a two-stage process. First, we sum the columns from left to right. To complete the operation, we add the column values.

```
    125
  +  89
  + 376     Step 1 – column addition
    400
  + 170
  +  20     Step 2 – final sum
    590
```

The column addition method is also a two-stage process. First, we add the digits in each column. To complete the operation, we perform the place carries from right to left.

```
    1 |  2|  5
  +   |  8|  9     Stage 1 – column addition
  + 3 |  7|  6
    4| 17| 20
    4| 19|  0     First carry
    5|  9|  0 = 590   Second carry = final answer
```

The fast method of addition is the traditional method of right-to-left addition. We sum the columns from left to right, performing carries mentally or writing them down.

```
    12        Carries
    125
  +  89
  + 376
    590
```

Multi-digit Subtraction

Three common algorithms of integer subtraction are left-to-right subtraction, partial differences, and the same change rule. In left-to-right subtraction, we decompose the second number into smaller values and perform the individual subtractions. For example, to solve $335 - 78$, we break down 78 into $70 + 8$.

```
    335
  -  70
    265
  -   8
    257
```

The partial differences method is a two-stage process. First, we operate on each column individually, being careful to record the sign of each result. Then, we sum the results to yield the final answer.

$$
\begin{array}{r}
335 \\
-78 \\
\hline
+300 \\
-40 \\
-3 \\
\hline
257
\end{array}
$$

The same change rule takes advantage of the knowledge that subtraction is easier if the smaller number ends in zero. Thus, we change each number by the same amount to produce a smaller number ending in zero.

$$
\begin{array}{rr}
335 & 333 \\
-78 & -80 \\
& \hline
& 257
\end{array}
$$

Like the addition algorithms, the subtraction algorithms rely on the commutative and associative properties of addition (because subtraction is addition of a negative number).

Skill 3.5   **Differentiate between problem-solving strategies that use models, properties of operations, and the inverse relationship of operations**

As mentioned earlier, to promote problem solving is to encourage and accept different strategies to arrive at the same answer. Having multiple tools at a student's disposal will not only increase chances at success but also allow a deeper understanding of the relationship between mathematical patterns and operations.

Young children are accustomed to expressing situations through drawings, so making a picture or model can be an easily accepted problem solving technique. For instance, if a quantity of items needs to be grouped, the child can make a diagram in which each item is represented; the items can then be circled to differentiate groups. For additional problem-solving techniques, see Skills 1.2 and 2.4.

In the abstract sense, the concept of inverses may be difficult to understand for the young mathematician.

Inverse: Finding a number such that when added to the number it results in zero or when multiplied by the number results in 1.

> For addition: $a - a = 0$
> For multiplication: $a \cdot (1/a) = 1$
>
> $(-a)$ is the additive inverse of a; $(1/a)$, also called the reciprocal, is the multiplicative inverse of a.
>
>
> <u>Example</u>: $25 - 25 = 0$
>
> <u>Example</u>: $5 \times \frac{1}{5} = 1$

Students can perform repeated calculations with examples of inverses to gain familiarity with the patterns.

Additionally, when students are allowed to solve problems in multiple ways, the inverse relationship can be understood on a different level. Consider the following problem solved by two different students:

Sara goes to the school store to buy a pen and a notebook. If she pays $4 in total, and the pen costs $1, what is the cost of the notebook?

> Student A recreates the totaling structure of the problem and recalls addition facts to find the missing value of 3.
>
> Student B decides to subtract the cost of the pen from the total to be left with the cost of the notebook: $4 - 1 = 3$.

Each student has used an acceptable strategy to solve the problem, and together they have demonstrated that addition and subtraction are inverse operations. Similar discoveries should be promoted through problem solving with multiplication and division.

Skill 3.6   Use area, set, and linear fraction models (e.g., number lines) to represent fractions, including fractions greater than one

The use of shaded regions is a legitimate way to represent a number (whether a whole number or a fraction). The shaded region below represents 47 out of 100 total area units, which also equals 0.47, $\frac{47}{100}$, or 47%.

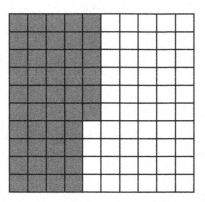

Fraction strips are another method of representing numbers, as shown below. Each strip could, for instance, represent unity. The number of equal subdivisions is the denominator of the fraction; the number of subdivisions that are shaded (for example) could represent the numerator.

1
2
4

5
10

Number lines are also a common method for representing fractions. An example of a number line with multiple labeling scales is shown below.

0	$\frac{1}{4}$	$\frac{3}{4}$	1	$1\frac{1}{2}$	2
			$\frac{4}{4}$	$\frac{3}{2}$	$\frac{4}{2}$

Diagrams are yet another representational method. One particular diagram involves a given number of objects of the same type to represent that number. If each box represents a whole, shading can indicate partial units, or fractions.

Skill 3.7   **Relate the size of the fractional part to the number of equal-sized pieces in the whole**

$$\frac{4}{4} = \frac{7}{7} = \frac{10}{10} = 1 \text{ and } \frac{8}{4} = 2$$

Teachers should include these fraction equivalency relationships in their modeling and diagramming examples. Additionally, students should experience the notion that dividing the whole into more or fewer pieces will change the value of the fraction. For example, when sharing a cake, dividing the cake among 4 people and get $1/4^{th}$ of the cake gives each person a larger portion than dividing the cake among 20 people, who each get only $1/20^{th}$ of the cake.

Skill 3.8   **Use models to represent equivalent fractions, including fractions greater than one, and numerical representation of equivalents (e.g., 1/2 = 2/4 = 3/6, the same amount is shaded in the whole)**

$$1/3 \quad = \quad 2/6 \qquad\qquad\qquad 4/2 \qquad = \qquad 2$$

Models resembling the above diagrams can be shared with children in picture or puzzle form. Providing students with such tactile opportunities to compare fractions will lead to a better understanding of the relative magnitude of fractions.

COMPETENCY 4.0   KNOWLEDGE OF MEASUREMENT AND DATA COLLECTION AND ANALYSIS

Skill 4.1   Identify the use of measurable attributes and the appropriate use of metric and customary units to measure and compare length, area, perimeter, and volume

One of the most important things that must be emphasized when beginning measurement activities is that this is a world of approximations. No measurement can ever be exact, and teachers should refrain from using the word *exact* in connection with measurements. Many adults are confused about this concept, so it is important to set the children straight from the outset.

The stages of measuring something are: (1) Determine what to measure, (2) decide on an appropriate tool, (3) select a reasonable unit of measure, (4) estimate how much or how long the measurement will be, (5) measure, and finally (6) check the reasonableness of the results.

Studying temperature is one appropriate measurement activity for students. Most children are aware of temperature as it is given on TV, in Fahrenheit degrees in the United States. Introduce them to the thermometer with the actual device and then with a large reproduction on paper showing the degree marks. Talk about how air temperature is physically measured. For example, ask, Should one put a thermometer in direct sunlight? What would be a comfortable temperature? What would be very hot? Very cold? Have them estimate air temperature each day and then measure it with the thermometer. Again, point out that to say the temperature is 75 degrees only means that it is closer to 75 than to 74 or 76. Point this out on the paper diagram of a thermometer scale. With older students this is a good chance to briefly introduce the idea of negative numbers. Students can also work with the Celsius (or centigrade) scale.

Another type of measurement is length. A great deal of time needs to be spent here. First, the students need to be convinced that there is need for a standard unit. Does "foot" mean the length of just anybody's foot? Get some objects for them to measure that are very close to 3 feet or 5 feet, for example. Then introduce something smaller so that they will see the need for a smaller unit. A paperclip is a good choice. Students are taught to use the paperclip as a unit, and by laying the paperclips end to end, they can measure an object longer than the paperclip (repetition of a single unit to measure something larger than the unit). Most physical objects would have a length, although even here there are choices to be made. Since the world is three-dimensional, you have to choose which dimension will be the length, which the width, and which the height. Those words are used to distinguish the three dimensions, but of course all three would be measured in length units.

Have students practice measuring objects to the nearest inch. After they have been measuring for a few weeks, introduce the millimeter as a still smaller unit. Most rulers have metric units on one side and standard English units on the other.

Once the idea of measuring length is understood, it is natural to advance to the measurement of perimeters. The students can measure sides and total the lengths, or, in the case of a circle (the perimeter of a circle is its circumference), mark off the perimeter with a string or measuring tape.

Similarly, measuring length can connect to the concept of area. The area of objects can be calculated with dimensions or measured directly with physical representations of square units. A 12-inch by 12-inch piece of paper, for instance, represents one square foot. Groups of students equipped with collections of square foot measurers can work together to approximate the area of a tabletop by finding how many papers it will take to cover the table.

Some work can be done occasionally with weights. Pounds would be the obvious starting unit, then ounces for a smaller unit and tons for a larger one. Fairly early on in this work, introduce the kilogram and the gram. Students can try to guess the weights of objects before actually weighing them.

Another thing to measure is liquids. Introduce the idea of gallons and quarts, but fairly soon also work with liters and milliliters. Bring in soda bottles and notice that both metric and English units are given. Briefly talk about pints and cups as used in recipes.

For all of these measurement activities, bring examples from newspapers and TV to class and discuss them. Have the children be on the lookout for such examples. What would they like to measure? What would be easy to measure? Hard to measure? Keep reinforcing the idea that no measurement is ever exact.

Additionally, students should be able to determine what unit of measurement is appropriate for a particular problem, as indicated by the following table.

Problem Type	Unit (Customary System)	Unit (Metric System)
Length	Inch Foot Yard	Millimeter Centimeter Meter
Distance	Mile	Kilometer
Area	Square inches Square feet Square yards Square miles	Square millimeters Square centimeters Square meters Square kilometers
Volume	Cubic inches Cubic feet Cubic yards	Cubic millimeters Cubic centimeters Cubic meters
Liquid volume	Fluid ounces Cups Pints Quarts Gallons	Milliliters Liters
Mass		Milligrams Centigrams Grams Kilograms
Weight	Ounces Pounds Tons	Milligrams Centigrams Grams Kilograms
Temperature	Degrees Fahrenheit	Degrees Celsius or Kelvin

It is necessary to be familiar with both the metric and customary systems to estimate measurements.

Some common equivalents include:

ITEM	APPROXIMATELY EQUAL TO	
	METRIC	CUSTOMARY
large paper clip	1 gram	1 ounce
	1 quart	1 liter
average-sized man	75 kilograms	170 pounds
	1 yard	1 meter
math textbook	1 kilogram	2 pounds
	1 mile	1 kilometer
	1 foot	30 centimeters
thickness of a dime	1 millimeter	0.1 inches

Estimate the measurement of the following items:

length of an adult cow = _____ meters
thickness of a compact disc = _____ millimeters
your height = _____ meters
length of your nose = _____ centimeters
weight of your math textbook = _____ kilograms
weight of an automobile = _____ kilograms
weight of an aspirin = _____ grams

Skill 4.2   **Identify effective instructional activities for estimating, telling, and writing time; calculating elapsed time; and counting money**

The measurement of time is an appropriate learning activity based on a concept already familiar to students. When you start the lesson, give students the opportunity to show you what they already know about time. Most people measure time with clocks or watches. Why do we need to measure or tell time? What are the units? Most children are familiar with hours and minutes, but lessons should be developed to incorporate additional units.

Measurement of time

1 minute	=	60 seconds
1 hour	=	60 minutes
1 day	=	24 hours
1 week	=	7 days
1 year	=	365 days
1 century	=	100 years

Timed athletic events like running, swimming, and horse races will get students further involved in the lesson. At this point, they would probably see the need for a smaller unit, so seconds and even tenths of seconds can be introduced.

Constantly point out that 10.3 seconds only means that the time in question is closer to 10.3 than it is to 10.2 or 10.4.

A stopwatch can be used to have students actively experience time measurement. The stopwatch can help students understand the duration of time and equivalent periods of time.

Other possibilities for measurement activities can concern money. In kindergarten, students learn to recognize a penny, nickel, dime, quarter, and $1 bill. In Grade 1, they learn how different combinations of coins have equivalent values; for example, that 10 pennies are the same as 1 dime. Teaching children that money has value can start with a simple exercise of counting pennies to understand their monetary value. From here, students can advance to counting nickels, dimes, and so on. The next step might be to have students combine different coins and compute the value of the combination. As students advance in their understanding of the value of money, shopping math can be introduced, in which students see that money has value in exchange for goods. They can also learn to make change and count change.

| Skill 4.3 | Select effective methods to organize, represent, and interpret data (e.g., bar graphs, line plots) |

Organizing data occurs on multiple levels. When collecting the data, it makes sense to use a list or table. When presenting data for further representation and interpretation, it is logical to use charts and graphs. In this way, the data and its comparable values can be more easily visualized and interpreted.

A **bar graph** or a **pictograph** can be a good tool for displaying data. To construct the graph, first determine the scale to be used. Then determine the length of each bar on the graph or determine the number of pictures needed to represent each piece of information. Be sure to include an explanation of the scale in the legend.

<u>Example:</u>
A class had the following grades: 4 As, 9 Bs, 8 Cs, 1 D, 3 Fs. Graph these on a bar graph and a pictograph.

Pictograph

Grade	Number of Students
A	
B	
C	
D	
F	

Bar graph

To read a bar graph or a pictograph, read the explanation of the scale that is used in the legend. Compare the length of each bar with the dimensions on the axes and calculate the value each bar represents. On a pictograph, count the number of pictures used in the chart and calculate the value of all the pictures.

To make a **line graph**, determine appropriate scales for both the vertical and horizontal axes (based on the information to be graphed). Describe what each axis represents and mark the scale periodically on each axis. Graph the individual points of the graph and connect the points on the graph from left to right.

<u>Example:</u>

Graph the following information using a line graph.

The number of National Merit finalists/school year

	1990–91	1991–92	1992–93	1993–94	1994–95	1995–96
Central	3	5	1	4	6	8
Wilson	4	2	3	2	3	2

Skill 4.4 **Solve problems analyzing data sets, drawing conclusions, and making predictions**

Collecting, describing, and analyzing data are fun activities in the early childhood classroom. There are numerous exciting and playful methods for collecting data for use in various classroom lessons. The following are some fun ways to collect data:

- Have students drop a piece of cereal into a bowl that is their favorite color.
- Have students draw a tally mark under their lunch choice on a bulletin board.
- Utilize a thumbs up or thumbs down approach for students' responses when asking whole-group questions.
- Use wipe boards.
- Have the students stand in lines to form a human graph to show a particular set of data.

The following are ideas of data to collect, organize, describe, and analyze:

- favorite colors
- birthdays
- hair/eye/clothing colors
- favorite foods
- favorite books
- ending to a story (like/don't like)
- shoe size (type/color/style)
- favorite songs

Once the data has been collected, it needs to be organized into a format easily analyzed by the students. This can involve tables, tally charts, and graphs. Using the real objects to form the bars of the graphs can provide the students with immediate results. This can be very important to young children. It also provides a concrete representation. In contrast, transferring the data to paper to create the graph, table, or chart is more abstract.

Once the graph, table, or chart is completed it is important to utilize mathematical language to describe and analyze the information. Comparing two different bars on the graph, finding the greatest, finding the smallest/least, or other types of analysis help students develop their critical thinking skills. The students also need to be exposed to vocabulary terms that mean the same thing (such as *smallest* and *least*).

As students learn to examine data sets, they should be able to:

- describe what the data set shows
- describe parts of the data set
- compare sets of data or parts of the data set
- represent data in a visual manner (chart/graph/table)
- sort parts of the data set
- organize the data
- ask and answer questions about the data

Students who are presented with data should make concrete statements and comments about the data with guidance from the teacher. As they progress, students should be guided to begin to make inferences and predictions based on the information presented.

The skill of making inferences and predictions is the same whether predicting events in a story or making mathematical inferences and predictions. Students need to consider the information or facts available and use that information to formulate a logical prediction. Students will often begin this process with wild and outlandish guesses rather than making true inferences and predictions.

It is a skilled teacher who guides students through the dialogue and experiences necessary to base predictions and inferences on available information. This process takes patience and repetitions for students to become skilled.

COMPETENCY 5.0   KNOWLEDGE OF GEOMETRIC AND SPATIAL CONCEPTS

Skill 5.1   **Identify and classify two-dimensional and three-dimensional shapes according to defining attributes (e.g., number of sides, length of sides, measure of angles)**

AND

Skill 5.2   **Identify the composition of a complex figure using basic two-dimensional and three-dimensional shapes (e.g., squares, circles, triangles, spheres, cones, prisms)**

Start the investigation of geometry by asking students what they already know about shapes. Most students will be able to recognize and name many two-dimensional shapes, like triangle, rectangle, square, and circle.

Each of these shapes can be labeled with further attributes. For instance, a **triangle** is defined as a polygon (a simple closed figure composed of line segments) with three sides. Triangles can be classified by the types of their angles or by the lengths of their sides.

Classifying by angles:

- An **acute** triangle has exactly three *acute* angles. (An *acute* angle is less than 90 degrees.)
- A **right** triangle has one *right* angle. (A *right* angle measures exactly 90 degrees.)
- An **obtuse** triangle has one *obtuse* angle. (An *obtuse* angle is greater than 90 degrees but less than 180 degrees.)

Classifying by sides:

- *All three* sides of an **equilateral** triangle are the same length.
- *Two* sides of an **isosceles** triangle are the same length.
- *None* of the sides of a **scalene** triangle are the same length.

A study of four-sided polygons, or quadrilaterals, can also focus on classification.

- A **quadrilateral** must have four sides.
- When a quadrilateral has four right angles and opposite sides of equal length, it is called a **rectangle**.
- If all four sides are of equal length and all angles are right angles, the quadrilateral is a **square**.

These quadrilateral categories actually overlap; every square is a rectangle, but not every rectangle is a square. Sorting various examples into a Venn diagram would help students begin to understand such classification.

Once students have a good understanding of two-dimensional shapes, they can explore shapes in three dimensions. Start with some of the most easily recognized three-dimensional objects, or solids.

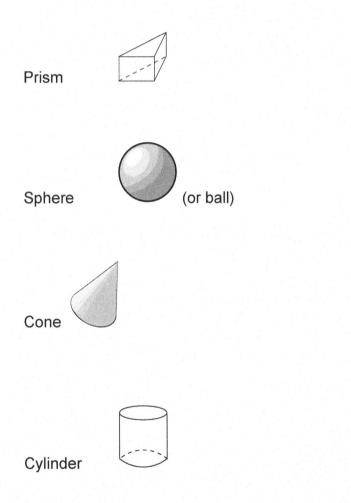

Prism

Sphere   (or ball)

Cone

Cylinder

Formally, the union of all points on a simple closed surface and all points in its interior form a space figure called a **solid**. The five regular (having all sides of equal length) solids, or **polyhedra**, are the cube, tetrahedron, octahedron, icosahedron, and dodecahedron. A **net** is a two-dimensional figure that can be cut out and folded up to make a three-dimensional solid. Below are models of the five regular solids with their corresponding face polygons and nets.

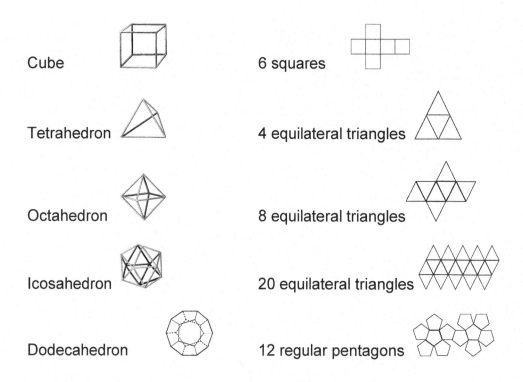

Cube   6 squares

Tetrahedron   4 equilateral triangles

Octahedron   8 equilateral triangles

Icosahedron   20 equilateral triangles

Dodecahedron   12 regular pentagons

Models such as these help students see how three-dimensional solids are composed of two-dimensional shapes.

As students grow in their knowledge of shapes, they will need to increase their critical thinking skills to include the development of mathematical arguments about the relationships among shapes. After the beginning levels of being able to identify, name, and create basic two- and three-dimensional shapes, students need to begin to compare and sort shapes.

During this comparison, students will need to examine the various attributes of shapes to help them make predictions. Students should explore and make predictions about how shapes can be combined to make new shapes, what would happen if parts were taken off shapes, and other extrapolations about the shapes. This exploration provides students the basis for later, more complex understanding of geometric relationships.

Tangrams, or puzzle pieces, are excellent manipulatives for children to use to explore geometric shapes and relationships. They allow students to transform shapes through flips and rotations and to take them apart and put them together in different formations. Tangrams can be tangible pieces that students manipulate with their hands, or they can be virtual pieces on the computer that students manipulate to visualize geometric shape changes.

For tactile experiences in three dimensions, use a classroom set of geometric blocks, or bring in common household items (such as canned goods and cereal boxes). Students can build arrangements composed of multiple solids and begin to appreciate the idea of geometrical structural representation.

Skill 5.3   Analyze and distinguish examples of symmetry and non-symmetry in two dimensions

Symmetry is exact similarity between two parts or halves, as if one were a mirror image of the other. As an introduction to symmetry, the teacher could discuss the fact that human bodies have right-left symmetry: two arms, two legs, two eyes, and a nose and mouth in the middle. Explain the idea of imagining a line down the middle of the body and seeing that the two sides roughly match. Then discuss the idea that if there was a drawing on paper of a body, students could actually draw a line vertically and then fold on that line, and the two sides would match.

Next, have the students guess what kinds of symmetry a square has, then a rectangle. Then give them a worksheet with different geometric figures on it. Have them cut out the figures and try folding on different lines. What can they conclude about symmetry for each of these figures? Try an exercise in which a line of symmetry is given and one side is drawn. Then ask the children to draw the other side. Recognizing when an image or shape does *not* have symmetry should be part of student exploration as well. Exercises available on the Internet and computer software activities can provide good symmetry lessons.

As children progress in their mathematical education, they can be introduced to the idea of radial symmetry. Interesting discussions can arise when they are asked about the kind of symmetry they find in a circle. The idea of transformations is a bit more advanced. Luckily for today's teachers, there are computer programs to help with this. Teachers can start with making things proportionately larger or smaller. This is a relatively easy concept for the students. A bit of imagination, which children are terrifically good at, will allow for more types of transformations. For example, a Halloween unit on transformations lends itself to ones such as those done by funhouse mirrors.

Skill 5.4   Identify spatial concepts (e.g., above, below, hidden view, through) and vocabulary (e.g., line, angle, ray, plane) useful for teaching geometry in real-world situations

Students love to explore their homes, cupboards, classrooms, and play areas in search of various shapes. Finding the shapes around their environment can help students better reflect on the world around them. In this way, they can also begin to identify the relationships among shapes (squares and rectangles both have four sides and four corners, but they are not the same). These real-world examples also provide perfect opportunity to reinforce geometry concepts such as sides, angles, rays, and planes.

A **point** is a dimensionless location and has no length, width, or height.

A **line** connects a series of points and continues straight infinitely in two directions. Lines extend in one dimension. A line is defined by any two points that fall on the line; therefore, a line may have multiple names.

A **line segment** is a portion of a line. A line segment is the shortest distance between two endpoints and is named using those endpoints. Line segments therefore have exactly two possible names (for example, $\overline{AB}$ or $\overline{BA}$). Because line segments have two endpoints, they have a defined length or distance.

A **ray** is a portion of a line that has only one endpoint and continues infinitely in one direction. Rays are named using the endpoint as the first point and any other point on the ray as the second.

An **angle** is formed by the intersection of two rays.

A **plane** is a flat surface defined by three points. Planes extend infinitely in two dimensions. A common example of a plane is x-y plane used in the Cartesian coordinate system.

Show students where these geometric features are located on everyday items such as a cereal box, pizza slice, or windowpane. Students can also make creative drawings win which rays, angles, and lines may be highlighted. Another crafty geometry activity is to use materials such as Popsicle sticks, play dough, or pipe cleaners to build shapes. Students can use straws or toothpicks to create three-dimensional structures made of various shapes. These activities give students concrete ways to apply geometry to their surroundings.

When choosing literature for the classroom, find stories with visually descriptive passages that can help develop a student's spatial sense. Pay special attention to moments in the text and illustrations that show an object's relative location (above, below, behind, and so on). Additionally, students would love to act out these descriptors by following directions to "stand *behind* your chair" or "crawl *under* your desk."

SUBAREA 4   **SCIENCE**

COMPETENCY 1.0   **KNOWLEDGE OF EFFECTIVE SCIENCE INSTRUCTION**

Skill 1.1   **Analyze developmentally appropriate strategies for teaching science practices (e.g., observing, questioning, designing and carrying out investigations, developing and using models, constructing and communicating explanations)**

It is critical that scientific curricula be selected for the intended audience. Just as one would not use a college-level textbook in preschool education, one should not present science topics beyond the comprehension or preparation level of students. The educator must adapt the curricula to a broad audience and attempt to meet the needs of all students.

Every student presents a unique educational need. Not all students learn at a similar rate in a given environment. Each student represents a unique fusion of educational needs and learning potential. The need to accommodate disparate student needs is critical to successful education. It is also often exceptionally challenging. Educational presentation often becomes entrenched in established methods that work fairly well most of the time for most students. This is unfortunate inasmuch as it suggests that established methodology is optimal, whereas some beneficial change can nearly always be implemented.

When it becomes apparent that students are struggling with a particular topic, the teacher should take the time to review underlying principles. Generally, it is insufficient to present material solely based on educational grade level. Teachers should use a variety of teaching techniques and methodologies to fully engage students' interest, increase their knowledge, challenge their understanding, and expand their scientific thinking abilities. Activities are particularly useful in science, as simple experimentation or observation can be engrossing and instructive.

Teachers should exercise particular care in helping students develop a thorough understanding of scientific language and process. Words with specific scientific meanings must be carefully defined so students do not mistakenly associate them with their broader, popular meanings. For example, in biology the word *gene* has a specific and fairly exact meaning, whereas in the popular media the word has very little meaning beyond indicating an association with inherited traits. Similarly, scientific processes may be foreign to many students, who may lack background training in rigorous experimentation to establish support for hypotheses. Special care should be taken in the basic instruction of the scientific method. Again, simple activities in scientific experimentation are helpful and can maintain student interest.

Since the laboratory experience is of critical importance in the process of enhancing students' cognitive and affective understanding of science, the National Science Teachers Association makes the following recommendations.

PRESCHOOL/ELEMENTARY LEVEL

- Preschool/elementary science classes must include activity-based, hands-on experiences for all children. Teachers should select activities that allow students to discover and construct science concepts; and, after the concept is labeled and developed, activities should allow for application of the concept to the real lives of students. Teachers should also provide activities in which students manipulate one variable while holding others constant and establish experimental and control groups.

- Children at all developmental levels benefit from science experiences. Appropriate hands-on experiences must be provided for children with special needs who are unable to participate in classroom activities.

- A minimum of 60 percent of the science instruction time should be devoted to hands-on activities, in which children are manipulating, observing, exploring, and thinking about science using concrete materials. Reading about science, using computer programs, and observing teacher demonstrations are all important but should not be substituted for hands-on experiences.

- Evaluation and assessment of student performance must reflect hands-on experience. The testing program should measure the full range of student experience in science.

- Hands-on activities should be revised and adapted to meet student needs and to enhance curricular goals and objectives. There should be ongoing dissemination of elementary science education research results and information about supplementary science curricula.

- Hands-on activities must be supported with a yearly building science budget, including a petty cash fund for immediate materials purchase. Teachers should purchase enough supplies (such as magnets, cells, and hand lenses) to allow each child to have hands-on experiences. Many science activities can be taught using easily accessible, free, and inexpensive materials.

- Reasonable and prudent safety precautions should always be taken when teachers and students are interacting with manipulative materials. (See the NSTA publication *Safety in the Elementary Science Classroom*.)

- Preschool/elementary science should be taught in a classroom with sufficient workspace to include flat, moveable desks or tables/chairs; equipment; and hands-on materials. Consideration should be given to the purchase and storage of materials and to convenient access to water and electricity.

Computers and other electronic tools should be available for children's use as an integral part of science activities.

- Parents, members of the community, and members of parent/teacher organizations should be enlisted to assist preschool/elementary teachers with science activities and experiences. For example, these individuals could act as field-trip chaperones, science fair assistants, material collectors, or science classroom aides.

- There should not be more than 24 children assigned to each class. Teachers and children must have immediate access to one another for children to have a safe and effective learning environment.

Skill 1.2   **Identify strategies and skills for facilitating children's experiences in ways that support their active inquiry, naturalistic exploration, talk and argument, and conceptual development**

Learning can be broadly divided into two kinds: active and passive. Active learning involves, as the name indicates, a learning atmosphere full of action. In passive learning, students are taught in a non-stimulating and inactive atmosphere. Active learning involves and draws students into it, thereby interesting them to the point of participating and purposely engaging in learning.

It is crucial that students are actively engaged, not entertained. They should be taught the answers for "How" and "Why" questions and encouraged to be inquisitive and interested.

Active learning is conceptualized as follows:

A Model of Active Learning

Experience of	Dialogue with
Doing	Self
Observing	Others

This model suggests that all learning activities involve some kind of experience or some kind of dialogue. The two main kinds of dialogue are dialogue with self and dialogue with others. The two main kinds of experience are observing and doing.

Dialogue with self: This is what happens when learners think reflectively about a topic. They ask themselves a number of things about the topic.

Dialogue with others: When the students are listening to a book being read by another student or when the teacher is teaching, a partial dialogue takes place because the dialogue is one-sided. When they are listening to one another and when there is an exchange of ideas back and forth, it is said to be a dialogue with others.

Observing: This is a very important skill in science. This occurs when a learner carefully watches or observes someone else doing an activity or experiment. This is a good experience, although it is not quite like doing something for oneself.

Doing: This refers to any activity in which a learner actually does something, giving the learner a firsthand experience that is very valuable.

The scientific attitude is to be curious, open to new ideas, and skeptical. In science, there are always new discoveries, new research, and new theories. Sometimes, old theories are disproved. To view these changes rationally, one must have openness, curiosity, and skepticism. (*Skepticism* is a Greek word, meaning a method of obtaining knowledge through systematic doubt and continual testing. A scientific skeptic is one who refuses to accept certain types of claims without subjecting them to a systematic investigation.)

The students may not have these attitudes inherently, but it is the responsibility of the teacher to encourage, nurture, and practice these attitudes so that students will have a good role model.

Inquiry-based learning provides opportunities for students to experience and acquire thought processes that enable them to gather information about the world. This requires a higher level of interaction among the learner, the teacher, the area of study, available resources, and the learning environment. Students become actively involved in the learning process as they:

1. act upon their curiosity and interests
2. develop questions that are relevant
3. think their way through controversies or dilemmas
4. analyze problems
5. develop, clarify, and test hypotheses
6. draw conclusions
7. find possible solutions

The most important element in inquiry-based learning is questioning. Students must ask relevant questions and develop ways to search for answers and generate explanations. Higher-order thinking is encouraged.

INQUIRY STRATEGIES

Deductive Inquiry

The main goal of this strategy is to move students from generalized principles to specific instances. The strategy stresses the process of testing general assumptions, applying them, and exploring the relationships among specific elements. The teacher coordinates the information and presents important principles, themes, or hypotheses. Students are actively engaged in testing generalizations, gathering information, and applying it to specific examples.

Inductive Inquiry

The information-seeking process of the inductive inquiry method helps students establish facts, determine relevant questions, and develop ways to pursue these questions and build explanations. Students are encouraged to develop and support their own hypotheses. Through inductive inquiry, students experience the thought processes that require them to move from specific facts and observations to inferences.

Interactive Instruction

This strategy relies heavily on discussion and sharing among participants. Students develop social skills, learning from the teacher and their peers. They also learn organizational skills. Examples of this type of instruction include debates, brainstorming, discussions, and laboratory groups.

Skill 1.3	Identify and analyze strategies for formal and informal learning experiences to provide science curriculum that promotes children's natural curiosity about the world (e.g., active hands-on experiences, active engagement in the physical world, student interaction)

In every educational setting, a variety of rules and regulations apply that must direct instructor behavior in practices and activities appropriate to the setting. Financial constraints will largely dictate technologies and materials available. Within this framework, instructors should endeavor to provide effective and appropriate educational activities to further students' scientific knowledge and stimulate their inquisitiveness about natural processes.

Many simple but profound experiments can be demonstrated with near complete safety and very little financial outlay; these should always be used because they invite students to engage and interact with the physical world. While some students learn solely from lectures, notes, and reading, most students benefit from personal interaction with scientific processes. For example, the classic states of matter can easily be demonstrated with balloons, wood or plastic blocks, and water. For more advanced lessons, non-Newtonian fluids can be safely and cheaply demonstrated with starch (such as cornstarch) and water mixtures. No amount of lecture or reading will ever engage a student's interest as much as a bowl of non-Newtonian fluid.

Various other inexpensive but instructive demonstrations are easy to arrange. Of course, the hands-on experiences must be age appropriate and designed to conform to student needs. Safety equipment should always be used, and instructors should use caution to protect students' clothing and other personal belongings.

Engaging young learners in the process of the scientific method is a positive way to engage them in active learning.

THE SCIENTIFIC METHOD

The scientific method is the basic process of scientific investigation. It begins with the posing of a question and ends with the drawing of a conclusion based on reproducible experimental results.

Posing a Question

Although many discoveries happen by chance, the standard thought process of a scientist begins with forming a question to research. The more limited the question, the easier it is to set up an experiment to answer it.

Forming a Hypothesis

Once the question is formulated, the researcher makes an educated guess about the answer to the problem or question. This best educated guess is the hypothesis.

Conducting the Experiment

Ensuring experiments are fair requires that they have a variable or condition that can be changed (such as temperature or mass). A good experiment manipulates as few variables as possible to see which variable is responsible for the result. Depending on the type of research being conducted, a control may be necessary to prove that the results occurred because of the changed conditions and would not have happened otherwise.

Observing and Recording Data

Observations and results of the experiment should be recorded. Drawings, graphs, and illustrations should be included to support the gathered information. Observations are objective, whereas analysis and interpretation are subjective.

Reporting of the data should include specific information about how the measurements were calculated.

Drawing a Conclusion

After recording the data, it is compared with data from other groups. A conclusion is the judgment derived from the results. A conclusion should explain why the results of the experiment either proved or disproved the hypothesis.

Graphing Data

Graphing utilizes numbers to demonstrate patterns. The patterns offer a visual representation of the information, making it easier to draw conclusions.

Communicating Results

Conclusions must be communicated by clearly describing the information using accurate data, visual presentations, and other appropriate media such as a Power Point presentation. Examples of visual presentations are graphs (bar/line/pie), tables/charts, diagrams, and artwork.

Skill 1.4	Identify ways to organize and manage the early childhood classroom for safe, effective science teaching and learning (e.g., procedures, equipment, layout)

Safety in the science classroom and laboratory is of great importance to the science educator. One key to maintaining a safe learning environment is proactive training and regular in-service updates for all staff and students who utilize the science laboratory. This training should include how to identify and evaluate potential hazards as well as how to prevent or respond to them.

Right-to-know laws cover science teachers who work with potentially hazardous chemicals. Briefly, the laws state that employees must be informed of potentially toxic chemicals. An inventory must be made available, if requested. The inventory must contain information about the hazards and properties of the chemicals. Training must be provided in the safe handling and interpretation of the material safety data sheet (MSDS).

Schools should consider the following types of training:

- Right-to-know training (OSHA training on the importance and benefits of properly recognizing and safely working with hazardous materials) along with some basic chemical hygiene and instruction in how to read and understand a material safety data sheet
- Instruction in how to use a fire extinguisher

- Instruction in how to use a chemical fume hood
- General guidance on when and how to use personal protective equipment (such as safety glasses or gloves)
- Instruction in how to monitor activities for potential impact on indoor air quality

It is also important for the instructor to use **material safety data sheets (MSDS).** MSDSs include information on substances such as physical data (melting point, boiling point, and so on), toxicity, health effects, first aid, reactivity, storage, disposal, protective gear, and spill/leak procedures. They are particularly important to have available if a spill or other accident occurs. You should have an MSDS in the lab for every item in your chemical inventory. They will assist you in determining how to store and handle your materials. In most cases the manufacturer provides recommendations with regard to protective equipment, ventilation, and storage.

In addition to requirements set forth by your place of employment, the National Association of Biology Teachers (NABT) and International Science Education Foundation (ISEF) have set parameters for the science classroom.

All science labs should contain the following items of safety equipment (*required by law*):

- Fire blanket that is visible and accessible
- Ground fault circuit interrupters (GFCIs) within two feet of water supplies
- Emergency shower capable of providing a continuous flow of water
- Signs designating room exits
- Emergency eyewash station that can be activated by the foot or forearm
- Eye protection for every student and a means of sanitizing equipment
- Emergency exhaust fans providing ventilation to the outside of the building
- Master cutoff switches for gas, electric, and compressed air. Switches must have permanently attached handles. Cutoff switches must be clearly labeled.
- An ABC fire extinguisher
- Storage cabinets for flammable materials

The following are also recommended, but are not required by law:

- Chemical spill control kit
- Fume hood with a motor that is sparkproof
- Protective laboratory aprons made of flame-retardant material
- Signs that will alert people to potentially hazardous conditions
- Containers for broken glassware, flammables, corrosives, and waste
- Containers should be labeled

In addition to the safety laws set forth by the government for equipment necessary to the lab, the Occupational Safety and Health Administration (OSHA) has helped make environments safer by creating signs for the laboratory. Of particular importance are diamond safety signs, prohibitive signs, and triangle danger signs. Each sign encloses a descriptive picture.

It is the teacher's responsibility to provide a safe environment for his or her students. Proper supervision greatly reduces the risk of injury. A teacher should never leave a class for any reason without providing alternate supervision. When an accident occurs, two factors are always considered: foreseeability and negligence. Foreseeability is the anticipation that an event may occur under certain circumstances. Negligence is the failure to exercise ordinary or reasonable care. Safety procedures should be built in to the science curriculum, and a well-managed classroom is critical to avoiding potential problems.

Skill 1.5	Identify and select developmentally appropriate formal and informal assessments to evaluate prior knowledge, to guide instruction, and to evaluate the impact of science experiences on student learning

Some assessment methods can be both formal and informal. For example, observation may incorporate structured observation instruments as well as other informal observation procedures, including professional judgment. When evaluating a child's developmental level, a professional may use a formal adaptive rating scale as well as his or her professional judgment to assess the child's motivation and behavior.

CURRICULUM-BASED ASSESSMENT

Curriculum-based assessment is assessment of an individual's performance of objectives within a curriculum such as a reading, math, or science program. The individual's performance is measured in terms of which objectives were mastered. This type of testing can be verbal, written, or demonstration based. Its general structure may include such factors as amount of time to complete, amount to complete, and whether it was group or individual testing. The level of response may be multiple choice, essay, or recall of facts.

MOMENTARY TIME SAMPLING

Momentary time sampling is a technique used for measuring behaviors of a group of individuals or several behaviors of the same individual. Time samples are usually brief and can be conducted at fixed or variable intervals. The advantage of using variable intervals is increased reliability, as the students will not be able to predict when the time sample will be taken.

COMMUNICATING WITH STUDENTS

How can a teacher provide good feedback so students will learn from their assessments? First, the teacher's language should be helpful and constructive. Critical language does not usually help students learn. Language that is constructive and helpful recommendations will guide students to specific actions that will help them improve in the future.

When teachers provide timely feedback, they increase the chances that students will reflect on the thought processes they went through when they originally produced the work. When feedback comes weeks after an assignment was produced, the student may not remember what caused him or her to respond in a particular way.

Specific feedback is particularly important. Comments like, "This should be clearer" and "Your grammar needs work" provide information that students may already know. Students benefit from comments that include specific actions they can take to make something clearer or to improve their grammar.

When teachers provide feedback on a set of assignments, for example, they enhance students' learning by teaching them how to use the feedback. Teachers can ask students to do additional things to work with their original products, or they can ask students to take small sections and rewrite them based on the feedback. While written feedback enhances student learning, having students do something with the feedback encourages even deeper learning and reflection.

Teachers can also show students how to use scoring guides and rubrics to evaluate their own work, particularly before they turn it in. One particularly effective way of doing this is to have students examine models and samples of proficient work. Teachers should collect samples of good work, remove names and other identifying features, and show these to students so that they understand what is expected of them. Often, when teachers do this, they are surprised to see how much students gain in terms of their ability to assess their own performance.

Finally, teachers can help students develop plans to revise and improve their work, even if the teacher does not evaluate it in the preliminary stages. For example, teachers can have students keep track of words they commonly misspell or make their own lists of areas they feel they need to focus on.

MULTIPLE BASELINE DESIGN

Multiple baseline design can be used to test the effectiveness of an intervention in the performance of a skill or to determine if the intervention accounted for the observed changes in a target behavior. First, the initial baseline data are collected, followed by the data during the intervention period. To get the second baseline, the intervention is stopped for a period of time and data are collected again. The intervention is then restarted or reapplied, and data are collected on the target behavior.

GROUP TESTS AND INDIVIDUAL TESTS

The obvious distinction between a group test and an individual test is that individual tests must be administered to only one person at a time, whereas group tests are administered to several people simultaneously or can be administered individually. However, there are several other subtle differences.

When administering an individual test, the tester has the opportunity to observe the individual's responses and to determine how such things as problem solving are accomplished. Within limits, the tester is able to control the pace and tempo of the testing session and to rephrase and probe responses to elicit the individual's best performance. If a child becomes tired, the examiner can give the child a break between parts of the test or end the test; if the child loses his or her place on the test, the tester can help the child regain it; if the child dawdles or loses interest, the tester can encourage or redirect him or her. If the child lacks self-confidence, the examiner can reinforce the child's efforts. In short, individual tests allow the examiner to encourage a child's best efforts and to observe how a student uses his or her skills to answer questions. Thus, individual tests provide for the gathering of both quantitative and qualitative information.

It is vital for teachers to track student performance using a variety of methods. Teachers should be able to assess students on a daily basis using informal assessments such as monitoring during work time, class discussions, and note taking. Often these assessments are an excellent way to determine whether students are on track and learning selected objectives. Generally, teachers can assess students by their participation in class discussion, and often this is a good way to give students credit for participation, especially those students who have special needs and who participate well in class but may struggle with other assignments.

More formal assessments are necessary to ensure that students fully understand selected objectives. Regular grading using selected performance skills is necessary; however, teachers should develop personal ways of grading using a variety of assessment tools. For example, students could keep a science journal, tracking the progress of their ongoing assignments, projects, and labs. Other tools for observing and evaluating students are rubrics and checklists. Student profiles and checklists are an excellent way to quickly determine whether students are meeting selected objectives. It is easy for a teacher to check off students who are meeting objectives, using a checklist while monitoring students' work done in class. See the example below.

Student Name	Objective #1	Objective #2	On Task
Joe Student	X	X	X
Jan Student		X	X

Checklists provide an easy way for teachers to quickly see who is behind or who needs to review a lesson or objective.

Skill 1.6	Select and analyze small- and large-group strategies to help students explain the concepts they are learning, provide opportunities to introduce formal science terms, and to clarify scientific concepts and misconceptions

The scientific process assumes that rational explanations (hypotheses) can be offered for observable phenomena. Experiments are then performed to generate data that support or refute a given hypothesis. Once sufficient data have been amassed to strongly support a given hypothesis and refute competing hypotheses, the supported hypothesis is termed a theory. If substantive alternative hypotheses can be established for a given phenomenon, even a strongly supported hypothesis cannot be accepted as conclusive.

Good scientific investigation should seek to provide a number of plausible hypotheses for any given phenomenon and then identify the correct hypothesis as established by experimental results. It is therefore critical that students approach a given scientific phenomenon with an open mind and a willingness to accept logical conclusions even when they are unanticipated.

Additionally, a variety of explanations may be correct for a given phenomenon if they seek to explain the phenomenon as resulting from different causation. For example, proximate causation of a given animal behavior may result from stimuli and responses controlled by internal mechanisms, while ultimate causation of the same animal behavior may result from evolutionary pressures. In this situation, both explanations may be correct. Students should be encouraged to analyze the phenomenon from a variety of viewpoints to fully understand it.

To draw conclusions, we need to study the data on hand. The data tell us whether the hypothesis is correct. If the hypothesis is not correct, another hypothesis has to be formulated and another experiment has to be done.

If a hypothesis is tested and the results are repeated in further experimentation, a theory can be formulated. A theory is a hypothesis that is tested repeatedly by different scientists and yields the same results. A theory has more validity than a hypothesis because it can be used to predict future events.

Scientific inquiries should end in formulating an explanation or model. Models should be physical, conceptual, and mathematical. While drawing conclusions, a lot of discussion and arguments are generated. There may be several possible explanations for any given set of results, but not all of them are reasonable. Carefully evaluating and analyzing the data creates a reasonable conclusion. The conclusion needs to be backed up by scientific criteria.

Skill 1.7	Select and apply safe and effective instructional strategies when using curricular and instructional tools and resources such as physical and conceptual models, scientific equipment, regalia, and print and digital representations to support and enhance science instruction

Scientists start with a problem and solve it in an orderly fashion following the scientific method. The key to the success of the scientific method lies in minimizing human prejudice. The steps consist of identifying the problem, gathering information, formulating a hypothesis, designing an experiment, interpreting data, and drawing conclusions.

The first step in a science investigation is identifying the problem. As we observe, we notice interesting things that arouse our curiosity. We ask ourselves the basic questions: how, why, what, when, which, and where. The two most important questions are how and why.

We can classify observations into two types. The first is qualitative, which we describe in words ("the water is hot" or "the solution is sour"). The second is quantitative, in which we use numbers and quantities to describe our observations ("the mass is 125 kilograms" or "the distance is 500 kilometers").

The second step is gathering information. We collect as much information as possible from various sources such as the Internet, books, journals, newspapers, and experts in the field. This lays a solid foundation for formulating a hypothesis.

The third step is hypothesizing. This is making a statement about the problem with the knowledge acquired and using the two important words, *if* and *when*.

The next step is designing an experiment. Before we do this, however, we need to identify the control, the constants, the independent variables, and the dependent variable.

For beginners, the simplest investigation would be to manipulate only one variable at a time. This way, the experiment doesn't get too complicated and is easier to handle. We have to identify the control and then the variable that can affect the outcome of the experiment. For an experiment to be authentic and reliable, controls have to be identified and kept constant throughout the experiment. Finally, we have to identify the dependent variable, which is dependent on the independent variable. The dependent variable is the factor that is being measured in an experiment; for example, the height of a plant or the number of leaves.

For an experiment to be successful, it should be completed in 10 to 12 days. The results should be noted carefully. At the end of the experiment, the data have to be analyzed and searched for patterns. Any scientific investigation has to be repeated at least twice to ensure reproducible results. After the analysis, conclusions must be drawn based on the data.

Systematic observation emphasizes gathering quantitative data on certain specific behaviors. Researchers are interested in a limited set of behaviors. This allows them to study and test specific hypotheses.

The first step is to develop a coding system, which is a description of behaviors and how they will be recorded. They key idea is to delimit the range of behaviors that are observed. The operational definitions of each behavior to be recorded are defined, and the occurrence and duration of each behavior are recorded.

For example, consider the recording of animal behavior. Potential problems that can occur during the observation include the following:

- **Remaining vigilant:** Following an animal in its natural habitat is difficult, especially when human presence is required. Recording devices (audio and video) are used to deal with this problem.

- **Reactivity:** Humans and animals often change their behavior when they are being observed. The observer must take steps to remain unobtrusive or become a participant observer.

- **Reliability:** To ensure that the coding of behavior is accurate, two or more observers are used consistently and their results are compared. This is known as inter-rater or inter-observer reliability.

- **Sampling:** Setting up a schedule of observation intervals and using multiple observations over a range of time provides a good measure of the behavior of an animal over a period of time and is considered to be reliable.

Skill 1.8   **Apply scientifically and professionally responsible decision making regarding the selection of socially and culturally sensitive content and activities**

Scientists are expected to show good conduct in their scientific pursuits. Conduct here refers to all aspects of scientific activity including experimentation, testing, education, data evaluation, data analysis, data storage, peer review, government funding, staff, and so on.

The influence of social and cultural factors on science can be profound. Some early societies had trouble accepting science, especially when the science exposed some cultural beliefs as myths. This created a dilemma concerning whether to accept the facts provided by scientific investigations or to cling to cultural norms. This struggle went on for centuries. It took a long time for societies to accept scientific facts and to leave some of the cultural beliefs behind or modify them.

It can be extremely difficult for some societies to come to terms with technological advances. Even today, some cultures are not using modern technology, but, at the same time, they are using technology in principle (for example, using simple machines for farming rather than complex machines like tractors).

Other cultures have so readily adapted to technology that lives are intertwined with it to the extent that individuals utilize the computer, television, microwave, dishwasher, washing machine, cell phone, and so on a daily basis. It is surprising to realize that we began with no technology and now are surrounded by it.

The religious beliefs and institutions of a culture can greatly influence scientific research and technological innovation. Political factors affect scientific advancement as well, especially in cultures that partially support scientific research with public money. Warfare has traditionally been a strong driver of technological advancement as cultures strive to outpace their neighbors with better weapons and defenses. Technologies developed for military purposes often find their way into the mainstream. Significant advances in flight technology, for example, were made during the two world wars.

Many cultures have come to value innovation and welcome new products as well as improvements to older products. The desire to always be advancing and obtaining the latest, newest technology creates economic incentives for innovation.

COMPETENCY 2.0   KNOWLEDGE OF THE NATURE OF SCIENCE

Skill 2.1   Identify and apply basic process skills (e.g., observing, inferring, classifying, measuring) and developmentally appropriate science practices (e.g., analyzing and interpreting data, constructing explanations, engaging in argument from evidence)

SEE Skill 1.6

Skill 2.2   Evaluate and interpret pictorial representations, charts, tables, and graphs of authentic data from scientific investigations to make predictions, construct explanations, and support conclusions

GRAPHING DATA

Graphing is an important skill to visually display collected data for analysis. It utilizes numbers to demonstrate patterns. The patterns offer a visual representation, making it easier to draw conclusions.

The two types of graphs most commonly used are the **line graph** and the **bar graph** (histogram). Line graphs are set up to show two variables represented by one point on the graph. The x-axis is the horizontal axis; it represents the dependent variable. Dependent variables are those that would be present independently of the experiment. A common example of a dependent variable is time. Time proceeds regardless of anything else occurring. The y-axis is the vertical axis; it represents the independent variable. Independent variables, such as the amount of light or the height of a plant, are manipulated by the experiment.

Graphs should be calibrated at equal intervals. If one space represents one day, the next space may not represent 10 days. A *best fit* line can be drawn to join the points, and it does not always include all the points in the data. Axes must always be labeled for the graph to be meaningful. A good title will describe both the dependent and the independent variable.

Bar graphs are set up similarly in regards to axes, but points are not plotted. Instead, the dependent variable is set up as a bar where the x-axis intersects the y-axis. Each bar is a separate item of data and is not joined by a continuous line.

APPLY KNOWLEDGE OF DESIGNING AND PERFORMING INVESTIGATIONS

Normally, knowledge is integrated in the form of a lab report. A report has many sections. It should include a specific **title** that tells exactly what is being studied. The **abstract** is a summary of the report; it is written at the beginning of the paper. The **purpose** should always be defined because it will state the problem.

The purpose should include the **hypothesis** (educated guess) of what is expected from the outcome of the experiment. The entire experiment should relate to this problem.

A scientific theory is an explanation of a set of related observations based on a proven hypothesis. A scientific law usually lasts longer than a scientific theory and has more experimental data to support it.

SEE also Skill 1.3

METRIC SYSTEM

Science uses the metric system, as it is accepted worldwide and allows easier comparison among experiments done by scientists around the world. It is important to learn the following basic units and prefixes:

Meter: measure of length
Liter: measure of volume
Gram: measure of mass

deca-(meter, liter, gram) = 10× the base unit   *deci*- = 1/10 the base unit
hecto-(meter, liter, gram) = 100× the base unit   *centi*- = 1/100 the base unit
kilo-(meter, liter, gram) = 1000× the base unit   *milli*- = 1/1000 the base unit

Skill 2.3	Analyze the dynamic nature of science as a way of understanding the world (e.g., tentativeness, replication, reliance on evidence)

SEE Skill 1.8

Skill 2.4	Identify and select appropriate tools, including digital technologies, and units of measurement for various science tasks

Biological science is closely connected to technology and the other sciences; it greatly impacts society and everyday life. Scientific discoveries often lead to technological advances and, conversely, technology is often necessary for scientific investigation. Biology and the other scientific disciplines share several unifying concepts and processes that help unify the study of science. Because biology is the science of living systems, biology directly impacts society and everyday life.

Science and technology, while two distinct concepts, are closely related. Science attempts to investigate and explain the natural world, while technology attempts to solve human adaptation problems. Technology often results from the application of scientific discoveries, and advances in technology can increase the impact of scientific discoveries. For example, Watson and Crick used science to discover the structure of DNA; their discovery led to many biotechnological advances in the manipulation of DNA. These technological advances greatly influenced the medical and pharmaceutical fields. The success of Watson and Crick's experiments, however, was dependent on the technology available. Without the necessary technology, the experiments would not have been possible.

Biologists use a variety of tools and technologies to perform tests, to collect and display data, and to analyze relationships. Examples of commonly used tools include computer-linked probes, spreadsheets, and graphing calculators.

Biologists use **computer-linked probes** to measure various environmental factors including temperature, dissolved oxygen, pH, ionic concentration, and pressure. The advantage of computer-linked probes, as compared to more traditional observational tools, is that the probes automatically gather data and present it in an accessible format. This property of computer-linked probes eliminates the need for constant human observation and manipulation.

Biologists use **spreadsheets** to organize, analyze, and display data. For example, conservation ecologists use spreadsheets to model population growth and development, to apply sampling techniques, and to create statistical distributions to analyze relationships. Spreadsheet use simplifies data collection and manipulation, and it also allows the presentation of data to be done in a logical and understandable format.

Graphing calculators are another technology with many applications to biology. For example, biologists use algebraic functions to analyze growth, development, and other natural processes. Graphing calculators can manipulate algebraic data and create graphs for analysis and observation. In addition, biologists use the matrix function of graphing calculators to model problems in genetics. The use of graphing calculators simplifies the creation of graphical displays, including histograms, scatter plots, and line graphs. Biologists can transfer data and displays to computers for further analysis. Finally, biologists also connect computer-linked probes, used to collect data, to graphing calculators to ease the collection, transmission, and analysis of data.

The combination of biology and technology has improved the human standard of living in many ways. However, the negative impact of increasing human life expectancy and population on the environment is problematic. In addition, advances in biotechnology (such as genetic engineering and cloning) produce ethical dilemmas that society must consider.

Skill 2.5   **Evaluate the relationship between claims (e.g., including predictions), evidence (i.e., scientific knowledge, observations) and explanations (i.e., linking claims to evidence, drawing conclusions)**

Science is a process of checks and balances. It is expected that scientific findings will be challenged, and in many cases retested. Often one experiment serves as the starting point for another. While bias does exist, the use of controlled experiments and awareness on the part of the scientist can go far to ensure a sound experiment. Even if the science is sound, however, it may still be questioned. It is through this continual search that hypotheses become theories, which sometimes become laws. It is also through this search that new information is discovered.

Although the concept of biology as a field of science arose only in the nineteenth century, the origin of the biological sciences can be traced back to the ancient Greeks. It is important for teachers to stress diversity among scientists. Great contributions have been made by a wide variety of cultures.

During the Renaissance and the Age of Discovery, renewed interest in the rapidly increasing number of known organisms generated considerable interest in biology.

Andreas Vesalius (1514–1564) was a Belgian anatomist and physician whose dissections of the human body and descriptions of his findings helped correct the misconceptions of science. The books Vesalius wrote on anatomy are the most accurate and comprehensive anatomical texts to date.

Anton van Leeuwenhoek is known as the father of microscopy. In the 1650s, Leeuwenhoek began making tiny lenses that gave magnifications up to 300x. He was the first to see and describe bacteria, yeast, and the microscopic life found in water. Over the years, light microscopes have advanced to produce greater clarity and magnification. The scanning electron microscope (SEM) was developed in the 1950s. Instead of light, a beam of electrons passes through the specimen. Scanning electron microscopes have a resolution about one thousand times greater than light microscopes. The disadvantage of the SEM is that the chemical and physical methods used to prepare the sample results in the death of the specimen.

Robert Hooke (1635–1703) was a renowned inventor, natural philosopher, astronomer, experimenter, and cell biologist. He is remembered mainly for Hooke's law, an equation describing elasticity that is still used today, but he made other lesser-known contributions as well. He was the type of scientist who was called a virtuoso, able to contribute findings of major importance in many fields of science. Hooke published *Micrographia* in 1665. He devised the compound microscope and illumination system, one of the best such microscopes of his time, and used it in demonstrations at the Royal Society's meetings. With it he observed organisms as diverse as insects, sponges, bryozoans, foraminifera, and bird feathers. *Micrographia* is an accurate and detailed record of his observations, illustrated with magnificent drawings.

Carl von Linnaeus (1707–1778), a Swedish botanist, physician, and zoologist, is well known for his contributions in ecology and taxonomy. Linnaeus is famous for his binomial system of nomenclature, in which each living organism has two names, a genus and a species name. He is considered the father of modern ecology and taxonomy.

In the late 1800s, Louis Pasteur discovered the role of microorganisms in the cause of disease, invented the process that came to be called pasteurization, and created the rabies vaccine. Robert Koch took Pasteur's observations one step further by formulating the hypothesis that specific diseases were caused by specific pathogens. **Koch's postulates** are still used as guidelines in the field of microbiology. They state that the same pathogen must be found in every diseased person; that the pathogen must be isolated and grown in culture; that the disease is induced in experimental animals from the culture; and that the same pathogen must be isolated from the experimental animal.

Matthias Schleiden, a German botanist, is famous for his cell theory. He observed plant cells microscopically and concluded that the cell is the common structural unit of plants. He proposed the cell theory along with Theodor Schwann, a zoologist, who observed cells in animals.

In the eighteenth century, many fields of science like botany, zoology, and geology began to evolve as scientific disciplines in the modern sense.

In the twentieth century, the rediscovery of Gregor Mendel's work led to the rapid development of genetics by Thomas Hunt Morgan and his students.

DNA structure was another key event in biological study. In the 1950s, James Watson and Francis Crick discovered the structure of a DNA molecule to be a double helix. The discovery of this structure made it possible to explain DNA's ability to replicate and to control the synthesis of proteins.

Following the cracking of the genetic code, biology has largely split between organismal biology (ecology, ethology, systematics, paleontology, evolutionary biology, developmental biology, and other disciplines that deal with whole organisms or group of organisms) and the disciplines related to molecular biology (cell biology, biophysics, biochemistry, neuroscience, immunology, and many other overlapping subjects).

The use of animals in biological research has expedited many scientific discoveries. Animal research has allowed scientists to learn more about animal biological systems, including the circulatory and reproductive systems. One significant use of animals is for the testing of drugs, vaccines, and other products before use or consumption by humans.

There are significant arguments against the use of animals in research. The debate about the ethical treatment of animals has been ongoing since scientists began testing with them. Many people believe the use of animals in research is cruel and unnecessary. There are now a number of federal and local regulations in place regarding the use of animals for research purposes.

Skill 2.6	Identify and analyze attitudes and dispositions underlying scientific thinking (e.g., curiosity, openness to new ideas, appropriate skepticism, cooperation)

To understand scientific ethics, we need to have a clear understanding of ethics in general. Ethics is defined as a system of public, general rules for guiding human conduct (Gert 1988). The rules are general because they are supposed to apply to all people at all times, and they are public because they are not secret codes or practices.

Philosophers have proposed a number of moral theories to justify moral rules, including the following:

- **Utilitarianism:** A theory of ethics that prescribes the quantitative maximization of good consequences for a population. Utilitarianism is a form of consequentialism. This theory was proposed by Mozi, a Chinese philosopher who lived from 471 to 381 BCE.
- **Kantianism:** A theory proposed by Immanuel Kant, a German philosopher who lived from 1724 to 1804, which ascribes intrinsic value to rational beings and is the philosophical foundation of contemporary human rights.
- **Social contract theory:** A view of the ancient Greeks that states that a person's moral and/or political obligations are dependent upon a contract or agreement among people to form society.

The guiding principles of scientific ethics include the following:

1. **Scientific honesty:** Not to commit fraud; not to fabricate or misinterpret data for personal gain
2. **Caution:** To avoid errors and sloppiness in all scientific experimentation
3. **Credit:** To give credit where credit is due and not to copy
4. **Responsibility:** To report only reliable information to the public and not to mislead in the name of science
5. **Freedom:** The freedom to criticize old ideas, question new research, and conduct research

SEE also Skill 1.8

Skill 2.7   **Identify and analyze ways in which science is an interdisciplinary process and interconnected to STEM disciplines (i.e., science, technology, engineering, mathematics)**

Science can be related to all disciplines. This can be done through a variety of teaching methods.

One of the most significant methods of improving educational presentation is the utilization of a variety of teaching methods. These methods allow students with a variety of learning styles to gain from the educational experience. One of the best teaching methods available is the use of activities that encourage direct student involvement. There is clearly a major role for lecture in the classroom, but there is also an obvious need for hands-on project work to motivate students. Lecture itself can be delivered in a variety of ways to add and maintain interest. Some students respond well to relatively straightforward lecture, while others respond to question-and-answer sessions, review sessions, object lessons, or other common types of presentation. Care should be taken to plan a variety of activities that include all students. Activities should also be planned in accordance with law and school policy.

While planning lectures and activities in advance is critical to success, plans should remain flexible enough to adapt to emerging classroom needs. In most structured learning environments, predefined (such as by standardized testing or policy) critical outcomes exist, and the instruction supporting these outcomes must not be eliminated. Instead, the plan should adequately address these critical outcomes and simultaneously remain flexible in other areas addressing secondary or supplementary outcomes. In this way the plan is adaptable—content can be added, expanded, eliminated, or reduced—and still addresses all areas supporting critical outcomes.

It is important that young learners understand the ways science is relatable to other subjects. Teachers can tie core concepts in from all disciplines through the use of interactive lessons that incorporate problem solving, communication, and technology.

Learners can complete guided experiments, use mathematical tools, and organize data in systematic ways. The teacher will use good modeling to demonstrate how science is related to technology and problem solving.

Problem solvers will understand the relationships between cause and effect and communicate the results in writing and through organized charts and graphs. Although learners are young, basic information can be conveyed in a variety of ways, including labeled pictures from observations, bar and line graphs, and short written explanations when appropriate.

STEM ties four disciplines together: **S**cience, **T**echnology, **E**ngineering, and **M**athematics. Teachers should aim to provide the opportunity for all learners to partake in lessons that deliver aspects of all four areas.

Skill 2.8	Analyze considerations of science technology in society including cultural, ethical, economic, political, and global implications

USES OF GENETIC ENGINEERING

Many microorganisms are used to detoxify toxic chemicals and to recycle waste. Sewage treatment plants use microbes to degrade organic compounds. Some compounds, like chlorinated hydrocarbons, cannot be easily degraded. Scientists are working on genetically modifying microbes to be able to degrade the harmful compounds that the current microbes cannot.

Genetic engineering has also benefited agriculture. For example, many dairy cows are given bovine growth hormone to increase milk production. Commercially grown plants are often genetically modified for optimal growth.

Strains of wheat, cotton, and soybeans have been developed to resist herbicides used to control weeds. This allows for the successful growth of the plants while destroying the weeds. Crop plants are also being engineered to resist infections and pests. Scientists can genetically modify crops to contain a viral gene that does not affect the plant but will vaccinate the plant from a virus attack. Crop plants are now being modified to resist insect attacks. This allows farmers to reduce the amount of pesticide used on plants.

NATURAL HAZARDS AND DISASTERS

An important topic in science is the effect of natural disasters on society and the effect human activity has had on inducing such events. Naturally occurring geological, weather, and environmental events can greatly affect people's lives. In addition, the activities of humans can induce such events that would not otherwise occur.

Types of Hazards

Nature-induced hazards include the following:

- Floods
- Landslides
- Avalanches

- Volcanic eruptions
- Wildfires
- Earthquakes
- Hurricanes
- Tornadoes
- Droughts
- Disease

Such events often occur naturally, because of changing weather patterns or geological conditions. Property damage, resource destruction, and the loss of human life are possible outcomes of natural hazards. Thus, natural hazards are often extremely costly on both an economic and personal level.

Human Influence

While many natural disasters occur naturally, human activity can often stimulate such events. For example, destructive land-use practices such as mining have induced landslides and avalanches when not properly planned and monitored. In addition, human activities can cause other hazards including climate change and waste contamination.

GLOBAL WARMING AND CLIMATE CHANGE

Global warming is an increase in Earth's average temperature, resulting, at least in part, from the burning of fuels by humans. Global warming is hazardous because it disrupts Earth's environmental balance and can negatively affect weather patterns. Ecological and weather pattern changes, referred to as climate change, can promote the natural disasters listed above.

CONTAMINATION

Finally, improper **hazardous waste disposal** can also contaminate the environment. Hazardous waste contamination can cause disease in humans. Thus, hazardous waste contamination negatively affects both the environment and the people who live in it.

SCIENCE AND CONSUMER PRODUCTS

An important application of science and technology is the production, storage, use, management, and disposal of consumer products and energy. Scientists from many disciplines work to produce a vast array of consumer products. Energy production and management is another area in which science plays a key role.

Production and Use

The **production** of a large number of popular consumer products requires scientific knowledge and technology. The following are few examples of science-based consumer goods:

- Genetically modified foods
- Pharmaceuticals
- Plastics
- Nylon
- Cosmetics
- Household cleaning products
- Color additives

Disposal

The management and disposal of consumer products is also an important concern. Scientists help establish limits for the safe use of potentially hazardous consumer products. For example, household cleaning products are potentially hazardous if used improperly. Scientific testing determines the proper uses and potential hazards of such products.

Disposal of waste from consumer product production and use is of great concern. Proper disposal of hazardous waste and recycling of durable materials is important for the health and safety of human populations as well as the long-term sustainability of Earth's resources and environment.

Energy

Energy production and management is an increasingly important topic in scientific research because of the increasing scarcity of energy-yielding resources, such as petroleum. With traditional sources of energy becoming more scarce and costly, a major goal of scientific energy research is the creation of alternative, efficient means of energy production. Examples of potential sources of alternative energy include the following:

- Wind
- Water
- Solar
- Nuclear
- Geothermal
- Biomass

An important concern in the production and use of energy, both from traditional and alternative sources, is the effect on the environment and the safe disposal of waste products. Scientific research and study helps determine the best methods for energy production, use, and waste product disposal, balancing the need for energy with the associated environmental and health concerns.

COMPETENCY 3.0   KNOWLEDGE OF EARTH AND SPACE SCIENCES

Skill 3.1   Identify the living and nonliving composition of Earth's surface and the properties of the nonliving materials that make up Earth's surface (e.g., soil, minerals, rocks, water)

ROCK CYCLE

There is a great deal of interaction between Earth's mantle and crust. The slow convection of rocks in the mantle is responsible for the shifting of tectonic plates on the crust. Matter can also move between the layers, as occurs during the rock cycle. Within the rock cycle, igneous rocks are formed when magma escapes from the mantle as lava during volcanic eruption. Rocks can also be forced back into the mantle, where the high heat and pressure recreate them as metamorphic rocks.

ROCKS

There are three major subdivisions of rocks:

- **Sedimentary rocks:** When fluid sediments are transformed into solid sedimentary rocks, the process is known as **lithification**. A common process that affects sediments is compaction, when the weight of overlying materials compresses and compacts the deeper sediments. The compaction process leads to cementation. **Cementation** is when sediments are converted to sedimentary rock.

- **Igneous rocks:** Igneous rocks can be classified according to their texture, their composition, and the way they formed. Molten rock is called magma. When molten rock pours out onto Earth's surface, it is called lava. As magma cools, the elements and compounds begin to form crystals. The more slowly the magma cools, the larger the crystals grow. Rocks with large crystals are said to have a coarse-grained texture. Granite is an example of a coarse-grained rock. Rocks that cool rapidly before any crystals can form have a glassy texture like obsidian, commonly known as volcanic glass.

- **Metamorphic rocks**: Metamorphic rocks are formed by high temperatures and great pressures. The process by which the rocks undergo these changes is called **metamorphism**. The outcome of metamorphic changes includes deformation by extreme heat and pressure, compaction, destruction of the original characteristics of the parent rock, bending and folding while in a plastic stage, and the emergence of completely new and different minerals due to chemical reactions with heated water and dissolved minerals. Metamorphic rocks are classified into two groups, foliated (leaflike) rocks and unfoliated rocks. Foliated rocks consist of compressed, parallel bands of minerals, which give the rocks a striped appearance. Examples of such rocks are slate, schist, and gneiss. Unfoliated rocks are not banded; examples of unfoliated rocks are quartzite, marble, and anthracite.

MINERALS

Minerals are natural, nonliving solids with a definite chemical composition and a crystalline structure. **Ores** are minerals or rock deposits that can be mined for profit. **Rocks** are earth materials made of one or more minerals.

Minerals must adhere to five criteria. They must:

- be nonliving
- be formed in nature
- be solid in form
- have atoms that form a crystalline pattern
- have a chemical composition fixed within narrow limits

There are more than 3,000 minerals in Earth's crust. Minerals are classified by composition. The major groups of minerals are silicates, carbonates, oxides, sulfides, sulfates, and halides. The largest group of minerals is the silicates. Silicates are made of silicon, oxygen, and one or more other elements.

SOILS

Soils are composed of particles of sand, clay, various minerals, tiny living organisms, and humus, plus the decayed remains of plants and animals. Soils are divided into three classes according to their texture:

- **Sandy soils** are gritty, and their particles do not bind together firmly. Sandy soils are porous: Water passes through them rapidly. Sandy soils do not hold much water.

- **Clay soils** are smooth and greasy; their particles bind together firmly. Clay soils are moist and usually do not allow water to pass through easily.

- **Loamy soils** feel somewhat like velvet, and their particles clump together. Loamy soils are made up of sand, clay, and silt. Loamy soils holds water but allow some water to pass through.

In addition to the three main classes, soils are further grouped into three major types based upon their composition:

- **Pedalfers** form in the humid, temperate climate of the eastern United States. Pedalfer soils contain large amounts of iron oxide and aluminum-rich clays, making the soil a brown to reddish-brown color. These soils support forest-type vegetation.

- **Pedocals** are found in the western United States where the climate is dry and temperate. These soils are rich in calcium carbonate. These soils support grasslands and brush vegetation.

- **Laterites** are found where the climate is wet and tropical. Large amounts of water flow through these soils. Laterites are red-orange soils rich in iron and aluminum oxides. There is little humus in these soils, and they are not very fertile.

Skill 3.2   **Identify the processes that change the surface of Earth**

MOUNTAINS

Orogeny is the term given to natural mountain building.

A mountain is terrain that has been raised high above the surrounding landscape by volcanic action or some form of tectonic plate collision. The physical composition of mountains includes igneous, metamorphic, and sedimentary rocks; some may have rock layers that are tilted or distorted by plate collision forces.

Folded mountains (Alps, Himalayas) are produced by the folding of rock layers during their formation. The Himalayas are the highest mountains in the world and include Mount Everest, which rises almost 9 kilometers above sea level. The Himalayas were formed when India collided with Asia. The movement that created this collision is still in process at the rate of a few centimeters per year.

Fault-block mountains (in Utah, Arizona, and New Mexico) are created when plate movement produces tension forces instead of compression forces. The area under tension produces normal faults; rock along these faults is displaced upward.

Dome mountains are formed as magma tries to push up through the crust but fails to break the surface. Dome mountains resemble huge blisters on Earth's surface.

Upwarped mountains (Black Hills of South Dakota) are created in association with a broad arching of the crust. They can also be formed by rock thrust upward along high-angle faults.

Volcanism is the term given to the movement of magma through the crust as well as its emergence as lava onto Earth's surface. Volcanic mountains are built up by successive deposits of volcanic materials.

An **active volcano** is one that is presently erupting or building to an eruption. A **dormant volcano** is one that is between eruptions but still shows signs of internal activity that might lead to an eruption in the future. An **extinct volcano** is said to be no longer capable of erupting.

There are three types of volcanic mountains: shield volcanoes, cinder cones, and composite volcanoes.

Shield volcanoes are associated with quiet eruptions. Lava emerges from the vent or opening in the crater and flows freely out over Earth's surface until it cools and hardens into a layer of igneous rock. A repeated lava flow builds this type of volcano into the largest volcanic mountain. Mauna Loa in Hawaii is the largest shield volcano on Earth.

Cinder cone volcanoes are associated with explosive eruptions as lava is hurled high into the air in a spray of droplets of various sizes. These droplets cool and harden into cinders and particles of ash before falling to the ground. The ash and cinder pile up around the vent to form a steep, cone-shaped hill called the cinder cone. Cinder cone volcanoes are relatively small but may form quite rapidly.

Composite volcanoes are built by both lava flows and layers of ash and cinders. Mount Fuji in Japan, Mount St. Helens in Washington State, and Mount Vesuvius in Italy are all famous composite volcanoes.

Mechanisms of Producing Mountains

Mountains are produced by different types of mountain-building processes. Most major mountain ranges are formed by the processes of folding and faulting. **Folded mountains** are produced by the folding of rock layers. **Faults** are fractures in Earth's crust that have been created by either tension or compression forces transmitted through the crust. These forces are produced by the movement of separate blocks of crust. **Fault lines** are categorized on the basis of the relative movement between the blocks on both sides of the fault plane. The movement can be horizontal, vertical, or oblique.

GLACIATION

A glacier is a large mass of ice that moves or flows over the land in response to gravity. Glaciers form among high mountains and in other cold regions. There are two main types of glaciers: valley glaciers and continental glaciers.

NATURAL DISASTERS

SEE Skill 2.8

EARTH AND WATER INTERACTIONS

Erosion is the inclusion and transportation of surface materials by another moveable material (usually water, wind, or ice). The most important cause of erosion is running water. Streams, rivers, and tides are constantly at work removing weathered fragments of bedrock and carrying them away from their original location.

A stream erodes bedrock through the grinding action of sand, pebbles, and other rock fragments. This grinding is called **abrasion**. Streams also erode rocks by dissolving or absorbing their minerals. Limestone and marble are readily dissolved by streams.

The breaking down of rocks at or near Earth's surface is known as **weathering**. Weathering breaks down these rocks into smaller and smaller pieces. There are two types of weathering: physical weathering and chemical weathering.

Skill 3.3	Analyze the effects of the law of gravity on objects on Earth and in space

DYNAMICS AND MOTION

Dynamics is the study of the relationship between motion and the forces affecting motion. **Force** causes motion.

Mass and weight are not the same quantities. An object's **mass** gives it a reluctance to change its current state of motion. It is also the measure of an object's resistance to acceleration. The force that Earth's gravity exerts on an object with a specific mass is called the object's weight on Earth. Weight is a force that is measured in newtons. Weight (W) = mass times acceleration due to gravity (W = mg).

Newton's Laws of Motion

Newton's first law of motion is also called the law of inertia. It states that an object at rest will remain at rest and an object in motion will remain in motion at a constant velocity unless acted upon by an external force.

Newton's second law of motion states that if a net force acts on an object, it will cause the acceleration of the object. The relationship between force and motion is: force equals mass times acceleration (F = ma).

Newton's third law states that for every action there is an equal and opposite reaction. Therefore, if an object exerts a force on another object, that second object exerts an equal and opposite force on the first.

Surfaces that touch each other have a certain resistance to motion. This resistance is **friction**.

1. The materials that make up the surfaces will determine the magnitude of the frictional force.
2. The frictional force is independent of the area of contact between the two surfaces.
3. The direction of the frictional force is opposite to the direction of motion.
4. The frictional force is proportional to the normal force between the two surfaces in contact.

Static friction describes the force of friction of two surfaces that are in contact but do not have any motion relative to each other, such as a block sitting on an inclined plane. **Kinetic friction** describes the force of friction of two surfaces in contact with each other when there is relative motion between the surfaces.

When an object moves in a circular path, a force must be directed toward the center of the circle to keep the motion going. This constraining force is called **centripetal force**. Gravity is the centripetal force that keeps a satellite circling Earth.

Push and pull—Pushing a volleyball or pulling a bowstring applies muscular force as the muscles expand and contract. Elastic force occurs when any object returns to its original shape (for example, when the bow is released).

Rubbing—Friction opposes the motion of one surface past another. Friction is common when slowing down a car or sledding down a hill.

Pull of gravity—The pull of gravity is a force of attraction between two objects. Gravity questions can be raised not only on Earth but also between planets and even in black hole discussions.

Inertia and circular motion—Centripetal force is provided, for example, by the high banking of a curved road and by friction between a vehicle's wheels and the road. The inward force that keeps an object moving in a circle is another example of a centripetal force.

Forces on objects at rest—The formula $F = m/a$ is shorthand for force equals mass over acceleration. An object will not move unless the force is strong enough to move the mass. Also, there can be opposing forces holding the object in place. For instance, a boat may want to be forced by the currents to drift away, but an equal and opposite force is a rope holding it to a dock.

Forces on a moving object—Overcoming inertia is the tendency of any object to oppose a change in motion. An object at rest tends to stay at rest. An object that is moving tends to keep moving.

Work is done on an object when an applied force moves through a distance.

Power is the work done divided by the amount of time that it took to do it.

(Power = Work/time)

Conserving Energy

The law of **conservation of energy** states that energy can neither be created nor destroyed. Therefore, the sum of all energy in a system remains constant. The law of **momentum conservation** states that when two objects collide in an isolated system, the total momentum of the two objects before the collision is equal to the total momentum of the two objects after the collision. That is, the momentum lost by object 1 is equal to the momentum gained by object 2.

STRAIGHT-LINE, CIRCULAR, AND PERIODIC MOTION

Matter can move in a straight line, in a circular pattern, and in a periodic fashion. The Greeks were the first civilization on record to think about motion. They thought that matter wanted to be stopped and were under the impression that after an object moved, it would not keep moving. They thought that the object would slow down and stop because its nature was to be at rest. These early scientists considered that matter moves. Galileo was the first to realize the error in the early scientists' thought process. Galileo concluded that an object keeps moving, even against the force of gravity.

Straight-Line Motion

To make an object move, a force must be applied. Friction must also be taken into account, because friction makes moving objects slow down. Galileo was also the first to notice this characteristic. This is Newton's first law of motion, which states that an object at rest stays at rest unless acted upon by an outside force. Force can have varied effects on moving objects. Force makes objects move, slow down, stop, increase their speed, decrease their speed, and so on. A moving object has speed, velocity, and acceleration. To summarize, when force is applied to an object, the object moves in a straight line (Newton's first law), and adding force can make the object go faster or slow down.

Circular Motion

Circular motion is defined as acceleration along a circle, a circular path, or a circular orbit. Circular motion involves acceleration of the moving object by a centripetal force that pulls the moving object toward the center of the circular orbit. Without acceleration, the object would move in a straight line, according to Newton's first law of motion. Circular motion is accelerated even though the speed is constant, because the object's velocity is constantly changing direction.

Periodic Motion

Periodic motion occurs when an object moves back and forth in a regular motion. Some examples of periodic motion are a weight on a string swinging back and forth (a pendulum) and a ball bouncing up and down. Periodic motion has three characteristics: velocity, period, and amplitude. There are many devices that use the characteristics of periodic motion. A clock is the most common example of periodic motion.

Skill 3.4　　　　Identify and distinguish distant objects seen in the daytime and nighttime sky (e.g., Sun, stars, planets, moon)

There are eight established planets in our solar system: Mercury, Venus, Earth, Mars, Jupiter, Saturn, Uranus, and Neptune. Pluto was an established planet in our solar system, but as of summer 2006, it is considered a dwarf planet. The planets are divided into two groups based on their distance from the Sun. The inner planets include Mercury, Venus, Earth, and Mars. The outer planets include Jupiter, Saturn, Uranus, and Neptune.

PLANETS

- **Mercury:** The closest planet to the Sun. Its surface has craters and rocks. The atmosphere is composed of hydrogen, helium, and sodium. Mercury was named after the Roman messenger god.

- **Venus:** Has a slow rotation compared to Earth. Venus and Uranus rotate in opposite directions from the other planets. This opposite rotation is called retrograde rotation. The surface of Venus is not visible due to the extensive cloud cover. The atmosphere is composed mostly of carbon dioxide. Sulfuric acid droplets in the dense cloud cover give Venus a yellow appearance. Venus has a greater greenhouse effect than that observed on Earth. The dense clouds combined with the carbon dioxide gas trap heat. Venus was named after the Roman goddess of love.

- **Earth:** Considered a water planet, with 70 percent of its surface covered by water. Gravity holds the water in place. The different temperatures observed on Earth allow for the different states (solid, liquid, and gas) of water to exist. The atmosphere is composed mainly of oxygen and nitrogen. Earth is the only planet known to support life.

- **Mars:** The surface of Mars contains numerous craters, active and extinct volcanoes, ridges, and valleys with extremely deep fractures. Iron oxide found in the dusty soil makes the surface rust-colored and the skies pink. The atmosphere is composed of carbon dioxide, nitrogen, argon, oxygen, and water vapor. Mars has polar regions with ice caps composed of water. Mars has two satellites. Mars was named after the Roman war god.

- **Jupiter:** Largest planet in the solar system. Jupiter has 16 moons. The atmosphere is composed of hydrogen, helium, methane, and ammonia. There are white bands of clouds indicating rising gas and dark bands of clouds indicating descending gas. The gas movement is caused by heat resulting from the energy of Jupiter's core. Jupiter has a large red spot that is thought to be a hurricane-type cloud. Jupiter has a strong magnetic field.

- **Saturn:** The second largest planet in the solar system. Saturn has rings of ice, rock, and dust particles circling it. Saturn's atmosphere is composed of hydrogen, helium, methane, and ammonia. Saturn has more than 20 satellites. Saturn was named after the Roman god of agriculture.

- **Uranus:** The third largest planet in the solar system. Uranus has retrograde revolution. Uranus is a gaseous planet. It has 10 dark rings and 15 satellites. Its atmosphere is composed of hydrogen, helium, and methane. Uranus was named after the Greek god of the heavens.

- **Neptune:** Another gaseous planet with an atmosphere consisting of hydrogen, helium, and methane. Neptune has three rings and two satellites. Neptune was named after the Roman sea god because its atmosphere is the same color as the seas.

- **Pluto:** Once considered the smallest planet in the solar system, it is now categorized as a dwarf planet. Pluto's atmosphere probably contains methane, ammonia, and frozen water. Pluto has one satellite. Pluto revolves around the Sun every 250 years. Pluto was named after the Roman god of the underworld.

COMETS, ASTEROIDS, AND METEORS

Astronomers believe that rocky fragments may be the remains of the birth of the solar system that never formed into planets. **Asteroids** are found in the region between Mars and Jupiter.

Comets are masses of frozen gases, cosmic dust, and small rocky particles. Astronomers think most comets originate in a dense comet cloud beyond Pluto. Comets consist of a nucleus, a coma, and a tail. A comet's tail always points away from the Sun. The most famous comet, **Halley's comet,** is named after the person who first discovered it in 240 BCE. It returns to the skies near Earth every 75 to 76 years.

Meteoroids are composed of particles of rock and metal of various sizes. When a meteoroid travels through Earth's atmosphere, friction causes its surface to heat up, and it begins to burn. The burning meteoroid falling through Earth's atmosphere is called a **meteor** (also known as a shooting star).

Meteorites are meteors that strike Earth's surface. A physical example of a meteorite's impact on Earth's surface is the Barringer Crater, a huge meteor crater in Arizona. There are many other meteor craters throughout the world.

Skill 3.5   **Identify and analyze the causes and effects of atmospheric processes (e.g., weather, wind, water cycle)**

AIR MASSES

Air masses moving toward or away from Earth's surface are called air currents. Air moving parallel to Earth's surface is called **wind**. Weather conditions are generated by winds and air currents carrying large amounts of heat and moisture from one part of the atmosphere to another. Wind speeds are measured by instruments called anemometers.

Wind Belts

The wind belts in each hemisphere consist of convection cells that encircle Earth like belts. There are three major wind belts on Earth:

1. Trade winds
2. Prevailing westerlies
3. Polar easterlies

Wind belt formation depends on the differences in air pressures that develop in the doldrums, the horse latitudes, and the polar regions. The doldrums surround the equator; within this belt, heated air usually rises straight up into Earth's atmosphere. The horse latitudes are regions of high barometric pressure with calm and light winds. Finally, the polar regions contain cold, dense air that sinks to Earth's surface.

Breezes and Monsoons

Winds caused by local temperature changes include sea breezes and land breezes.

Sea breezes are caused by the unequal heating of the land and an adjacent, large body of water. Since land heats up faster than water, it creates the movement of cool, ocean air toward the land, which is called a sea breeze. Sea breezes usually begin blowing about midmorning and end about sunset.

A breeze that blows from the land to the ocean or a large lake is called a **land breeze**.

Monsoons are huge wind systems that cover large geographic areas and that reverse direction seasonally. The monsoons of India and Asia are examples of these seasonal winds, where they alternate wet and dry seasons. As denser, cooler air over the ocean moves inland, a steady, seasonal wind called a summer, or wet, monsoon is produced.

CLOUDS

The following are the major types of clouds:

- **Cirrus**—white and feathery; high in the sky.
- **Cumulus**—thick, white, fluffy.
- **Stratus**—layers of clouds that cover most of the sky.
- **Nimbus**—heavy, dark clouds that represent thunderstorm clouds.

There are also some variations of these could types:

- **Cumulonimbus**—formed from cumulus clouds; tall, dense clouds involved in extreme weather.
- **Stratonimbus**—dark, flat, low clouds, mostly containing liquid droplets.

The air temperature at which water vapor begins to condense is called the **dew point**.

Relative humidity is the actual amount of water vapor in a certain volume of air compared to the maximum amount of water vapor this air could hold at a given temperature.

TYPES OF STORMS

A **thunderstorm** is a brief, local storm produced by the rapid upward movement of warm, moist air within a cumulonimbus cloud. Thunderstorms always produce lightning and thunder and are accompanied by strong wind gusts and heavy rain and/or hail.

A severe storm with swirling winds that may reach speeds of hundreds of kilometers per hour is called a **tornado**. Such a storm is also referred to as a twister. The sky is covered by large cumulonimbus clouds and violent thunderstorms, and a funnel-shaped swirling cloud may extend downward from a cumulonimbus cloud and reach the ground. Tornadoes leave a path of destruction on the ground.

A swirling, funnel-shaped cloud that extends downward and touches a body of water is called a **waterspout**.

Hurricanes are storms that develop when warm, moist air carried by trade winds rotate around a low-pressure "eye." A large, rotating, low-pressure system accompanied by heavy precipitation and strong winds is called a tropical cyclone (better known as a hurricane). In the Pacific region, a hurricane is called a typhoon.

Storms that occur only in the winter are known as blizzards or ice storms. A **blizzard** is a storm with strong winds, blowing snow, and frigid temperatures. An **ice storm** consists of falling rain that freezes when it strikes the ground, covering everything with a layer of ice.

Skill 3.6	Interpret and predict the direct and indirect effects of the Sun's energy on Earth, including plants, animals, water, land, and air

THE SUN

The **Sun** is the nearest star to Earth, and it produces solar energy. By the process of nuclear fusion, the Sun converts hydrogen gas to helium gas. Energy flows out of the Sun's core to the surface, allowing radiation to escape into space.

The parts of the Sun include the following:

1. **Core**—the inner portion of the Sun where fusion takes place.
2. **Photosphere**—the surface of the Sun that produces **sunspots**, which are cool, dark areas that can be seen on its surface.
3. **Chromosphere**—hydrogen gas causes this portion to be red in color. Also found here are solar flares (sudden brightness of the chromosphere) and solar prominences (gases that shoot outward from the chromosphere).
4. **Corona**—the transparent area of Sun visible only during a total eclipse.

Solar radiation is energy traveling from the Sun that radiates into space. **Solar flares** produce excited protons and electrons that shoot outward from the chromosphere at great speeds, reaching Earth. These particles disturb radio reception and also affect the magnetic field on Earth.

Interrelationships of Sun, Moon, and Earth

The mass of any celestial object may be determined by using Newton's laws of motion and his law of gravity.

For example, to determine the mass of the Sun, use the following formula:

$$M = \frac{4\pi^2}{G} = \frac{a^3}{P^2}$$

where M = the mass of the Sun, G = a constant measured in laboratory experiments, a = the distance of a celestial body in orbit around the Sun from the Sun, and P = the period of the body's orbit.

Skill 3.7	**Identify the components and significance of space research and exploration (e.g., timelines, tools and equipment, benefits and cost to society)**

SATELLITES AND SPACE EXPLORATION

Life Support

The health of astronauts depends on the quality of food they consume. Long space travels must have packaged food that is lightweight, is nutritious, will endure temperature and pressure changes, and is easily disposable. The water astronauts consume is filtered from their own breath, urine, and portable water brought on board. The purified water that astronauts use is cleaner than most systems on Earth. Earth's atmosphere is composed of roughly 78 percent nitrogen, 21 percent oxygen, and 1 percent argon and carbon dioxide. In a spacecraft, you would find liquid oxygen and liquid nitrogen; the cabin pressurization systems regulate the use of oxygen and nitrogen. Fire safety is essential to the life support of the astronauts. Fire does not react the same way in space as it does on Earth. The operating temperatures are maintained by varied means such as covering the spaceship with thermal blankets, paints, and specially made products that reduce both shrinking and expansion.

Unmanned Missions

Unmanned missions are carried out if they are deemed too dangerous for humans to undertake. *Sputnik* was the first unmanned mission. It was a Russian mission launched on October 4, 1957, during the cold war. The United States was driven to compete and enhance its space program. The following is a list of unmanned missions:

- *Mariner 10*: This American mission was the first to use the gravitational pull of one planet to reach another planet.
- **Deep Space 1:** This American mission tested 12 advanced technologies to lower the cost and risk of future space travel.
- *Magellan*: The Magellan mission took pictures of and collected information on Venus to help understand the geological structure of that planet.
- **Mars Exploration Rover:** The two Mars Exploration Rovers landed in January 2004 to robotically explore the geology of Mars. They were also used to explore the possibility of ancient water on Mars.
- *Mars Pathfinder*: The *Mars Pathfinder* landed July 4, 1997. The *Sojourner* rover onboard was used to analyze the atmosphere, climate, and geology of Mars.
- *Sputnik 1*: The Soviet Union launched *Sputnik 1* on October 4, 1957. It was the first artificial satellite in space. The launch of *Sputnik* ignited the Space Race between Russia and the United States and strengthened the cold war.
- *Sputnik 2*: Soviet Union scientists sent *Sputnik 2* into space along with the first live space traveler, a dog named Laika, to demonstrate that organisms from Earth could survive in orbit.
- *Voyager 1* and *Voyager 2*: *Voyager 1* and *Voyager 2* were spacecraft designed to explore the outer planets and interstellar space. Launched in 1977, these spacecraft transmitted information about the gas giants and are currently reaching the edge of our solar system.

Manned Missions

Throughout history there have been many manned missions, including many "firsts," such as first animal, first man on the moon, first woman in space, first preventable catastrophe, and first fatal catastrophe. As of 2007, manned missions have been limited to orbiting Earth and landing on the moon. With new knowledge of propulsion, it would be possible to reach Mars with a manned mission. Previously, unmanned missions have used land rovers to collect over 17,000 images and rock and soil samples.

- *Soyuz TM-32*: The *Russian Soyuz TM-32* was to be kept at the International Space Station as a lifeboat, and the crew that brought it returned to Earth on the *Soyuz TM-31* stored there.
- *Vostok 6*: The Russian *Vostok 6* was launched to continue experiments for joint spaceflights and also to observe the effect of space travel on the female body.
- *Apollo-Soyuz*: This mission involved a docking of ships between the American *Apollo* and Russian *Soyuz* to develop techniques for emergency rescues and to perform some experiments.

- *Challenger:* The American *Challenger* explosion occurred on the tenth mission of this space shuttle on January 28, 1986.
- *Vostok 1:* This Russian mission was the first manned spaceflight in history, signifying the first time anyone had journeyed into orbit.
- *Apollo 13:* This American mission was to gather information and pictures from the moon. This was the third manned mission to land in outer space. The explosion onboard the spacecraft was caused by a problem in the oxygen tank.
- *Apollo 11:* This American mission was the first lunar landing that also brought the first man on the moon.

CONSTELLATIONS AND GALAXIES

Astronomers use groups or patterns of stars, called **constellations,** as reference points to locate other stars in the sky. Familiar constellations include Ursa Major (meaning big bear) and Ursa Minor (meaning little bear). A smaller constellation, the Big Dipper, is found within Ursa Major. The Little Dipper, a smaller constellation, is found within the Ursa Minor. Different constellations appear as Earth continues its revolution around the Sun with the seasonal changes.

Vast collections of stars are **galaxies**. Galaxies are classified as irregular, elliptical, or spiral.

DEEP SPACE

Here are some important terms related to deep space:

- A **pulsar** is a variable radio source that emits signals in very short, regular bursts; it is believed to be a rotating neutron star.
- A **quasar** is an object that photographs like a star but has an extremely large red shift and a variable energy output; it is believed to be the active core of a very distant galaxy.
- **A black hole** is an object that has collapsed to such a degree that light cannot escape from its surface; that light is trapped by the intense gravitational field.

REMOTE SENSING

Remote sensing is the measurement or acquisition of information about an object or phenomenon by a recording device that is not in physical or intimate contact with the object. Examples of remote sensing include

- an aircraft taking pictures
- Earth observation and weather satellites
- monitoring a fetus in the womb through ultrasound

- a space probe

Skill 3.8   **Identify and describe repeated patterns in the Sun-Earth-moon system (e.g., the day-night cycle, phases of the moon, seasons)**

SEASONS

The **tilt of Earth's axis** creates the seasonable changes called summer, spring, autumn, and winter. Earth's orbit around the Sun and Earth's axis of rotation determine the seasons of the year. When the northern and southern hemispheres of Earth are pointed toward the Sun, it is summer, and when they are pointed away from the Sun, it is winter. Because of the axis of rotation, both hemispheres cannot be in the same season simultaneously. The two hemispheres have opposite seasons at all times.

- **The summer solstice** occurs when the North Pole is tilted toward the Sun on June 21 or 22, providing increased daylight hours for the Northern Hemisphere and shorter daylight hours for the Southern Hemisphere.
- **The winter solstice** occurs when the South Pole is tilted toward the Sun on December 21 or 22, providing shorter daylight hours in the Northern Hemisphere and longer daylight hours in the Southern Hemisphere.
- The **spring, or vernal, equinox** occurs on March 20 or 21, when the direct energy from the Sun falls on the equator, providing equal day and night hours in both hemispheres.
- The **autumnal equinox** occurs on September 22 or 23, providing equal day and night hours in both hemispheres.

Moon

The **moon** is a sphere that is always half illuminated by the Sun. The moon phase we see is dependent on the position of the moon in relation to Earth. During each lunar orbit (a lunar month), we see the moon's appearance change from not visibly illuminated to partially illuminated to fully illuminated, then back through partially illuminated to not illuminated. Although this cycle is a continuous process, there are eight distinct, traditionally recognized stages, called **phases**. The phases designate both the degree to which the moon is illuminated and the geometric appearance of the illuminated part.

New moon: This occurs when the moon's non-illuminated side is facing Earth. The moon is not visible (except during a solar eclipse).

Waxing crescent: This is when the moon appears to be less than one-half illuminated by direct sunlight. The fraction of the moon's disk that is illuminated is increasing.

First quarter: One-half of the moon appears to be illuminated by direct sunlight during this time. The fraction of the moon's disk that is illuminated is increasing.

Waxing gibbous: In this phase, the moon appears to be more than one-half but not fully illuminated by direct sunlight. The fraction of the moon's disk that is illuminated is increasing.

Full moon: This occurs when the moon's illuminated side is facing Earth. The moon appears to be completely illuminated by direct sunlight.

Waning gibbous: This is when the moon appears to be more than one-half but not fully illuminated by direct sunlight. The fraction of the moon's disk that appears to be illuminated is decreasing.

Last quarter: One-half of the moon appears to be illuminated by direct sunlight in this phase. The fraction of the moon's disk that appears to be illuminated is decreasing.

Waning crescent: During this phase, the moon appears to be less than one-half illuminated by direct sunlight. The fraction of the moon's disk that appears to be illuminated is decreasing.

The moon, Earth, and the Sun affect ocean tides. Along the west coast of the United States, there are four different tides per day: two highs and two lows. When the moon, Earth, and the Sun are in a line, **spring tides** occur. During these tides, one may observe tides that are higher or lower than normal. In other words, there will be very high tides and very low tides. When the moon, Earth, and Sun are at right angles to one another, **neap tides** occur. During these tides, one is not able to observe a great deal of difference in the heights of the high and low tides.

Skill 3.9	Analyze the impact of human activity on renewable and nonrenewable resources and natural events, including preparation for severe weather related events (e.g., hurricanes, tornadoes, flooding)

Natural phenomena affect the makeup and functioning of ecosystems both directly and indirectly. For example, floods and volcanic eruptions can destroy the fixed portions of an ecosystem, such as plants and microbes. Mobile elements, such as animals, must evacuate or risk injury or death. After a catastrophic event, species of microbes and plants begin to repopulate the ecosystem, beginning a line of secondary succession that eventually leads to the return of higher-level species. Often the area affected by the event returns to something like its original state.

Volcanic eruptions produce large amounts of molten lava and expel large amounts of ash and gas. Molten lava kills and destroys any living organisms it contacts. However, when lava cools and hardens, it provides a rich environment for the growth of microbes and plants. Volcanic eruptions also affect ecosystems indirectly. Studies show that the ash and gas released by eruptions can cause a reduction in the area's temperature for several years. The volcanic aerosol reflects the Sun's rays and creates clouds that have the same effect. In addition, sulfuric acid released by the volcano suppresses the production of greenhouse gases that damage the ozone layer.

Floods destroy microbes and vegetation and kill or force the evacuation of animals. Only when floodwaters recede can an ecosystem begin to return to normal. Floods also have indirect effects. For example, floods can cause permanent soil erosion and nutrient depletion. Such disruptions of the soil can delay and limit an ecosystem's recovery.

COMPETENCY 4.0   KNOWLEDGE OF THE PHYSICAL SCIENCES

Skill 4.1   **Sort matter by its observable qualitative properties (e.g., shape, color, states, texture, hardness) and quantitative properties (e.g., mass, volume, temperature, weight, density)**

The **phase of matter** (solid, liquid, or gas) is identified by the matter's shape and volume. Characteristics of each phase are described below.

SOLIDS

The following are characteristics of solids:

- They ave a definite shape that can be changed in some way.
- They have a definite volume that cannot be changed.
- Their mass can be changed when the physical shape is diminished; for example, sawing a board into two pieces.
- They can be any color and temperature.
- Some will melt under high temperatures, in which case they become liquid.
- They are very hard.

LIQUIDS

The following are characteristics of liquids:

- They take the shape of the container into which they are poured.
- When a liquid results from melting a solid, it has the same color as the solid.
- They flow.
- They cannot be compressed and keep the same volume.
- Their weight may be lighter than that of a solid because of evaporation.
- They are soft.

GASES

The following are characteristics of gases:

- They do not keep their shape; they fill a container.
- They flow very quickly.
- They are colorless.
- They can be compressed and take on a different volume than that of a solid or liquid.
- They are of high temperature.
- They are extremely light and do not have weight.

Skill 4.2 **Categorize matter as an element, compound, or mixture and compare the similarities and differences among them**

An **atom** is the smallest particle of an element that retains the properties of that element. All of the atoms of a particular element are the same. The atoms of each element are different from the atoms of other elements.

An **element** is a substance that cannot be broken down into other substances. To date, scientists have identified 109 elements; 89 are found in nature and 20 are synthetic. Elements are assigned an identifying symbol of one or two letters. For example, the symbol for oxygen is O, which stands for one atom of oxygen. However, because oxygen atoms in nature are joined in pairs, the symbol O_2 represents oxygen as we know it.

This pair of oxygen atoms is a molecule. A **molecule** is the smallest particle of substance that can exist independently and has all of the properties of that substance. A molecule of most elements is made up of one atom. However, oxygen, hydrogen, nitrogen, and chlorine molecules are made of two atoms each.

A **compound** is made of two or more elements that have been chemically combined. Each element's atoms join together when they bind chemically; the result is that the elements lose their individual identities. The compound that they become has different properties.

We use a formula to show the elements of a chemical compound. A **chemical formula** is a shorthand way of showing what is in a compound by using symbols and subscripts. The letter symbols let us know which elements are involved, and the number subscripts tell how many atoms of each element are involved. No subscript is used if there is only one atom involved. For example, carbon dioxide is made up of one atom of carbon (C) and two atoms of oxygen (O_2), so the formula is CO_2.

Substances can combine without a chemical change. A **mixture** is any combination of two or more substances in which the substances keep their own properties. A fruit salad is a mixture. So is an ice cream sundae, although you might not recognize each part if it is stirred together. Colognes and perfumes are other examples. You may not readily recognize the individual elements; however, they can be separated.

Compounds and mixtures are similar in that they are made up of two or more substances. However, they have the following distinct characteristics:

Compounds

1. Made up of one kind of particle
2. Formed during a chemical change
3. Broken down only by chemical changes
4. Properties are different from their parts
5. Have a specific amount of each ingredient

Mixtures

1. Made up of two or more particles
2. Not formed by a chemical change
3. Can be separated by physical changes
4. Properties are the same as their parts
5. Do not have a definite amount of each ingredient

Skill 4.3	Identify and differentiate between physical and chemical changes in matter

Everything in the world is made up of **matter**, whether it is a rock, a building, an animal, or a person. Matter is defined by its characteristics: *It takes up space and it has mass.*

Mass is a measure of the amount of matter in an object. Two objects of equal mass will balance each other on a simple balance scale no matter where the scale is located. For instance, two rocks with the same amount of mass that are in balance on Earth will also be in balance on the moon. They will feel **heavier** on Earth than on the moon because of the gravitational pull of Earth. So, although the two rocks have the same mass, they will have different weight.

Weight is the measure of Earth's pull of gravity on an object. It can also be defined as the pull of gravity between other bodies. The units of weight commonly used are the pound in English measure and the **kilogram** in metric measure.

In addition to mass, matter also has the property of volume. **Volume** is the amount of cubic space that an object occupies. Volume and mass together give a more exact description of the object. Two objects may have the same volume but different mass, the same mass but different volumes, and so on. For instance, consider two cubes that are each one cubic centimeter, one made from plastic, one from lead. They have the same volume, but the lead cube has more mass. The measure that we use to describe the cubes takes into consideration both the mass and the volume. **Density** is the mass of a substance contained per unit of volume. If the density of an object is less than the density of a liquid, the object will float in the liquid. If the object is denser than the liquid, the object will sink.

Density is stated in grams per cubic centimeter (g/cm^3), where the gram is the standard unit of mass. To find an object's density, one must measure its mass and its volume, then divide the mass by the volume (D = m/V).

To find an object's density, first use a balance to find its mass. Then calculate its volume. If the object is a regular shape, one can find the volume by multiplying the length, width, and height together. However, if it is an irregular shape, one can find the volume by seeing how much water it displaces. Measure the water in the container before and after the object is submerged. The difference will be the volume of the object.

Specific gravity is the ratio of the density of a substance to the density of water. For instance, the specific density of one liter of turpentine is calculated by comparing its mass (0.81 kg) to the mass of one liter of water (1 kg):

$$\frac{\text{mass of 1 L turpentine}}{\text{mass of 1 L water}} = \frac{0.81 \text{ kg}}{1.00 \text{ kg}} = 0.81$$

Physical properties and chemical properties of matter describe the appearance or behavior of a substance. A **physical property** can be observed without changing the identity of a substance. For instance, one can describe the color, mass, shape, and volume of a book. **Chemical properties** describe the ability of a substance to be changed into new substances. Baking powder goes through a chemical change as it changes into carbon dioxide gas during the baking process.

Matter constantly changes. A **physical change** is a change that does not produce a new substance. The freezing and melting of water is an example of a physical change. A **chemical change** (or **chemical reaction**) changes the inherent properties of a substance. This includes things such as burning materials that turn into smoke or a seltzer tablet that fizzes into gas bubbles when submerged in water.

Energy is the ability to cause change in matter. Applying heat to a frozen liquid changes it from solid back to liquid. Continue heating it, and it will boil and give off steam, a gas.

Evaporation is the change in phase from liquid to gas. **Condensation** is the change in phase from gas to liquid.

SEE also Skill 4.1

Skill 4.4   Identify and compare types, characteristics, and functions of energy

The relationships between heat, forms of energy, and work (mechanical, electrical, and so on) are the **laws of thermodynamics**. These laws deal strictly with systems in thermal equilibrium and not those within the process of rapid change or in a state of transition. Systems that are nearly always in a state of equilibrium are called **reversible systems**.

The **first law of thermodynamics** is a restatement of the conservation of energy. The change in heat energy supplied to a system (Q) is equal to the sum of the change in the internal energy (U) and the change in the work done by the system against internal forces.

$$DQ = DU + DW$$

The **second law of thermodynamics** is stated in two parts:

1. No machine is 100 percent efficient. It is impossible to construct a machine that only absorbs heat from a heat source and performs an equal amount of work because some heat will always be lost to the environment.
2. Heat cannot spontaneously pass from a colder to a hotter object. An ice cube sitting on a hot sidewalk will melt into a little puddle, but it will never spontaneously cool and form the same ice cube. Certain events have a preferred direction called the **arrow of time**.

Entropy is the measure of how much energy or heat is available for work. Work occurs only when heat is transferred from hotter to cooler objects. Once this is done, no more work can be extracted. The energy is still being conserved, but it is not available for work when the objects are the same temperature. Theory has it that, eventually, all things in the universe will reach the same temperature. If this happens, energy will no longer be usable.

Remember that the law of conservation of energy states that energy is neither created nor destroyed. Thus, energy changes form when energy transactions occur in nature. The following are the major forms energy can take:

- **Thermal energy** is the total internal energy of objects created by the vibration and movement of atoms and molecules. Heat is the transfer of thermal energy.
- **Acoustical energy**, or sound energy, is the movement of energy through an object in waves. Energy that forces an object to vibrate creates sound.
- **Radiant energy** is the energy of electromagnetic waves. Light—visible and otherwise—is an example of radiant energy.
- **Electrical energy** is the movement of electrical charges in an electromagnetic field. Examples of electrical energy are electricity and lightning.

- **Chemical energy** is the energy stored in the chemical bonds of molecules. For example, the energy derived from gasoline is chemical energy.
- **Mechanical energy** is the potential and kinetic energy of a mechanical system. Rolling balls, car engines, and body parts in motion exemplify mechanical energy.
- **Nuclear energy** is the energy present in the nucleus of atoms. The division, combination, or collision of nuclei release nuclear energy.

Skill 4.5   **Identify and analyze ways energy is transferred between objects or the surrounding air**

The **law of conservation of energy** states that energy is neither created nor destroyed. Thus, energy changes form whenever energy transactions occur in nature. Because the total energy in the universe is constant, energy continually transitions between forms. For example, an engine burns gasoline, converting the chemical energy of the gasoline into mechanical energy. A plant converts radiant energy of the Sun into chemical energy found in glucose. A battery converts chemical energy into electrical energy.

Chemical reactions are the interactions of substances that result in chemical changes and changes in energy. Chemical reactions involve changes in electron motion as well as the breaking up and formation of chemical bonds. **Reactants** are the original substances that interact to form distinct products. **Endothermic** chemical reactions consume energy, while **exothermic** chemical reactions release energy with product formation. Chemical reactions occur continually in nature and are also induced by humans for many purposes.

Nuclear reactions, or **atomic reactions**, are reactions that change the composition, energy, or structure of atomic nuclei. Nuclear reactions change the number of protons and neutrons in the nucleus. The two main types of nuclear reactions are **fission** (splitting of nuclei) and **fusion** (joining of nuclei). Fusion reactions are exothermic, releasing heat energy. Fission reactions are endothermic, absorbing heat energy. Fission of large nuclei (such as uranium) releases energy because the products of fission undergo further fusion reactions. Fission and fusion reactions can occur naturally, but are most recognized as human-made events. Particle acceleration and bombardment with neutrons are two methods of inducing nuclear reactions.

The law of conservation can also be applied to physical and biological processes. For example, when a rock is weathered, it does not just lose pieces; instead, it is broken down into its composite minerals, many of which enter the soil. Biology takes advantage of decomposers to recycle decaying material. Since energy is neither created nor destroyed, we know that it must change form. An animal may die, but its body will either be consumed by other animals or decay into the ecosystem. Either way, the animal enters another form and the matter still exists in some form or another.

Skill 4.6	Analyze and compare the relationship between forces (e.g., push or pull) and an object's change in position, direction, and/or speed

FORCES

SEE Skill 3.3

MACHINES

Simple machines include the following:

1. Inclined plane
2. Lever
3. Wheel and axle
4. Pulley

Compound machines are two or more simple machines working together. A wheelbarrow is an example of a complex machine. It uses a lever and a wheel and axle. Machines of all types ease workload by changing the size or direction of an applied force. The amount of effort saved when using simple or complex machines is called mechanical advantage, or MA.

COMPETENCY 5.0   KNOWLEDGE OF THE LIFE SCIENCES

Skill 5.1   Identify how plants and animals respond to their environment

HOMEOSTASIS

All living organisms respond and adapt to their environments. **Homeostasis** is the result of regulatory mechanisms that help maintain an organism's internal environment within tolerable limits. For example, in humans and mammals, constriction and dilation of blood vessels near the skin help maintain body temperature.

RESPONSE TO STIMULI

Response to stimuli is one of the key characteristics of any living thing. Any detectable change in the internal or external environment (the stimulus) may trigger a response in an organism. Just like physical characteristics, organisms' responses to stimuli are adaptations that allow them to better survive. While these responses may be more noticeable in animals that can move quickly, all organisms are capable of responding to changes.

Single-Celled Organisms

These organisms are able to respond to basic stimuli such as the presence of light, heat, or food. Changes in the environment are typically sensed via **cell surface receptors**. These organisms may respond to such stimuli by making changes in internal biochemical pathways or initiating reproduction or **phagocytosis**. Those capable of **simple motility**, for instance, using flagella, may respond by moving toward food or away from heat.

Plants

Plants typically do not possess sensory organs, so individual cells recognize stimuli through a variety of pathways. When many cells respond to stimuli together, the response becomes apparent. Logically then, the responses of plants occur on a longer timescale that those of animals. Plants are capable of responding to a few basic stimuli including light, water and gravity. Some common examples include the way plants turn and grow toward the Sun, the sprouting of seeds when exposed to warmth and moisture, and the growth of roots in the direction of gravity.

Animals

Lower members of the animal kingdom have responses similar to those seen in single-celled organisms. However, higher animals have developed complex systems to detect and respond to stimuli. The **nervous system**, **sensory**

organs (eyes, ears, skin, and so on), and **muscle tissue** all allow animals to sense and quickly respond to changes in their environment.

As in other organisms, many responses to stimuli in animals are **involuntary**. For example, pupils dilate in response to the reduction of light. Such reactions are typically called **reflexes**. However, many animals are also capable of **voluntary response**. In many animal species, voluntary reactions are **instinctual**. For instance, a zebra's response to a lion is a voluntary one, but, instinctually, it will flee quickly as soon as the lion's presence is sensed. Complex responses, which may or may not be instinctual, are typically termed **behavior**. An example is the annual migration of birds when seasons change. Even more complex social behavior is seen in animals that live in large groups.

Skill 5.2   Identify basic concepts of heredity (e.g., why offspring resemble their parents)

DNA AND DNA REPLICATION

The modern definition of a gene is a unit of genetic information. DNA makes up genes, which in turn make up the chromosomes. DNA is wound tightly around proteins to conserve space. The DNA/protein combination makes up the chromosome. DNA controls the synthesis of proteins, thereby controlling the total cell activity. DNA is capable of making copies of itself.

DNA Structure

DNA is made of nucleotides, which are composed of a five-carbon sugar, phosphate group, and nitrogen base (either adenine, guanine, cytosine, or thymine). The amount of adenine equals the amount of thymine, and the amount of cytosine equals the amount of guanine.

DNA consists of a sugar/phosphate backbone that is covalently bonded. The bases are joined down the center of the molecule and attached by hydrogen bonds that are easily broken during replication.

The shape of DNA is called a double helix and looks like a twisted ladder. The sugar/phosphates make up the sides of the ladder and the base pairs make up the rungs of the ladder.

DNA Replication

Enzymes control each step of the replication of DNA. The DNA molecule untwists. The hydrogen bonds between the bases break and serve as a pattern for replication. Free nucleotides inside the nucleus join on to form a new strand. Two new pieces of DNA are formed that are identical. This is a very accurate process. There is only one mistake for every billion nucleotides added. This is because there are enzymes (polymerases) present that proofread the molecule. In eukaryotes, replication occurs in many places along the DNA at once. The molecule may open up at many places like a broken zipper. In prokaryotic circular plasmids, replication begins at a point on the plasmid and goes in both directions until the circle is complete.

Base-pairing rules are important in determining a new strand of DNA sequence. For example, say our original strand of DNA had the following sequence:

A T C G G C A A T A G C

This can be called our sense strand, as it contains a sequence that makes sense or codes for something. The complementary strand (or other side of the ladder) would follow base-pairing rules (A bonds with T, and C bonds with G) and would read:

T A G C C G T T A T C G

When the molecule opens up and nucleotides join on, the base-pairing rules create two new identical strands of DNA:

A T C G G C A A T A G C   and   A T C G G C A A T A G C
T A G C C G T T A T C G   T A G C C G T T A T C G

PROTEIN SYNTHESIS

It is necessary for cells to manufacture new proteins for growth and repair of the organism. Protein synthesis is the process that allows the DNA code to be read and carried out of the nucleus into the cytoplasm in the form of RNA. This is where the ribosomes are found, which are also the sites of protein synthesis. The protein is then assembled according to the instructions on the DNA. There are several types of RNA:

- **Messenger RNA** (mRNA): Copies the code from DNA in the nucleus and takes it to the ribosomes in the cytoplasm.

- **Transfer RNA** (tRNA): Free floating in the cytoplasm. Its job is to carry and position amino acids for assembly on the ribosome.

- **Ribosomal RNA** (rRNA): Found in the ribosomes. They make a place for the proteins to be made. rRNA is believed to have many important functions, so much research is currently being done in this area.

Along with enzymes and amino acids, the RNA's function is to assist in the building of proteins. There are two stages of protein synthesis:

- **Transcription:** This phase allows for the assembly of mRNA and occurs in the nucleus where the DNA is found. The DNA splits open and the mRNA reads the code and transcribes the sequence onto a single strand of mRNA. For example, if the code on the DNA is T A C C T C G T A C G A, the mRNA will make a complementary strand reading: A U G G A G C A U G C U (remember that uracil replaces thymine in RNA.) Each group of three bases is called a **codon**. The codon will eventually code for a specific amino acid to be carried to the ribosome. "Start" codons begin the building of the protein and "stop" codons end transcription. When the stop codon is reached, the mRNA separates from the DNA and leaves the nucleus for the cytoplasm.

- **Translation:** This is the assembly of the amino acids to build the protein and occurs in the cytoplasm. The nucleotide sequence is translated to choose the correct amino acid sequence. As the rRNA translates the code at the ribosome, tRNA that contains an **anticodon** seek out the correct amino acid and bring it back to the ribosome. For example, using the codon sequence from the example above:

   The mRNA reads: A U G / G A G / C A U / G C U
   The anticodons are: U A C / C U C / G U A / C G A
   The amino acid sequence would be: Methionine (start) - Glu - His - Ala

This whole process is accomplished through the assistance of **activating enzymes**. Each of the 20 amino acids has its own enzyme. The enzyme binds the amino acid to the tRNA. When the amino acids get close to each other on the ribosome, they bond together using peptide bonds. The start and stop codons are called nonsense codons. There is one start codon (AUG) and three stop codons (UAA, UGA, and UAG). Addition mutations will cause the whole code to shift, thereby producing the wrong protein or, at times, no protein at all.

Irregularities or Interruptions of Mitosis and Meiosis

Since it's not a perfect world, mistakes happen. Inheritable changes in DNA are called **mutations**. Mutations can be errors in replication or a spontaneous rearrangement of one or more segments by factors like radioactivity, drugs, or chemicals. The amount of change is not as critical as where the change is.

Mutations can occur on somatic or sex cells. Usually the ones on sex cells are more dangerous since they contain the basis of all information for the developing offspring. Mutations are not always bad. They are the basis of evolution, and if they make a more favorable variation that enhances the organism's survival, then they are beneficial. But mutations can also lead to abnormalities, birth defects, and even death. There are several types of mutations. Let's suppose a normal sequence was as follows:

Normal: A B C D E F

Duplication: One gene is repeated (A B C C D E F).

Inversion: A segment of the sequence is flipped around (A E D C B F).

Deletion: A gene is left out (A B C E F).

Insertion or translocation: A segment from another place on the DNA is inserted in the wrong place (A B C R S D E F).

Breakage: A piece is lost (A B C) DEF is lost.

Nondisjunction: This occurs during meiosis when chromosomes fail to separate properly. One sex cell may get both genes and another may get none. Depending on the chromosomes involved, this may or may not be serious. Offspring end up with either an extra chromosome or a missing one. An example of nondisjunction is Down syndrome, in which there are three copies of chromosome 21 instead of two.

Skill 5.3	Classify plants and animals into major groups according to characteristics (e.g., physical features, behaviors, development)

Carolus Linnaeus is considered the father of taxonomy. **Taxonomy** is the science of classification. **Classifying** is the grouping of items according to their similarities. It is important for students to realize relationships and similarity as well as differences to reach a reasonable conclusion in a lab experience. The modern classification system uses binomial nomenclature. This consists of a two-word name for every species. The genus is the first part of the name and the species is the second part. Notice in the levels explained below that Homo sapiens is the scientific name for humans. Starting with the kingdom, the groups get smaller and more alike as one moves down the levels in human classification:

Kingdom: Animalia
Phylum: Chordata
Subphylum: Vertebrata
Class: Mammalia
Order: Primate
Family: Hominidae
Genus: Homo
Species: sapiens

Species are defined by the ability to successfully reproduce with members of their own kind.

Members of the five different kingdoms of the classification system of living organisms often differ in their basic life functions. Here we compare and analyze how members of the five kingdoms obtain nutrients, excrete waste, and reproduce.

Bacteria are prokaryotic, single-celled organisms that lack cell nuclei. The different types of bacteria obtain nutrients in a variety of ways. Most bacteria absorb nutrients from the environment through small channels in their cell walls and membranes (chemotrophs), while some perform photosynthesis (phototrophs). Chemoorganotrophs use organic compounds as energy sources, while chemolithotrophs can use inorganic chemicals as energy sources. Depending on the type of metabolism and energy source, bacteria release a variety of waste products (such as alcohols, acids, or carbon dioxide) to the environment through diffusion.

All bacteria reproduce through binary fission (asexual reproduction), producing two identical cells. Bacteria reproduce very rapidly, dividing or doubling every 20 minutes in optimal conditions. Asexual reproduction does not allow for genetic variation, but bacteria achieve genetic variety by absorbing DNA from ruptured cells and conjugating or swapping chromosomal or plasmid DNA with other cells.

Animals are multicellular, eukaryotic organisms. All animals obtain nutrients by eating food (ingestion). Different types of animals derive nutrients from eating plants, other animals, or both. Animal cells perform respiration, which converts food molecules—mainly carbohydrates and fats—into energy. The excretory systems of animals, like animals themselves, vary in complexity. Simple invertebrates eliminate waste through a single tube, while complex vertebrates have a specialized system of organs that process and excrete waste.

Most animals, unlike bacteria, exist in two distinct sexes. Members of the female sex give birth or lay eggs. Some less developed animals can reproduce asexually. For example, flatworms can divide into two, and some unfertilized insect eggs can develop into viable organisms. Most animals reproduce sexually through various mechanisms.

Plants, like animals, are multicellular, eukaryotic organisms. Plants obtain nutrients from the soil through their root systems and convert sunlight into energy through photosynthesis. Many plants store waste products in vacuoles or organs (such as leaves and bark) that are discarded. Some plants also excrete waste through their roots. More than half of the plant species reproduce by producing seeds from which new plants grow. Depending on the type of plant, flowers or cones produce seeds. Other plants reproduce by spores, tubers, bulbs, buds, and grafts.

Fungi are eukaryotic, mostly multicellular organisms. All fungi are heterotrophs, obtaining nutrients from other organisms. More specifically, most fungi obtain nutrients by digesting and absorbing nutrients from dead organisms. Fungi secrete enzymes outside their body to digest organic material and then absorb the nutrients through their cell walls.

Most fungi can reproduce asexually and sexually. Different types of fungi reproduce asexually by mitosis, budding, sporification, or fragmentation. Sexual reproduction of fungi is different from sexual reproduction of animals. The two mating types of fungi are plus and minus, not male and female.

Protists are eukaryotic, single-celled organisms. Most protists are heterotrophic, obtaining nutrients by ingesting small molecules and cells and digesting them in vacuoles. All protists reproduce asexually by either binary or multiple fission. Like bacteria, protists achieve genetic variation by exchange of DNA through conjugation.

Skill 5.4	Compare the ways living things meet their basic needs through interaction with and dependence on one another when sharing an environment (e.g., competition, predation, pollination)

There are many interactions that may occur between different species living together. Predation, parasitism, competition, commensalisms, and mutualism are the different types of relationships populations have with one another.

Predation and **parasitism** result in a benefit for one species and a detriment for the other. Predation occurs when a predator eats its prey. The number of predators determines the number of prey, which in turn affects the number of predators. The common conception of predation is of a carnivore consuming other animals. This is one form of predation. Although not always resulting in the death of the plant, herbivory is a form of predation. Some animals eat enough of a plant to cause death. However, many plants and animals have defenses against predators. Some plants have poisonous chemicals that will harm the predator if ingested, and some animals are camouflaged so they are harder to detect.

Parasitism involves a predator that lives on or in its host, causing detrimental effects to the host but not the parasite. Insects and viruses living off and reproducing in their hosts is an example of parasitism.

Competition occurs when two or more species in a community use the same resources. Competition is usually detrimental to both populations. It is often difficult to find in nature, because competition between two populations is not continuous. Either the weaker population will no longer exist, or one population will evolve to utilize other available resources.

Symbiosis is when two species live close together. Parasitism, described above, is one example of symbiosis. Another example of symbiosis is commensalism. **Commensalism** occurs when one species benefits from the other without harming the other. **Mutualism** is when both species benefit from the other. Species involved in mutualistic relationships must coevolve to survive; as one species evolves, the other must as well. For example, grouper and a species of shrimp live in a mutualistic relationship. The shrimp feed off parasites living on the grouper; thus the shrimp are fed and the grouper stays healthy and parasite-free. Many microorganisms are in mutualistic relationships.

Niche and Carrying Capacity

The term **niche** describes the relational position of a species or population in an ecosystem. Niche includes how a population responds to the abundance of its resources and its enemies (such as growing when resources are abundant and predators, parasites, and pathogens are scarce).

Niche also indicates the life history of an organism, its habitat, and its place in the food chain. According to the competitive exclusion principle, no two species can occupy the same niche in the same environment for a long time.

The full range of environmental conditions (biological and physical) under which an organism can exist describes its **fundamental niche**. Because of the pressure from superior competitors, organisms that survive over the long term are driven to occupy a niche that is narrower than their previous one. This is known as the **realized niche**.

Examples of niches include the following:

Oak trees
- live in forests
- absorb sunlight by photosynthesis
- provide shelter for many animals
- act as support for creeping plants
- serve as a source of food for animals
- cover their ground with dead leaves in autumn

If the oak trees were cut down or destroyed by fire or storms, they would no longer be doing these jobs. In turn, this would have a disastrous effect on all the other organisms living in the same habitat.

Hedgehogs
- eat a variety of insects and other invertebrates that live underneath the dead leaves and twigs in the garden
- have spines that are a superb environment for fleas and ticks
- put the nitrogen back into the soil when they urinate
- eat slugs and protect plants from them

If the hedgehog population was drastically reduced, the number of slugs would explode and the nutrients in the dead leaves and twigs would not recycle.

A **population** is a group of individuals of one species that live in the same general area. Many factors can affect the population size and its growth rate. For example, population size depends on the total amount of life a habitat can support. This is called the **carrying capacity** of the environment. Once the habitat runs out of food, water, shelter, or space, the carrying capacity decreases and then stabilizes.

Limiting factors can also affect population growth. As a population increases, the competition for resources is more intense, and the growth rate declines. This is a **density-dependent** growth factor. The carrying capacity can be determined by the density-dependent factor.

Density-independent factors affect individuals regardless of population size. The weather and climate are good examples. Temperatures that are too hot or too cold may kill many individuals from a population even if it has not reached its carrying capacity.

Biotic factors are living things in an ecosystem: plants, animals, bacteria, fungi, and so on. **Abiotic factors** are nonliving aspects of an ecosystem: soil quality, rainfall, temperature, and so on.

Human population increased slowly until 1650. Since 1650, the human population has grown almost exponentially, reaching the current population of over 6 billion. Factors that have led to this increased growth rate include improved nutrition, sanitation, and health care. In addition, advances in technology, agriculture, and scientific knowledge have made the use of resources more efficient and readily available.

Skill 5.5   Identify basic characteristics of living and nonliving things

The organization of living systems builds by levels from small to increasingly larger and more complex. All aspects, whether they are cells or ecosystems, have the same requirements to sustain life. Life is organized from simple to complex in the following way:

Organelles make up **cells**, which make up **tissues**. Tissues make up **organs**, and groups of organs make up **organ systems**. Organ systems work together to provide life for the **organism**.

Several characteristics have been described to identify living versus nonliving substances.

1. **Living things are made of cells**. They grow, are capable of reproduction, and respond to stimuli.
2. **Living things must adapt to environmental changes or perish**.
3. **Living things carry out metabolic processes**. They use and make energy.

All organic life has a common element: carbon. Carbon is recycled through the ecosystem through both biotic and abiotic means. It is the link between biological processes and is the chemical makeup of life.

Skill 5.6   Identify and describe the basic structures, behaviors, and functions of plants and animals that allow them to carry out their life processes (e.g., grow, reproduce, and survive)

Definitions of Feeding Relationships

SEE Skill 5.4

Biogeochemical Cycles

Essential elements are recycled through an ecosystem. At times, the element needs to be "fixed" in a useable form. Some cycles are dependent on plants, algae, and bacteria to fix nutrients for use by animals.

Water cycle: Two percent of all the available water is fixed and unavailable in ice or the bodies of organisms. Available water includes surface water (lakes, ocean, and rivers) and groundwater (aquifers, wells). Ninety-six percent of all available water is from groundwater. Water is recycled through the processes of evaporation and precipitation. The water present on Earth now is the water that has been here since Earth's atmosphere formed.

Carbon cycle: Ten percent of all available carbon in the air (from carbon dioxide gas) is fixed by photosynthesis. Plants fix carbon in the form of glucose, and animals then eat the plants and are able to obtain carbon. When animals release carbon dioxide through respiration, the plants have a source of carbon to fix once more.

Nitrogen cycle: Eighty percent of the atmosphere is nitrogen gas. Nitrogen must be in nongaseous form to be incorporated into an organism. Only a few genera of bacteria have the correct enzymes to break the triple bond between nitrogen atoms. These bacteria live within the roots of legumes (peas, beans, alfalfa) and add bacteria to the soil so that it can be taken up by plants. Nitrogen is necessary to make amino acids and the nitrogenous bases of DNA.

Phosphorus cycle: Phosphorus is a mineral; it is not found in the atmosphere. Fungi and plant roots have structures called mycorrhizae that are able to fix insoluble phosphates into useable phosphorus. Urine and decayed matter return phosphorus to the earth where it can be incorporated in the plant. Phosphorus is needed for the backbone of DNA and for ATP manufacture.

Ecological Problems

Nonrenewable resources are fragile and must be conserved for use in the future. Humans' impact on the environment and knowledge of conservation will determine the future.

Biological magnification: Chemicals and pesticides accumulate in the food chain. Tertiary consumers have more accumulated toxins than animals at the bottom of the food chain.

Simplification of the food web: Three major crops feed the world (rice, corn, and wheat). Planting these crops wipes out other habitats and pushes animals into smaller areas, causing overpopulation or extinction.

Fuel sources: Strip mining and the overuse of oil reserves have depleted these resources. At the current rate of consumption, conservation or alternate fuel sources will be key to our future.

Pollution: Although technology gives us many advances, pollution is a side effect of production. Waste disposal and the burning of fossil fuels have polluted our land, water, and air. Climate change and acid rain are two results of the burning of hydrocarbons and sulfur.

Climate change: Rain forest depletion, fossil fuels, and aerosols have caused an increase in carbon dioxide production. This leads to a decrease in the amount of oxygen, which is directly proportional to the amount of ozone. As the ozone layer depletes, more heat enters Earth's atmosphere and is trapped. This causes an overall warming effect that may eventually melt the polar ice caps, causing a rise in water levels and changes in climate. This will, in turn, affect weather systems.

Endangered species: Construction to house our overpopulated world has caused a destruction of habitats for other animals, often leading to their extinction.

Overpopulation: The human population is still growing at an exponential rate. Carrying capacity has not been met due to our ability to use technology to produce more food.

Skill 5.7   **Identify and compare the structure and functions of major systems of the human body**

The following are some important terms related to the anatomy and physiological systems of humans:

- **Skeletal system:** The skeletal system functions for support. Vertebrates have an endoskeleton, with muscles attached to bones. Skeletal proportions are controlled by area to volume relationships. Body size and shape is limited due to the forces of gravity. Surface area is increased to improve efficiency in all organ systems.

- **Muscular system:** Its function is movement. There are three types of muscle tissue. Skeletal muscle is for voluntary motion, and these muscles are attached to bones. Smooth muscle is involuntary motion, and it is found in organs and enables functions such as digestion and respiration. Cardiac muscle is a specialized type of smooth muscle.

- **Nervous system:** The neuron is the basic unit of the nervous system. It consists of an axon, which carries impulses away from the cell body; the dendrite, which carries impulses toward the cell body; and the cell body, which contains the nucleus. Synapses are spaces between neurons. Chemicals called neurotransmitters are found close to the synapse. The myelin sheath, composed of Schwann cells, covers the neurons and provides insulation.

- **Digestive system:** The function of the digestive system is to break down food and absorb it into the bloodstream, where it can be delivered to all cells of the body for use in cellular respiration. As animals evolved, digestive systems changed from simple absorption to systems with a separate mouth and anus, allowing the animal to become independent of a host.

- **Respiratory system:** This system functions in the gas exchange of oxygen (needed) and carbon dioxide (waste). It delivers oxygen to the bloodstream and picks up carbon dioxide for release out of the body. Simple animals diffuse gases from and to their environment. Gills allow aquatic animals to exchange gases in a fluid medium by removing dissolved oxygen from the water. Lungs maintain a fluid environment for gas exchange in terrestrial animals.

- **Circulatory system:** The function of the circulatory system is to carry oxygenated blood and nutrients to all cells of the body and return carbon dioxide waste to be expelled from the lungs. Animals evolved from an open system to a closed system with vessels leading to and from the heart.

- **Respiration:** This process takes in oxygen and gives off waste gases. Respiration without oxygen is called anaerobic respiration. Anaerobic respiration in animal cells is also called lactic acid fermentation. The end product is lactic acid.

Skill 5.8   **Identify and compare the predictable ways plants and animals change as they grow, develop, and age**

Gregor Mendel is recognized as the father of genetics. His work in the late 1800s is the basis of our knowledge of genetics. Although unaware of the presence of DNA or genes, Mendel realized there were factors (now known as **genes**) that were transferred from parents to their offspring. Mendel worked with pea plants, fertilizing them himself and keeping track of subsequent generations. His findings led to the Mendelian laws of genetics. Mendel found that two factors governed each trait, one from each parent. Traits or characteristics came in several forms, known as **alleles**. For example, the trait for flower color had both white alleles and purple alleles.

Mendel formed three laws:

Law of dominance: In a pair of alleles, one trait may cover up the allele of the other trait. Example: Brown eyes are dominant to blue eyes.

Law of segregation: Only one of the two possible alleles from each parent is passed on to the offspring. (During meiosis, the haploid number insures that half the sex cells get one allele, and half get the other.)

Law of independent assortment: Alleles sort independently of each other. (Many combinations are possible depending on which sperm ends up with which egg. Compare this to the many combinations of hands possible when dealing a deck of cards).

Punnet squares are used to show the possible ways that genes combine and indicate the probability of the occurrence of a certain genotype or phenotype. One parent's genes are put at the top of the box and the other parent's are put at the side of the box. Genes combine on the square just like numbers that are added in addition tables learned in elementary school. Below is an example of a **monohybrid cross**, which is a cross using only one trait—in this case, a trait labeled g.

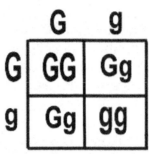

In a **dihybrid cross**, 16 gene combinations are possible, as each cross has two traits.

Key Terms

- **Dominant:** The stronger of the two traits. If a dominant gene is present, it is expressed as a capital letter.
- **Recessive:** The weaker of the two traits. For the recessive gene to be expressed, there must be two recessive genes present. It is expressed as a lowercase letter.
- **Homozygous:** Also known as purebred; having two of the same genes present. An organism may be homozygous dominant, with two dominant genes, or homozygous recessive, with two recessive genes.
- **Heterozygous:** Also known as hybrid; having one dominant gene and one recessive gene. The dominant gene is the one that is expressed.
- **Genotype:** The genes the organism has. Genes are represented with letters. AA, Bb, and tt are examples of genotypes.
- **Phenotype:** How the trait is expressed in an organism. Blue eyes, brown hair, and red flowers are examples of phenotypes.
- **Incomplete dominance:** Neither gene masks the other, so a new phenotype is formed. For example, the genes for red flowers and white flowers may have equal strength. A heterozygote (Rr) would have pink flowers. If a problem occurs with a third phenotype, incomplete dominance is occurring.
- **Codominance:** Genes may form new phenotypes. The ABO blood grouping is an example of codominance. A and B are of equal strength and O is recessive. Therefore, type A blood may have the genotypes of AA or AO, type B blood may have the genotypes of BB or BO, type AB

blood has the genotype A and B, and type O blood has two recessive O genes.

- **Linkage:** Genes that are found on the same chromosome usually appear together unless crossing over has occurred in meiosis (for example, blue eyes and blonde hair often show up together).
- **Lethal alleles:** Usually recessive due to the early death of the offspring. If a 2:1 ratio of alleles is found in offspring, a lethal gene combination is usually the reason. Some examples of lethal alleles include sickle cell anemia, Tay-Sachs disease, and cystic fibrosis. In these cases, the coding for an important protein is usually affected.
- **Inborn errors of metabolism:** The affected protein is an enzyme. Examples include PKU (phenylketonuria) and albinism.
- **Polygenic characters:** Many alleles code for a phenotype. There may be as many as 20 genes that code for skin color. This is why there is such a variety of skin tones. Another example is height. A couple of medium height may have very tall offspring.
- **Sex-linked traits:** The Y chromosome found only in males (XY) carries very little genetic information, whereas the X chromosome found in females (XX) carries very important information. Since men have no second X chromosome to cover up a recessive gene, the recessive trait is expressed more often in men. Women need the recessive gene on both X chromosomes to show the trait. Examples of sex-linked traits include hemophilia and colorblindness.
- **Sex-influenced traits:** Traits that are influenced by the sex hormones. Male pattern baldness is an example of a sex-influenced trait. Testosterone influences the expression of the gene. Men lose their hair mainly due to this trait.

Skill 5.9   Identify and compare processes of sexual and asexual reproduction in plants, animals, and microorganisms

REPRODUCTION

Sexual reproduction greatly increases diversity because of the many combinations possible through meiosis and fertilization. All organisms (except twins or clones) are genetically unique and represent a unique combination of genetic heritable variation.

Variation is generated by mutation and, in sexually reproducing species, sexual recombination. Mutations can be errors in replication or a spontaneous rearrangement of one or more segments of DNA, and ultimately mutations are responsible for all innovative heritable variation. Mutations contribute a minimal but constant amount of variation in a population. In sexually reproducing species, the unique recombination of existing alleles causes the majority of genetic difference among individuals. Genetic variability is caused by independent assortment during meiosis, random fertilization, and crossing over during meiosis.

Gametogenesis is the production of the sperm and egg cells. **Spermatogenesis** begins at puberty in the male. One spermatozoa produces four sperm. The sperm mature in the seminiferous tubules located in the testes. **Oogenesis**, the production of egg cells, is usually complete by the birth of a female. Egg cells are not released until menstruation begins at puberty. Meiosis (division of sex cells) forms one ovum with all the cytoplasm and three polar bodies, which are reabsorbed by the body. The ovum are stored in the ovaries and released each month from puberty to menopause.

Path of the Sperm

Sperm are stored in the seminiferous tubules in the testes, where they mature. Mature sperm are found in the epididymis, located on top of the testes. After ejaculation, the sperm travel up the vas deferens, where they mix with semen made in the prostate and seminal vesicles and travel out the urethra.

Path of the Egg

Eggs are stored in the ovaries. Ovulation releases an egg into the fallopian tubes, which are ciliated to move the egg along. Fertilization normally occurs in the fallopian tube. If pregnancy does not occur, the egg passes through the uterus and is expelled through the vagina. Levels of progesterone and estrogen stimulate menstruation. In the event of pregnancy, hormonal levels are affected by the implantation of a fertilized egg, so menstruation does not occur.

Pregnancy

If fertilization occurs, the zygote implants in about two to three days in the uterus. Implantation promotes secretion of human chorionic gonadotropin (HCG). This is the hormone detected in pregnancy tests. The HCG keeps the level of progesterone elevated to maintain the uterine lining to feed the developing embryo until the umbilical cord forms. Labor is initiated by oxytocin, which causes labor contractions and dilation of the cervix. Prolactin and oxytocin cause the production of milk.

CELL DIVISION

The purpose of cell division is to provide growth and repair in body (somatic) cells and to replenish or create sex cells for reproduction. There are two forms of cell division: **Mitosis** is the division of somatic cells and **meiosis** is the division of sex cells (eggs and sperm). The table below summarizes the major differences between the two processes.

MITOSIS

1. Division of somatic cells.
2. Two cells result from each division.
3. Chromosome number is identical to parent cells.
4. Division occurs for cell growth and repair.

MEIOSIS

1. Division of sex cells.
2. Four cells or polar bodies result from each division.
3. Chromosome number is half the number of parent cells.
4. Recombinations provide genetic diversity.

Key Terms

- **Gamete:** Sex cell or germ cell; eggs and sperm.
- **Chromatin:** Mass of DNA and associated proteins that condenses to form chromosomes during cell division.
- **Chromosomes:** Strands of coiled DNA and associated proteins. Carries genetic information in a linear sequence.
- **Homologues:** Chromosomes that contain the same information. They are of the same length and contain the same genes.
- **Diploid:** 2n number; diploid chromosomes are a pair of chromosomes (somatic cells).
- **Haploid:** 1n number; haploid chromosomes are half of a pair (sex cells).

COMMON LIFE CYCLES

Bacteria are commonly used in laboratories for research. Bacteria reproduce by binary fission. This asexual process is simply a division of the bacterium in half. All new organisms are exact clones of the parent. The obvious advantage of asexual reproduction is that it does not require a partner. This is a huge advantage for organisms that do not move around; not having to move around to reproduce allows organisms to conserve energy. Asexual reproduction also tends to be faster. However, as asexual reproduction produces only exact copies of the parent organism, it does not allow for genetic variation, which means that mutations, or weaker qualities, will always be passed on.

Butterflies actually go through four different stages of life, but they only look like butterflies in the final stage. In the first stage, the adult butterfly lays an egg. In the second stage, the egg hatches into a caterpillar or larva. The third stage is when the caterpillar forms the chrysalis or pupa. Finally, the chrysalis matures and the adult butterfly emerges.

Frogs also have multiple stages in their life cycle. Initially, an adult frog lays its eggs in the water (all amphibians require water for reproduction). In the second stage, tadpoles hatch from the eggs. The tadpoles swim in the water and use gills for breathing. Tadpoles have a tail that is used for locomotion, but they will grow legs as well. Somewhere between two and four months old, the tadpole is known as a froglet. You can recognize a froglet because the rim around its tail, which appears fish-like, has disappeared; its tail is shorter; and its four legs have grown to the extent that its rear legs are bent underneath it. The final stage of a frog's life is spent as an adult. Its tail has been entirely reabsorbed, it has a chubby frog-like appearance instead of the tadpole's fish-like appearance, and as a mature frog it can lay eggs.

| Skill 5.10 | Identify the variety of habitats within ecosystems and analyze how they meet the needs of the organisms that live there |

Ecology is the study of organisms, where they live, and their interactions with the environment. A **population** is a group of the same species in a specific area. A **community** is a group of populations residing in the same area. Communities that are ecologically similar in regards to temperature, rainfall, and the species that live there are called **biomes**. Specific biomes include the following:

- **Marine:** This biome covers 75 percent of the earth. It is organized by the depth of water. The *intertidal* zone is located from the tide line to the edge of the water. The *littoral* zone is found from the water's edge to the open sea. It includes coral reef habitats, and it is the most densely populated area of the marine biome. The open sea zone is divided into the *epipelagic* zone and the *pelagic* zone. The epipelagic zone receives more sunlight and has a larger number of species. The ocean floor is called the *benthic* zone. It is populated with bottom-feeders.

- **Tropical rain forest:** Here, temperature is fairly constant (25 degrees C) and rainfall exceeds 200 centimeters per year. Located around the equator, rain forests have abundant, diverse species of plants and animals.

- **Savanna:** The temperatures range from 0 to 25 degrees C depending on the location. Rainfall is from 90 to 150 centimeters per year. Plants include shrubs and grasses. The savanna is a transitional biome between the rain forest and the desert.

- **Desert:** Temperatures range from 10 to 38 degrees C in the desert. Rainfall is under 25 centimeters per year. Plant species include xerophytes and succulents. Lizards, snakes, and small mammals are common animals.

- **Temperate deciduous forest:** In this biome, temperatures range from –24 to 38 degrees C. Rainfall is 65 to 150 centimeters per year. Deciduous trees are common, as well as deer, bear, and squirrels.

- **Taiga:** Here, temperatures range from –24 to 22 degrees C. Rainfall is 35 to 40 centimeters per year. Taiga is located north and south of the equator, close to the poles. Plant life includes conifers and plants that can withstand harsh winters. Animals include weasels, mink, and moose.
- **Tundra:** Temperatures range from –28 to 15 degrees C in the tundra. Rainfall is limited, ranging from 10 to 15 centimeters per year. The tundra is located even further north and south than the taiga. Common plants include lichens and mosses. Animals include polar bears and musk ox.

- **Polar or permafrost:** This is where temperatures range from –40 to 0 degrees C. It rarely gets above freezing. Rainfall is below 10 centimeters per year. Most water is bound up as ice. Life is limited.

- **Succession** is an orderly process of replacing a community that has been damaged or has begun where no life previously existed. **Primary succession** occurs after a community has been totally wiped out by a natural disaster or in a place where life never existed before, as in a flooded area. **Secondary succession** takes place in communities that were once flourishing but were disturbed by some force, either human or natural, but not totally stripped. A **climax community** is a community that is established and flourishing.

Sample Test

DEVELOPMENTAL KNOWLEDGE

1. **Which of the following is a sign of child abuse? (Skill 1.1; Average)**

   A. Awkward social behavior around other children
   B. Bruises
   C. Withdrawn behavior
   D. All of the above

2. **If child abuse is suspected, what action should the teacher take? (Skill 1.1; Average)**

   A. Wait to see if the child talks about it again.
   B. Talk to your supervisor about your concerns.
   C. Call the child's parent.
   D. Talk to another teacher about your suspicions.

3. **A preschool teacher is concerned because the three-year-olds in her class do not play with one another. Each student plays without interacting with others in the class. What advice would you give her? (Skill 1.2; Rigorous)**

   A. Contact the parents immediately so they can talk to their doctors about medications that might help.
   B. Plan more activities that require interactions among the children.
   C. Tell the children that you expect them to share and play together. If they don't, then punish them.
   D. Don't worry. It is typical for young children engage in "parallel" activities, playing alongside their peers without directly interacting with one another.

4. **Which of the following is a true statement? (Skill 1.2; Rigorous)**

   A. Physical development does not influence social development.
   B. Social development does not influence physical development.
   C. Cognitive development does not influence social development.
   D. All domains of development (physical, social, and cognitive) are integrated and influence other domains.

5.   Which of the following is a true statement? (Skill 1.3; Rigorous)

   A.   Younger children tend to process information at a slower rate than older children (age eight and older).
   B.   Older children tend to process information at a slower rate than younger children (younger than age 8).
   C.   Children process information at the same rate as adults.
   D.   All children process information at exactly the same rate.

6.   A child exhibits the following symptoms: a lack of emotional responsiveness, indifference to physical contact, abnormal social play, and abnormal speech. What is the likely diagnosis for this child? (Skill 1.3; Average)

   A.   Separation anxiety
   B.   Mental retardation
   C.   Autism
   D.   Hypochondria

7.   Marcus is a first-grade boy of good developmental attainment. His learning progress is good for the first half of the year. He shows no indicators of emotional distress. After the holiday break, he returns much changed. He is quieter, sullen even, tending to play alone. He has moments of tearfulness, sometimes almost without cause. He avoids contact with adults as often as he can. Even play with his friends has become limited. He has episodes of wetting not seen before, and he often wants to sleep in school. What approach is appropriate for this sudden change in behavior? (Skill 1.4; Rigorous)

   A.   Give him some time to adjust. He's probably having a difficult time adjusting to school after the fun of the holiday break.
   B.   Report this change immediately to administration. Do not call the parents until administration decides a course of action.
   C.   Document his daily behavior carefully as soon as you notice such a change, then report to administration the next month or so in a meeting.
   D.   Make a courtesy call to the parents to let them know he is not acting like himself, being sure to tell them he is not making trouble for others.

8. **An effective teacher will recognize that: (Skill 1.5; Easy)**

   A. all students in the classroom can be taught all materials regardless of race, culture, or ethnicity.
   B. if one student is unable to participate in a lesson due to religious reasons, the lesson must be omitted for all students.
   C. a phone call to the caregivers of the student will help clarify the parts of a lesson in which a student might be able to participate
   D. none of the above

9. **Learning activities for young students (below age eight) should focus on short time frames because: (Skill 1.6; Average)**

   A. Younger children tend to process information at a slower rate than older children (age eight and older)
   B. Young children have long attention spans
   C. Young children can understand complex instructional activities
   D. Young children need to sit quietly and listen to learn

10. **Involving parents in the school setting should be done in the following way: (Skill 1.7; Easy)**

    A. Through inviting them into the classroom casually after school during dismissal time
    B. By ghosting school events like activity night, family BINGO, or a school carnival
    C. By holding one large celebration at the end of the school year
    D. Both A and C

11. **Researchers have shown that school involvement and connections with community institutions yield greater retention rates of students graduating and seeking higher education experiences. What is a current barrier to community involvement? (Skill 1.8; Rigorous)**

    A. The current disconnect and autonomy that has become commonplace in today's society
    B. The amount of gang activity in many communities
    C. The tough economic times we are facing
    D. None of the above

12. **Assigning a student an adult mentor is an effective tool for addressing student achievement because: (Skill 1.8; Average)**

    A. the mentor can reinforce learning through tutorial instruction
    B. it provides the student with an appropriate adult role model
    C. the mentor can help the student with the practical application of the lesson
    D. all of the above

13. **With state and federal educational funding becoming increasingly subject to legislative budget cuts, what can the school community provide to support the school? (Skill 1.8; Average)**

    A. Money to supplement teacher salaries
    B. Free notebooks, backpacks, and student supplies for low-income students who may have difficulty obtaining the basic supplies for school
    C. Advice on how to save money when running a school
    D. All of the above

14. **According to Piaget, when does the development of symbolic functioning and language take place? (Skill 2.1; Rigorous)**

    A. Concrete operational stage
    B. Formal operational stage
    C. Sensorimotor stage
    D. Preoperational stage

15. **According to Piaget, what is a child born with? (Skill 2.1; Rigorous)**

    A. The tendency to actively relate pieces of information acquired
    B. The ability to adapt
    C. Primary emotions
    D. Desire

16. **Effective curriculum models for early childhood programs should include which of the following? (Skill 2.2; Average)**

    A. Cognitive development
    B. Social development
    C. Both cognitive and social development
    D. None of the above

17. **Head Start programs were created in the early 1960s to provide: (Skill 2.2; Average)**

    A. a comprehensive curriculum model for preparation of low-income students for success in school communities
    B. a national curriculum that ensures that "no child is left behind"
    C. a parent involvement program in every school
    D. Prek-Kindergarten for every four-year-old

18. **It is important to make a report when abuse or neglect is suspected because: (Skill 2.3; Average)**

    A. failure to do so could result in revocation of certification and license
    B. failure to do so could result in a monetary fine
    C. both A and B
    D. none of the above

19. **IDEA sets policies that provide for inclusion of students with disabilities. What does *inclusion* mean? (Skill 2.3; Rigorous)**

    A. Inclusion is the name of the curriculum that must followed in special education classes.
    B. Inclusion is the right of students with disabilities to be placed in the regular classroom.
    C. Inclusion refers to the quality of instruction necessary for student academic success.
    D. Inclusion means that students with disabilities should always be placed in classes for gifted and talented students.

20. **Under IDEA, Congress provides safeguards for students against schools' actions, including the right to sue in court, and encourages states to develop hearing and mediation systems to resolve disputes. This is known as: (Skill 2.3; Rigorous)**

    A. due process
    B. mediation
    C. Safe Schools Initiative
    D. parent involvement

21. **Why should teachers view the Websites of professional organizations like the IRA? (Skill 2.4; Average)**

    A. To find new digital games for teaching children
    B. To chat with other early childhood educators
    C. To find quality strategies to improve early childhood education for students
    D. To post student work for parent viewing

22. **Which of the following organizations target improvement of education specifically for young children? (Skill 2.5; Rigorous)**

    A. SPCA, NCTM, and NAACP
    B. NAEYC, SECA, and ACEI
    C. NAACP, IRA, and NCTM
    D. None of the above

23. **You've received a job offer to teach Pre-Kindergarten, but you've never taught children this young. What professional organization might publish journal articles that would be useful to you? (Skill 2.5; Rigorous)**

    A. FCRR
    B. IRA
    C. NAEYC
    D. AERA

24. **When considering the comprehensive cost of educating students, what is a hidden cost that may not be often considered? (Skill 2.6; Rigorous)**

    A. The increase in the number of students for whom English is not a first language
    B. Federal mandates
    C. The cost of technology
    D. Teacher turnover rate

25. **What two things have contributed to a reduction in teaching and instructional time for young learners? (Skill 2.6; Rigorous)**

    A. Increased expectations for learning coupled with increasing numbers of teachers who are alternatively certified
    B. Increased early violence in communities coupled with classroom management issues
    C. Increased expectations for learning coupled with a decrease in parent involvement
    D. Increasing numbers of alternatively certified teachers coupled with a decrease in parent involvement

26. When students are able to share their daily experiences and understanding of their world in a safe and nurturing learning environment, they are able to: (Skill 2.7; Average)

   A. evaluate and redirect their own ethical issues that occur during the school day
   B. build character
   C. both A and B
   D. neither A nor B

27. What is one component of the instructional planning model that must be given careful evaluation? (Skill 3.1; Average)

   A. Students' prior knowledge and skills
   B. The script the teacher will use in instruction
   C. Future lesson plans
   D. Parent participation

28. When is utilization of instructional materials most effective? (Skill 3.1; Average)

   A. When the activities are sequenced
   B. When the materials are prepared ahead of time
   C. When the students choose the pages to work on
   D. When the students create the instructional materials

29. What is evaluation of the instructional activity based on? (Skill 3.1; Average)

   A. Student grades
   B. Teacher evaluation
   C. Student participation
   D. Specified criteria

30. What should a teacher do when students have not responded well to an instructional activity? (Skill 3.1; Rigorous)

   A. Reevaluation of learner needs
   B. Skill-building and analysis of outcomes
   C. Interaction with students and manipulation of subject matter
   D. Management techniques and levels of questioning

31. The teacher states, "We will work on the first page of vocabulary words. On the second page we will work on the structure and meaning of the words. We will go over these together and then you will write out the answers to the exercises on your own. I will be circulating to give help if needed." What is this an example of? (Skill 3.1; Rigorous)

A. Evaluation of instructional activity
B. Analysis of instructional activity
C. Identification of expected outcomes
D. Pacing of instructional activity

32. The teacher states that the lesson in which the students will be engaged will consist of a review of the material from the previous day, a demonstration of the scientific aspects of an electronic circuit, and small-group work setting up an electronic circuit. What has the teacher demonstrated? (Skill 3.2; Rigorous)

A. The importance of reviewing
B. Giving the general framework for the lesson to facilitate learning
C. Giving students the opportunity to leave if they are not interested in the lesson
D. Providing momentum for the lesson

33. Which of the following can directly relate to a student's learning? (Skill 3.3; Average)

A. Lighting
B. Noise levels
C. Room temperature
D. All of the above

34. Objectives should be: (Skill 3.4; Average)

A. adaptable to timelines and concise and to the point
B. clear and observable
C. both A and B
D. neither A nor B

35. As teachers select instructional materials, it is important that teachers remember: (Skill 3.6; Average)

A. it is unlawful for students to study from textbooks or materials that are brought from home
B. it is unlawful for students to study from textbooks or materials that are more than 10 years old
C. it is unlawful to require students to study from textbooks or materials other than those approved by the state Department of Education
D. none of the above

36. **Prior experiences influence the individual's cognitive style, or method of accepting, processing, and retaining information. According to Marshall Rosenberg, students can be categorized as: (Skill 3.6; Rigorous)**

   A. rigid-inhibited, undisciplined, acceptance-anxious, or creative
   B. hyperactive, well-behaved, disinterested, or cognitively delayed
   C. visual, auditory, kinesthetic, or multimodality learners
   D. none of the above

37. **Grouping flexibly allows teachers to:**

   A. utilize various levels of differentiating learning when it is needed
   B. have a permanent way to group the students right at the beginning of the year
   C. have rigorous lesson plans
   D. use fewer resources

38. **When teachers plan lessons around broad themes with which students can identify, such as "The Environment," this is known as: (Skill 3.8; Average)**

   A. environmental curriculum
   B. integrated curriculum
   C. practical curriculum
   D. child-centered curriculum

39. **A child learns the following skills from playing: (Skill 3.9; Easy)**

   A. Basic values and fine motor skills
   B. How to compete in today's world
   C. How to boss others around
   D. How to read and do math

40. **The teacher's goal should be: (Skill 3.10; Easy)**

   A. to build rapport with his or her students
   B. to be best friends with each student
   C. to be consistently strict and unwelcoming so students understand who is in charge
   D. none of the above

41. **Once a teaching method has been established, it: (Skill: 3.11; Average)**

   A. should be used for at least the next three years
   B. should be used for a month or two and then changed
   C. must be changed when data shows another method is more effective
   D. can be changed when the teacher feels like changing it according to his or her current lesson objectives

42. **An effective teacher will: (Skill 4.1; Average)**

    A. never introduce political topics to young learners due to the topics being too difficult and controversial
    B. always introduce political topics in the classroom and share his or her voting choices
    C. consider introducing political topics, but consider both parent and student needs first
    D. help students always avoid political topics

43. **To enhance their students' effective listening skills, teachers can encourage which of the following strategies? (Skill 4.2; Average)**

    A. Associate
    B. Visualize
    C. Repeat
    D. All of the above

44. **When children learn more complex motor patterns including running, climbing, and jumping, they are said to be in the _____ stage of motor development. (Skill 4.3; Average)**

    A. A. first
    B. B. second
    C. C. third
    D. D. fourth

45. **Which style of teaching physical skills involves the entire group of students taking part in the same task regardless of individual skill level? (Skill 4.4; Rigorous)**

    A. Command style
    B. Practice style
    C. Reciprocal style
    D. Inclusion style

46. **In which type of learning situation is learned helplessness likely to have the greatest impact on students? (Skill 4.4; Rigorous)**

    A. One in which students lack the motivation to succeed
    B. One in which students have little control over how well they perform
    C. One in which competition among students is encouraged
    D. One in which rewards are in place to motivate students

47. **What should be the first thing taught when introducing dance? (Skill 4.5; Easy)**

    A. Rhythm
    B. Feelings
    C. Empathy
    D. Texture

48. When discussing color, the intensity of a color refers to the color's _____. (Skill 4.5; Average)

    A. strength
    B. value
    C. lightness or darkness
    D. associated emotions

49. What is a benefit of distance learning? (Skills 4.6, 4.7; Average)

    A. Students do not have to deal with social issues in the school setting.
    B. Teachers do not have to make any lesson plans.
    C. Administrators can employ fewer teachers because there are fewer students.
    D. Students feel more comfortable and may communicate more freely with teachers than they would otherwise.

50. What are the most powerful factors influencing students' academic focus and success? (Skill 5.1; Average)

    A. Teachers' knowledge and training
    B. Teachers' preparation and planning
    C. Students' attitudes and perceptions
    D. Students' interests and goals

51. The three areas of differentiated instruction are content, process, and _____. (Skill 5.1; Easy)

    A. application
    B. product
    C. assessment
    D. structure

52. Which strategy for adapting the curriculum would be most useful for the purpose of reducing the effect of a student's learning disability on completing an assessment task? (Skill 5.1; Rigorous)

    A. Differentiated instruction
    B. Alternative assessments
    C. Testing modifications
    D. Total physical response

53. Which of the following characteristics are considerations when identifying children with diverse needs? (Skill 5.2; Easy)

    A. Ethnicity
    B. Socioeconomic status
    C. Physical disability
    D. All of the above

54. What is it most important for a teacher to consider when planning homework assignments? (Skill 5.2; Average)

    A. Access to technology
    B. Ethnicity
    C. Language difficulties
    D. Gender

55. When dealing with a difficult family, what is it most important for a teacher to display? (Skill 5.3; Average)

A. Strength
B. Excitement
C. Authority
D. Patience

56. In regards to dealing with parents, which term best describes the role that teachers should play in the education of children? (Skill 5.3; Average)

A. Friends
B. Leaders
C. Partners
D. Managers

57. How is a student who has extreme trouble spelling most likely to be identified? (Skill 5.4; Average)

A. Dyslexic
B. Gifted
C. Autistic
D. Hyperactive

58. What should interventions for exceptional students be focused on? (Skill 5.5; Rigorous)

A. Caring
B. Curing
C. Academics
D. Both caring and curing

59. What type of problems are children who have been abandoned or neglected most likely to have? (Skill 5.6; Average)

A. Behavioral problems
B. Medical problems
C. Social problems
D. Physical problems

60. If a school nurse is not available, who should assume responsibility for the administration of medication? (Skill 5.7; Average)

A. A qualified teacher
B. The parent or guardian of the student
C. The prescriber of the medication
D. The principal of the school

61. Professionals in a school setting can best meet student needs by: (Skill 5.8; Easy)

A. working individually
B. collaborating
C. checking in on the classroom teacher to see if he or she needs any help
D. keeping the student after school for tutoring

62. **Which type of test is most likely to be a true indication of the content knowledge of ESOL students? (Skill 5.9; Average)**

    A. Oral test
    B. Written test
    C. Timed test
    D. Practical test

63. **What is the term for a structured, infrequent measure of learner achievement that involves the use of a test and an exam? (Skill 6.1; Average)**

    A. Informal continuous assessment
    B. Observation
    C. Formal continuous assessment
    D. Formal assessment

64. **Which of the following best explains why teachers should carefully consider observations recorded by other teachers? (Skill 6.2; Average)**

    A. Teachers may be manipulative.
    B. Teachers may be biased.
    C. Teachers may be dishonest.
    D. Teachers may be indifferent.

65. **Why are student records often a good indicator of student progress? (Skill 6.2; Easy)**

    A. They contain information from several people.
    B. They show changes over time.
    C. They contain information gathered over a period of time.
    D. All of the above

66. **Which of the following statements would not be appropriate in an anecdotal record about a student? (Skill 6.2; Rigorous)**

    A. Jasmine completed only half of the homework assigned.
    B. Jasmine contributed only slightly to class discussions.
    C. Jasmine was not interested in learning the material.
    D. Jasmine did not volunteer to answer any questions.

67. **Which type of assessment is most likely to be used to assess student interest and motivation? (Skill 6.3; Average)**

    A. Rating scales
    B. Questioning
    C. Portfolio assessment
    D. Anecdotal records

68. **What does a student's portfolio typically contain? (Skill 6.3; Easy)**

   A. Results of standardized tests
   B. Competed self-appraisal checklists
   C. Samples of work
   D. Results of all assessment activities completed to date

69. **What does portfolio assessment typically provide? (Skill 8.4; Average)**

   A. Opportunities for teachers to assess students' progress
   B. Opportunities for students to reflect on their own progress
   C. Opportunities for students to consider their approaches to problem solving
   D. All of the above

70. **Which of the following is portfolio assessment most likely to encourage? (Skill 6.4; Average)**

   A. Self-esteem
   B. Self-directed learning
   C. Conflict management skills
   D. Time management skills

71. **When addressing issues of concern in a parent-teacher conference, what is it best to focus on? (Skill 6.5; Easy)**

   A. Likely explanations
   B. Personal opinions
   C. Statements from other students
   D. Observable behaviors

72. **Which statement would it be most appropriate to make when speaking to parents about an issue of concern? (Skill 6.5; Rigorous)**

   A. Sandra is often distracted easily.
   B. Sandra irritates other students.
   C. Sandra is a frustrating student.
   D. While completing the exam, Sandra started conversations with other students.

73. **When sending a follow-up note to parents following a conference, which of the following is it best to include? (Skill 6.5; Average)**

   A. Further details on the student's strengths and weaknesses
   B. A summary of the agreed plan of action
   C. A description of how the student has progressed since the conference
   D. Praise for the parents on becoming involved in their child's education

74. **When is it appropriate for a teacher to talk to parents about another student's performance? (Skill 6.5; Rigorous)**

    A. When the parents of the student have been invited to participate
    B. When the student is having a negative impact on other students
    C. When the student is performing well and only positive information will be communicated
    D. When permission to discuss the student has been given by the principal

75. **Why is repetition an important part of a child's play? (Skill 6.6; Rigorous)**

    A. It allows the child to master the skill and then move into creativity.
    B. It allows the child to stress the caregiver who is bored with playing the same thing over and over.
    C. It is a creative outlet for the child.
    D. None of the above

76. **Which type of assessments would be used to determine if students are meeting national and state learning standards? (Skill 6.7; Average)**

    A. Norm-referenced assessments
    B. Criterion-referenced assessments
    C. Performance-based assessments
    D. Observation-based assessments

77. **RTI stands for: (Skill 6.8; Easy)**

    A. Rigorous Testing Interventions
    B. Reading Theme Interactions
    C. Readiness Thinking Initiative
    D. Response to Intervention

78. **When should procedures that use social humiliation be used as behavior management techniques? (Skill 7.1; Average)**

    A. Never
    B. Only in severe situations
    C. Only when the student is a danger to himself or herself or others
    D. Only when all other methods have been ineffective

79. **Which of the following is NOT a recommended token for use in a token economy? (Skill 7.1; Easy)**

    A. Stamps
    B. Stickers
    C. Point cards
    D. Poker chips

80. Which type of social skill assessment involves students ranking their classmates on set criteria? (Skill 7.2; Average)

    A. Direct observation
    B. Paired-comparison
    C. Peer nomination
    D. Peer rating

81. A student is punished by taking five stars from his tally in the token economy. What type of punishment is this an example of? (Skill 7.2; Average)

    A. Time-out
    B. Suspension
    C. Overcorrection
    D. Response cost

82. Consistency is important when managing the behavior of adolescents because it reduces _____. (Skill 7.3; Average)

    A. emotional responses
    B. unpredictable reactions
    C. consequences
    D. power struggles

83. Which type of student is seclusion time-out least likely to be effective with? (Skill 7.3; Average)

    A. Outgoing
    B. Intelligent
    C. Shy
    D. Aggressive

84. What is a common source of interpersonal conflict for students? (Skill 7.4; Average)

    A. Disagreements over values or decisions
    B. Family relationships
    C. Competition
    D. All of the above

85. Which of the following is NOT a common character development trait? (Skill 7.5; Easy)

    A. Self-discipline
    B. Respect
    C. Patriotism
    D. Decision making

86. Which classroom activity would be most useful for teaching character development? (Skill 7.5; Average)

    A. Exam
    B. Discussion
    C. Project
    D. Quiz

87. Which of the following is a common sign that a student is experiencing stress? (Skill 7.6; Easy)

    A. Behavioral problems
    B. Episodes of sadness
    C. Aggressive behavior
    D. All of the above

88. **What should a teacher do first when he or she notices that a student appears stressed? (Skill 7.6; Average)**

A. Ask the student what the problem is.
B. Praise the student.
C. Hold a class discussion.
D. Inform the parents.

LANGUAGE ARTS AND READING

1. Which of the following explains a significant difference between phonics and phonemic awareness? (Skill 1.1; Average)

    A. Phonics involves print; phonemic awareness involves language.
    B. Phonics is more difficult than phonemic awareness.
    C. Phonics involves sounds; phonemic awareness involves letters.
    D. Phonics is the application of sounds to print; phonemic awareness is oral.

2. An early warning sign of emergent literacy difficulties is: (Skill 1.2; Average)

    A. a student's failure to identify the letters in his or her own name
    B. a student's inability to count to 10
    C. a student's trouble singing the ABC song correctly
    D. a student's difficulty tying his or her shoes

3. Young children often spell words they write according to the way the letters sound. This process, which may be used as an activity to draw upon background knowledge, is called: (Skill 1.3; Rigorous)

    A. spelling lists
    B. incorrect spelling
    C. developmental spelling
    D. invented spelling

4. Which of the following is the most commonly practiced strategy to encourage literacy growth? (Skill 1.4; Average)

    A. Storybook reading
    B. Teaching phonics
    C. Teaching fluency
    D. Letter identification

5. Instructional methods of grouping should be: (Skill 1.5; Average)

    A. based on ability solely
    B. used for small groups of students who need more instruction on an objective
    C. used to introduce new materials and strategies to the whole class
    D. B and C

6. A print-rich environment would have which of the following components? (Skill 1.6; Easy)

A. A word wall
B. Classroom libraries
C. Labels for objects in the room
D. All of the above

7. A delegation from the United Kingdom has come to the United States, and since they are considering adapting the balanced literacy approach, they are very interested in seeing the small group demonstrated. Mr. Adams, the principal, knows that he should bring them into Greg's room when Greg is doing which activity? (Skill 1.7; Rigorous)

A. A mini lesson
B. A conference with individual students
C. A time when the children are divided into small and independent study groups
D. A read-aloud

8. Environmental print is available in all of the following places except: (Skill 1.8; Easy)

A. within a newspaper
B. on the page of a library book
C. on a supermarket circular
D. in a commercial flyer

9. Which of the following are effective methods and strategies to integrate language arts into the content areas of the curriculum? (Skill 1.9; Rigorous)

A. Introduce content-area topics by reading from a picture book about the topic.
B. Use oral reports.
C. Use cartoons in writing assignments.
D. All of the above

10. Monthly book clubs, book fairs, read-a-thons, and the class library are all examples of: (Skill 1.10; Rigorous)

A. ways to foster reading outside class
B. ways to raise money for the school library
C. ways to raise money for the classroom library
D. none of the above

11. Which of the following varieties of text are appropriate for building language skills and concept development? (Skill 2.1; Easy)

A. Concept books
B. Predictable texts or pattern books
C. Board books
D. All of the above

12. Historical fiction, mythology, folklore, realistic fiction, mystery, and legends are: (Skill 2.2; Easy)

A. reading styles
B. young adult topics
C. genres
D. booklists

13. Which of the following activities does NOT help show children what people with different viewpoints and cultural perspectives have in common? (Skill 2.3; Average)

A. Making a graph showing the sizes of families represented in the classroom
B. Making classroom books about My Family after reading a book such as Rebecca Doltich's *A Family Like Yours*
C. Providing children with play dough and a variety of powdered colors, along with a mirror, then allowing them to match their skin colors
D. Using English in all signs, labels, posters, and environmental print so that students all use one language

14. When applying the strategy of analyzing the narrator's point of view as part of literary analysis, it is important to consider: (Skill 2.4; Rigorous)

A. whether the narrator is inside or outside the story
B. whether the narrator is one of the characters
C. whether the narrator can "see" into anyone else's mind
D. all of the above

15. One of the many ways in which children can be encouraged to respond to literature and informational texts is: (Skill 2.5; Average)

A. dramatizing a historical document or song
B. retelling the story orally
C. making up a prequel or sequel
D. all of the above

16. The use of newspapers in the classroom aids children in all the specific uses and purposes for multiple representations of information except which of the following? (Skill 2.6; Rigorous)

A. Chronology, such as a calendar of events for the week
B. Timelines
C. Comparison/contrast news writings
D. Cause/effort diagramming

17. **Making inferences from the text means that the reader: (Skill 2.7; Average)**

 A. is making informed judgments based on available evidence
 B. is making a guess based on prior experiences
 C. is making a guess based on what he or she would like to be true of the text
 D. all of the above

18. **The five types of expository texts (also called text structures) include all but which of the following? (Skill 2.8; Rigorous)**

 A. Description text
 B. Collection text
 C. Call and response text
 D. Comparison text

19. **Teaching students how to interpret _____ involves evaluating a text's headings, subheadings, bolded words, and side notes. (Skill 2.9; Rigorous)**

 A. graphic organizers
 B. text features
 C. textual marking
 D. summaries

20. **Which of the following is NOT one of the four basic features of the alphabetic principle? (Skill 3.1; Rigorous)**

 A. Students must be able to hear the separate sounds in spoken words.
 B. Students must be able to blend separate sounds together to make words.
 C. Teachers must use a systematic, effective program to teach children to decode.
 D. The teaching of the alphabetic principle usually begins in Grade 1.

21. **When students begin to master prosody, their reading aloud sounds more like _____. (Skill 3.2; Rigorous)**

 A. natural speech
 B. a performance
 C. reciting a poem
 D. correct word identification

22. **The following is an example of an explicit context clue for the word *jovial*. (Skill 3.3; Average)**

 A. I feel jovial.
 B. A jovial person is good-humored.
 C. Santa Claus is a jovial character.
 D. Dad was is a jovial mood.

23. **A topic sentence is usually: (Skill 3.4; Easy)**

    A. the first sentence in a paragraph
    B. more general than the other sentences in a paragraph
    C. supported by details in sentences that follow it
    D. all of the above

24. **Teaching students how to interpret _____ involves evaluating a text's headings, subheadings, bolded words, and side notes. (Skill 3.5; Average)**

    A. text structure
    B. graphic organizers
    C. textual marking
    D. summaries

25. **To find out what students already know about a topic they are about to read, the teacher should help them: (Skill 3.6; Average)**

    A. question the text
    B. discuss the illustrations
    C. activate their prior knowledge
    D. read the text critically

26. **Which of the following does NOT support reading fluency for beginning readers? (Skill 3.7; Average)**

    A. Listening to teachers read aloud
    B. Reading from frustration-level material
    C. Rereading familiar stories
    D. Shared and choral reading

27. **For Pre-K–Grade 3 students, reading nonfiction is a challenge because: (Skill 3.8; Easy)**

    A. they have inadequate background knowledge
    B. graphic aids and organizers are unfamiliar to them
    C. they need to be taught to take notes
    D. all of the above

28. **In the _____ stage of writing, students write in scribbles and can assign meaning to the markings. (Skill 4.1; Rigorous)**

    A. role-play
    B. experimental
    C. early
    D. conventional

29. **When students know that letters stand for a message, they are said to be in the _____ stage of spelling. (Skill 4.2; Rigorous)**

    A. non-phonemic
    B. pre-phonemic
    C. early phonemic
    D. letter-name

30. **When students correct misspellings and check punctuation, they are: (Skill 4.3; Average)**

    A. revising
    B. drafting
    C. proofreading
    D. prewriting

31. Most content area texts are written in the _____ mode. (Skill 4.4; Average)

   A. narrative
   B. persuasive
   C. descriptive
   D. expository

32. Which of the following describes a narrative writing project? (Skill 4.5; Easy)

   A. Tell about what happened on a family outing this summer.
   B. Compare two books by your favorite author.
   C. Create an invitation to a class art show.
   D. Describe the most delicious meal you've ever had.

33. Adding the transition words *of course* to their writing during the revision and editing stage will help students to: (Skill 4.6; Rigorous)

   A. contrast similar things
   B. highlight an important idea
   C. show what causes something to happen
   D. indicate a time sequence

34. A good discussion about a text does NOT require: (Skill 4.7; Average)

   A. having a Group Artist
   B. listening carefully to others
   C. following group discussion rules
   D. stimulating ideas

35. What best describes the key element in student presentations? (Skill 4.8; Rigorous)

   A. Visual aids
   B. Auditory enhancements
   C. Multimedia
   D. Computer-based

36. The sentence *Many teachers have been using a balanced literacy approach over the last decade and a half* is written in the _____ tense. (Skill 4.9; Rigorous)

   A. present
   B. present perfect
   C. future
   D. past perfect

37. A shopping list is an example of: (Skill 4.10; Easy)

   A. informal oral language
   B. formal oral language
   C. formal written language
   D. informal written language

38. What is one of the main advantages of portfolio assessment for students? (Skill 5.1; Average)

   A. It promotes creativity.
   B. It generates opportunities to use diverse skills.
   C. It encourages students to reflect on their own work.
   D. It develops communication skills.

39. **It may be said of norm-referenced tests that they: (Skill 5.2; Average)**

    A.   give information only about the local sample's results

    B.   provide information about how the local test-takers did compared to a representative sampling of national test-takers

    C.   make no comparisons to national test-takers

    D.   D) none of the above

MATHEMATICS

1. **Which is NOT a behavior demonstrating concrete understanding of mathematics? (Skill 1.1; Average)**

   A. Representing an unknown quantity with a variable
   B. Sorting objects into equally sized groups
   C. Giving one pencil to each student in the class
   D. Counting the number of books on each shelf

2. **Which of the following is NOT the most effective math teaching strategy? (Skill 1.1; Rigorous)**

   A. To be clear about instructional goals (topics)
   B. To progress experiences and understanding from the concrete to the abstract stage
   C. To communicate to students what is expected of them and why
   D. To keep math separate from other subject areas

3. **Which of the following is NOT a basic assumption of the criteria for teaching problem solving in mathematics? (Skill 1.2; Rigorous)**

   A. A teacher can expect students to approach problems with varied strategies
   B. Problem solving can be applied to subject areas other than math
   A. Students can help one another investigate possible problem-solving strategies
   B. Problem solving is always a uniform, predictable process

4. **Which of the following classroom experiences demonstrates a meaningful way to show math integrated with another subject area? (Skill 1.3; Easy)**

   A. Reorganizing the day's schedule so that math problems are worked during what is normally language arts time
   B. Giving students extra time to complete their unfinished seatwork from any subject
   C. Teaching a math lesson outside
   D. Having students read a short story and record how many times they come across a given set of sight words, then working with the class to construct a bar graph representing the data

5. In the fall, the kindergarten students interviewed their classmates about how students arrive at school: walking, bus, or car. Then they made a pictograph of the results. This math activity is appropriate for young children because: (Skill 1.4; Average)

    A. it shows them how math is used in their own lives
    B. it gives them a chance to participate directly in the lesson
    C. it provides the opportunity to quantify results and compare values
    D. all of the above

6. Why are manipulatives, models, and technology used by math teachers? (Skill 1.5; Average)

    A. To promote interest
    B. To address diverse learning needs
    C. To give hands-on math experience
    D. All of the above

7. Which of the following best promotes understanding of math operations? (Skill 1.6; Rigorous)

    A. The teacher promoting a single best solution
    B. Students verbalizing their reasoning and solutions to problems
    C. Speed tests
    D. Providing solutions to textbook tests

8. Alternative assessment in math may include: (Skill 1.7; Easy)

    A. student explanation of reasoning behind the answer
    B. analysis of data
    C. multimedia
    D. all of the above

9. Open-ended questions, portfolios, and writing activities can: (Skill 1.7; Rigorous)

    A. only be used in early childhood assessment
    B. be used as assessment of mathematical skill and knowledge
    C. only be used for language arts assessment
    D. none of the above

10. **What is NOT one of the advantages of collaborative or small-group learning? (Skill 1.8; Average)**

A. Students who work together in groups or teams develop their skills in organizing, leadership, research, communication, and problem solving.

B. Working in teams can help students overcome anxiety in distance learning courses and contribute a sense of community and belonging for the students.

C. Students working in a small group have more opportunities to be directly involved with concepts in the lesson than when the same information is taught to a large group.

D. Teachers reduce their workloads and the amount of time spent on helping students and planning lessons.

11. **When introducing students to a new math topic, a teacher should: (Skill 1.9; Average)**

A. show students the hardest problems first, so they know what to expect

B. tell the class that some of the students may not understand the material as well as others

C. save the math lesson until the end of the school day.

D. provide opportunities for students to investigate and explore the new material in small groups and individually

12. **What number comes next in this pattern? (Skill 2.1; Easy)**

3, 8, 13, 18, ____

A. 21
B. 26
C. 23
D. 5

13. Students in a kindergarten class are placing colored cards in the following order: red-yellow-red-yellow. What is the overall importance of this type of activity? (Skill 2.1; Rigorous)

A. The students are learning a beautiful pattern for art class.
B. The students are practicing patterns, which will help them build a foundation for algebraic thinking.
C. The students are playing a sorting game to see which color has more.
D. The students are practicing counting sets of two.

14. Students in a kindergarten class are curious about which toy is heavier: a plastic doll or a metal truck. They use a balance and wooden cubes to determine their answer. The toy that requires more cubes to hold the balance even will be the heavier toy. Which math principles does this activity demonstrate? (Skill 2.2; Rigorous)

A. Subtraction, meaningful counting
B. Problem solving, number sense
C. Addition, problem solving
D. Problem solving, subtraction

15. Which expression best characterizes the shaded area in the graph below? (Skill 2.2; Rigorous)

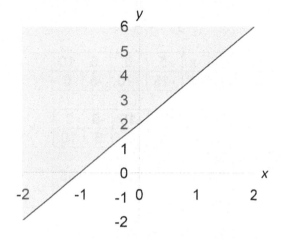

A. $y \le -x + 2$
B. $y \ge 2x + 2$
C. $y = 2x + 2$
D. $y \ge 2x - 1$

16. Which table(s) represent solutions of the following equation?
(Skill 2.3; Average)

$$y = x - 10$$

I

x	-5	0	5	10
y	-15	-10	-5	0

II

x	-15	-10	-5	0
y	-5	0	5	10

III

x	20	25	30	35
y	10	15	20	25

A. I
B. II
C. II and III
D. I and III

17. If the operation of a function machine is described by the phrase "increases inputs by 8," which variable equation below best represents the function? (Skill 2.3; Rigorous)

A. $y = 8x$
B. $y = 8$
C. $y = x + 8$
D. $y + x = 8$

18. A teacher knows that a burning candle will lose 1 inch in height every hour. The original height of the candle is 10 inches. After letting the candle burn for 4 hours, the teacher wants students to predict how long it would take the candle to burn down to a height of 2 inches. What should students do to analyze the candle's behavior? (Skill 2.4; Rigorous)

A. Write down the height of the candle at the beginning of the day and its height after recess.
B. Make a table recording the candle's height at each hour mark.
C. Draw a picture of the candle when it is first lit.
D. Compare the height of the candle to their own height.

19. A teacher shows the class the following graph comparing the height of a person to the span of the person's arms.

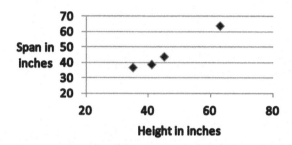

Height in inches

What could students do next to learn more about the pattern of the data? (Skill 2.4; Rigorous)

A. Draw the best fit line through the points.
B. Measure one another and add their data to the graph.
C. Record the data in a table.
D. All of the above

20. What is the main purpose of having kindergarten students count by twos? (Skill 3.1; Rigorous)

A. To hear a rhythm
B. To recognize patterns in numbers
C. To practice addition
D. To become familiar with equations

21. Using a number line is an appropriate strategy to introduce which of the following?

I. Skip counting
II. Counting backward
III. Finding doubles

(Skill 3.1; Easy)

A. I and II
B. I and III
C. II and III
D. I, II, and III

22. Which of the following skills would a student develop first? (Skill 3.2; Average)

A. Understanding place value
B. Recognizing number patterns
C. Counting objects
D. Solving number problems

23. A Pre-K student is distributing napkins for snack. He passes out 15 napkins, which is not enough for the 18 students. After checking how many students still need napkins, he determines that they need three more. Which math principles are demonstrated in this activity? (Skill 3.2; Rigorous)

A. Addition, rote counting
B. Rote counting, one-to-one correspondence
C. One-to-one correspondence, pre-subtraction skills
D. Pre-subtraction skills, rote counting

24. Look at this number: 4,087,361. What number represents the ten-thousandths place? (Skill 3.3; Easy)

   A. 4
   B. 6
   C. 0
   D. 8

25. If students can use place value blocks to represent the quantity 16 as "16 ones" as well as "1 ten and 6 ones," they are demonstrating an understanding of: (Skill 3.3; Average)

   A. doubles
   B. function machines
   C. the distributive property
   D. place value

26. Which of the following is NOT true about multiplication? (Skill 3.4; Easy)

   A. Multiplication is only used in algebra.
   B. Multiplication represents repeated addition.
   C. Multiplication is commutative and associative.
   D. Multiplication can be modeled with area diagrams.

27. Which of the following is an example of the additive identity? (Skill 3.4; Average)

   A. $a(b + c) = ab + bc$
   B. $a + 0 = a$
   C. $(a + b) + c = a + (b + c)$
   D. $a + b = b + a$

28. Which of the following problems would be a good example to use to explain the idea of "doubles plus one" to students? (Skill 3.4; Rigorous)

   A. $2 + 1 = 3$
   B. $5 + 6 = 11$
   C. $1 + 1 = 2$
   D. $22 - 11 = 11$

29. The second-grade class has 14 boys and 12 girls. How many more boys are in the class? (Skill 3.5; Easy)

   A. 26 more boys
   B. 2 more boys
   C. 14 more boys
   D. 12 more boys

30. Students are asked to use numbers and operations to represent the following: *If a teacher needs to give each of her 20 students a pencil, and already has 15 pencils in her hand, how many more pencils will she need?* Some students respond with $20 - 15 = 5$, while others propose $p + 15 = 20$. Comparing these problem-solving choices shows students that: (Skill 3.5; Rigorous)

   A. sometimes a problem can be solved in more than one way
   B. addition and subtraction are inverse operations
   C. a letter can stand in place of an unknown number when solving a problem
   D. all of the above

31. First-grade students are arranging four small squares of identical size to form a larger square. Each small square represents what part of the larger square? (Skill 3.6; Average)

    A. One half
    B. One whole
    C. One fourth
    D. One fifth

32. A teacher gives each student a copy of a number line, labeled with the whole numbers. Students are then directed to take a red crayon and put a mark between each whole number on the number line. Which set of numbers are they adding to the number line? (Skill 3.6; Rigorous)

    A. $\left\{\frac{1}{2}, \frac{1}{3}, \frac{1}{4}, \frac{1}{5}, \dots\right\}$
    B. $\left\{\frac{1}{2}, 1\frac{1}{2}, 2\frac{1}{2}, 3\frac{1}{2}, \dots\right\}$
    C. The set of negative integers
    D. The set of irrational numbers

33. Which statement is FALSE? (Skill 3.7; Rigorous)

    A. $\frac{1}{3} < 1$

    B. $\frac{1}{3} > \frac{1}{8}$

    C. $\frac{1}{3} < \frac{1}{8}$

    D. $\frac{1}{3} < \frac{2}{3}$

34. The model above can be used to show students that: (Skill 3.8; Average)

    A. $\frac{2}{4} = \frac{1}{2}$

    B. $2 = 1$

    C. $\frac{1}{2} = 0.5$

    D. all boxes should be shaded in

35. What is the area of a square whose side is 13 feet long? (Skill 4.1; Rigorous)

    A. 169 feet
    B. 169 square feet
    C. 52 feet
    D. 52 square feet

36. What measure could be used to report the distance traveled in walking around a track? (Skill 4.1; Easy)

    A. Degrees
    B. Square meters
    C. Kilometers
    D. Cubic feet

37. **Third-grade students are recording the length of the hallway. Which unit of measure would be used? (Skill 4.1; Average)**

    A. Inches
    B. Centimeters
    C. Yards
    D. Miles

38. **The mass of a cookie is closest to: (Skill 4.1; Average)**

    A. 500 grams
    B. 0.5 grams
    C. 15 grams
    D. 1.5 grams

39. **A teacher wants students to measure certain items in the school and calculate their perimeter. Which item below should NOT be included in the list of items to be measured? (Skill 4.1; Rigorous)**

    A. The rectangular classroom carpet
    B. The top of the teacher's desk
    C. The classroom door
    D. The flagpole in front of the school

40. **A first-grade class is learning how to count money. A good way to create a concrete learning experience for students is to: (Skill 4.2; Average)**

    A. give each student a debit card
    B. give students an assortment of coins to sort and count
    C. show students different kinds of wallets
    D. ask students to convert between different values of currency

41. **Which type of graphs would best be used to represent the number of students who like red, green, or yellow best? (Skill 4.3; Average)**

    A. A bar graph or pictograph
    B. A pictograph or line graph
    C. A stem-and-leaf plot or bar graph
    D. A line graph or stem-and-leaf plot

42. The following chart shows the yearly average number of international tourists visiting Palm Beach for 1990–1994. How many more international tourists visited Palm Beach in 1994 than in 1991? (Skill 4.4; Average)

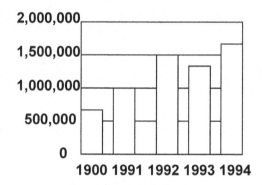

1900 1991 1992 1993 1994

A. 100,000
B. 600,000
C. 1,600,000
D. 8,000,000

43. All of the following are measurements of obtuse angles EXCEPT: (Skill 5.1; Easy)

A. 110 degrees
B. 90 degrees
C. 135 degrees
D. 91 degrees

44. Which angle would measure less than 90 degrees? (Skill 5.1; Easy)

A. Acute
B. Obtuse
C. Right
D. Straight

45. A "shape set" in a preschool classroom contains an assortment of squares, triangles, rectangles, and circles in various sizes and colors. Which of the student activities listed below would represent an appropriate math learning experience? (Skill 5.2; Rigorous)

A. Arranging the pieces in a repeating pattern
B. Sorting the pieces in the set by shape
C. Using the set's pieces to make a model of a real-life object (such as a house, tree, or ice cream cone)
D. All of the above

46. Where can a teacher expect students to find items representing the shape of a rectangle? (Skill 5.2; Average)

A. In the classroom
B. In their room at home
C. In a picture book
D. All of the above

47. Which letter does NOT demonstrate symmetry? (Skill 5.3; Average)

A. T
B. A
C. O
D. F

48. Kindergarten students are doing a butterfly art project. They fold paper in half. On one half, they paint a design. Then they fold the paper closed and reopen it. The resulting picture is a butterfly with matching halves. What math principle does this demonstrate? (Skill 5.3; Average)

    A. Slide
    B. Rotate
    C. Symmetry
    D. Transformation

49. Using scissors to cut a piece of paper represents which of the following spatial concepts? (Skill 5.4; Rigorous)

    A. An angle intersecting a plane
    B. A point above a line
    C. A set of parallel lines
    D. Two points determining a line

50. Reading a story out loud about two children playing hide-and-seek would: (Skill 5.4; Average)

    A. strengthen students' understanding of spatial concepts such as behind, under, and inside
    B. show the students a one-to-one correspondence
    C. confuse the children
    D. frighten most children

SCIENCE

1. **What type of science instruction will young learners benefit from most? (Skill 1.1; Easy)**

   A. Paper-and-pencil assessment
   B. Lecture and note taking
   C. Hands-on experiments
   D. Reading about science

2. **Which is always true of active learning? (Skill 1.2; Average)**

   A. Learning takes place in the classroom.
   B. Learning takes place in the subject of science.
   C. Learning takes place over a long period of time.
   D. Learning is active, safe, and effective.

3. **In schools in which science materials are in demand, teachers should: (Skill 1.3; Easy)**

   A. avoid science instruction because the materials are unavailable
   B. allow students to listen to a lecture delivered by the teacher
   C. complete experiments even if some safety equipment is lacking
   D. plan hands-on activities using the materials and environment around them, including those found in nature when possible

4. **Managing the early childhood science classroom must include: (Skill 1.4; Average)**

   A. the teacher allowing the students to partake in all parts of each experiment
   B. safety materials being used throughout the lesson
   C. allowing only up to 20 students to be a part of any lesson
   D. safety rules being followed when needed

5. **How can a teacher provide the most effective feedback to students? (Skill 1.5; Average)**

   A. The teacher should provide feedback on a monthly basis by providing a report to each student.
   B. The teacher should provide specific feedback, focusing not only on science concepts but also on other interdisciplinary subjects related to the assignment.
   C. The teacher should always provide positive comments.
   D. The teacher can allow peer groups to evaluate one another's work.

6. **How can a teacher provide students with effective instruction in both small- and large-group settings? (Skill 1.6; Average)**

   A. Engage students in scientific vocabulary knowledge via note taking in a large group.
   B. Partake in experiments in small groups that will allow for data results to be formed.
   C. Place students in two groups: boys in one group and girls in another group.
   D. Place students in one large group so the teacher can do all the experiments and the students can observe.

7. **Which of the following tools would you be least likely to employ as an elementary science teacher? (Skill 1.7; Average)**

   A. Microscope
   B. Centrifuge
   C. Ruler
   D. Test tube

8. **Culture and religion may play a part in the ability of a teacher to engage in some science lessons. What is true about this reality? (Skill 1.8; Rigorous)**

   A. Teachers should partake in all science lessons without regard to culture and religion within the science classroom.
   B. Teachers should not teach any science objectives that relate to any cultural or religious matters if any member of the class might have concerns regarding his or her beliefs.
   C. Teachers should teach whatever information is provided by the school or district, regardless of any religious or cultural concerns within the classroom.
   D. Teachers should avoid all science topics to ensure that all students feel comfortable with regards to religion and culture within the science classroom.

9. **Scientific inquiry begins with _____. (Skill 2.1; Easy)**

   A. a hypothesis
   B. an observation
   C. research
   D. a theory

10. A _____ would be a good choice when graphing the percent of time students spend on various after-school activities. (Skill 2.2; Average)

    A. line graph
    B. pie chart
    C. histogram
    D. bar graph

11. Which of the following statements about scientific knowledge best explains what scientific knowledge is? (Skill 2.3; Average)

    A. Scientific knowledge is based on experiments.
    B. Science knowledge is empirical.
    C. Scientific knowledge is tentative.
    D. Scientific knowledge is based on reason.

12. Students are observing pumpkins during science class in an early childhood classroom. Which type of measurement will be important in allowing the students to graph how heavy each pumpkin is? (Skill 2.4; Average)

    A. Density
    B. Shape
    C. Volume
    D. Weight

13. Which of the following individuals developed the principal of elasticity that is still used today? (Skill 2.5; Average)

    A. Robert Hooke
    B. Lev Vygotsky
    C. Andreas Vesalius
    D. Carl von Linnaeus

14. Which view of the ancient Greeks that affects scientific thinking states that moral and political obligations of an individual are dependent upon an agreement among people to form society? (Skill 2.6; Rigorous)

    A. Scientific political ethics principal
    B. Utilitarianism
    C. Kantianism
    D. Social contract theory

15. Incorporating problem solving, communication, and technology into science lessons are ways to ensure that the _____ disciplines are being taught. (Skill 2.7; Average)

    A. STEM
    B. synthesized
    C. unified
    D. NSF

16. Destructive land-use practices can induce _____ when not properly planned. (Skill 2.8; Easy)

    A. global warming
    B. avalanches
    C. hurricanes
    D. volcanic eruptions

17. Rocks formed from magma are _____. (Skill 3.1; Average)

    A. igneous
    B. metamorphic
    C. sedimentary
    D. none of the above

18. Which types of volcanoes have been built from lava flows as well as cinders and ash? (3.2; Rigorous)

    A. Cinder cone volcanoes
    B. Shield volcanoes
    C. Warped volcanoes
    D. Composite volcanoes

19. Which of the following does NOT determine the frictional force of a box sliding down a ramp? (3.3; Average)

    A. The weight of the box
    B. The area of the box
    C. The angle of the ramp
    D. The chemical properties of the two surfaces

20. The planet with retrograde rotation is: (Skill 3.4; Rigorous)

    A. Mars
    B. Uranus
    C. Venus
    D. Saturn

21. _____ are areas of weakness in the plates of Earth's crust. (Skill 3.5; Easy)

    A. Faults
    B. Ridges
    C. Earthquakes
    D. Volcanoes

22. Surface ocean currents are caused by which of the following? (Skill 3.6; Rigorous)

    A. Temperature
    B. Changes in density of water
    C. Wind
    D. Tidal forces

23. The goal of which U.S. space mission was to gather information and pictures from the moon? (Skill 3.7; Average)

    A. Challenger
    B. Apollo11
    C. Apollo 13
    D. None of the above

24. The phases of the moon are the result of its _____ in relation to the Sun. (Skill 3.8; Rigorous)

    A. revolution
    B. rotation
    C. position
    D. inclination

25. Which of the following is the most accurate definition of a nonrenewable resource? (Skill 3.9; Average)

  A. A nonrenewable resource is never replaced once used.
  B. A nonrenewable resource is replaced on a timescale that is very long relative to human lifespans.
  C. A nonrenewable resource is a resource that can only be manufactured by humans.
  D. A nonrenewable resource is a species that has already become extinct.

26. Which type of matter is extremely light and does not have any weight? (Skill 4.1; Average)

  A. Solid
  B. Liquid
  C. Gas
  D. All of the above

27. Oxygen, hydrogen, nitrogen, and chlorine are unusual because they: (Skill 4.2; Rigorous)

  A. are made of two atoms each
  B. are made of three atoms that have been chemically combined
  C. have no identifying symbols
  D. none of the above

28. The ability of a substance to be changed into a new substance is a _____. (Skill 4.3; Average)

  A. chemical condition
  B. physical condition
  C. mechanical property
  D. chemical property

29. Internal energy that is created by the vibration and movement of atoms and molecules is classified as _____. (Skill 4.4; Rigorous)

  A. mechanical energy
  B. acoustical energy
  C. radiant energy
  D. thermal energy

30. A teacher explains to the class that energy is neither created nor destroyed. Therefore, this means that _____. (Skill 4.5; Average)

  A. matter never changes form
  B. matter must change form
  C. matter changes form only if it is a liquid
  D. none of the above

31. Resistance of motion of surfaces that touch each other is considered _____. (Skill 4.6; Average)

  A. friction
  B. inertia
  C. gravity
  D. force

32. When humans shiver to keep warm, this is an example of _____. (Skill 5.1; Average)

    A. translation
    B. synthesis
    C. motility
    D. homeostasis

33. These are the basis of evolution and may enhance an organism's survival. (Skill 5.2; Rigorous)

    A. Species
    B. Mutation
    C. DNA
    D. Instincts

34. The science of classification is referred to as: (Skill 5.3; Easy)

    A. subgroups
    B. systems
    C. taxonomy
    D. class

35. A _____ describes the relational position of a species or population. (Skill 5.4; Average)

    A. class
    B. phylum
    C. predator
    D. niche

36. _____ make up _____, which make up tissues. (Skill 5.5; Rigorous)

    A. Cells; DNA
    B. Cells; organelles
    C. Organisms; organelles
    D. Organelles; cells

37. Eighty percent of Earth's atmosphere is _____. (Skill 5.6; Average)

    A. carbon dioxide
    B. phosphorus
    C. water
    D. nitrogen gas

38. _____ maintain a fluid environment for _____ exchange in mammals. (Skill 5.7; Average)

    A. Lungs; gas
    B. Blood vessels; blood
    C. Carbon dioxide molecules; air
    D. None of the above

39. _____ is known as the father of genetics. (Skill 5.8; Easy)

    A. Matthias Schleiden
    B. Andreas Vesalius
    C. Robert Punnet
    D. Gregor Mendel

40. Which is true of meiosis? (Skill 5.9; Rigorous)

    A. Recombination provides genetic diversity.
    B. The chromosome number is half the number of parent cells.
    C. Both A and B
    D. Neither A nor B

41. **Which type of ecosystem is located close to the poles, both north and south of the equator? (Skill 5.10; Average)**

    A. Tundra
    B. Savanna
    C. Taiga
    D. Temperate deciduous forest

Sample Test Answer Key

DEVELOPMENTAL KNOWLEDGE

1. D	31. B	61. B
2. B	32. B	62. A
3. D	33. D	63. D
4. D	34. C	64. B
5. A	35. C	65. D
6. C	36. A	66. C
7. B	37. A	67. A
8. C	38. B	68. C
9. A	39. A	69. D
10. B	40. A	70. B
11. A	41. C	71. D
12. D	42. C	72. D
13. B	43. D	73. B
14. D	44. B	74. A
15. A	45. D	75. A
16. C	46. B	76. B
17. A	47. A	77. D
18. C	48. A	78. A
19. B	49. D	79. D
20. A	50. C	80. D
21. C	51. B	81. D
22. B	52. C	82. D
23. C	53. D	83. C
24. D	54. A	84. D
25. B	55. D	85. D
26. C	56. C	86. B
27. A	57. A	87. D
28. A	58. A	88. A
29. D	59. B	
30. A	60. D	

LANGUAGE ARTS

1. D	14. D	27. D
2. A	15. D	28. A
3. D	16. D	29. B
4. A	17. A	30. C
5. D	18. C	31. D
6. D	19. B	32. A
7. C	20. D	33. B
8. B	21. A	34. A
9. D	22. B	35. C
10. A	23. D	36. B
11. D	24. A	37. D
12. C	25. C	38. C
13. D	26. B	39. B

MATHEMATICS

1. A	18. B	35. B
2. D	19. D	36. C
3. D	20. B	37. C
4. D	21. A	38. C
5. D	22. C	39. D
6. D	23. C	40. B
7. B	24. D	41. A
8. D	25. D	42. B
9. B	26. A	43. B
10. D	27. B	44. A
11. D	28. B	45. D
12. C	29. B	46. D
13. B	30. D	47. D
14. B	31. C	48. C
15. B	32. B	49. A
16. D	33. C	50. A
17. C	34. A	

SCIENCE

1.	C	15.	A	29.	D
2.	D	16.	B	30.	B
3.	D	17.	A	31.	A
4.	B	18.	D	32.	D
5.	B	19.	B	33.	B
6.	B	20.	C	34.	C
7.	B	21.	A	35.	D
8.	B	22.	C	36.	D
9.	B	23.	C	37.	D
10.	B	24.	C	38.	A
11.	B	25.	B	39.	D
12.	D	26.	C	40.	C
13.	A	27.	A	41.	C
14.	D	28.	D		

RATIONALE

Developmental Knowledge

1. **Which of the following is a sign of child abuse? (Skill 1.1; Average)**

   A. Awkward social behavior around other children
   B. Bruises
   C. Withdrawn behavior
   D. All of the above

   Answer D: All of the above
   While the symptoms of abuse are usually thought to be physical (and therefore visible, like bruises), mental and emotional abuse is also possible. The impact of abuse on a child's development in other domains is often extensive. Abused children can be socially withdrawn, and typically, as one might suspect, their minds will not always be on their schoolwork. All three answers are signs of child abuse.

2. **If child abuse is suspected, what action should the teacher take? (Skill 1.1; Average)**

   A. Wait to see if the child talks about it again.
   B. Talk to your supervisor about your concerns.
   C. Call the child's parent.
   D. Talk to another teacher about your suspicions.

   Answer B: Talk to your supervisor about your concerns.
   The child who is undergoing the abuse is the one whose needs must be served first. A suspected case gone unreported may destroy a child's life and his or her subsequent life as a functional adult. It is the duty of any citizen who suspects abuse and neglect to make a report, and it is especially important and required for state licensed and certified persons to make a report. If you contact the parent first and the parent is the abuser, then the child's life may be endangered.

3. **A preschool teacher is concerned because the three-year-olds in her class do not play with one another. Each student plays without interacting with others in the class. What advice would you give her? (Skill 1.2; Rigorous)**

    A. Contact the parents immediately so they can talk to their doctors about medications that might help.
    B. Plan more activities that require interactions among the children.
    C. Tell the children that you expect them to share and play together. If they don't, then punish them.
    D. Don't worry. It is typical for young children to engage in "parallel" activities, playing alongside their peers without directly interacting with one another.

Answer D: Don't worry. It is typical for young children to engage in "parallel" activities, playing alongside their peers without directly interacting with one another.
At age three, children are happier in the presence of a few other children their own age, but seldom play together with them. This type of play is known as parallel play and is a typical social development for this age.

4. **Which of the following is a true statement? (Skill 1.2; Rigorous)**

    A. Physical development does not influence social development.
    B. Social development does not influence physical development.
    C. Cognitive development does not influence social development.
    D. All domains of development (physical, social, and cognitive) are integrated and influence other domains.

Answer D: All domains of development (physical, social and cognitive) are integrated and influence other domains
The answer to this question explains its reasoning.

5. **Which of the following is a true statement? (Skill 1.3; Rigorous)**

    A. Younger children tend to process information at a slower rate than older children (age eight and older).
    B. Older children tend to process information at a slower rate than younger children (younger than age 8).
    C. Children process information at the same rate as adults.
    D. All children process information at exactly the same rate.

Answer A: Younger children tend to process information at a slower rate than older children (age eight and older)
Because of this, the learning activities selected for younger students (below age eight) should focus on short time frames in highly simplified form. The nature of the activity and the context in which the activity is presented affects the approach that the students will take in processing the information.

6. **A child exhibits the following symptoms: a lack of emotional responsiveness, indifference to physical contact, abnormal social play, and abnormal speech. What is the likely diagnosis for this child? (Skill 1.3; Average)**

    A.   Separation anxiety
    B.   Mental retardation
    C.   Autism
    D.   Hypochondria

Answer C: Autism
According to many psychologists who have been involved with treating autistic children, it seems that these children have built a wall between themselves and everyone else, including their families and even their parents. They do not make eye contact with others and do not even appear to hear the voices of those who speak to them. Treatment may include outpatient psychotherapy, medication, or long-term treatment in a residential center, but neither the form of treatment or even the lack of treatment seems to make a difference in the long run for many, but not all, children.

7. **Marcus is a first-grade boy of good developmental attainment. His learning progress is good for the first half of the year. He shows no indicators of emotional distress. After the holiday break, he returns much changed. He is quieter, sullen even, tending to play alone. He has moments of tearfulness, sometimes almost without cause. He avoids contact with adults as often as he can. Even play with his friends has become limited. He has episodes of wetting not seen before, and he often wants to sleep in school. What approach is appropriate for this sudden change in behavior? (Skill 1.4; Rigorous)**

    A. Give him some time to adjust. He's probably having a difficult time adjusting to school after the fun of the holiday break.
    B. Report this change immediately to administration. Do not call the parents until administration decides a course of action.
    C. Document his daily behavior carefully as soon as you notice such a change, then report to administration the next month or so in a meeting.
    D. Make a courtesy call to the parents to let them know he is not acting like himself, being sure to tell them he is not making trouble for others.

    Answer B: Report this change immediately to administration. Do not call the parents until administration decides a course of action.
    Anytime a child's disposition, attitude, or habits change significantly, teachers and parents need to seriously consider the existence of emotional difficulties. Emotional disturbances in childhood are not uncommon and take a variety of forms. Usually these problems show up in the form of uncharacteristic behaviors. Most of the time, children respond favorably to brief treatment programs of psychotherapy. At other times, disturbances may need more intensive therapy and are harder to resolve. All stressful behaviors need to be addressed, and any type of chronic antisocial behavior needs to be examined as a possible symptom of deep-seated emotional upset. In a case in which the change is sudden and dramatic, administration needs to become involved.

8. **An effective teacher will recognize that: (Skill 1.5; Easy)**

   A. all students in the classroom can be taught all materials regardless of race, culture, or ethnicity
   B. if one student is unable to participate in a lesson due to religious reasons, the lesson must be omitted for all students
   C. a phone call to the caregivers of the student will help clarify the parts of a lesson in which a student might be able to participate
   D. none of the above

   Answer C: a phone call to the caregivers of the student will help clarify the parts of a lesson in which a student might be able to participate
   The effective teacher will recognize the diversity in a group of students and through strong communication with the parents within the classroom, a teacher will understand what the student is allowed to participate in for religious and cultural reasons and what must be avoided. Students who cannot participate can be given alternate projects or lessons to complete.

9. **Learning activities for young students (below age eight) should focus on short time frames because: (Skill 1.6; Average)**

   A. younger children tend to process information at a slower rate than older children (age eight and older)
   B. young children have long attention spans
   C. young children can understand complex instructional activities
   D. young children need to sit quietly and listen to learn

   Answer A: younger children tend to process information at a slower rate than older children (age eight and older)
   Because of this, the learning activities selected for younger students (below age eight) should focus on short time frames in highly simplified form. The nature of the activity and the context in which the activity is presented affects the approach that the students will take in processing the information.

10. **Involving parents in the school setting should be done in the following way: (Skill 1.7; Easy)**

    A. Through inviting them into the classroom casually after school during dismissal time
    B. By ghosting school events like activity night, family BINGO, or a school carnival
    C. By holding one large celebration at the end of the school year
    D. Both A and C

    Answer B: By ghosting school events like activity night, family BINGO, or a school carnival
    Planning community events at the school is a great way to encourage active involvement with parents. Well-planned events that allow for some interaction among administrators, teachers, parents, and students might include activity nights, family BINGO, school carnivals, musical performances, plays, or athletic events.

11. **Researchers have shown that school involvement and connections with community institutions yield greater retention rates of students graduating and seeking higher education experiences. What is a current barrier to community involvement? (Skill 1.8; Rigorous)**

    A. The current disconnect and autonomy that has become commonplace in today's society
    B. The amount of gang activity in many communities
    C. The tough economic times we are facing
    D. None of the above

    Answer A: The current disconnect and autonomy that has become commonplace in today's society
    Daily life is more isolated than it used to be. With the ability to communicate easily and cheaply, families have scattered all over the globe, with few living in one community their whole life. Neighbors are isolated from neighbors and no longer share community activities. The general disconnectedness in our society is a barrier to community involvement in schools.

12. **Assigning a student an adult mentor is an effective tool for addressing student achievement because: (Skill 1.8; Average)**

    A. the mentor can reinforce learning through tutorial instruction
    B. it provides the student with an appropriate adult role model
    C. the mentor can help the student with the practical application of the lesson
    D. all of the above

    Answer D: all of the above
    Mentoring has become an instrumental tool in addressing student achievement and access to learning. Adult mentors work individually with identified students on specific subject areas to reinforce the learning through tutorial instruction and application of knowledge. Providing students with adult role models to reinforce learning has become a crucial instructional strategy for teachers seeking to maximize student learning beyond the classroom.

13. **With state and federal educational funding becoming increasingly subject to legislative budget cuts, what can the school community provide to support the school? (Skill 1.8; Average)**

    A. Money to supplement teacher salaries
    B. Free notebooks, backpacks, and student supplies for low-income students who may have difficulty obtaining the basic supplies for school
    C. Advice on how to save money when running a school
    D. All of the above

    Answer B: Free notebooks, backpacks, and student supplies for low-income students who may have difficulty obtaining the basic supplies for school
    With state and federal educational funding becoming increasingly subject to legislative budget cuts, school communities welcome the financial support that community resources can provide in terms of discounted prices on high-end supplies (such as computers, printers, and technology supplies) along with free notebooks, backpacks, and student supplies for low-income students who may have difficulty obtaining the basic supplies for school.

14. **According to Piaget, when does the development of symbolic functioning and language take place? (Skill 2.1; Rigorous)**

    A.   Concrete operational stage
    B.   Formal operational stage
    C.   Sensorimotor stage
    D.   Preoperational stage

    Answer D: Preoperational stage
    Although there is no general theory of cognitive development, the most historically influential theory was developed by Jean Piaget, a Swiss psychologist (1896–1980). His theory provided many central concepts in the field of developmental psychology. His theory concerned the growth of intelligence, which for Piaget meant the ability to more accurately represent the world and perform logical operations on representations of concepts grounded in the world. His theory concerns the emergence and acquisition of schemata—schemes of how one perceives the world—in developmental stages, times during which children are acquiring new ways of mentally representing information. His theory is considered constructivist, meaning that, unlike nativist theories (which describe cognitive development as the unfolding of innate knowledge and abilities) or empiricist theories (which describe cognitive development as the gradual acquisition of knowledge through experience), it asserts that we construct our cognitive abilities through self-motivated action in the world. For his development of the theory, Piaget was awarded the Erasmus Prize.

15. **According to Piaget, what is a child born with? (Skill 2.1; Rigorous)**

    A.   The tendency to actively relate pieces of information acquired
    B.   The ability to adapt
    C.   Primary emotions
    D.   Desire

    Answer A: The tendency to actively relate pieces of information acquired
    Piaget believed that a child is capable of relating small pieces of information to help with learning.

16. **Effective curriculum models for early childhood programs should include which of the following? (Skill 2.2; Average)**

   A. Cognitive development
   B. Social development
   C. Both cognitive and social development
   D. None of the above

   Answer C: Both cognitive and social development
   Early childhood and elementary education programs must incorporate both the cognitive and social development of young learners in designing effective curriculum models. The most important premise of child development is that all domains of development (physical, social, and academic) are integrated. Development in each dimension is influenced by development in the other dimensions.

17. **Head Start programs were created in the early 1960s to provide: (Skill 2.2; Average)**

   A. a comprehensive curriculum model for preparation of low-income students for success in school communities
   B. a national curriculum that ensures that "no child is left behind"
   C. a parent involvement program in every school
   D. Pre-Kindergarten for every four-year-old

   Answer A: a comprehensive curriculum model for preparation of low-income students for success in school communities
   The answer to this question explains its reasoning.

18. **It is important to make a report when abuse or neglect is suspected because: (Skill 2.3; Average)**

   A. failure to do so could result in revocation of certification and license
   B. failure to do so could result in a monetary fine
   C. both A and B
   D. none of the above

   Answer C: Both A and B
   For state-licensed personnel (teachers and school staff), failure to make a report when abuse or neglect is suspected is also punishable by the filing of criminal charges.

19. **IDEA sets policies that provide for inclusion of students with disabilities. What does _inclusion_ mean? (Skill 2.3; Rigorous)**

    A. Inclusion is the name of the curriculum that must followed in special education classes.
    B. Inclusion is the right of students with disabilities to be placed in the regular classroom.
    C. Inclusion refers to the quality of instruction necessary for student academic success.
    D. Inclusion means that students with disabilities should always be placed in classes for gifted and talented students.

    Answer B: Inclusion is the right of students with disabilities to be placed in the regular classroom.
    Although inclusion could mean that students with disabilities can be placed in classes for gifted and talented students (answer D), they would not always be placed there. Explanation of this policy also includes references to "least restrictive environment" and "mainstreaming." Least restrictive environment is the mandate that children be educated to the maximum extent appropriate with their non-disabled peers. Mainstreaming is a policy through which disabled students can be placed in the regular classroom as long as such placement does not interfere with the student's educational plan. Until this law was passed, many students with disabilities were provided instruction in separate classrooms and separate programs and never had access to the curriculum in the regular classroom.

20. **Under IDEA, Congress provides safeguards for students against schools' actions, including the right to sue in court, and encourages states to develop hearing and mediation systems to resolve disputes. This is known as: (Skill 2.3; Rigorous)**

    A. due process
    B. mediation
    C. Safe Schools Initiative
    D. parent involvement

    Answer A: due process
    States are required to develop hearing and mediation systems to resolve disputes. No students or their parents/guardians can be denied due process because of disability.

21. **Why should teachers view the Websites of professional organizations like the IRA? (Skill 2.4; Average)**

    A. To find new digital games for teaching children
    B. To chat with other early childhood educators
    C. To find quality strategies to improve early childhood education for students
    D. To post student work for parent viewing

    Answer C: To find quality strategies to improve early childhood education for students
    It is important to stay current with the latest research and teaching strategies to meet the needs of all children. The best information can be found in a variety of books, Websites, and journal articles provided by professional organizations devoted to the education of young children.

22. **Which of the following organizations target improvement of education\specifically for young children? (Skill 2.5; Rigorous)**

    A. SPCA, NCTM, and NAACP
    B. NAEYC, SECA, and ACEI
    C. NAACP, IRA, and NCTM
    D. None of the above

    Answer B: NAEYC, SECA, and ACEI
    The focus of the National Association for the Education of Young Children (**NAEYC**) is on improving and developing programs and services for children from birth through the age of eight. The Southern Early Childhood Association (**SECA**) is dedicated to improving the quality of life for the South's children and families. To assume that responsibility, this organization follows the progress of public policy debate and legislation, both nationally and in the 14 Southern states. The Association for Childhood Education International (**ACEI**) promotes and supports the global community to optimize the education and development of children from birth through early adolescence and to influence the professional growth of educators and the efforts of others who are committed to the needs of children in a changing society.

23. You've received a job offer to teach Pre-Kindergarten, but you've never taught children this young. What professional organization might publish journal articles that would be useful to you? (Skill 2.5; Rigorous)

    A. FCRR
    B. IRA
    C. NAEYC
    D. AERA

    Answer C: NAEYC
    The focus of the National Association for the Education of Young Children (NAEYC) is on improving and developing programs and services for children from birth through the age of eight. The other three organizations focus on the improvement of reading instruction at the state, national, and international level. Although information from FCRR (Florida Center for Reading Research), IRA (International Reading Association), and AERA (American Educational Research Association) would be valuable, only the NAEYC would have comprehensive information about teaching young children.

24. When considering the comprehensive cost of educating students, what is a hidden cost that may not be often considered? (Skill 2.6; Rigorous)

    A. The increase in the number of students for whom English is not a first language
    B. Federal mandates
    C. The cost of technology
    D. Teacher turnover rate

    Answer D: Teacher turnover rate
    While we are all familiar with unfunded federal mandates, the cost of technology, and the increase in the number of students for whom English is not a first language, there is a hidden cost not often considered. The cost of teacher turnover in school communities has been estimated to be in the range of $5–7 billion, which further impacts the legislature's ability to provide enough funding for all educational communities. When considering the comprehensive cost of educating students, more attention may need to be given to retaining current teachers through ongoing professional development training and support.

25. **What two things have contributed to a reduction in teaching and instructional time for young learners? (Skill 2.6; Rigorous)**

    A. Increased expectations for learning coupled with increasing numbers of teachers who are alternatively certified

    B. Increased early violence in communities coupled with classroom management issues

    C. Increased expectations for learning coupled with a decrease in parent involvement

    D. Increasing numbers of alternatively certified teachers coupled with a decrease in parent involvement

Answer B: Increased early violence in communities coupled with classroom management issues

Early violence in elementary school communities coupled with classroom management issues have contributed to a reduction in teaching and instructional time for young learners. Providing young learners with ethical and social strategies to improve cooperative learning and communication will go a long way in reducing the time spent on conflict and increasing the time spent on learning acquisition.

Lack of parent involvement and increased learning expectations may influence young children's behavior, but if children are taught strategies for resiliency and self-management, then learning time can be increased. All teachers, not just those who are trained through alternative certification programs, need continued training in strong classroom management skills to effectively teach today's learners.

26. **When students are able share their daily experiences and understanding of their world in a safe and nurturing learning environment, they are able to: (Skill 2.7; Average)**

    A. evaluate and redirect their own ethical issues that occur during the school day

    B. build character

    C. both A and B

    D. neither A nor B

Answer C: both A and B

Sharing experiences in a safe place is a way for students to evaluate and redirect their own ethical issues and build character.

27. **What is one component of the instructional planning model that must be given careful evaluation? (Skill 3.1; Average)**

   A.   Students' prior knowledge and skills
   B.   The script the teacher will use in instruction
   C.   Future lesson plans
   D.   Parent participation

   Answer A: Students' prior knowledge and skills
   The teacher will, of course, have certain expectations regarding where the students will be physically and intellectually when he or she plans for a new class. However, there will be wide variations in the actual classroom. If the teacher doesn't make the extra effort to understand where there are deficiencies and where there are strengths in the individual students, the planning will probably miss the mark, at least for some members of the class. Students' deficiencies and strengths can be obtained by reviewing student records, by observation, and by testing.

28. **When is utilization of instructional materials most effective? (Skill 3.1; Average)**

   A.   When the activities are sequenced
   B.   When the materials are prepared ahead of time
   C.   When the students choose the pages to work on
   D.   When the students create the instructional materials

   Answer A: When the activities are sequenced
   Most assignments will require more than one educational principle. It is helpful to explain to students the proper order in which these principles must be applied to complete the assignment successfully. Subsequently, students should also be informed of the nature of the assignment (such as cooperative learning, group project, or individual assignment). This is often done at the start of the assignment.

29. **What is evaluation of the instructional activity based on? (Skill 3.1; Average)**

   A. Student grades
   B. Teacher evaluation
   C. Student participation
   D. Specified criteria

Answer D: Specified criteria
The ways that a teacher uses test data is a meaningful aspect of instruction and may increase the motivation level of the students, especially when this information takes the form of feedback to the students. However, for a test to be an accurate measurement of student progress, the teacher must know how to plan and construct tests. Perhaps the most important caveat in creating and using tests for classroom purposes is the old adage to test what you teach. Actually, it is better stated that you should teach what you plan to test. This second phrasing more clearly reflects the need for thorough planning of the entire instructional program. Before you begin instruction, you should have the assessment planned and defined. One common method of matching the test to the instruction is to develop a table of specifications, a two-way grid in which the objectives of instruction are listed on one axis and the content that has been presented is listed on the other axis. Then the individual cells are assigned percentages that reflect the focus and extent of instruction in each area. The final step is to distribute the number of questions to be used on the test among the cells of the table in proportion to the identified percentages.

30.   **What should a teacher do when students have not responded well to an instructional activity? (Skill 3.1; Rigorous)**

A.   Reevaluation of learner needs
B.   Skill-building and analysis of outcomes
C.   Interaction with students and manipulation of subject matter
D.   Management techniques and levels of questioning

Answer A: Reevaluation of learner needs
The value of teacher observations cannot be overestimated. It is through the use of observations that the teacher is able to informally assess the needs of the students during instruction. These observations will drive the lesson and determine the direction that the lesson will take based on student activity and behavior. After a lesson is carefully planned, teacher observation is the single most important component of an instructional presentation. If the teacher observes that a particular student is not on-task, he or she will change the method of instruction accordingly. The teacher may change from a teacher-directed approach to a more interactive approach. The teacher will increase questioning to increase the participation of the students. If appropriate, the teacher will introduce manipulative materials to the lesson. In addition, teachers may switch to a cooperative group activity, thereby removing the responsibility of instruction from the teacher and putting it on the students.

31.   **The teacher states, "We will work on the first page of vocabulary words. On the second page we will work on the structure and meaning of the words. We will go over these together and then you will write out the answers to the exercises on your own. I will be circulating to give help if needed." What is this an example of? (Skill 3.1; Rigorous)**

A.   Evaluation of instructional activity
B.   Analysis of instructional activity
C.   Identification of expected outcomes
D.   Pacing of instructional activity

Answer B: Analysis of instructional activity
The successful teacher carefully plans all activities and foresees any difficulties in executing the plan. This also assures that the directions given to students will be clear, avoiding any misunderstanding.

32. **The teacher states that the lesson in which the students will be engaged will consist of a review of the material from the previous day, a demonstration of the scientific aspects of an electronic circuit, and small-group work setting up an electronic circuit. What has the teacher demonstrated? (Skill 3.2; Rigorous)**

   A. The importance of reviewing
   B. Giving the general framework for the lesson to facilitate learning
   C. Giving students the opportunity to leave if they are not interested in the lesson
   D. Providing momentum for the lesson

   Answer B: Giving the general framework for the lesson to facilitate learning
   If children know where they're going, they're more likely to be engaged in getting there. It's important to give them a road map whenever possible for what is coming in their classes.

33. **Which of the following can directly relate to a student's learning? (Skill 3.3; Average)**

   A. A. Lighting
   B. B. Noise levels
   C. C. Room temperature
   D. D. All of the above

   Answer D: All of the above
   Environmental preferences such as lighting, noise level, and room temperature are factors that can affect students in various ways and are often directly related to individual learning styles. A number of students learn best in bright light, but others learn considerably better in low-lighted areas. Bright light can actually cause some students to become restless and hyperactive. Teachers can provide listening stations with headsets for children who need sound and quiet, comfortable study areas for those who learn best in a silent environment. Teachers should encourage students to dress according to their body's temperature to assure that students are not uncomfortable and can concentrate fully on their schoolwork.

34.   **Objectives should be: (Skill 3.4; Average)**

A.   adaptable to timelines and concise and to the point
B.   clear and observable
C.   both A and B
D.   neither A nor B

Answer C: both A and B
Objectives are the measurements that support goals, and they should be adaptable to timelines, concise and to the point, clear, and observable.

35.   **As teachers select instructional materials, it is important that teachers remember: (Skill 3.6; Average)**

A.   it is unlawful for students to study from textbooks or materials that are brought from home
B.   it is unlawful for students to study from textbooks or materials that are more than 10 years old
C.   it is unlawful to require students to study from textbooks or materials other than those approved by the state Department of Education
D.   none of the above

Answer C: it is unlawful to require students to study from textbooks or materials other than those approved by the state Department of Education
In considering suitable learning materials for the classroom, the teacher must have a thorough understanding of the state-mandated, competency-based curriculum. According to state requirements, certain objectives must be met in each subject taught at every designated level of instruction. It is necessary that the teacher become well acquainted with the curriculum to which he or she is assigned. The teacher must also be aware that it is unlawful to require students to study from textbooks or materials other than those approved by the state Department of Education.

36. **Prior experiences influence the individual's cognitive style, or method of accepting, processing, and retaining information. According to Marshall Rosenberg, students can be categorized as: (Skill 3.6; Rigorous)**

    A. rigid-inhibited, undisciplined, acceptance-anxious, or creative
    B. hyperactive, well-behaved, disinterested, or cognitively delayed
    C. visual, auditory, kinesthetic or multimodality learners
    D. none of the above

    Answer A: rigid-inhibited, undisciplined, acceptance-anxious, or creative
    In choosing materials, teachers should keep in mind that students not only learn at different rates but also bring a variety of cognitive styles to the learning process. Prior experiences influence the individual's cognitive style, or method of accepting, processing, and retaining information.

    According to Rosenberg, "The creative learner is an independent thinker, one who maximizes his/her abilities, can work by him/herself, enjoys learning, and is self-critical." This category constitutes the ideal, but teachers should make every effort to use materials that will stimulate and hold the attention of learners of all types.

37. **Grouping flexibly allows teachers to:**

    A. utilize various levels of differentiating learning when it is needed
    B. have a permanent way to group the students right at the beginning of the year
    C. have rigorous lesson plans
    D. use fewer resources

    Answer A: utilize various levels of differentiating learning when it is needed
    Teachers can utilize grouping flexibility to differentiate to meet the needs of all learners. Lessons and materials can be adjusted for one group and reformulated for the next group when needed.

38. **When teachers plan lessons around broad themes with which students can identify, such as "The Environment," this is known as: (Skill 3.8; Average)**

    A.   environmental curriculum
    B.   integrated curriculum
    C.   practical curriculum
    D.   child-centered curriculum

Answer B: integrated curriculum
An integrated curriculum is a program of study that describes a movement toward integrated lessons that enables students to make connections across curricula. This curriculum links lessons among the humanities, art, natural sciences, mathematics, music, and social studies.

39. **A child learns the following skills from playing: (Skill 3.9; Easy)**

    A.   Basic values and fine motor skills
    B.   How to compete in today's world
    C.   How to boss others around
    D.   How to read and do math

Answer A: Basic values and fine motor skills
Play is an activity that helps teach basic values such as sharing and cooperation. Play helps develop very important attributes in children. For example, children learn and develop personal interests and practice particular skills. The play in which children engage may even develop future professional interests. Finally, playing with objects helps develop motor skills.

40. **The teacher's goal should be: (Skill 3.10; Easy)**

    A.   to build rapport with his or her students
    B.   to be best friends with each student
    C.   to be consistently strict and unwelcoming so students understand who is in charge
    D.   none of the above

Answer A: to build rapport with his or her students
The teacher should build a rapport with students by being firm but fair, consistent, and thorough.

41. **Once a teaching method has been established, it: (Skill: 3.11; Average)**

    A. should be used for at least the next three years
    B. should be used for a month or two and then changed
    C. must be changed when data shows another method is more effective
    D. can be changed when the teacher feels like changing it according to his or her current lesson objectives

    Answer C: must be changed when data shows another method is more effective
    Teachers and administrators are responsible for implementing the most effective practices within the classroom. Outdated practices do a disservice to students and should be changed when applicable.

42. **An effective teacher will: (Skill 4.1; Average)**

    A. never introduce political topics to young learners due to the topics being too difficult and controversial
    B. always introduce political topics in the classroom and share his or her voting choices
    C. consider introducing political topics but consider both parent and student needs first
    D. Help students always avoid political topics

    Answer C: consider introducing political topics but consider both parent and student needs first
    Developmentally appropriate curriculum is important in guiding instruction in the classroom. The curriculum should be age-appropriate, relevant to the students' real lives, and in their realm of anticipated interest. When deciding whether politically controversial issues should be introduced or avoided, the teacher must make these decisions deliberatively on the basis of feedback from his or her students while keeping sight of his or her objectives.

43. **To enhance their students' effective listening skills, teachers can encourage which of the following strategies? (Skill 4.2; Average)**

    A. Associate
    B. Visualize
    C. Repeat
    D. All of the above

    Answer D: All of the above
    Associating, visualizing, repeating, and concentrating are four strategies to increase listening skills in students.

44. When children learn more complex motor patterns including running, climbing, and jumping, they are said to be in the _____ stage of motor development. (Skill 4.3; Average)

    A.   first
    B.   second
    C.   third
    D.   fourth

Answer B: second
Stage 1 includes basic reflexes and movements; Stage 2 includes more complex patterns of movement such as running; Stage 3 occurs later in childhood when the Stage 2 movements become more fluid; and in Stage 4, adolescents develop specialized movements, and practice, talent, and motivation affect their performance of these movements.

45. Which style of teaching physical skills involves the entire group of students taking part in the same task regardless of individual skill level? (Skill 4.4; Rigorous)

    A.   Command style
    B.   Practice style
    C.   Reciprocal style
    D.   Inclusion style

Answer D: Inclusion style
Inclusion style involves all students taking part in the same task regardless of individual skill level. With this style, the students make decisions on how to practice and develop their skills, with the teacher exerting very little control over the activities.

46. In which type of learning situation is learned helplessness likely to have the greatest impact on students? (Skill 4.4; Rigorous)

    A.   One in which students lack the motivation to succeed
    B.   One in which students have little control over how well they perform
    C.   One in which competition among students is encouraged
    D.   One in which rewards are in place to motivate students

Answer B: One in which students have little control over how well they perform
Learning helplessness occurs when students' continued failure inhibits them from trying again. Learned helplessness most often occurs in situations in which people experience events and feel they have little control over what happens to them.

47. **What should be the first thing taught when introducing dance? (Skill 4.5; Easy)**

   A. Rhythm
   B. Feelings
   C. C. Empathy
   D. D. Texture

   Answer A: Rhythm
   Rhythm is the basis of dance. Teaching dance should begin by focusing on rhythm. This can be achieved through activities such as children clapping their hands or tapping their feet to express rhythm.

48. **When discussing color, the intensity of a color refers to the color's _____. (Skill 4.5; Average)**

   A. strength
   B. value
   C. lightness or darkness
   D. associated emotions

   Answer A: strength
   Color is an important consideration when viewing art. Color can be considered in more depth by focusing on intensity, which is the strength of the color, and value, which is the lightness or darkness of the color.

49. **What is a benefit of distance learning? (Skills 4.6, 4.7; Average)**

   A. Students do not have to deal with social issues in the school setting.
   B. Teachers do not have to make any lesson plans.
   C. Administrators can employ fewer teachers because there are fewer students.
   D. Students feel more comfortable and may communicate more freely with teachers than they would otherwise.

   Answer D: Students feel more comfortable and may communicate more freely with teachers than they would otherwise.
   Distance learning is a technological strategy that keeps students and teachers communicating about issues in the classroom and beyond. Students might communicate more freely using technology to ask teachers or adult mentors questions than they would in a classroom of peers.

50. **What are the most powerful factors influencing students' academic focus and success? (Skill 5.1; Average)**

   A. Teachers' knowledge and training
   B. Teachers' preparation and planning
   C. Students' attitudes and perceptions
   D. Students' interests and goals

   Answer C: Students' attitudes and perceptions
   Students' attitudes and perceptions about learning are the most powerful factors influencing academic focus and success. The key is to ensure that objectives are focused on students' interests and are relevant to their lives. It is also important that students believe that they have the ability to perform tasks.

51. **The three areas of differentiated instruction are content, process, and _____. (Skill 5.1; Easy)**

   A. application
   B. product
   C. assessment
   D. structure

   Answer B: product
   Differentiated instruction includes content, process, and product. Content focuses on what is going to be taught. Process focuses on how the content is going to be taught. Product focuses on the expectations and requirements placed on students; the product is what is expected of students.

52. **Which strategy for adapting the curriculum would be most useful for the purpose of reducing the effect of a student's learning disability on completing an assessment task? (Skill 5.1; Rigorous)**

   A. Differentiated instruction
   B. Alternative assessments
   C. Testing modifications
   D. Total physical response

   Answer C: Testing modifications
   Testing modifications are changes made to assessments that allow students with disabilities equal opportunity to demonstrate their knowledge and ability on the task.

53. **Which of the following characteristics are considerations when identifying children with diverse needs? (Skill 5.2; Easy)**

A. Ethnicity
B. Socioeconomic status
C. Physical disability
D. All of the above

Answer D: All of the above
Diversity can be based on distinctive features such as race, ethnicity, and gender. Diversity can also be based on other differences such as physical or intellectual disability and socioeconomic status.

54. **What is it most important for a teacher to consider when planning homework assignments? (Skill 5.2; Average)**

A. Access to technology
B. Ethnicity
C. Language difficulties
D. Gender

Answer A: Access to technology
When planning homework assignments, teachers must take into account students' access to technology. If socioeconomic status or other factors make it likely that some students do not have access to technology such as a computer or the Internet, assessments that require this technology would not give these students equal opportunity to succeed in the task.

55. **When dealing with a difficult family, what is it most important for a teacher to display? (Skill 5.3; Average)**

A. Strength
B. Excitement
C. Authority
D. Patience

Answer D: Patience
When dealing with difficult families, teachers need to be patient. Teachers must also be aware that methods of criticism such as verbal attacks are not acceptable.

56. **In regards to dealing with parents, which term best describes the role that teachers should play in the education of children? (Skill 5.3; Average)**

    A. Friends
    B. Leaders
    C. Partners
    D. Managers

    Answer C: Partners
    It is important for teachers to act as partners in the education of children. This means accepting that parents know their children best and utilizing the feedback, information, and advice received from parents.

57. **How is a student who has extreme trouble spelling most likely to be identified? (Skill 5.4; Average)**

    A. Dyslexic
    B. Gifted
    C. Autistic
    D. Hyperactive

    Answer A: Dyslexic
    Dyslexia is a common learning disability that requires intervention strategies. Students with dyslexia often have difficulty reading and have extreme trouble spelling.

58. **What should interventions for exceptional students be focused on? (Skill 5.5; Rigorous)**

    A. Caring
    B. Curing
    C. Academics
    D. Both caring and curing

    Answer A: Caring
    Interventions for exceptional students should be focused on caring for the children rather than curing the children. This means accepting that children have unique needs and implementing interventions that aim to allow exceptional students to have similar opportunities as students who do not have learning disabilities.

59.   **What type of problems are children who have been abandoned or neglected most likely to have? (Skill 5.6; Average)**

   A.   Behavioral problems
   B.   Medical problems
   C.   Social problems
   D.   Physical problems

   Answer B: Medical problems
   Children who have been abandoned or neglected or often have medical problems. They may also experience problems due to poor nutrition. Schools can address these problems by providing healthy school lunches and medical attention.

60.   **If a school nurse is not available, who should assume responsibility for the administration of medication? (Skill 5.7; Average)**

   A.   A qualified teacher
   B.   The parent or guardian of the student
   C.   The prescriber of the medication
   D.   The principal of the school

   Answer D: The principal of the school
   If a school district has school nurses available on a daily basis, the school nurse should take responsibility for the administration of medication. If a school nurse is not available, the principal should take responsibility for the administration of medication.

61.   **Professionals in a school setting can best help to meet student needs by: (Skill 5.8; Easy)**

   A.   working individually
   B.   collaborating
   C.   checking in on the classroom teacher to see if he or she needs any help
   D.   keeping the student after school for tutoring

   Answer B: collaborating
   To meet student needs, the school may utilize professional personnel including the classroom teacher, guidance counselors, a school nurse, physical therapists, occupational therapists, related arts teachers, ELL teachers, and speech and language teachers, among others. By collaborating to meet student needs, these professionals can help to ensure that each child is getting the best education possible.

62. **Which type of test is most likely to be a true indication of the content knowledge of ESOL students? (Skill 5.9; Average)**

    A. Oral test
    B. Written test
    C. Timed test
    D. Practical test

    Answer A: Oral test
    In many cases, written tests may not provide teachers with any indication of an ESOL student's content knowledge. An oral test is much more likely to provide a true indication of content knowledge.

63. **What is the term for a structured infrequent measure of learner achievement that involves the use of a test and an exam? (Skill 6.1; Average)**

    A. Informal continuous assessment
    B. Observation
    C. Formal continuous assessment
    D. Formal assessment

    Answer D: Formal assessment
    A formal assessment is a structured infrequent measure of learner achievement. It involves the use of a test and an exam. Exams are used to measure the learner's progress.

64. **Which of the following best explains why teachers should carefully consider observations recorded by other teachers? (Skill 6.2; Average)**

    A. Teachers may be manipulative.
    B. Teachers may be biased.
    C. Teachers may be dishonest.
    D. Teachers may be indifferent.

    Answer B: Teachers may be biased.
    When reading another teacher's observations of a student, teachers must be aware that the teacher may be biased. This could result in either a more positive or a more negative assessment.

65. **Why are student records often a good indicator of student progress? (Skill 6.2; Easy)**

    A. They contain information from several people.
    B. They show changes over time.
    C. They contain information gathered over a period of time.
    D. All of the above

    Answer D: All of the above
    Student records are often a good indicator of student progress because they contain information from more than one person, they contain information gathered over a period of time, and they show progress over time as well as current results.

66. **Which of the following statements would not be appropriate in an anecdotal record about a student? (Skill 6.2; Rigorous)**

    A. Jasmine completed only half of the homework assigned.
    B. Jasmine contributed only slightly to class discussions.
    C. Jasmine was not interested in learning the material.
    D. Jasmine did not volunteer to answer any questions.

    Answer C: Jasmine was not interested in learning the material.
    Anecdotal records of a student should include observable behaviors. Anecdotal records should not include assumptions or speculations about the student's motivation or interest. "Jasmine was not interested in learning the material" is not appropriate to include because it is speculation.

67. **Which type of assessment is most likely to be used to assess student interest and motivation? (Skill 6.3; Average)**

    A. Rating scales
    B. Questioning
    C. Portfolio assessment
    D. Anecdotal records

    Answer A: Rating scales
    Rating scales are often used to assess behavior and effective areas. They can be used to assess interest and motivation, whereas most other assessment types are not appropriate for this purpose.

68.   **What does a student's portfolio typically contain? (Skill 6.3; Easy)**

A.   Results of standardized tests
B.   Competed self-appraisal checklists
C.   Samples of work
D.   Results of all assessment activities completed to date

Answer C: Samples of work
A student's portfolio typically contains samples of work created throughout the year. These can be selected by the teacher or by the student, or they can be samples linked to learning objectives.

69.   **What does portfolio assessment typically provide? (Skill 8.4; Average)**

A.   Opportunities for teachers to assess students' progress
B.   Opportunities for students to reflect on their own progress
C.   Opportunities for students to consider their approaches to problem solving
D.   All of the above

Answer D: All of the above
Portfolio assessment has a number of purposes. It provides opportunities for teachers to assess students' progress, opportunities for students to reflect on their own progress, and opportunities for students to consider their approaches to problem solving.

70.   **Which of the following is portfolio assessment most likely to encourage? (Skill 6.4; Average)**

A.   Self-esteem
B.   Self-directed learning
C.   Conflict management skills
D.   Time management skills

Answer B: Self-directed learning
One of the main advantages of portfolio assessment for students is that it provides them the opportunity to assess and reflect on their own work. This encourages self-directed learning.

71. When addressing issues of concern in a parent-teacher conference, what is it best to focus on? (Skill 6.5; Easy)

    A. Likely explanations
    B. Personal opinions
    C. Statements from other students
    D. Observable behaviors

    Answer D: Observable behaviors
    When addressing issues of concern in a parent-teacher conference, teachers should focus on observable behaviors and concrete examples.

72. Which statement would it be most appropriate to make when speaking to parents about an issue of concern? (Skill 6.5; Rigorous)

    A. Sandra is often distracted easily.
    B. Sandra irritates other students.
    C. Sandra is a frustrating student.
    D. While completing the exam, Sandra started conversations with other students.

    Answer D: While completing the exam, Sandra started conversations with other students.
    When addressing issues of concern in a parent-teacher conference, teachers should focus on providing concrete examples and avoid making judgments. "While completing the exam, Sandra started conversations with other students" is the most appropriate statement to make because it provides concrete information and avoids judging Sandra.

73. When sending a follow-up note to parents following a conference, which of the following is it best to include? (Skill 6.5; Average)

    A. Further details on the student's strengths and weaknesses
    B. A summary of the agreed plan of action
    C. A description of how the student has progressed since the conference
    D. Praise for the parents on becoming involved in their child's education

    Answer B: A summary of the agreed plan of action
    A follow-up note to parents should be sent around two days after the conference. It should briefly summarize the plan of action. It should be professional and should not be chatty.

74. **When is it appropriate for a teacher to talk to parents about another student's performance? (Skill 6.5; Rigorous)**

    A. When the parents of the student have been invited to participate
    B. When the student is having a negative impact on other students
    C. When the student is performing well and only positive information will be communicated
    D. When permission to discuss the student has been given by the principal

    Answer A: When the parents of the student have been invited to participate
    Information about a student's school performance is confidential and falls under the Privacy Act. Information can be given only to the student's parents or guardians. If another student must be discussed, that student's parents or guardians must be invited to participate.

75. **Why is repetition an important part of a child's play? (Skill 6.6; Rigorous)**

    A. It allows the child to master the skill and then move into creativity.
    B. It allows the child to stress the caregiver who is bored with playing the same thing over and over.
    C. It is a creative outlet for the child.
    D. None of the above

    Answer A: It allows the child to master the skill and then move into creativity.
    Repetition is an important aspect of children's play. Doing the same thing over and over may be boring to the adult caregiver, but the repetition allows the child to master the new skill and then move on to experimentation and creativity.

76. **Which type of assessments would be used to determine if students are meeting national and state learning standards? (Skill 6.7; Average)**

    A. Norm-referenced assessments
    B. Criterion-referenced assessments
    C. Performance-based assessments
    D. Observation-based assessments

    Answer B: Criterion-referenced assessments
    Criterion-referenced assessments are used to assess how each student compares with a norm group of student learners. These are often used to determine if students and schools are meeting state and national standards.

77. **RTI stands for: (Skill 6.8; Easy)**

    A. Rigorous Testing Interventions
    B. Reading Theme Interactions
    C. Readiness Thinking Initiative
    D. Response to Intervention

    Answer D: Response to Intervention
    The process known as RTI, or Response to Intervention, is a way to strategize how to get a student back on track.

78. **When should procedures that use social humiliation be used as behavior management techniques? (Skill 7.1; Average)**

    A. Never
    B. Only in severe situations
    C. When the student is a danger to himself or herself or others
    D. Only when all other methods have been ineffective

    Answer A: Never
    Procedures that use social humiliation should never be used as behavior management techniques. Procedures that involve withholding of basic needs, pain, or extreme discomfort should also never be used.

79. **Which of the following is NOT a recommended token for use in a token economy? (Skill 7.1; Easy)**

    A. Stamps
    B. Stickers
    C. Point cards
    D. Poker chips

    Answer D: Poker chips
    A token economy should use tokens such as stamps, stickers, stars, or point cards. Poker chips should not be used as they increase the likelihood of theft and loss.

80. **Which type of social skill assessment involves students ranking their classmates on set criteria? (Skill 7.2; Average)**

A. Direct observation
B. Paired-comparison
C. Peer nomination
D. Peer rating

Answer D: Peer rating
There are many ways to assess students' social skills. Peer rating is a method in which students rate their peers on set criteria.

81. **A student is punished by taking five stars from his tally in the token economy. What type of punishment is this an example of? (Skill 7.2; Average)**

A. Time-out
B. Suspension
C. Overcorrection
D. Response cost

Answer D: Response cost
Response cost is a type of punishment in which there is a cost to the student by having something taken away. When a token economy is in place, the student has points taken away.

82. **Consistency is important when managing the behavior of adolescents because it reduces _____. (Skill 7.3; Average)**

A. emotional responses
B. unpredictable reactions
C. consequences
D. power struggles

Answer D: power struggles
Consistency is especially important when managing the behavior of adolescents. It reduces the likelihood of power struggles. It also teaches them that predictable consequences will follow their actions.

83. **Which type of student is seclusion time-out least likely to be effective with? (Skill 7.3; Average)**

    A. Outgoing
    B. Intelligent
    C. Shy
    D. Aggressive

    Answer C: Shy
    Seclusion time-out is often not effective with students who consider the seclusion a reward rather than a punishment. Shy, solitary, or withdrawn children may consider seclusion a reward and prefer it to being in the classroom.

84. **What is a common source of interpersonal conflict for a student? (Skill 7.4; Average)**

    A. Disagreements over values or decisions
    B. Family relationships
    C. Competition
    D. All of the above

    Answer D: All of the above
    Common sources of interpersonal conflict include problems with family relationships, competition, and disagreement over values or decisions.

85. **Which of the following is NOT a common character development trait? (Skill 7.5; Easy)**

    A. Self-discipline
    B. Respect
    C. Patriotism
    D. Decision making

    Answer D: Decision making
    There are various character development traits that are developed in children. These include responsibility, caring, self-discipline, citizenship, honesty, respect, and patriotism.

86. **Which classroom activity would be most useful for teaching character development? (Skill 7.5; Average)**

    A. Exam
    B. Discussion
    C. Project
    D. Quiz

    Answer B: Discussion
    Teaching character development has been found to be most effective when students take part in discussions focused on the moral implications of their everyday lives.

87. **Which of the following is a common sign that a student is experiencing stress? (Skill 7.6; Easy)**

    A. Behavioral problems
    B. Episodes of sadness
    C. Aggressive behavior
    D. All of the above

    Answer D: All of the above
    Various signs are indications that a student may be experiencing stress. These include behavioral problems, a drop in grades, episodes of sadness, nightmares, aggressive behavior, and an increase in physical complaints.

88. **What should a teacher do first when he or she notices that a student appears stressed? (Skill 7.6; Average)**

    A. Ask the student what the problem is.
    B. Praise the student.
    C. Hold a class discussion.
    D. Inform the parents.

    Answer A: Ask the student what the problem is.
    The first thing a teacher should do when he or she notices that a student appears stressed is to ask the student what the problem is. This simple step can reduce the student's stress.

RATIONALE

Language Arts and Reading

1. **Which of the following explains a significant difference between phonics and phonemic awareness? (Skill 1.1; Average)**

    A.   Phonics involves print; phonemic awareness involves language.
    B.   Phonics is more difficult than phonemic awareness.
    C.   Phonics involves sounds; phonemic awareness involves letters.
    D.   Phonics is the application of sounds to print; phonemic awareness is oral.

    Answer D: Phonics is the application of sounds to print; phonemic awareness is oral.
    Both phonics and phonemic awareness activities involve sounds, but it is with phonics that the application of these sounds is applied to print. Phonemic awareness is an oral activity.

2. **An early warning sign of emergent literacy difficulties is: (Skill 1.2; Average)**

    A.   a student's failure to identify the letters in his or her own name
    B.   a student's inability to count to 10
    C.   a student's trouble singing the ABC song correctly
    D.   a student's difficulty tying his or her shoes

    Answer A: a student's failure to identify the letters in his or her own name
    Parents and teachers should be aware of early warning signs of emergent literacy difficulties. These include

    - failure in identifying/recognizing letters in the child's own name
    - lack of interest in singsong rhymes
    - difficulty remembering/learning names and shapes of letters
    - trouble comprehending simple instructions

3. **Young children often spell words they write according to the way the letters sound. This process, which may be used as an activity to draw upon background knowledge, is called: (Skill 1.3; Rigorous)**

    A. spelling lists
    B. incorrect spelling
    C. developmental spelling
    D. invented spelling

    Answer D: invented spelling
    Spelling is of utmost importance in the writing process. At first, young children will use invented spelling in which they write the words according to letter sounds, using their background knowledge.

4. **Which of the following is the most commonly practiced strategy to encourage literacy growth? (Skill 1.4; Average)**

    A. Storybook reading
    B. Teaching phonics
    C. Teaching fluency
    D. Letter identification

    Answer A: Storybook reading
    Reading stories and reading aloud to children is the most common literacy growth strategy implemented in classrooms across the country.

5. **Instructional methods of grouping should be: (Skill 1.5; Average)**

    A. based on ability solely
    B. used for small groups of students who need more instruction on an objective
    C. used to introduce new materials and strategies to the whole class
    D. B and C

    Answer D: B and C
    Although students should sometimes be grouped according to ability, this should not be the standard. Instructional methods using flexible grouping should be used. These include whole-class instruction (used to introduce new materials and strategies to the entire class) and small-group instruction (used for small groups of students who need more instruction on an objective).

6. **A print-rich environment would have which of the following components? (Skill 1.6; Easy)**

    A. A word wall
    B. Classroom libraries
    C. Labels for objects in the room
    D. All of the above

    Answer D: All of the above
    Components of a print-rich environment include classroom libraries, word walls, and labels for classroom objects.

7. **A delegation from the United Kingdom has come to the United States, and since they are considering adapting the balanced literacy approach, they are very interested in seeing the small group demonstrated. Mr. Adams, the school principal, knows that he should bring them into Greg's room when Greg is doing which activity? (Skill 1.7; Rigorous)**

    A. A mini-lesson.
    B. A conference with individual students
    C. A time when the children are divided into small and independent study groups
    D. A read-aloud

    Answer C: A time when the children are divided into small and independent study groups
    In a balanced literacy approach, small-group time is when small groups of students are pulled to work independently with focused direction from the teacher.

8. **Environmental print is available in all of the following places except: (Skill 1.8; Easy)**

    A. within a newspaper
    B. on the page of a library book
    C. on a supermarket circular
    D. in a commercial flyer

    Answer B: on the page of a library book
    Environmental print involves print from items such as signs and boxes. Magazines and catalogues that include ads for child-centered products are another source of environmental print. Supermarket circulars and coupons from the newspaper are also excellent for engaging children in using environmental print as reading, especially when combined with dramatic play centers or prop boxes.

9. **Which of the following are effective methods and strategies to integrate language arts into the content areas of the curriculum? (Skill 1.9; Rigorous)**

    A.   Introduce content area topics by reading from a picture book about the topic.
    B.   Use oral reports.
    C.   Use cartoons in writing assignments.
    D.   All of the above

Answer D: All of the above
In the early grades, incorporating language arts into the content areas of the curriculum is very fluid; picture books, oral reports, and cartoons in writing assignments all help children use and develop their skills in language arts across the curriculum.

10. **Monthly book clubs, book fairs, read-a-thons, and the class library are all examples of: (Skill 1.10; Rigorous)**

    A.   ways to foster reading outside class
    B.   ways to raise money for the school library
    C.   ways to raise money for the classroom library
    D.   none of the above

Answer A: ways to foster reading outside class
Providing students with opportunities to read outside class is a key component of reading success. These events allow students to build their own home libraries or to spend time reading with friends and family.

11. **Which of the following varieties of text are appropriate for building language skills and concept development? (Skill 2.1; Easy)**

    A.   Concept books
    B.   Predictable texts or pattern books
    C.   Board books
    D.   All of the above

Answer D: All of the above
Fine children's literature opens children up to vicarious experiences that enrich their worlds and build language skills and concept development. From being read to by parents and caregivers from the earliest ages, toddlers can handle **board books** with sturdy pages such as Kit Allen's *Sweater*. From ages three to seven, children enjoy a variety of nonfiction **concept books** combining language and pictures to show concrete examples of abstract concepts, such as Eric Carle's *Ten Little Rubber Ducks* (directions, numbers, and up and down), and **predictable texts or pattern books** allow the beginning reader to feel successful with the process of reading in a rapid manner.

12. **Historical fiction, mythology, folklore, realistic fiction, mystery, and legends are known as: (Skill 2.2; Easy)**

   A.   reading styles
   B.   young adult topics
   C.   genres
   D.   booklists

   Answer C: genres
   A genre is a particular category of literature.

13. **Which of the following activities does NOT help show children what people with different viewpoints and cultural perspectives have in common? (Skill 2.3; Average)**

   A.   Making a graph showing the sizes of families represented in the classroom
   B.   Making classroom books about My Family after reading a book such as Rebecca Doltich's *A Family Like Yours*.
   C.   Providing children with playdough and a variety of powdered colors, along with a mirror, then allowing them to match their skin colors
   D.   Using English in all signs, labels, posters, and environmental print so that students all use one language

   Answer D: Using English in all signs, labels, posters, and environmental print so that students all use one language
   In fact, just the opposite is true for promoting multicultural awareness and understanding of different viewpoints. Languages other than English, as well as pictures, posters, and books depicting other cultures and locations should all be included in a classroom that unifies children in an increasingly multicultural world.

14. **When applying the strategy of analyzing the narrator's point of view as part of literary analysis, it is important to consider: (Skill 2.4; Rigorous)**

   A.   whether the narrator is inside or outside the story
   B.   whether the narrator is one of the characters
   C.   whether the narrator can "see" into anyone else's mind
   D.   all of the above

   Answer D: all of the above
   In literary analysis, the strategy of analyzing the author's point of view includes considering whether the narrator is inside the story and one of the characters (first-person point of view), outside the story (third-person point of view), or outside the story and able to see into the minds of other characters to discern what they are thinking (third-person omniscient point of view).

15. **One of the many ways in which children can be encouraged to respond to literature and informational texts is: (Skill 2.5; Average)**

    A. dramatizing a historical document or song
    B. retelling the story orally
    C. making up a prequel or sequel
    D. all of the above

    Answer D: all of the above
    All are examples of ways to elicit from children a response to literature or informational texts. These methods may also help the teacher assess student understanding, but their primary purpose is to engage students to respond to to what they read.

16. **The use of newspapers in the classroom aids children in all the specific uses and purposes for multiple representations of information except which of the following? (Skill 2.6; Rigorous)**

    A. Chronology, such as a calendar of events for the week
    B. Timelines
    C. Comparison/contrast news writings
    D. Cause/effort diagramming

    Answer D: Cause/effort diagramming
    Answers A–C represent genuine multiple representations of information. Answer D would represent such too if it read "Cause/effect diagramming." There is no such thing as cause/effort diagramming.

17. **Making inferences from the text means that the reader: (Skill 2.7; Average)**

    A. is making informed judgments based on available evidence
    B. is making a guess based on prior experiences
    C. is making a guess based on what he or she would like to be true of the text
    D. all of the above

    Answer A: is making informed judgments based on available evidence
    Inference is a process that involves the reader making a reasonable judgment based on the information given. Inference engages children to construct meaning.

18. **The five types of expository texts (also called text structures) include all but which of the following? (Skill 2.8; Rigorous)**

   A. Description text
   B. Collection text
   C. Call and response text
   D. Comparison text

   Answer C: Call and response text
   Description text is factual and used in expository writing; collection text uses ideas in groups; and comparison test compares and contrasts two or more ideas. These are all types of expository text. Another type of expository text is response structure expository text, which presents a question or response followed by an answer or solution. The only similar word between Answer C and response structure expository text is the word *response*, making Answer C and invalid answer.

19. **Teaching students how to interpret _____ involves evaluating a text's headings, subheadings, bolded words, and side notes. (Skill 2.9; Rigorous)**

   A. graphic organizers
   B. text features
   C. textual marking
   D. summaries

   Answer B: text features
   Studying text features, including the table of contents, glossary, index, and headings, is an excellent way for students to increase comprehension of a text. Knowledge of these tools helps students understand the organization and flow of their reading.

20. **Which of the following is NOT one of the four basic features of the alphabetic principle? (Skill 3.1; Rigorous)**

   A. Students must be able to hear the separate sounds in spoken words.
   B. Students must be able to blend separate sounds together to make words.
   C. Teachers must use a systematic, effective program to teach children to decode.
   D. The teaching of the alphabetic principle usually begins in Grade 1.

   Answer D: The teaching of the alphabetic principle usually begins in Grade 1.
   Teaching the alphabetic principle starts in kindergarten or before, when teachers help students discover that written words have individual letters and spoken words have individual sounds. This is known as graphophonemic awareness.

21. **When students begin to master prosody, their reading aloud sounds more like _____. (Skill 3.2; Rigorous)**

    A.   natural speech
    B.   a performance
    C.   reciting a poem
    D.   correct word identification

    Answer A: natural speech
    Prosody in spoken discourse involves word accenting, intonation, and rhythm. When those elements are part of reading aloud, the content sounds like natural speech.

22. **The following is an example of an explicit context clue for the word *jovial*. (Skill 3.3; Average)**

    A.   I feel jovial.
    B.   A jovial person is good-humored.
    C.   Santa Claus is a jovial character.
    D.   Dad was in a jovial mood.

    Answer B: A jovial person is good-humored.
    When authors define words within text, they provide explicit context clues.

23. **A topic sentence is usually: (Skill 3.4; Easy)**

    A.   the first sentence in a paragraph
    B.   more general than the other sentences in a paragraph
    C.   supported by details in sentences that follow it
    D.   all of the above

    Answer D: all of the above
    A topic sentence is usually the first sentence in a paragraph, and it is more general than the detail sentences that usually follow it.

24. Teaching students how to interpret _____ involves evaluating a text's headings, subheadings, bolded words, and side notes. (Skill 3.5; Average)

    A. text structure
    B. graphic organizers
    C. textual marking
    D. summaries

    Answer A: text structure
    Nonfiction texts are structured differently from fiction, so It is important to point out to students features such as headings and sidebars -- important tools for understanding content-area reading.

25. To find out what students already know about a topic they are about to read, the teacher should help them: (Skill 3.6; Average)

    A. question the text
    B. discuss the illustrations
    C. activate their prior knowledge
    D. read the text critically

    Answer C: activate their prior knowledge
    Teachers should help their students make connections between what they already know (their prior knowledge) and what they are reading or about to read. In fact, it isn't possible for students to understand what they read without thinking about what they already know.

26. Which of the following does NOT support reading fluency for beginning readers? (Skill 3.7; Average)

    A. Listening to teachers read aloud
    B. Reading from frustration-level material
    C. Rereading familiar stories
    D. Shared and choral reading

    Answer B: Reading from frustration-level material
    Teachers help students develop fluency in reading by modeling fluent reading themselves, encouraging students to reread familiar material, using shared and choral reading, and providing appropriate level materials. Frustration-level materials are never appropriate for beginning readers.

27. **For Pre-K–Grade 3 students, reading nonfiction is a challenge because: (Skill 3.8; Easy)**

    A. they have inadequate background knowledge
    B. graphic aids and organizers are unfamiliar to them
    C. they need to be taught to take notes
    D. all of the above

    Answer D: all of the above
    Reading from nonfiction texts requires a great deal of support for younger students. Teachers at these levels are required to provide concrete, hands-on, before-reading experiences with aspects of the content to activate and add to prior knowledge. Teach children how nonfiction text looks different from stories, with its headings, sidebars, graphs, maps, charts, and the like. These aids help clarify the text and provide another format to help with comprehension. Help children learn note taking by finding the main ideas in a text and writing them as a text summary.

28. **In the _____ stage of writing, students write in scribbles and can assign meaning to the markings. (Skill 4.1; Rigorous)**

    A. role-play
    B. experimental
    C. early
    D. conventional

    Answer A: role-play
    In the role-play stage of writing, the child writes in scribbles and assigns a message to the symbols. Even though an adult would not be able to read the writing, the child can read what is written, although it may not be the same each time the child reads it. In experimental writing, the student writes in the simplest form of recognizable writing. In the early writing stage, children start to use a small range of familiar text forms and sight words in their writing. Finally, in the conventional writing stage, students have a sense of audience and purpose for writing.

29. **When students know that letters stand for a message, they are said to be in the _____ stage of spelling. (Skill 4.2; Rigorous)**

    A. non-phonemic
    B. pre-phonemic
    C. early phonemic
    D. letter-name

    Answer B: pre-phonemic
    The pre-phonemic stage of spelling is the first stage of spelling in which students know that letters stand for a message, but they cannot link the spelling to meaningful pronunciation yet. In the early phonemic stage, students are beginning to understand spelling and can start to write letters. Finally, letter-name spelling is when students spell some words correctly and they are developing a sight vocabulary. There is no non-phonemic stage of spelling.

30. **When students correct misspellings and check punctuation, they are: (Skill 4.3; Average)**

    A. revising
    B. drafting
    C. proofreading
    D. prewriting

    Answer C: proofreading
    Writing is a process and typically involves these five steps: prewriting, drafting, revising and editing, proofreading, and publishing. Prewriting involves brainstorming ideas to write about; drafting entails getting those ideas into a first draft; revising and editing look at that first draft to improve its ideas, flow, and completeness; proofreading assesses the grammar, usage, and spelling; and publishing is the creation of a final draft meant for others to read.

31. **Most content-area texts are written in the _____ mode. (Skill 4.4; Average)**

    A. narrative
    B. persuasive
    C. descriptive
    D. expository

    Answer D: expository
    Narrative writing tells a story, persuasive writing advances an opinion meant to change readers' minds, descriptive writing makes an experience available by inviting the five senses, and expository writing is primarily informative. Texts written in the content areas of science, literature, and social studies are informative in those disciplines and therefore expository.

32.   **Which of the following describes a narrative writing project? (Skill 4.5; Easy)**

A.   Tell about what happened on a family outing this summer.
B.   Compare two books by your favorite author.
C.   Create an invitation to a class art show.
D.   Describe the most delicious meal you've ever had.

Answer A: Tell about what happened on a family outing this summer.
Telling about something that happened, usually in sequence, is narrative writing. Comparing two books by the same author may be a combination of descriptive and expository writing. An invitation is usually persuasive because you want to motivate people to show up. A delicious meal can be mostly descriptive, and when the courses are discussed in order of presentation, it can also be narrative.

33.   **Adding the transition words of course to their writing during the revision and editing stage will help students to: (Skill 4.6; Rigorous)**

A.   contrast similar things
B.   highlight an important idea
C.   show what causes something to happen
D.   indicate a time sequence

Answer B: highlight an important idea
Transitional words help writing flow smoothly and enhance comprehension. Words like *in the same way* invite comparison. *Because, so,* and *then* indicate causation. *Next, later,* and *today* are sequence or time indicators. Words that help writers highlight or emphasize an important idea include *of course, I think,* and *clearly.*

34.   **A good discussion about a text does NOT require: (Skill 4.7; Average)**

A.   having a Group Artist
B.   listening carefully to others
C.   following group discussion rules
D.   stimulating ideas

Answer A: having a Group Artist
Small-group or whole-class discussion stimulates ideas about a text and gives students a larger picture of its social concepts. By following group rules, which entail listening carefully to their peers, students see the wide range of possible interpretations and thoughts regarding one text. Having a job such as Group Artist, Word Master, or Discussion Leader encourages multitasking, but isn't a requirement for a good discussion.

35. **What best describes the key element in student presentations? (Skill 4.8; Rigorous)**

    A. Visual aids
    B. Auditory enhancements
    C. Multimedia
    D. Computer-based

    Answer C: Multimedia
    What is most important is that students learn to use at least one element in their presentations that goes beyond the words they speak or read. Not only is that what's required of them in the twenty-first century, but a multimedia presentation of content also helps learners better understand and process the material.

36. **The sentence *Many teachers have been using a balanced literacy approach over the last decade and a half* is written in the _____ tense. (Skill 4.9; Rigorous)**

    A. present
    B. present perfect
    C. future
    D. past perfect

    Answer B: present perfect
    Present perfect tense is used to express action or a condition that started in the past and continues.

37. **A shopping list is an example of: (Skill 4.10; Easy)**

    A. informal oral language
    B. formal oral language
    C. formal written language
    D. informal written language

    Answer D: informal written language
    Conversation is an example of informal oral language. Formal oral language is not usually required of Pre-K–Grade 3 students; when they give presentations, they usually read from the formal written language of their reports. Informal written language includes shopping lists, notes, cards, and captions.

38. **What is one of the main advantages of portfolio assessment for students? (Skill 5.1; Average)**

   A. It promotes creativity.
   B. It generates opportunities to use diverse skills.
   C. It encourages students to reflect on their own work.
   D. It develops communication skills.

   Answer C: It encourages students to reflect on their own work.
   One of the main advantages of portfolio assessment for students is that it provides them with the opportunity to assess and reflect on their own work. It also encourages self-directed learning.

39. **It may be said of norm-referenced tests that they: (Skill 5.2; Average)**

   A. give information only about the local sample's results
   B. provide information about how the local test-takers did compared to a representative sampling of national test-takers
   C. make no comparisons to national test-takers
   D. none of the above

   Answer B: provide information about how the local test-takers did compared to a representative sampling of national test-takers
   A norm-referenced test is one in which the children are measured against one another. Scores on this test are reported in percentiles to compare children to others in their age group, usually on a large scale. Each percentile indicates the percent of the testing population whose scores were lower than or the same as a particular child's score. Percentile is defined as a score on a scale of 100 showing the percentage of a distribution that is equal to it or below it.

RATIONALE

Mathematics

1. **Which is NOT a behavior demonstrating concrete understanding of mathematics? (Skill 1.1; Average)**

   A. Representing an unknown quantity with a variable
   B. Sorting objects into equally sized groups
   C. Giving one pencil to each student in the class
   D. Counting the number of books on each shelf

   Answer A: Representing an unknown quantity with a variable
   Variable representation requires an abstract understanding of mathematics.

2. **Which of the following is NOT the most effective math teaching strategy? (Skill 1.1; Rigorous)**

   A. To be clear about instructional goals (topics)
   B. To progress experiences and understanding from the concrete to the abstract stage.
   C. To communicate to students what is expected of them and why
   D. To keep math separate from other subject areas

   Answer D: To keep math separate from other subject areas
   Children's understanding of math is enhanced when it can be connected to other subject areas or to their daily lives.

3. **Which of the following is NOT a basic assumption of the criteria for teaching problem solving in mathematics? (Skill 1.2; Rigorous)**

   A. A teacher can expect students to approach problems with varied strategies.
   B. Problem solving can be applied to subject areas other than math.
   C. Students can help each other investigate possible problem-solving strategies.
   D. Problem solving is always a uniform, predictable process.

   Answer D: Problem solving is always a uniform, predictable process.
   To develop good problem-solving skills, students should be given opportunities to experiment with multiple solving strategies to see how math strategies can apply to other subject areas and to work with others to achieve a successful solution. Teachers should be prepared to let students be flexible with their problem-solving approach.

4.   **Which of the following classroom experiences demonstrates a meaningful way to show math integrated with another subject area? (Skill 1.3; Easy)**

   A.   Reorganizing the day's schedule so that math problems are worked during what is normally language arts time
   B.   Giving students extra time to complete their unfinished seatwork from any subject
   C.   Teaching a math lesson outside
   D.   Having students read a short story and record how many times they come across a given set of sight words, then working with the class to construct a bar graph representing the data

   Answer D: Having students read a short story and record how many times they come across a given set of sight words, then working with the class to construct a bar graph representing the data.
   This activity gives students the opportunity to quantify the frequency of sight words that they are studying for reading and spelling. Students will improve their sight word recognition skills while applying counting and data analysis.

5.   **In the fall, the kindergarten students interviewed their classmates about how students arrive at school: walking, bus, or car. Then they made a pictograph of the results. This math activity is appropriate for young children because: (Skill 1.4; Average)**

   A.   it shows them how math is used in their own lives
   B.   it gives them a chance to participate directly in the lesson
   C.   it provides the opportunity to quantify results and compare values
   D.   all of the above

   Answer D: all of the above
   Preschoolers and kindergarteners need to experience numbers on multiple levels, from counting to analysis of data. Furthermore, appropriate math instruction for young children lets them participate in the lesson and gives them a chance to see how math is used in the real world.

6. **Why are manipulatives, models, and technology used by math teachers? (Skill 1.5; Average)**

    A. To promote interest
    B. To address diverse learning needs
    C. To give hands-on math experience
    D. All of the above

    Answer D: All of the above
    Some students, especially those in the early school years, show more interest in or have more need for concrete, hands-on experience. Manipulatives, models, and technology offer ways to address that in math.

7. **Which of the following best promotes understanding of math operations? (Skill 1.6; Rigorous)**

    A. The teacher promoting a single best solution
    B. Students verbalizing their reasoning and solutions to problems
    C. Speed tests
    D. Providing solutions to textbook tests

    Answer B: Students verbalizing their reasoning and solutions to problems
    Students best understand math operations when they can exercise reasonable thinking: making conjectures, choosing investigation models, and reaching conclusions. Verbalizing this process demonstrates their success.

8. **Alternative assessment in math may include: (Skill 1.7; Easy)**

    A. student explanation of reasoning behind the answer
    B. analysis of data
    C. multimedia
    D. all of the above

    Answer D: all of the above
    Alternative assessment is any type of assessment in which students express their understanding in a way other than just providing a question's answer.

9. Open-ended questions, portfolios, and writing activities can: (Skill 1.7; Rigorous)

    A. only be used in early childhood assessment
    B. be used as assessment of mathematical skill and knowledge
    C. only be used for language arts assessment
    D. none of the above

Answer B: be used as assessment of mathematical skill and knowledge
The key word in choices A and C is *only*, which implies that open-ended questions, portfolios, and writing activities would only apply to assessment in early childhood or in language arts. The best answer choice for this question is B.

10. What is NOT one of the advantages of collaborative or small-group learning?
(Skill 1.8; Average)

    A. Students who work together in groups or teams develop their skills in organizing, leadership, research, communication, and problem solving.
    B. Working in teams can help students overcome anxiety in distance learning courses and contribute a sense of community and belonging for the students.
    C. Students working in a small group have more opportunities to be directly involved with concepts in the lesson than when the same information is taught to a large group.
    D. Teachers reduce their workloads and the amount of time spent on helping students and planning lessons

Answer D: Teachers reduce their workloads and the amount of time spent on helping students and planning lessons
Teachers continue to expend time planning, monitoring, and evaluating students, their groups, and their activities.

11. **When introducing students to a new math topic, a teacher should: (Skill 1.9; Average)**

   A. show students the hardest problems first, so they know what to expect
   B. tell the class that some of the students may not understand the material as well as others
   C. save the math lesson until the end of the school day
   D. provide opportunities for students to investigate and explore the new material in small groups and individually

   Answer D: provide opportunities for students to investigate and explore the new material in small groups and individually
   To keep students' learning effective and positive, a teacher should build skills progressively, gradually increasing the difficulty level while still providing opportunities for success as students work with new concepts.

12. **What number comes next in this pattern? (Skill 2.1; Easy)**

   3, 8, 13, 18, _____

   A. 21
   B. 26
   C. 23
   D. 5

   Answer C: 23
   The pattern here is to add 5 to the previous number for the next number in sequence.

13. **Students in a kindergarten class are placing colored cards in the following order: red-yellow-red-yellow. What is the overall importance of this type of activity? (Skill 2.1; Rigorous)**

    A. The students are learning a beautiful pattern for art class.
    B. The students are practicing patterns, which will help them build a foundation for algebraic thinking.
    C. The students are playing a sorting game to see which color has more.
    D. The students are practicing counting sets of two.

    Answer B: The students are practicing patterns, which will help them build a foundation for algebraic thinking.
    Students in this activity are practicing the pattern A-B. Experimenting with patterns of objects will lead them to find patterns with numbers, which is the basis for algebraic development.

14. **Students in a kindergarten class are curious about which toy is heavier: a plastic doll or a metal truck. They use a balance and wooden cubes to determine their answer. The toy that requires more cubes to hold the balance even will be the heavier toy. Which math principles does this activity demonstrate? (Skill 2.2; Rigorous)**

    A. Subtraction, meaningful counting
    B. Problem solving, number sense
    C. Addition, problem solving
    D. Problem solving, subtraction

    Answer B: Problem solving, number sense
    In this activity, students are using math problem solving through experimentation. Because of their number sense, they are able to determine which toy is heavier (weighs the same as more blocks).

15. **Which expression best characterizes the shaded area in the graph below? (Skill 2.2; Rigorous)**

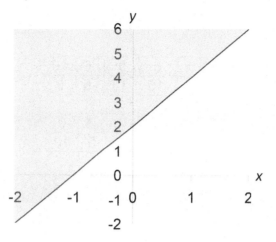

A. $y \leq -x + 2$
B. $y \geq 2x + 2$
C. $y = 2x + 2$
D. $y \geq 2x - 1$

Answer B: $y \geq 2x + 2$
The shaded region includes all the points above the line. Thus, we only need to find the equation for the line and then choose the correct symbol for the inequality. Note that the line has a slope of 2 (it increases by two units in the y direction for every one unit of increase in the x direction) and a y-intercept of 2. Thus, the equation for the line is

$y = 2x + 2$

Note that the shaded region is above the line; the best choice is then answer B, $y \geq 2x + 2$.

16. **Which table(s) represent solutions of the following equation?** (Skill 2.3; Average)

$$y = x - 10$$

I

x	-5	0	5	10
y	-15	-10	-5	0

II

x	-15	-10	-5	0
y	-5	0	5	10

III

x	20	25	30	35
y	10	15	20	25

A. I
B. II
C. II and III
D. I and III

Answer D: I and III
Substitute values for *x* and *y* into the equation. For example, if $x = -5$ and $y = -15$, then

$$-15 = (-5) - 10$$
$$-15 = (-5) + (-10)$$
$$-15 = -15$$

Since the equation is true, the values $x = -5$ and $y = -15$ are solutions of the equation. All other entries in table I will also test true.

In table II, substituting the values $x = 0$ and $y = 10$ gives a false statement since $10 = 0 - 10$ is not a true statement.

In table III, you can similarly check values by substitution and find them to be true, or you can recognize the pattern of each *y* output being 10 less than its *x* input.

17. If the operation of a function machine is described by the phrase "increases inputs by 8," which variable equation below best represents the function? (Skill 2.3; Rigorous)

A. $y = 8x$
B. $y = 8$
C. $y = x + 8$
D. $y + x = 8$

Answer C: $y = x + 8$
If x is the input, then this equation represents adding the quantity 8 to produce each increased output, y.

18. A teacher knows that a burning candle will lose 1 inch in height every hour. The original height of the candle is 10 inches. After letting the candle burn for 4 hours, the teacher wants students to predict how long it would take the candle to burn down to a height of 2 inches. What should students do to analyze the candle's behavior?
(Skill 2.4; Rigorous)

A. Write down the height of the candle at the beginning of the day and its height after recess.
B. Make a table recording the candle's height at each hour mark.
C. Draw a picture of the candle when it is first lit.
D. Compare the height of the candle to their own height.

Answer B: Make a table recording the candle's height at each hour mark.
A table will show how the values representing the candle's height decrease over time. An hourly entry should demonstrate the loss of one inch every hour.

19. A teacher shows the class the following graph comparing the height of a person to the span of the person's arms.

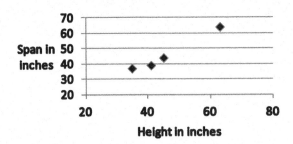

What could students do next to learn more about the pattern of the data? (Skill 2.4; Rigorous)

A. Draw the best fit line through the points.
B. Measure one another and add their data to the graph.
C. Record the data in a table.
D. All of the above

Answer D: All of the above
Each choice represents an appropriate way for students to make sense of the data in search of a pattern.

20. What is the main purpose of having kindergarten students count by twos? (Skill 3.1; Rigorous)

A. To hear a rhythm
B. To recognize patterns in numbers
C. To practice addition
D. To become familiar with equations

Answer B: To recognize patterns in numbers
Recognizing patterns in numbers is an early skill for multiplication. It will also help children recognize patterns in word families such as *bit, hit, fit.*

21. **Using a number line is an appropriate strategy to introduce which of the following?**

    I.   **Skip counting**
    II. **Counting backward**
    III. **Finding doubles**

    (Skill 3.1; Easy)

    A. I and II
    B. I and III
    C. II and III
    D. I, II, and III

    Answer A: I and II
    The skip-counting pattern adds the same number repeatedly. Counting backward subtracts 1 repeatedly. Each of these repetitions can be demonstrated on the number line.

22. **Which of the following skills would a student develop first? (Skill 3.2; Average)**

    A. Understanding place value
    B. Recognizing number patterns
    C. Counting objects
    D. Solving number problems

    Answer C: Counting objects
    As with phonemic awareness skills in reading, number sense is the foundation upon which all future math topics will be built. While in this beginning stage, children will be able to identify how many objects are in a group.

23. **A Pre-K student is distributing napkins for snack. He passes out 15 napkins, which is not enough for the 18 students. After checking how many students still need napkins, he determines that they need three more. Which math principles are demonstrated in this activity? (Skill 3.2; Rigorous)**

   A. Addition, rote counting
   B. Rote counting, one-to-one correspondence
   C. One-to-one correspondence, pre-subtraction skills
   D. Pre-subtraction skills, rote counting

   Answer C: One-to-one correspondence, pre-subtraction skills
   The student demonstrates one-to-one correspondence when giving each student a napkin. By determining the number of students left without napkins, he is demonstrating pre-subtraction skills. 18 students – 15 napkins = 3 additional napkins needed.

24. **Look at this number: 4,087,361.**
   What number represents the ten-thousands place? (Skill 3.3; Easy)

   A. 4
   B. 6
   C. 0
   D. 8

   Answer D: 8
   Listed from right to left, the place values are ones, tens, hundreds, thousands, ten-thousands, hundred-thousands, millions.

25. **If students can use place value blocks to represent the quantity 16 as "16 ones" as well as "1 ten and 6 ones," they are demonstrating an understanding of: (Skill 3.3; Average)**

   A. doubles
   B. function machines
   C. the distributive property
   D. place value

   Answer D: place value
   To have an understanding of place value, students must know that a digit's value depends on its location within a multi-digit number.

26.   Which of the following is NOT true about multiplication? (Skill 3.4; Easy)

   A.   Multiplication is only used in algebra.
   B.   Multiplication represents repeated addition.
   C.   Multiplication is commutative and associative.
   D.   Multiplication can be modeled with area diagrams.

   Answer A: Multiplication is only used in algebra.
   Multiplication is an operation naturally developing from (repeated) addition, and it is used in all levels of mathematics.

27.   Which of the following is an example of the additive identity? (Skill 3.4; Average)

   A. $a(b + c) = ab + bc$
   B. $a + 0 = a$
   C. $(a + b) + c = a + (b + c)$
   D. $a + b = b + a$

   Answer B: $a + 0 = a$
   The additive identity states that when zero is added to any number, the number is unchanged.

28.   Which of the following problems would be a good example to use to explain the idea of "doubles plus one" to students? (Skill 3.4; Rigorous)

   A. $2 + 1 = 3$
   B. $5 + 6 = 11$
   C. $1 + 1 = 2$
   D. $22 - 11 = 11$

   Answer B: $5 + 6 = 11$
   If students know the double of 5, or that $5 + 5 = 10$, they can use flexibility of numbers and the commutative and associative properties to see that the problem $5 + 6$ can be restructured as $5 + (1 + 5)$ or $(5 + 5) + 1 = 11$.

29. **The second-grade class has 14 boys and 12 girls. How many more boys are in the class? (Skill 3.5; Easy)**

    A. 26 more boys
    B. 2 more boys
    C. 14 more boys
    D. 12 more boys

    Answer B: 2 more boys
    Students identify the words *how many more* as indicating a subtraction problem. They use their knowledge of the number operation of subtraction to determine that there are 2 more boys. It is important that students include the label word(s)—in this case, *more boys*—for a complete answer.

30. **Students are asked to use numbers and operations to represent the following: *If a teacher needs to give each of her 20 students a pencil, and already has 15 pencils in her hand, how many more pencils will she need?* Some students respond with 20 – 15 = 5, while others propose *p* + 15 = 20. Comparing these problem-solving choices shows students that: (Skill 3.5; Rigorous)**

    A. sometimes a problem can be solved in more than one way
    B. addition and subtraction are inverse operations
    C. a letter can stand in place of an unknown number when solving a problem
    D. all of the above

    Answer D: all of the above.
    All of the choices represent sound principles regarding number operations, properties, and problem solving.

31. **First-grade students are arranging four small squares of identical size to form a larger square. Each small square represents what part of the larger square? (Skill 3.6; Average)**

    A. One half
    B. One whole
    C. One fourth
    D. One fifth

    Answer C: One fourth
    Four of the small squares make up the area of the large square. Each small square is one-fourth of the larger square.

32. A teacher gives each student a copy of a number line, labeled with the whole numbers. Students are then directed to take a red crayon and put a mark between each whole number on the number line. Which set of numbers are they adding to the number line? (Skill 3.6; Rigorous)

A. $\left\{\frac{1}{2}, \frac{1}{3}, \frac{1}{4}, \frac{1}{5}, \ldots\right\}$

B. $\left\{\frac{1}{2}, 1\frac{1}{2}, 2\frac{1}{2}, 3\frac{1}{2}, \ldots\right\}$

C. The set of negative integers

D. The set of irrational numbers

Answer B: $\left\{\frac{1}{2}, 1\frac{1}{2}, 2\frac{1}{2}, 3\frac{1}{2}, \ldots\right\}$
Each new mark made by the students represents a half between each of the whole numbers.

33. Which statement is FALSE? (Skill 3.7; Rigorous)

A. $\frac{1}{3} < 1$

B. $\frac{1}{3} > \frac{1}{8}$

C. $\frac{1}{3} < \frac{1}{8}$

D. $\frac{1}{3} < \frac{2}{3}$

Answer C: $\frac{1}{3} < \frac{1}{8}$
One piece of the whole divided into 3 portions represents a quantity greater than one piece of the whole divided into 8 portions.

34. The model above can be used to show students that: (Skill 3.8; Average)

A. $\frac{2}{4} = \frac{1}{2}$

B. $2 = 1$

C. $\frac{1}{2} = 0.5$

D. all boxes should be shaded in

Answer A: $\frac{2}{4} = \frac{1}{2}$
Because each whole fraction strip is the same size, students can visually confirm that the space representing 2 of the 4 shaded boxes covers the same amount of space as the space representing 1 of the 2 shaded boxes.

35. What is the area of a square whose side is 13 feet long? (Skill 4.1; Rigorous)

A. 169 feet
B. 169 square feet
C. 52 feet
D. 52 square feet

Answer B: 169 square feet
Since a square has four equal sides, multiplying length times width in this problem means multiplying 13 by 13, resulting in 169.

36. What measure could be used to report the distance traveled in walking around a track? (Skill 4.1; Easy)

A. Degrees
B. Square meters
C. Kilometers
D. Cubic feet

Answer C: Kilometers
Degrees are used for temperature, square meters represent area, and cubic feet show volume.

37. **Third-grade students are recording the length of the hallway. Which unit of measure would be used? (Skill 4.1; Average)**

   A. Inches
   B. Centimeters
   C. Yards
   D. Miles

   Answer C: Yards
   For a length of this magnitude, yards are the most practical measure of the choices listed.

38. **The mass of a cookie is closest to: (Skill 4.1; Average)**

   A. 500 grams
   B. 0.5 grams
   C. 15 grams
   D. 1.5 grams

   Answer C: 15 grams
   Science utilizes the metric system, and the unit of grams is used when measuring mass, the amount of matter in an object. A common estimation of mass used in elementary schools is that a paperclip has a mass of approximately 1 gram, which eliminates choices B and D because they are very close to 1 gram. A common estimation of 1 kilogram is equal to 1 liter of water. Half of one liter of water is still much more than one cookie, eliminating choice A. Therefore, the best estimation for one cookie is narrowed to 15 grams, or choice C.

39. **A teacher wants students to measure certain items in the school and calculate their perimeter. Which item below should NOT be included in the list of items to be measured? (Skill 4.1; Rigorous)**

   A. The rectangular classroom carpet
   B. The top of the teacher's desk
   C. The classroom door
   D. The flagpole in front of the school

   Answer D: The flagpole in front of the school
   Not only is the flagpole too tall for students to measure, it's three-dimensional, or cylindrical; nature is not conducive to the measure of perimeter.

40. A first-grade class is learning how to count money. A good way to create a concrete learning experience for students is to: (Skill 4.2; Average)

   A. give each student a debit card
   B. give students an assortment of coins to sort and count
   C. show students different kinds of wallets
   D. ask students to convert between different values of currency

   Answer B: give students an assortment of coins to sort and count.
   Students at this age are learning to recognize the appearance and value of coins and will do best with this tangible opportunity.

41. Which type of graphs would best be used to represent the number of students who like red, green, or yellow best? (Skill 4.3; Average)

   A. A bar graph or pictograph
   B. A pictograph or line graph
   C. A stem-and-leaf plot or bar graph
   D. A line graph or stem-and-leaf plot

   Answer A: A bar graph or pictograph
   A line graph is the most effective way to show change over time. Bar graphs and pictographs show quantity and can be a good way to show the results of a survey—in this case, a survey of the color that each student likes best. Stem-and-leaf plots show lists of numbers such as test scores in a specialized format.

42. The following chart shows the yearly average number of international tourists visiting Palm Beach for 1990–1994. How many more international tourists visited Palm Beach in 1994 than in 1991? (Skill 4.4; Average)

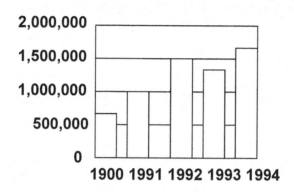

2,000,000				
1,500,000				
1,000,000				
500,000				
0				

1900 1991 1992 1993 1994

A. 100,000
B. 600,000
C. 1,600,000
D. 8,000,000

Answer B: 600,000.
Subtracting 1991's tourist count of 100,000 from 1994's tourist count of 1,600,000 yields 600,000.

43. All of the following are measurements of obtuse angles EXCEPT: (Skill 5.1; Easy)

A. 110 degrees
B. 90 degrees
C. 135 degrees
D. 91 degrees

Answer B: 90 degrees
An obtuse angle measures less than 180 degrees and more than 90 degrees. An angle with an exact measure of 90 degrees is a right angle.

44. Which angle would measure less than 90 degrees? (Skill 5.1; Easy)

A. Acute
B. Obtuse
C. Right
D. Straight

Answer A: Acute
An acute angle is an angle that measures than 90 degrees.

45. A "shape set" in a preschool classroom contains an assortment of squares, triangles, rectangles, and circles in various sizes and colors. Which of the student activities listed below would represent an appropriate math learning experience? (Skill 5.2; Rigorous)

   A. Arranging the pieces in a repeating pattern
   B. Sorting the pieces in the set by shape
   C. Using the set's pieces to make a model of a real-life object (such as a house, tree, or ice cream cone)
   D. All of the above

   Answer D: All of the above
   Using the pieces to make a pattern promotes development of algebraic thinking (Skill 2.1). Shape recognition (Skill 5.1) promotes geometry concepts, and creating a unique configuration of shapes helps students recognize shapes as parts of structures.

46. Where can a teacher expect students to find items representing the shape of a rectangle? (Skill 5.2; Average)

   A. In the classroom
   B. In their room at home
   C. In a picture book
   D. All of the above

   Answer D: All of the above
   Teachers should emphasize that the shapes exist everywhere in their world and should encourage students to be constantly on the lookout for them.

47. Which letter does NOT demonstrate symmetry? (Skill 5.3; Average)

   A. T
   B. A
   C. O
   D. F

   Answer D: F
   If printed on a piece of paper, each of the other letters could be folded in half to create identical halves.

48. Kindergarten students are doing a butterfly art project. They fold paper in half. On one half, they paint a design. Then they fold the paper closed and reopen it. The resulting picture is a butterfly with matching halves. What math principle does this demonstrate? (Skill 5.3; Average)

    A. Slide
    B. Rotate
    C. Symmetry
    D. Transformation

    Answer C: Symmetry
    By folding the painted paper in half, the design is mirrored on the other side, creating symmetry and reflection. The butterfly design is symmetrical about the center.

49. Using scissors to cut a piece of paper represents which of the following spatial concepts? (Skill 5.4; Rigorous)

    A. An angle intersecting a plane
    B. A point above a line
    C. A set of parallel lines
    D. Two points determining a line

    Answer A: An angle intersecting a plane.
    The scissors are a good representation of an angle (even one that can change in size) and the paper demonstrates the concept of a plane, or flat surface.

50. Reading a story out loud about two children playing hide-and-seek would: (Skill 5.4; Average)

    A. strengthen students' understanding of spatial concepts such as behind, under, and inside
    B. show the students a one-to-one correspondence
    C. confuse the children
    D. frighten most children

    Answer A: strengthen the children's understanding of spatial concepts such as behind, under, and inside
    A student's geometric understanding encompasses knowledge of shapes and their attributes as well as comprehension of spatial concepts.

Rationale

Science

1. **What type of science instruction will young learners benefit from most? (Skill 1.1; Easy)**

    A.   A. Paper-and-pencil assessment
    B.   B. Lecture and note taking
    C.   C. Hands-on experiments
    D.   D. Reading about science

    Answer C: Hands-on experiments
    Young learners require hands-on learning to fully understand science concepts. By uses hands-on methods, students are able to participate fully in lessons. Students at the early childhood level do not benefit from the other answer choices as much, as these are not developmentally appropriate for them at this stage of learning.

2. **Which is always true of active learning? (Skill 1.2; Average)**

    A.   Learning takes place in the classroom.
    B.   Learning takes place in the subject of science.
    C.   Learning takes place over a long period of time.
    D.   Learning is active, safe, and effective.

    Answer D: Learning is active, safe, and effective.
    Active learning is just that—active. Students who are engaged in active learning are also in safe and effective situations. Active learning may take place in settings other than the classroom and within all subjects, and it may occur over both short and long periods of time.

3. **In schools in which science materials are in demand, teachers should: (Skill 1.3; Easy)**

    A. avoid science instruction because the materials are unavailable
    B. allow students to listen to a lecture delivered by the teacher
    C. complete experiments even if some safety equipment is lacking
    D. plan hands-on activities using the materials and environment around them, including those found in nature when possible

    Answer D: plan hands-on activities using the materials and environment around them, including those found in nature when possible
    Teachers may have difficulty getting access to all materials that would be most beneficial to lessons. However, educators can creatively utilize what is available within the classroom and outside the school building. Many early childhood lessons focus on materials found in nature. It is important not to become discouraged because of a lack of resources. Lessons can be taught in other ways, as long as all safety measures are in place.

4. **Managing the early childhood science classroom must include: (Skill 1.4; Average)**

    A. the teacher allowing the students to partake in all parts of each experiment
    B. safety materials being used throughout the lesson
    C. allowing only up to 20 students to be a part of any lesson
    D. safety rules being followed when needed

    Answer B: safety materials being used throughout the lesson
    All lessons should have the safety of students in mind first and foremost. The teacher should allow students to take part in appropriate aspects of experiments and should manage the lesson in accordance with how many learners are taking part.

5. **How can a teacher provide the most effective feedback to students? (Skill 1.5; Average)**

    A. The teacher should provide feedback on a monthly basis by providing a report to each student.
    B. The teacher should provide specific feedback, focusing not only on science concepts but also on other interdisciplinary subjects related to the assignment.
    C. The teacher should always provide positive comments.
    D. The teacher can allow peer groups to evaluate one another's work.

    Answer B: The teacher should provide specific feedback, focusing not only on science concepts but also on other interdisciplinary subjects related to the assignment.
    The teacher must focus on providing specific feedback, related not only to science but also to other core subjects and focuses. Feedback should be positive, but a teacher should be sure to note mistakes where applicable. It is inappropriate for students to evaluate one another's work. This can lead to problematic social issues in the classroom.

6. **How can a teacher provide students with effective instruction in both small- and large-group settings? (Skill 1.6; Average)**

    A. Engage students in scientific vocabulary knowledge via note taking in a large group.
    B. Partake in experiments in small groups that will allow for data results to be formed.
    C. Place students in two groups: boys in one group and girls in another group.
    D. Always place students in one large group so the teacher can do all the experiments and the students can observe.

    Answer B: Partake in experiments in small groups that will allow for data results to be formed.
    Large class sizes are common, and it is important that a teacher is able to figure out the best and most effective management plan possible. Note taking and dividing students by gender are both ineffective procedures for young students. Teachers may choose to utilize large-group learning, but this should not always be the case.

7. **Which of the following tools would you be least likely to employ as an elementary science teacher? (Skill 1.7; Average)**

   A. Microscope
   B. Centrifuge
   C. Ruler
   D. Test tube

   Answer B: Centrifuge
   Microscopes and rulers are very common scientific tools, often used for introductory science lessons. A centrifuge is used for separating liquids through a high rate of spin; it is used in a laboratory setting or advanced classroom.

8. **Culture and religion may play a part in the ability of a teacher to engage in some science lessons. What is true about this reality? (Skill 1.8; Rigorous)**

   A. Teachers should partake in all science lessons without regard to culture and religion within the science classroom.
   B. Teachers should not teach any science objectives that relate to any cultural or religious matters if any member of the class might have concerns regarding his or her beliefs.
   C. Teachers should teach whatever information is provided by the school or district, regardless of any religious or cultural concerns within the classroom.
   D. Teachers should avoid all science topics to ensure that all students feel comfortable with regards to religion and culture within the science classroom.

   Answer B: Teachers should not teach any science objectives that relate to any cultural or religious matters if any member of the class might have concerns regarding his or her beliefs.
   Teachers will need to be cautious when teaching lessons that may affect a student's religion or culture. Communicating with families ahead of time will ensure that the teacher meets the needs of all learners, while avoiding potential issues. This does not necessarily mean that all students need to miss out on such objectives. The teacher can work with the child's family to engage the student in an alternate lesson instead.

9.   Scientific inquiry begins with _____. (Skill 2.1; Easy)

        A.   a hypothesis
        B.   an observation
        C.   research
        D.   a theory

Answer B: an observation
Scientific inquiry begins with an observation. Observation is an important skill by itself, since it leads to experimentation then to communicating the experimental findings to the public. After observing, a question is formed, which starts with "why" or "how." To answer these questions, experimentation is necessary.

10.   A _____ would be a good choice when graphing the percent of time students spend on various after-school activities. (Skill 2.2; Average)

        A.   line graph
        B.   pie chart
        C.   histogram
        D.   bar graph

Answer B: pie chart
Graphing utilizes numbers to demonstrate patterns. The patterns offer a visual representation, making it easier to draw conclusions. The type of graphic representation used to display observations depends on the data that is collected. Line graphs are used to compare different sets of related data or to predict data that has not yet be measured. A bar graph or histogram is used to compare different items and make comparisons based on this data. A pie chart is useful when organizing data as part of a whole.

11.   Which of the following statements about scientific knowledge best explains what scientific knowledge is? (Skill 2.3; Average)

        A.   Scientific knowledge is based on experiments.
        B.   Science knowledge is empirical.
        C.   Scientific knowledge is tentative.
        D.   Scientific knowledge is based on reason.

Answer B: Scientific knowledge is empirical.
Experiments involve observing two quantities to determine the relationship between them. Observing means gaining knowledge from one of the five senses, which is another word for *empirical knowledge.* Scientific knowledge in some areas is tentative because new and different observations are always possible. Science is based on reason, but so are other types of knowledge.

12. **Students are observing pumpkins during science class in an early childhood classroom. Which type of measurement will be important in allowing the students to graph how heavy each pumpkin is? (Skill 2.4; Average)**

    A. Density
    B. Shape
    C. Volume
    D. Weight

    Answer D: Weight
    Students will need to learn the weight of each pumpkin. This can be done with a scale. Density, shape, and volume will not allow students to learn how heavy an object is.

13. **Which of the following individuals developed the principal of elasticity that is still used today? (Skill 2.5; Average)**

    A. Robert Hooke
    B. Lev Vygotsky
    C. Andreas Vesalius
    D. Carl von Linnaeus

    Answer A: Robert Hooke
    Robert Hooke (1635–1703) was a renowned inventor, natural philosopher, astronomer, experimenter, and cell biologist. He is remembered mainly for Hooke's law, an equation describing elasticity.

14. **Which view of the ancient Greeks that affects scientific thinking states that moral and political obligations of an individual are dependent upon an agreement among people to form society? (Skill 2.6; Rigorous)**

    A. Scientific political ethics principal
    B. Utilitarianism
    C. Kantianism
    D. Social contract theory

    Answer D: Social contract theory
    Social contract theory is a view of the ancient Greeks that a person's moral and/or political obligations are dependent upon a contract or agreement among people to form society.

15. Incorporating problem solving, communication, and technology into science lessons are ways to ensure that the _____ disciplines are being taught. (Skill 2.7; Average)

   A. STEM
   B. synthesized
   C. unified
   D. NSF

Answer A: STEM
STEM ties four disciplines together: science, technology, engineering, and mathematics. By engaging in STEM, students learn skills including problem solving, communication, and technology concepts.

16. Destructive land-use practices can induce _____ when not properly planned. (Skill 2.8; Easy)

   A. global warming
   B. avalanches
   C. hurricanes
   D. volcanic eruptions

Answer B: avalanches
Destructive land-use practices such as mining have induced landslides and avalanches when not properly planned and monitored. Other destructive practices from human activities include global warming and waste contamination, but these are unrelated to land-use practices. Hurricanes are nature-induced and not caused by humans.

17. Rocks formed from magma are _____. (Skill 3.1; Average)

   A. igneous
   B. metamorphic
   C. sedimentary
   D. none of the above

Answer A: igneous
Igneous rocks are rocks that have formed from cooled magma. They are further classified as extrusive or intrusive according to the location in which they were formed. Metamorphism is the process of changing a preexisting rock into a new rock by heat and/or pressure. Sedimentary rocks are named for their source: They are rocks that form from sediments that become solid rock. Sedimentary rock is especially important because it contains fossils.

18. **Which types of volcanoes have been built from lava flows as well as cinders and ash? (Skill 3.2; Rigorous)**

    A. Cinder cone volcanoes
    B. Shield volcanoes
    C. Warped volcanoes
    D. Composite volcanoes

    Answer D: Composite volcanoes
    Composite volcanoes are volcanoes that have been built by both lava flows and layers of ash and cinders. The other three types of volcanoes have different characteristics from those of composite volcanoes.

19. **Which of the following does NOT determine the frictional force of a box sliding down a ramp? (Skill 3.3; Average)**

    A. The weight of the box
    B. The area of the box
    C. The angle of the ramp
    D. The chemical properties of the two surfaces

    Answer B: The area of the box
    The frictional force is caused by bonding between the molecules of the box and the molecules of the ramp. At a small number of points, there is contact between the molecules. While there may be a small increase in the frictional force as the area increases, it is not noticeable. The main determinants of the frictional force are the weight of the box and the nature of the two surfaces.

20. **The planet with retrograde rotation is: (Skill 3.4; Rigorous)**

    A. Mars
    B. Uranus
    C. Venus
    D. Saturn

    Answer C: Venus
    Venus has an axial tilt of only 3 degrees and a very slow rotation. It spins in the direction opposite of the other planets (that spin in the same direction as the Sun). Uranus has retrograde revolution, not retrograde rotation.

21. _____ are areas of weakness in the plates of Earth's crust. (Skill 3.5; Easy)

   A.   Faults
   B.   Ridges
   C.   Earthquakes
   D.   Volcanoes

   Answer A: Faults
   Faults are cracks in Earth's crust that often cause earthquakes when Earth's crust moves. Faults may lead to mismatched edges of ground that form ridges.

22. **Surface ocean currents are caused by which of the following? (Skill 3.6; Rigorous)**

   A.   Temperature
   B.   Changes in density of water
   C.   Wind
   D.   Tidal forces

   Answer C: Wind
   A current is a large mass of continuously moving oceanic water. Surface ocean currents are mainly wind-driven and occur in all of the world's oceans (for example, the Gulf Stream). This is in contrast to deep ocean currents, which are driven by changes in density. Surface ocean currents are classified by temperature. Tidal forces cause changes in ocean levels; however, they do not affect surface currents.

23. **The goal of which U.S. space mission was to gather information and pictures from the moon? (Skill 3.7; Average)**

   A.   *Challenger*
   B.   *Apollo 11*
   C.   *Apollo 13*
   D.   None of the above

   Answer C: *Apollo 13*
   Apollo 13 was U.S. mission to gather information and pictures from the moon. This was the third manned mission to land in outer space. An explosion occurred during the mission onboard the spacecraft, which was caused by a problem in the oxygen tank.

24. The phases of the moon are the result of its _____ in relation to the Sun. (Skill 3.8; Rigorous)

   A. revolution
   B. rotation
   C. position
   D. inclination

   Answer C: position
   The moon is visible in varying amounts during its orbit around Earth. One-half of the moon's surface is always illuminated by the Sun (appears bright), but the amount observed can vary from a full moon to no illumination at all.

25. Which of the following is the most accurate definition of a nonrenewable resource? (Skill 3.9; Average)

   A. A nonrenewable resource is never replaced once used.
   B. A nonrenewable resource is replaced on a timescale that is very long relative to human life spans.
   C. A nonrenewable resource is a resource that can only be manufactured by humans.
   D. A nonrenewable resource is a species that has already become extinct.

   Answer B: A nonrenewable resource is replaced on a timescale that is very long relative to human lifespans.
   Nonrenewable resources are fragile and must be conserved for use in the future. They cannot be replaced after they have been used up.

26. Which type of matter is extremely light and does not have any weight? (Skill 4.1; Average)

   A. Solid
   B. Liquid
   C. Gas
   D. All of the above

   Answer C: Gas
   The characteristics of a gas include being extremely light and being weightless. Solids can be either light or heavy, but they have a definite weight. Liquids also have a weight, although they might be lighter than a similar solid (for example, water and ice).

27. Oxygen, hydrogen, nitrogen, and chlorine are unusual because they: (Skill 4.2; Rigorous)

   A. are made of two atoms each
   B. are made of three atoms that have been chemically combined
   C. have no identifying symbols
   D. none of the above

   Answer A: are made of two atoms each
   A molecule of most elements is made up of one atom. However, oxygen, hydrogen, nitrogen, and chlorine molecules are made of two atoms each.

28. The ability of a substance to be changed into a new substance is a _____. (Skill 4.3; Average)

   A. chemical condition
   B. physical condition
   C. mechanical property
   D. chemical property

   Answer D: chemical property
   Chemical properties describe the ability of a substance to be changed into new substances. For example, baking powder goes through a chemical change as it changes into carbon dioxide gas during the baking process.

29. Internal energy that is created by the vibration and movement of atoms and molecules is classified as _____. (Skill 4.4; Rigorous)

   A. mechanical energy
   B. acoustical energy
   C. radiant energy
   D. thermal energy

   Answer D: thermal energy
   Thermal energy is the total internal energy of objects created by the vibration and movement of atoms and molecules. Heat is the transfer of thermal energy. Acoustical energy, or sound energy, is the movement of energy through an object in waves, and radiant energy is the energy of electromagnetic waves. Electrical energy is the movement of electrical charges in an electromagnetic field.

30. **A teacher explains to the class that energy is neither created nor destroyed. Therefore, this means that: (Skill 4.5; Average)**

   A. matter never changes form
   B. matter must change form
   C. matter changes form only if it is a liquid
   D. none of the above

   Answer B: matter must change form
   The law of conservation of energy states that energy is neither created nor destroyed. Since energy is neither created nor destroyed, it must change form. For example, an animal may die, but its body will either be consumed by other animals or will decay into the ecosystem. Either way, it enters another form and the matter still exists in some form.

31. **Resistance of motion of surfaces that touch each other is considered _____. (Skill 4.6; Average)**

   A. friction
   B. inertia
   C. gravity
   D. force

   Answer A: friction
   Surfaces that touch each other have a certain resistance to motion. This resistance is friction.

32. **When humans shiver to keep warm, this is an example of _____. (Skill 5.1; Average)**

   A. translation
   B. synthesis
   C. motility
   D. homeostasis

   Answer D: homeostasis
   Homeostasis is the result of regulatory mechanisms that help maintain an organism's internal environment within tolerable limits. Another example, in humans and in mammals, is constriction and dilation of blood vessels near the skin to help maintain body temperature.

33. **These are the basis of evolution and may enhance an organism's survival. (Skill 5.2; Rigorous)**

     A. Species
     B. Mutations
     C. DNA
     D. Instincts

     Answer B: Mutations
     Inheritable changes in DNA are called mutations. Mutations are not always bad. They are the basis of evolution, and if they make a more favorable variation that enhances the organism's survival, then they are beneficial. But mutations can also lead to abnormalities, birth defects, and even death.

34. **The science of classification is referred to as: (Skill 5.3; Easy)**

     A. subgroups
     B. systems
     C. taxonomy
     D. class

     Answer C: taxonomy
     Taxonomy is the science of classification and was developed by Carolus Linnaeus, who is known as the father of taxonomy. Taxonomy allows items to be grouped according to their similarities.

35. **A _____ describes the relational position of a species or population. (Skill 5.4; Average)**

     A. class
     B. phylum
     C. predator
     D. niche

     Answer D: niche
     Niche describes the relational position of a species or population in an ecosystem. Niche includes how a population responds to the abundance of its resources and its enemies (for example, growing when resources are abundant and predators, parasites, and pathogens are scarce). Niche also indicates the life history of an organism, its habitat, and its place in the food chain.

36. _____ make up _____, which make up tissues. (Skill 5.5; Rigorous)

    A. Cells; DNA
    B. Cells; organelles
    C. Organisms; organelles
    D. Organelles; cells

Answer D: Organelles; cells
Organelles make up cells, which make up tissues. Tissues make up organs, and groups of organs make up organ systems. Organ systems work together to provide life for the organism.

37. Eighty percent of Earth's atmosphere is _____. (Skill 5.6; Average)

    A. carbon dioxide
    B. phosphorus
    C. water
    D. nitrogen gas

Answer D: nitrogen gas
Eighty percent of Earth's atmosphere is nitrogen gas. Nitrogen must be in nongaseous form to be incorporated into an organism.

38. _____ maintain a fluid environment for _____ exchange in mammals. (Skill 5.7; Average)

    A. Lungs; gas
    B. Blood vessels; blood
    C. Carbon dioxide molecules; air
    D. None of the above

Answer A: Lungs; gas
Lungs maintain a fluid environment for gas exchange in mammals, while gills allow aquatic animals to exchange gases in a fluid medium by removing dissolved oxygen from the water.

39. _____ is known as the father of genetics. (Skill 5.8; Easy)

    A. Matthias Schleiden
    B. Andreas Vesalius
    C. Robert Punnet
    D. Gregor Mendel

Answer D: Gregor Mendel
Gregor Mendel is known as the father of genetics. His work in the late 1800s is the basis of our knowledge of genetics.

40. **Which is true of meiosis? (Skill 5.9; Rigorous)**

    A. Recombination provides genetic diversity.
    B. The chromosome number is half the number of parent cells.
    C. Both A and B
    D. Neither A nor B

    Answer C: Both A and B
    Both answers A and B are true. In meiosis, recombination provides genetic diversity, and the chromosome number is half the number of parent cells.

41. **Which type of ecosystem is located close to the poles, both north and south of the equator? (Skill 5.10; Average)**

    A. Tundra
    B. Savanna
    C. Taiga
    D. Temperate deciduous forest

    Answer C: Taiga
    Taiga is located north and south of the equator, close to the poles, while the tundra is located even further north and south of the taiga

CPSIA information can be obtained
at www.ICGtesting.com
Printed in the USA
BVOW04s0320300717

490505BV00035B/278/P

9 781607 873860